S0-DSO-144

THE LETTERS
of
JAMES *and* PETER

THE LETTERS

of

JAMES *and* PETER

Translated,
with Introductions and Interpretations
by

WILLIAM BARCLAY

THE WESTMINSTER PRESS
PHILADELPHIA

First published by The Saint Andrew Press
Edinburgh, Scotland
James: First Edition, February, 1958
Second Edition, May, 1960
I and II Peter: First Edition, July, 1958
Second Edition, May, 1960

Library of Congress Catalog Card No. 61-7023

Typeset in Great Britain
Printed in the United States of America

GENERAL INTRODUCTION

IT may truly be said that this series of Daily Bible Studies began almost accidentally. A series which the Church of Scotland was using came to an end, and another series was immediately required. I was asked to write a volume on *Acts*, and, at the moment, had no intention beyond that. But one volume followed another, until the demand for one volume became a plan to write on the whole New Testament.

The translation which is given in each volume claims no special merit. It was included in order that the reader might be able to carry both the text of the New Testament and the comments on it wherever he went, and that he might be able to read it anywhere. While I was making the translation, the translations of Moffatt, Weymouth, and Knox were ever beside me. *The American Revised Standard Version, The Twentieth Century New Testament,* and *The New Testament in Plain English,* by Charles Kingsley Williams, have been in constant use. Since its publication, I have consistently consulted *The Authentic New Testament,* translated by Hugh J. Schonfield.

I cannot see another edition of these books going out to the public without expressing my very deep and sincere gratitude to the Church of Scotland Publications Committee for allowing me the privilege of first beginning, and then continuing, this series. And in particular I wish to express my very great gratitude to the convener, Rev. R. G. Macdonald, O.B.E., M.A., D.D., and to the committee's secretary and manager, Rev. Andrew McCosh, M.A., S.T.M., for constant encouragement and never-failing sympathy and help.

As these volumes went on, the idea of the whole series developed. The aim is to make the results of modern scholarship available to the non-technical reader in a form that it does not require a theological education to understand; and then to seek to make the teaching of the New Testament books relevant to life and work to-day. The whole aim of these books is summed up in Richard of Chichester's famous prayer; they are meant to enable men and women to know Jesus Christ more clearly, to love Him more dearly, and to follow Him more nearly. It is my prayer that they may do something to make that possible.

FOREWORD

James has always suffered from Martin Luther's strictures upon it. It is not readily forgotten that Luther called it " a right strawy epistle," and that he declared that he did not find Christ in it (Luther's Biblical Prefaces, including the Preface to James may be found in *Reformation Writings of Martin Luther*, vol. ii, translated by Bertram Lee Woolf). Inevitably one approaches *James* with the feeling that it is one of the lesser books of the New Testament. But the longer I companied with *James* the greater this short letter became to me. E. C. Blackman quotes Marty's verdict on *James*: " The Epistle is a masterpiece of virile and reverent simplicity." It may be that a reader will begin the study of *James* as a duty; he may well end, as I did, by finding it a joy.

James has been fortunate in its commentators. First, there are the commentaries on the Greek text. That of J. B. Mayor in the Macmillan Commentaries is one of the greatest commentaries in the English language. That of J. H. Ropes in the *International Critical Commentary* is a model of judicious and meticulous scholarship. That of W. O. E. Oesterley in the *Expositor's Greek Testament* is very helpful, and, as one would expect from that scholar, specially illuminating on the Jewish thought and belief behind the letter. That of A. Carr in the *Cambridge Greek Testament for Schools and Colleges* is on a smaller scale, but is still most useful.

Second, there are the commentaries on the English text. In the *Moffatt Commentary* James Moffatt did the volume on the *General Epistles* of which *James* is one. It is useful, but rather slight. Of the very recent commentaries that by R. V. G. Tasker in the *Tyndale Commentaries* is conservative scholarship at its best and is most helpful. The volume in the *Torch Bible Commentaries* by E. C. Blackman is one of the outstanding volumes in that series. The commentary by **B. S.** Easton in *The Interpreter's Bible* is stimulating and suggestive.

For myself *James* was a new discovery, and I hope that this commentary may help others also to discover this letter.

First and *Second Peter* are very different letters. In its warmth and in its simplicity *First Peter* is one of the best loved letters in the New Testament, but *Second Peter* (with *Jude* with which it is very closely connected) is a very largely neglected book. *Second Peter and Jude* move in a world that is largely strange to us. Their special problem is that they move in a world which is strange even to the student of the Bible, for they take much of their imagery, their thought and their illustrations not from the Old Testament, but from the literature which was written in between the Old and the New Testament, a literature which is largely unknown to us, but which was immensely popular in its day. For that reason the explanatory material on *Second Peter* has had to run to some length. I know that it will require an effort to move through *Second Peter*, but I also know that the effort will be more than worthwhile.

First and *Second Peter* and *Jude* are frequently taken together in commentaries. The three letters are dealt with in one volume in the *International Critical Commentary* by C. Bigg, and this volume is the product of sound, if conservative, scholarship. They are also edited in one volume by E. H. Plumptre in the *Cambridge Bible for Schools and Colleges*, a work which is now old, but still full of wise illumination. They are also treated together by James Moffatt in the volume on *The General Epistles* in the *Moffatt Commentary*.

On *First Peter* there are two outstanding modern commentaries. The massive work of E. G. Selwyn in the Macmillan Commentaries has already taken its place among the great commentaries in the English language. That of

F. W. Beare is much more radical in its conclusions but is of the first importance. I have myself been under a special debt of gratitude to the smaller exposition by C. E. B. Cranfield, which is a masterpiece of brief but lucid and illuminating exposition. My debt to this book appears on every page of my own book. In *The Interpreter's Bible* the exposition by A. M. Hunter is characteristically helpful. In the *Cambridge Greek Testament for Schools and Colleges* there is a scholarly and helpful volume on *First Peter* by G. W. Blenkin.

The material on *Second Peter* is much less abundant. In the Macmillan Commentaries there is a massive volume on *Second Peter* along with *Jude* by J. B. Mayor, which is a monument of New Testament and of classical scholarship and which ranks with that author's volume on *James*. In the *Cambridge Greek Testament for Schools and Colleges* there is an excellent short volume by M. R. James.

Nothing will ever lessen the attraction of *First Peter*. It may be true that *Second Peter* cannot have the same fascination, but there are few New Testament books which enable us better to see the insidious attacks which were made on the Christian Doctrine and the Christian Ethic in the days of the early Church, and against which the New Testament writers had to erect their defences, and for that reason it is intensely important.

It is my hope and prayer that this exposition will enable its readers to appreciate and value these letters a little better and to love them a little more.

WILLIAM BARCLAY.

TRINITY COLLEGE,
   GLASGOW,
      March, 1960.

CONTENTS

THE LETTER OF JAMES

THE FIRST LETTER OF PETER

CONTENTS

CONTENTS

THE SECOND LETTER OF PETER

CONTENTS

THE LETTER OF JAMES

THE LETTER OF JAMES

INTRODUCTION

The Epistle of James is one of the books which had a very
hard fight to get into the New Testament at all. Even
when it did come to be regarded as Scripture it is still
spoken of with a certain reserve and suspicion, and even
as late as the sixteenth century Luther would gladly have
banished it from the New Testament altogether.

The Doubts of the Fathers

In the Latin-speaking part of the Church it is not until
the middle of the fourth century that *James* emerges
in the writings of the fathers at all. The first list of New
Testament books ever to be compiled is the Muratorian
Canon, which dates to about A.D. 170, and *James* is absent
from it. Tertullian, who was writing in the middle of the
third century, is an immense quoter of Scripture; he has
7,258 quotations from the New Testament, but never one
from *James*. The first appearance of *James* in Latin is in a
Latin manuscript called the Codex Corbeiensis, which
dates to about A.D. 350. This manuscript attributes the
authorship of the book to James the son of Zebedee;
and includes it, not with the universally acknowledged
New Testament books, but with a collection of religious
tracts written by the early fathers. *James* has now emerged,
but it is accepted with a certain reservation. The first
Latin writer to quote James *verbatim* is Hilary of Poitiers
in a work *On the Trinity*, written about A.D. 357. If, then,
James was so late in emerging in the Latin Church, and
if, when it did emerge, it was still regarded with some
uncertainty, how did it become integrated into the New
Testament? The moving influence was that of Jerome,
for he unhesitatingly included *James* in his Vulgate version
of the New Testament. But even then there is an accent
of doubt. In his book *On Famous Men*, Jerome writes,

" James, who is called the brother of the Lord . . . wrote only one epistle, which is one of the seven catholic epistles, and which, some people say, was issued by someone else under James's name." So, then, there is still the accent of doubt. Jerome fully accepted the letter as Scripture, but he felt that there was some doubt as to who the writer was. How then was the doubt finally set at rest in the Latin Church? It was finally set at rest by the fact that Augustine fully accepted *James*, and was not in doubt that the James in question was the brother of our Lord. James was late in emerging in the Latin Church; for long there was a kind of question mark against it; but Jerome's inclusion of it in the Vulgate, and Augustine's full acceptance of it, brought it in the end, albeit after a struggle, full and final recognition.

The Syrian Church.

One would have thought that the Syrian Church would have been the first to accept *James*, if it was really written in Palestine, and if it was really the work of James, the brother of our Lord; but in the Syrian Church there is the same oscillation. The official New Testament of the Syrian Church is called the Peshitto. The Peshitto was to the Syrian Church what the Vulgate was to the Latin Church. This Peshitto version of the Scriptures in Syriac was made by Rabbula, the Bishop of Edessa, about A.D. 412. In it for the first time *James* was translated into Syriac; up to that time there was no Syriac version of *James*; and up to A.D. 451 there is no trace of *James* in Syriac religious literature. After that *James* was widely enough accepted, but as late as A.D. 545, Paul of Nisibis was still questioning the right of *James* to be in the New Testament, and was still classing it among the books which are under dispute. It was not, in fact, until midway through the eighth century that the great authority of John of Damascus did for *James* in the Syrian Church what Augustine had done for it in the Latin Church.

4

THE LETTER OF JAMES

The Greek Church

Although *James* emerged sooner in the Greek-speaking Church than it did in the Latin and Syrian Church, it was nonetheless late in making its definite appearance. The first writer to quote it by name is Origen, the great scholar and head of the school of Alexandria. He was writing almost midway through the third century, and he says, " If faith is called faith, but exists apart from works, such a faith is dead, as we read in the letter which is currently reported to be by James." It is true that in other works he quotes it as being without doubt by James, and shows that he believes the James to be the brother of our Lord; but once again there is the accent of doubt at the back of his use of it. Eusebius, the great scholar of Caesarea, investigated the position of the various books in the New Testament or on the fringe of it in his own day midway through the fourth century. He classes *James* amongst the books which are " disputed "; and he writes of it: " The first of the epistles called Catholic is said to be his (James's); but it must be noted that some regard it as spurious; and it is certainly true that very few of the ancient writers mention it." Here again is the accent of doubt. Eusebius himself accepted *James*, but he was well aware that there were those who did not. The decisive turning-point in the Greek-speaking Church came in A.D. 367. In that year Athanasius issued his famous Easter Letter in Egypt. The purpose of that letter was to inform his people what books were Scripture, and what books were not, because apparently the reading of his people had become too wide, or at least too many books were being regarded as Holy Writ. In that Letter *James* is without qualification included; and its position is thenceforth safe.

So, then, in the early Church no one really questioned the value of *James*; but in every branch of the Church it was late in emerging, and in every branch of the Church it had to go through a period when it was regarded with

5

questions, and when its right to be considered a New Testament book was under dispute.

In point of fact the history of *James* is still to be seen in its position in the Roman Catholic Church. In 1546 The Council of Trent once finally and for all laid down the Roman Catholic Bible. In it a list of books was given to which none could be added and from which none could be subtracted, and which had to be read in the Vulgate Version and in no other. The books were divided into two classes. There are those which are *proto-canonical*; that is to say, those about which there had never been any question and which had been unquestioningly accepted from the beginning; and there were those which were *deutero-canonical*, that is to say those which only gradually won their way into the New Testament. And although the Roman Catholic Church never had any doubts about *James*, it is nonetheless in the second class that it is included.

Luther and James

In our own day it is true to say that *James*, at least for most people, does not occupy a position in the forefront of the New Testament. There are few who would mention it in the same breath as *John* or *Romans*, or *Luke* or *Galatians*. There is still for many a kind of reservation or qualification about *James*. Why should that be? It cannot have to do with the doubt about *James* in the early Church, for the history of the New Testament books in these dim and distant days is not known to many people in the modern Church. The reason lies in this. In the Roman Catholic Church the position of *James* was finally settled by the Edict of the Council of Trent; but in the Protestant Church the history of *James* continued to be troubled, and indeed became even more troubled, because Luther attacked it, and would have ejected it from the New Testament altogether. In his printing of his German New Testament Luther had a contents page with the books set out and numbered. But at the end of the list there is a little group, separate from the others, and with no numbers assigned to them. That group comprised *James, Jude, Hebrews* and *Revelation*. These were books which Luther definitely held to be secondary.

Luther was specially severe on *James,* and the adverse judgment of a great man on any book can be a millstone round that book's neck for ever. It is in the concluding paragraph of his *Preface to the New Testament* that there stands Luther's famous verdict on James:

> In sum: the gospel and the first epistle of St. John, St. Paul's epistles, especially those to the Romans, Galatians and Ephesians; and St. Peter's first epistle, are the books which show Christ to you. They teach everything you need to know for your salvation, even if you were never to see or hear any other book or hear any other teaching. In comparison with these the epistle of James is an *epistle full of straw,* because it contains nothing evangelical. But more about this in other prefaces.

As he promised that he would do, Luther developed this verdict in the *Preface to the Epistles of St. James and St. Jude.* He begins: " I think highly of the epistle of *James,* and regard it as valuable although it was rejected in early days. It does not expound human doctrines, but lays much emphasis on God's law. Yet to give my own opinion, without prejudice to that of anyone else, I do not hold it to be of apostolic authorship." He then goes on to give his reasons for this rejection.

First, in direct opposition to Paul and to the rest of the Bible it ascribes justification to works, quoting Abraham wrongly as one who was justified by his works. This in itself proves that the epistle cannot be of apostolic origin.

Second, not once does it give to Christians any instruction or reminder of the Passion, Resurrection, or Spirit of Christ. It mentions Christ only twice. Then Luther goes on to state his own principle for testing any books: " The true touchstone for testing any book is to discover whether it emphasises the prominence of Christ or not. . . . What does not teach Christ is not apostolic, not even if taught by Peter or Paul. On the other hand what does preach Christ is apostolic, even if Judas, Annas, Pilate, or Herod does it." On that test *James* fails. So Luther goes on: " The epistle of *James* however only drives you to the law and its works. He mixes one thing to another to such an extent that I suspect some good and pious man assembled a few things said by disciples of the apostles, and put them down in black and white; or perhaps the epistle was written by someone else who made notes of a sermon of his. He calls the law a law of freedom (*James* 1: 25; 2: 12), although St. Paul calls it a law of slavery, wrath, death, and sin " (*Galatians* 3: 23f; *Romans* 4: 15; 7: 10f).

So Luther comes to his conclusion: " In sum: he wishes to guard against those who depended on faith without going on to works, but he had neither the spirit, nor the thought, nor the eloquence equal to the task. He does violence to Scripture, and so contradicts Paul and all Scripture. He tries to accomplish by emphasising law what the apostles bring about by attracting man to love. I therefore refuse him a place among the writers of the true canon of my Bible; but I would not prevent anyone else placing him or raising him where he likes, for the epistle contains many excellent passages. One man does not count as a man even in the eyes of the world; how then shall this single and isolated writer count against Paul and all the rest of the Bible? " Luther indeed does not spare *James*; and it may be that once we have studied *James* we may well think that for once Luther allowed personal prejudice to injure sound judgment.

Such, then, is the troubled history of *James*; and now we must proceed to try to answer the questions it poses regarding its authorship and its date.

THE LETTER OF JAMES

The Identity of James

First, then, let us consider the author of this letter. He gives us practically no information at all about himself. He calls himself simply: " James, a servant of God and of the Lord Jesus Christ " (*James* 1: 1). Who then is this James? In the New Testament there are apparently at least five people who bear the name James.

(i) There was the James who was the father of the member of the Twelve called Judas, not Iscariot (*Luke* 6: 16). He is nothing but a name, and cannot have had any connection with this letter.

(ii) There is James, the son of Alphaeus, who was a member of the Twelve (*Matthew* 10: 3; *Mark* 3: 18; *Luke* 6: 15; *Acts* 1: 13). A comparison of *Matthew* 9: 9 and *Mark* 2: 14 makes it certain that Matthew and Levi were one and the same person. Levi was also a son of Alphaeus, and therefore Matthew and this James must have been brothers. But of James, the son of Alphaeus, nothing whatever is known; and he also can have had no connection with this letter.

(iii) There is the James who is called *James the Little* (*James the Less* is an error in translation), who is mentioned in *Mark* 15: 40 (cp. *Matthew* 27: 56; *John* 19: 25). Again nothing is known of him, and he cannot have had any connection with this letter.

(iv) There is James, the brother of John, and the son of Zebedee, a member of the Twelve (*Matthew* 10: 2; *Mark* 3: 17; *Luke* 6: 14; *Acts* 1: 13). In the gospel story James never appears independently of his brother John (*Matthew* 4: 21; 17: 1; *Mark* 1: 19, 29; 5: 37; 9: 2; 10: 35, 41; 13: 3; 14: 33; *Luke* 5: 10; 8: 51; 9: 28, 54). This James was the first of the apostolic band to be martyred, for he was beheaded on the orders of Herod Agrippa the First in the year A.D. 44. He has been connected with the letter. The fourth century Latin Codex Corbeiensis at the end of the epistle has a note quite definitely ascribing it to James the son of Zebedee. The only place where this ascription of authorship was taken seriously was in the Spanish Church, in which, down to the end of the seventeenth century, James the son of Zebedee was often held to be the author of the letter. This was due to the fact that St. James of Compostella is the patron saint of Spain; he is identified with James the son of Zebedee; and it was very natural that the Spanish Church should be predisposed to wish that their country's patron saint should be the author of a New Testament letter. But the martyrdom of James came too early for him to have written the letter, and in any event there is nothing beyond the Codex Corbeiensis to connect him with it.

(v) Finally, there is James, who is called the brother of Jesus. Although the first definite connection of James with this letter does not emerge until Origen in the first half of the third century, it is to him that the letter has always been traditionally ascribed. It is to him that the Roman Catholic Church definitely ascribes the letter, for in 1546 the Council of Trent laid it down that *James* is canonical and that it is written by an apostle.

Let us then look at this James; and let us collect the evidence about him. From the New Testament we learn that he was one of the brothers of Jesus (*Mark* 6: 3; *Matthew* 13: 58). We shall later discuss in what sense the word brother is to be taken. During Jesus' ministry it is clear that the family of Jesus did not understand or sympathise with Him and that indeed they were hostile to Him, and would have wished to restrain Him (*Matthew* 12: 46-50; *Mark* 3: 21, 31-35; *John* 7: 3-9). John says bluntly, " Neither did His brethren believe in Him " (*John* 7: 5). So, then, during Jesus' earthly ministry James was numbered amongst His opponents.

But with *Acts* there comes a sudden and unexplained change. When *Acts* opens, Jesus' mother and His brethren are there with the little group of Christians (*Acts* 1: 14).

From there onwards it becomes clear that James has become the leader of the Jerusalem Church. How that came about is never explained, but the pre-eminence of James is clear. It is to James that Peter sends the news of his escape from prison (*Acts* 12: 17). Clearly James presides over the Council of Jerusalem which agreed to the entry of the Gentiles into the Christian Church (*Acts* 15). It is James and Peter whom Paul met when he first went to Jerusalem, and it is with Peter, James and John, the pillars of the Church, that he discussed and settled his sphere of work (*Galatians* 1: 19; 2: 9). It is to James that Paul comes with his collection from the Gentile Churches on the visit to Jerusalem which was destined to be his last and which led to his imprisonment (*Acts* 21: 18-25). This last episode is important, for it shows James very sympathetic to the Jews who still observed the Jewish law, and very eager that their scruples should not be offended, and actually persuading Paul to demonstrate his loyalty to the law by assuming responsibility for the expenses of certain Jews who were fulfilling a Nazirite vow.

It is quite clear that James was the leader of the Jerusalem Church. As might be expected, this was something which tradition and legend greatly sharpened and developed. Hegesippus, the early historian, says that James was the first bishop of the Church at Jerusalem. Clement of Alexandria goes further and says that he was chosen for that office by Peter and John. Jerome in his book, *On Famous Men*, quite definitely says, " After the Passion of the Lord, James was immediately ordained bishop of Jerusalem by the apostles. . . . He ruled the Church of Jerusalem for thirty years, that is, until the seventh year of the reign of Nero." *The Clementine Recognitions* take the final step in the development of the legend, for they say that James was ordained Bishop of Jerusalem by none other than Jesus Himself. Clement of Alexandria relates a strange tradition: " To James the Just, and

John and Peter, after the Resurrection, the Lord committed knowledge; they committed it to the other apostles; and the other apostles to the seventy." It is clear that the legend of the pre-eminence of James in the Church at Jerusalem grew and developed. We need not accept its later developments, but the basic fact remains, that James was the undisputed head of the Church at Jerusalem.

James and Jesus

Such a change must have some explanation. What changed James the unsympathetic opponent of Jesus into James the leader of the Christian Church, and in the end, as we shall see, the martyr of Christ? It may well be that we have the explanation of that change in a brief sentence in the New Testament itself. In I *Corinthians* 15, Paul gives us a list of the Resurrection appearances of Jesus, and in that list there occur the words: " After that, He was seen by James " (I *Corinthians* 15: 7). Now it so happens that there is a strange reference to James in the *Gospel according to the Hebrews*, which was one of the very early gospels which did not gain admittance to the New Testament, but which, to judge from its remaining fragments, had much of value in it. In that gospel there occurs the following passage, which is handed down to us by Jerome:

> Now the Lord, when He had given the linen cloth unto the servant of the High Priest, went unto James and appeared to him (for James had sworn that he would not eat bread from that hour, wherein he had drunk the Lord's cup, until he should see Him risen again from among them that sleep). And again after a little, " Bring ye," saith the Lord, "a table and bread," and immediately it is added: " He took bread and blessed and brake it and gave it unto James the Just and said unto him, ' My brother, eat thy bread, for the Son of Man is risen from among them that sleep.' "

That is a passage not without its difficulties. The beginning of it seems to mean that Jesus, when He rose from the dead and emerged from the tomb, handed the linen shroud, which He had been wearing in death, to the servant of the High Priest, and went to meet His brother James. It also seems to imply that James was present at the Last Supper. But although the passage has its obscurities, one thing is clear from it. Its point is that something about Jesus in the last days and hours had fastened on James's heart, and that he had vowed that he would not eat until Jesus had risen again; and so Jesus came to him, and gave him the assurance for which he waited. That there was a meeting of James and the Risen Christ is certain. What passed at that sacred and intimate moment we shall never know. But we do know this, that after it the James who had been the hostile and unsympathetic opponent of Jesus became His servant for life, and His martyr in death.

James the Martyr of Christ

That James died a martyr's death is the consistent statement of early tradition. The accounts of the circumstances of his death vary, but the fact that he was martyred remains constant. Josephus' account is very brief (*Antiquities* 20: 9.1):

> So Ananus, being that kind of man, and thinking that he had got a good opportunity because Festus was dead and Albinus not yet arrived, holds a judicial council; and he brought before it the brother of Jesus, who was called Christ—James was his name— and some others, and on the charge of violating the Law he gave them over to be stoned.

Ananus was a Jewish High Priest; Festus and Albinus were procurators of Palestine, holding the same position as Pilate had held. And the point of the story is that Ananus took advantage of the interregnum between the death of one procurator and the arrival of his successor to eliminate James and other leaders of the Christian Church.

This, in fact, well fits the character of Ananus as it is known to us. This would mean that James was martyred in A.D. 62.

A much longer account is given in the history of Hegesippus. Hegesippus' history is itself lost, but his account of the death of James has been preserved in full by Eusebius (*Ecclesiastical History* 2: 23). It is lengthy, but it is of such interest that it must be quoted in full.

To the government of the Church in conjunction with the apostles succeeded the Lord's brother, James, he whom all from the time of the Lord to our own day call the Just, as there were many named James. And he was holy from his mother's womb; wine and strong drink he drank not, nor did he eat flesh; no razor touched his head, he anointed himself not with oil, and used not the bath. To him alone was it permitted to enter the Holy Place, for neither did he wear wool, but linen clothes. And alone he would enter the Temple, and be found prostrate on his knees beseeching pardon for the people, so that his knees were callous like a camel's in consequence of his continual kneeling in prayer to God and beseeching pardon for the people. Because of his exceeding righteousness he was called the Just, and Oblias, which is in Greek Bulwark of the People, and Righteousness, as the prophets declare concerning him.

Therefore, certain of the seven sects among the people, already mentioned by me in the *Memoirs*, asked him: " What is the door of Jesus? " and he said that He was the Saviour—of whom some accepted the faith that Jesus is the Christ. Now the aforesaid sects were not believers either in a Resurrection or in One who should come to render to every man according to his deeds; but as many as believed did so because of James. So, since many of the rulers, too, were believers, there was a tumult of the Jews and Scribes and Pharisees, for they said there was danger that all the people would expect Jesus the Christ. Accordingly they said, when they had met together with James: " We entreat thee restrain the people since it has gone astray unto Jesus, holding him to be the Christ. We entreat thee to persuade concerning Jesus all those who come to the day of the Passover, for we all listen to thee. For we and all the people testify to thee that thou art just and that thou respectest not persons. So thou, therefore, persuade the people concerning Jesus, not to go astray, for all the people and all of us listen to thee. Take thy stand, therefore, on the pinnacle of the Temple, that up there thou mayest be well seen, and thy words audible to all the people. For because of the Passover all the tribes have come together and the gentiles also."

So the aforesaid Scribes and Pharisees set James on the pinnacle of the Temple and called to him: " O thou, the Just, to whom we all ought to listen, since the people is going astray after Jesus the crucified, tell us what is the door of Jesus? " And with a loud voice he answered: " Why do you ask me concerning the Son of Man? He sitteth Himself in heaven on the right hand of the great Power, and shall come on the clouds of heaven." And when many were convinced and gave glory for the witness of James, and said, " Hosanna to the Son of David," then again the same Scribes and Pharisees said to one another, " We were wrong to permit such a testimony to Jesus; but let us go up and cast him (James) down, that through fear they may not believe him." And they cried out saying, " Ho, Ho! even the Just has gone astray," and they fulfilled the Scriptures written in *Isaiah*: " Let us away with the Just, because he is troublesome to us; therefore they shall eat the fruits of their doings."

Accordingly they went up and cast the Just down. And they said to one another, " Let us stone James the Just," and they began to stone him, since he was not killed by the fall, but he turned and knelt down saying, " I beseech Thee, Lord God Father, forgive them, for they know not what they do." And so, as they were stoning him, one of the Priests of the sons of Rechab, the son of Rechabim, mentioned by Jeremiah the prophet, cried out saying, " Stop! what are ye doing? The Just prays for you." And a certain one of them, one of the fullers, taking the club with which he pounds clothes, brought it down on the head of the Just; and so he suffered martyrdom.

And they buried him there on the spot, near the Temple. A true witness has he become both to Jews and Greeks that Jesus is Christ. And immediately Vespasian besieges them.

The last sentence of this Hegesippus extract shows that Hegesippus had a different date for the death of James. Josephus makes the date A.D. 62; but, if this happened just before the siege of Vespasian, then the date is perhaps about A.D. 66.

It may well be that there is much in the story of Hegesippus that is legendary, but from it two things emerge. First, it is again evidence that James died a martyr's death. Second, it is evidence that, even after James became a Christian, he remained in complete loyalty to the orthodox Jewish Law. In fact, so loyal was James to the Law that they Jews regarded him as one of themselves. This, in fact, would fit well with James's attitude to Paul when Paul came to Jerusalem with the collection for the Jerusalem Church (*Acts* 21: 18-25), for we have already seen that on that occasion James urged Paul to take steps to show that he was not a destroyer of the Law by defraying the expenses of those who were engaged in the fulfilment of their Nazirite vow.

The Brother of our Lord

Before we leave James as a person there is one other question about him which we must try to solve. In *Galatians* 1: 19 Paul speaks of James as *the Lord's brother*. In *Matthew* 13: 55 and in *Mark* 6: 3 he is named among the brothers of Jesus; and in *Acts* 1: 14, although no names are given, the brothers of Jesus are said to be amongst the followers of Jesus in the earliest Church. The question we have to answer is: What is the meaning of the word *brother*? This is a question which must be answered for the Roman Catholic Church attaches a very great deal of importance to the answer, as does the Anglo-Catholic section of the Anglican Church. This is a question indeed on which, ever since the time of Jerome, there has been continuous argument in the Church. There are three theories of the relationship of these " brothers " to Jesus; and we shall consider them one by one.

The Hieronymian Theory

The Hieronymian theory takes its name from Jerome, who in Greek is Hieronymos. It was he who worked out this theory, and no one before him ever mentioned it. It is the theory which declares that the " brothers " of Jesus were in fact His *cousins*; and the importance of this theory is that it is the fixed and settled belief of the Roman Catholic Church; for that Church it is an article of faith. It was put forward by Jerome in A.D. 383. We shall best grasp Jerome's complicated argument by setting it out in a series of steps.

(i) James the brother of our Lord is included among the number of the apostles. Paul writes: " Other of the apostles saw I none, save James the Lord's brother " (*Galatians* I: 19). Therein lies the proof that James was an *apostle*.

(ii) Jerome insists that the word *apostle* can only be used of the Twelve; he insists that the title apostle is confined to them and to them alone. Now, if that be so, we must look for James among the Twelve. He cannot be identified with James the brother of John, and the son of Zebedee, who apart from anything else was martyred by the time of *Galatians* I: 19, as *Acts* 12: 2 plainly tells us; therefore he must be identified with the only other James among the Twelve, James the son of Alphaeus. So, then, James the brother of our Lord and James the son of Alphaeus are, on this theory, one and the same person.

(iii) Jerome proceeds to make still another identification. In *Mark* 6: 3 we read: " Is not this the carpenter, the son of Mary, the brother of James and Joses? "; and in *Mark* 15: 40 we find beside the Cross, Mary the mother of James the Little and of Joses. Here James the Little is the brother of Joses and the son of Mary, and must therefore be the same person as the James of *Mark* 6: 3. The James of *Mark* 6: 3 is the James who is the brother of our Lord; therefore, according to Jerome, James the brother of the Lord, James the son of Alphaeus, and James the Little are all the same person under different descriptions.

(iv) Jerome bases the next and final step of his argument on a deduction made from the lists of the women who were there when Jesus was crucified. Let us set down that list as it is given by the three gospel writers who give it.

In *Mark* 15: 40 the list is:
> Mary Magdalene, Mary the mother of James and Joses, and Salome.

In *Matthew* 27: 56 the list is:
> Mary Magdalene, Mary the mother of James the Little and of Joses, the mother of Zebedee's children.

In *John* 19: 25 the list is:
> Jesus' mother, His mother's sister, Mary the wife of Cleopas, and Mary Magdalene.

Now let us analyse these lists. In each of them Mary Magdalene appears by name. It is safe to identify Salome and the mother of Zebedee's children. But the real problem is John's list; and the question is *how many women are there in John's list?* Are there three, or are there four? Is the list to be read like this:

(i) Jesus' mother;
(ii) Jesus' mother's sister;
(iii) Mary the wife of Cleopas;
(iv) Mary Magdalene.

Or, is the list to be read like this:

(i) Jesus' mother;
(ii) Jesus' mother's sister, Mary the wife of Cleopas;
(iii) Mary Magdalene.

Jerome insists that the second way is correct, that there are three women, and that Jesus' mother's sister and Mary the wife of Cleopas are one and the same person. If that

be so Jesus' mother's sister must also be the Mary, who
in the other lists is the mother of James and of Joses.
Now this James is the same James as James the Less, and
as James the son of Alphaeus, and as James the apostle
who was known as the brother of our Lord. This means
that James is the son of Mary's sister and therefore is
Jesus' cousin.

There, then, is Jerome's argument. Against it at least
four criticisms can be levelled.

(i) Again and again James is called the *brother* of Jesus,
or he is numbered amongst the *brothers* of Jesus. The
word for *brother* is in each case *adelphos*, which is the
normal word for brother. True, *adelphos* can describe
people who belong to a common fellowship, as the
Christians called each other *brother*. True, it can be
used as a term of endearment, and we may call someone
with whom we enjoy personal intimacy a *brother*. But
when it is used of those who are related in kin or in
blood, it is, to say the least of it, very doubtful that it
can mean *cousin*. If James was the *cousin* of Jesus, it is
extremely unlikely—perhaps impossible—that he would
be called the *adelphos*, the *brother* of Jesus.

(ii) Jerome was quite wrong in proceeding on the
assumption that the term *apostle* can only be used of one
of the Twelve. Paul was an apostle (*Romans* I: I; I *Corinthians* I: I; 2 *Corinthians* I: I; *Galatians* I: I). Barnabas
was an apostle (*Acts* 14: 14; I *Corinthians* 9: 6). Silas
was an apostle (*Acts* 15: 22). Andronicus and Junia
were apostles (*Romans* 16: 7). It is quite impossible to
limit the word *apostle* to the Twelve; and, if that be so,
it is no longer necessary to look for James the Lord's
brother among the Twelve, and the whole argument of
Jerome collapses.

(iii) It is on the face of it much more likely that *John*
19: 25 is a list of four women, not three, for, if Mary the
wife of Cleopas is really the sister of Mary, Jesus' mother,

it would mean that there were two sisters in the same family both called Mary, which is extremely unlikely.

(iv) It must be remembered that the Church knew nothing of this theory until A.D. 383 when Jerome produced it; and it is quite certain that it would never have been produced for any other reason than to conserve and bolster the doctrine of the perpetual viginity of Mary. The whole point of the theory is to ensure that it will be believed that Mary had no children other than Jesus.

Even although the theory that those who are called Jesus' brothers were, in fact, His cousins is the official and accepted theory of the Roman Catholic Church, and even although there are Protestants who insist upon it, it must be dismissed as, on the facts, quite untenable.

The Epiphanian Theory

The second of the great theories concerning the relationship of Jesus and His " brothers " is called the Epiphanian Theory. It holds that those who are called the " brothers " of Jesus were, in fact, His half-brothers, and that they were sons of Joseph by a previous marriage. This theory is called the Epiphanian Theory after Epiphanius who strongly affirmed it about A.D. 370. He did not construct it. It existed long before this, and may indeed be said to be the most usual opinion in the early Church.

The substance of it already appears in an apocryphal book called the *Book of James* or the *Protevangelium* which dates back to the middle of the second century. That book tells how there was a devout husband and wife called Joachim and Anna. Their great grief was that they had no child. To their great joy in their old age a child was born to them, and this too, apparently from the story, was regarded as a virgin birth. The child was a girl and was called Mary and was to be the mother of Jesus. Joachim and Anna vowed their child to the Lord; and when she reached the age of three they took her to the Temple and left her there in the charge of the priests. She grew up in the Temple; and when she reached the age of twelve the priests took thought for her marriage. They called together the widowers of the people, telling each man to bring his rod with him. Among them came Joseph the carpenter. The High Priest took the rods, and Joseph's was last. To the other rods nothing happened; but from the rod of Joseph there flew a dove which came and settled on Joseph's head. Thus it was revealed that Joseph was to take Mary to wife. Joseph at first was very unwilling. " I have sons," he said, " and I am an old man, but she is a girl: lest I become a laughing-stock to the children of Israel " (*Protevangelium* 9: 1). But in the end he took her in obedience to the will of God, and in due time Jesus was born. The material of the *Protevangelium* is, of course, legendary; but it does show that by the middle of the second century the theory which was one day to bear the name of Epiphanius was widely known and widely held.

It has to be stated at the very outset that there is no direct evidence for this theory whatsoever. If it is to be supported, it must be indirectly supported. What then are the indirect pieces of evidence and the implications of Scripture which can be cited on its behalf?

(i) It is asked: Would Jesus have committed His mother to the care of John, if she had other sons besides Himself? (*John* 19: 26, 27). The answer to that is that, so far as we know, Jesus' family were quite out of sympathy with Him, and it would hardly have been possible to commit His mother to their care.

(ii) It is argued that the behaviour of Jesus' " brothers " to Him is that of elder brothers to a younger brother. They questioned His sanity, and wished to take Him home (*Mark* 3: 21, 31-35); they were actively hostile to Him (*John* 7: 1-5). But it could just as well be argued that their conduct was due to the fact that they found Him an embarrassment to the family irrespective of age.

(iii) It is argued that Joseph must have been older than Mary, because he vanishes completely from the gospel story and must, therefore, in all probability have died before Jesus' public ministry began. The mother of Jesus was at the wedding feast at Cana of Galilee, but there is no mention of Joseph (*John* 2: 1). Jesus is called, at least sometimes, the son of Mary, and the implication is that Joseph was dead and that Mary was a widow (*Mark* 6: 3; but cp. *Matthew* 13: 55). Further, Jesus' long stay in Nazareth, until He was thirty years of age (*Luke* 3: 22), is most easily to be explained by the assumption that Joseph had died and that Jesus became responsible for the support of the household. But the fact that Joseph was older than Mary does not by any means prove that he had no other children by Mary; and the fact that Jesus stayed in Nazareth as the village carpenter in order to support the family would much more naturally indicate that He was the eldest, and not the youngest, son.

To these arguments Lightfoot would add two more general arguments.

First, he says that this theory is the theory of Christian tradition; and, second, he claims that anything else is " abhorrent to Christian sentiment."

But basically this theory springs from the same origin as the Hieronymian theory. Its aim, and the reason for its existence, is to conserve the perpetual virginity of Mary. It springs from that tendency in the thought of the Church to magnify asceticism and to belittle the ordinary married state. There is no direct evidence whatsoever for it; and no one would ever have thought of it unless it had been desired to retain the conception of the perpetual viginity of the mother of our Lord.

The Helvidian Theory

The third theory is called the Helvidian theory. It states quite simply that the brothers and sisters of Jesus were in the full sense of the term His brothers and sisters, that, to use the technical term, they were His uterine brothers and sisters. Nothing whatever is known of the Helvidius with whose name this theory is connected. All that is known of him is that he wrote a treatise to support this theory which Jerome strongly opposed and contradicted. What then may be said in support of this Helvidian theory?

(i) As we see it, it is true to say that no one reading the New Testament story without theological presuppositions would ever think of anything else. On the face of it the New Testament narrative does not think of Jesus' brothers and sisters as anything else but His brothers and sisters in the full sense of the term.

(ii) The birth narratives both in *Matthew* and *Luke* presuppose that Mary had other children. Matthew writes: " Then Joseph being raised from sleep did as the angel of the Lord had bidden him, and took unto him his wife, and knew her not till she had brought forth her firstborn son " (*Matthew* 1: 24, 25). The clear implication is that Joseph entered into normal married relationships with Mary after the birth of Jesus. Tertullian, in fact, uses this passage to prove that both virginity and the married state are hallowed and consecrated in Christ by the fact that Mary was first a virgin and then a wife in the full sense of the term. Luke in writing of the birth of Jesus uses the same phrase as Matthew: " She brought forth her *firstborn* son " (*Luke* 2: 7). To call Jesus a firstborn son is plainly to indicate that there were other children to follow. The birth narratives in *Matthew* and *Luke* lend no support to any view other than that Jesus' brothers and sisters were also children of Joseph and Mary.

(iii) As we have already said, the fact that Jesus remained in Nazareth as the village carpenter until the age of thirty is at least an indication that He was the eldest son, and had to take upon Himself the responsibility of the support of the family, after the death of Joseph.

We believe that the brothers and sisters of Jesus were in truth and in fact His brothers and sisters. Any other theory ultimately springs from the glorification of asceticism and from a wish to regard Mary as for ever a virgin. It is surely a far more lovely thing to believe in the sanctity of the home than to insist that celibacy is a higher thing than married love.

We can then believe that James who is called the Lord's brother was in every sense the brother of Jesus.

James as the Author

Can we then say that the James who was the Lord's brother is also the author of this letter? The more we investigate the authorship and the date of this letter the more we shall find ourselves in difficulties; for again and again we shall find that the arguments on either side are amazingly evenly balanced. Let us then collect the evidence in favour of the view that James is the author.

(i) If James wrote a letter at all, that letter would most naturally be a general epistle, as this letter is. James was not, like Paul, a traveller and a man of many congregations. James was the leader of the Jewish section of the Church; and the only natural kind of letter for him to write would be a general epistle specially directed to all Jewish Christians.

(ii) There is scarcely anything in the letter that a good and orthodox Jew could not accept. So much so is this the case that there are those who think that this is actually a Jewish ethical tract which has found its way into the New Testament. A. H. McNeile has pointed out that in instance after instance there are phrases in *James* which can be read equally well in a Christian or a Jewish sense. The Twelve Tribes of the Dispersion (I: I) could be understood by a Jew of the exiled Jews who were scattered all over the world; and by a Christian as the Christian Church, the new Israel of God. " The Lord " can again

and again in this letter be understood equally well of
Jesus and God (1: 7; 4: 10, 15; 5: 7, 8, 10, 11, 14, 15).
Our begetting by God by the word of His truth that we
might be the first fruits of His creation (1: 18) can equally
well be understood of God's first act of the creation of the
world, or of His recreation of men in Jesus Christ. The
perfect law, and the royal law (1: 25; 2: 8), can equally
well be understood of the ethical law of the Ten Commandments or the new law of Christ. The elders of the Church,
the *ekklēsia* (5: 14) can equally well be understood as
meaning the elders of the Christian Church or the Jewish
elders, for in the Septuagint the word *ekklēsia* is the title
of the chosen nation of God. In 2: 2 " your *assembly* "
is spoken of. The word there used for *assembly* is in fact
sunagōgē, which of course can mean the *synagogue* even
more readily than it can mean *the Christian congregation*.
His habit of addressing his readers as *brothers* is thoroughly
Christian, but it is equally thoroughly Jewish. The parousia
of the Lord, and the picture of the Judge standing at the
door (5: 7, 9) are just as common in Jewish thought as
they are in Christian thought. The accusation that they
have murdered the just man (5: 6) is a picture and a
phrase which occurs again and again in the prophets, but
a Christian could read it as a statement of the Crucifixion
of Christ. There is nothing in this letter which an orthodox
Jew could not heartily accept, if he read it in his own
terms.

It could well be argued that all this perfectly suits
James. James was the leader of what might be called
Jewish Christianity; he was the leader of the part of the
Church which remained centred in Jerusalem. There
must have been a time when the Church was very close
to Judaism, when, in fact, it was rather more a reformed
and recreated Judaism than anything else. There was a
kind of Christianity which had not the width or the
universality which the mind of Paul put into it. Paul
himself said that the sphere of the Gentiles had been

allocated to him and the sphere of the Jews had been allocated to Peter, James and John (*Galatians* 2: 9). The letter of James may well represent a kind of Christianity which had remained static in its earliest form. This would explain two things. First, it would explain the frequency with which *James* repeats the teaching of the Sermon on the Mount. We may, out of many instances, compare *James* 2: 12, 13 and *Matthew* 6: 14, 15; *James* 3: 11-13 and *Matthew* 7: 16-20; *James* 5: 12 and *Matthew* 5: 34-37. Any Jewish Christian would be supremely interested in the ethical teaching of the Christian faith.

Second, it would help to explain the relationship of this letter to the teaching of Paul. At a first reading *James* 2: 14-26 reads like a direct attack on Paulinism. " By works a man is justified and not by faith " (*James* 2: 24). At first sight this seems a flat contradiction of the Pauline doctrine of justification by faith. What *James* is attacking is a so-called faith which has no ethical results and consequences. But one thing is quite clear—anyone who charges Paul with preaching such a faith cannot possibly have read Paul's letters. These letters are full of ethical demands. One has only to read a chapter like *Romans* 12 to see that Paul preached a faith which has the fullest ethical consequences. Now James died in A.D. 62, and, therefore, could not have read Paul's letters, because these letters did not become the common property of the Church until at least A.D. 90. It was not until then that they were edited and generally issued to the Church. Therefore what *James* is attacking is either a misunderstanding of what Paul said, or a perversion of it; and nowhere was such a misunderstanding or perversion more likely to arise than in Jerusalem, where Paul's stress on faith and grace, and Paul's attack on the law were likely to be regarded with more suspicion and more misunderstanding than anywhere else. It is highly unlikely that *James* is attacking Paul; what it is attacking is a false interpre-

tation of Paulinism; and nowhere was such a letter more
likely to be written than in Jerusalem.

The Jewish character of this letter well suits James.

(iii) It has been pointed out that the letter of James
and the letter of the Council of Jerusalem to the Gentile
Churches have at least two rather curious resemblances.
Both begin with the word *Greeting* (*James* 1: 1; *Acts*
15: 23). The word is *chairein*. Now this was the normal
Greek beginning to a letter, but nowhere else in all the
New Testament is it found other than in the beginning
of the letter of Claudius Lysias the military officer to the
governor of the province (*Acts* 23: 26). It is an odd fact
that the only two New Testament documents which use
this beginning to a letter are connected with the name of
James. Second, *Acts* 15: 17 has a phrase in the letter of the
Council of Jerusalem in which it speaks of the Gentiles
upon whom my name is called. This phrase occurs nowhere
else in the New Testament other than in *James* 2: 7
where it is translated *the name by which you are called*.
Although the Authorized Version translations in the two
passages are different, the phrase in the Greek is exactly
the same. It is curious that the letter of the Council of
Jerusalem presents us with two unusual phrases which
recur only in the letter of James, when we remember
that the letter of the Council of Jerusalem must have been
drafted by James.

There is then evidence on the one hand which would
lend colour to the belief that the Epistle of James is indeed
the work of James the Lord's brother, and the head of
the Jerusalem Church.

But on the other hand there are facts which make us
a little doubtful if James the Lord's brother is after all the
author of this letter.

(i) If the writer of this letter was the brother of our
Lord, we would have expected him to make some reference
to that fact. All he calls himself is " a servant of God and

of the Lord Jesus Christ " (1: 1). Such a reference would not have been in any sense for his own personal glory, but simply to lend authority to his letter. And such authority would have been specially useful outside Palestine, in countries where James could hardly have been known at all. If this James was indeed the Lord's brother, it is surprising that he makes no reference, direct or indirect, to that fact.

(ii) Failing a reference to his relationship to Jesus, we would have expected a reference to the fact that he was an apostle, if James the Lord's brother was the writer of this letter. That he was an apostle there is no doubt. It was Paul's regular custom to begin his letters with a reference to his apostleship. Again it is not a question of personal prestige; it is simply a guarantee of the authority by which he writes. If this James was indeed the Lord's brother, the head of the Jerusalem Church, and one of the apostolic band, we should have expected some reference at least at the beginning of the letter to that fact.

(iii) But the most surprising fact of all is that which made Luther question the right of this letter to a place in the New Testament at all. The most surprising thing is the almost complete absence of any references to Jesus Christ. Only twice in the whole letter is the name of Jesus mentioned, and these mentions are almost incidental (1: 1; 2: 1). There is no reference at all to the Resurrection of Jesus. We know well that the early Church was built on faith in the Risen Christ. If this letter is the work of James, then it is contemporary with the events of the Book of Acts, and in *Acts* the Resurrection is mentioned no fewer than twenty-five times. What makes it still more surprising is that James had a personal and private reason for not writing about the appearance of Jesus and, as we have seen, it may well have been that appearance which changed the direction of his whole life. It is surprising that anyone writing at such a time in the Church's history should write with no reference to the Resurrection of Jesus; and it is doubly surprising if the writer is James the brother of our Lord. Further, there is no reference to Jesus as Messiah. If James, the leader of the Jewish Church, was writing to Jewish Christians in these very early days, then one would have thought that his main aim would have been to present Jesus as Messiah, or that at least he would have made his belief in that fact plain; and yet in the letter there is no reference to it.

(iv) It is plain that the writer of this letter is steeped in the Old Testament; it is also plain that he was intimately acquainted with the Wisdom Literature; and that in James was only to be expected. There are in his letter twenty-three apparent quotations from the Sermon on the Mount; that too is easy to understand, because from the very beginning, long before the gospels were written, compendiums of Jesus' teaching must have circulated. It is argued by some that he must have known Paul's letters to the Romans and to the Galatians in order to write as he does about faith and works, and it is argued rightly that a Jew who had never been outside Palestine, and who died in A.D. 62 could not have known these letters. As we have seen, this argument will not stand, because the criticism of Paul's doctrine in *James* is criticism which could only have been offered by someone who had not read the actual letters of Paul at first hand, and who is dealing with a misunderstanding or a perversion of Pauline doctrine. But the phrase in 1: 17: " Every good gift and every perfect boon," is an hexametre line, and is clearly a quotation from some Greek poet; and the phrase in 3: 16; " the wheel of being," may be an Orphic phrase from the mystery religions. How did James of Palestine pick up quotations like these?

As we can see, there are things which are difficult to understand and to account for on the assumption that James, the brother of our Lord, was the actual author of this letter.

THE LETTER OF JAMES

We began by saying that time and time again when we consider the evidence for the authorship and date of this letter, we find the arguments extraordinarily evenly balanced. And the evidence for and against the authorship of the letter is like that. For the moment we must leave the matter in suspense, and turn to certain other questions.

The Date of the Letter

When we turn to the evidence for the date of the letter we find this same even balance. It is possible to argue that the letter is very early, and it is possible to argue that it is rather late. Let us set down the evidence.

(i) When James was writing, it is clear that the hope of the Second Coming of Jesus Christ was still very real (5: 7-9). Now the expectation of the Second Coming never left the Christian Church, but it did to some extent fade from the foreground of the Church's thought, when it was unexpectedly long delayed. It could, therefore, be argued on this ground that this letter must be dated very early in the history of the Church.

(ii) In the early chapters of the Book of Acts and in the letters of Paul, there is a continuous background of Jewish controversy against the accepting of the Gentiles into the Church on grounds of faith and grace alone. Wherever Paul went the Judaizers followed him, and the acceptance of the Gentiles was not a battle which was readily won. In the letter of James there is not even a hint of this Jewish-Gentile controversy, a fact which is doubly surprising when we remember that James, the Lord's brother, took a leading part in settling it at the Council of Jerusalem, described in *Acts* 15. If that is so, this letter could be either very early, and could have been written before that controversy emerged; or, it could be late, and it could have been written after the last echo of the controversy had died away and the Gentiles were unquestionably integrated into the Church. The fact that there is no mention of the

Jewish-Gentile controversy can be used as an argument either way.

(iii) The evidence from the Church order, which is in the background of the letter, is equally conflicting. The meeting place of the Church is still called the *sunagōgē* (2: 2). That points to an early date, for later an assembly of Christians would definitely have been called the *ekklēsia*, for the Jewish term was soon dropped. The elders of the Church are mentioned (5: 14), but there is no mention of either deacons or bishops. This again indicates an early date, and possibly a Jewish connection, for the eldership was a Jewish institution before it was a Christian one. James is worried about the existence of *many teachers* (3: 1). This could well indicate a very early situation, before the Church had systematized its ministry and introduced some kind of order; or, it could indicate a late date, when many false and heretical teachers had arisen to plague the Church.

But there are two general facts which seem on the whole to indicate that *James* is late. As we have seen there is hardly any mention of Jesus at all. The subject of the letter is, in fact, the faults and the failings, the inadequacies and the imperfections, the sins and the mistakes of the members of the Church. This seems definitely to point to a fairly late date. The early preaching was ablaze with the grace and the glory of the Risen Christ; later preaching, becomes, as it so often is today, a tirade against the imperfections of the members of the Church. The second general fact is the condemnation of the rich (2: 1-3; 5: 1-6). The flattery of the rich and the arrogance of the rich seem to have been real problems when this letter was written. Now in the very early Church there were few or no rich men at all (I *Corinthians* 1: 26, 27). *James* seems to indicate a later time when the once poor Church was being threatened with the spirit of worldliness in its members. That is a situation which suits a later date much better than it does an earlier one.

THE LETTER OF JAMES

The Preachers of the Ancient World

It will help us to place this so-called letter of James and it may also help us to identify its author, if we place it in its context in the ancient world.

The sermon is identified with the Christian Church, but the sermon was by no means the invention of the Christian Church. The sermon had its roots in both the Hellenistic and the Jewish world. And when we set *James* beside both these Hellenistic and these Jewish sermons we cannot fail to be struck by the resemblances.

1. Let us look first at the Greek preachers and their sermons. The wandering philosopher was a common figure in the ancient world. Sometimes he was a Stoic; far more often he was a Cynic. Wherever men were gathered together you would find him there calling them to virtue. You would find him at the street corner and in the city squares; you would find him at the vast concourses which gathered for the games; you would even find him at the gladiatorial games, sometimes even directly addressing the emperor, rebuking him for luxury and tyranny, and calling him to virtue and justice. The ancient preacher, the philosopher-missionary, was a regular figure in the ancient world. There was a time when philosophy had been the business of the schools, but now the voice of philosophy and its ethical demands was to be heard daily in the market-place.

These ancient sermons had certain characteristics. The method was always the same, and that method had deeply influenced Paul's presentation of the gospel, and James too was in the same line of descent. Let us list some of the tricks of the trade of these ancient preachers, and let us see how they occur in *James*, and let us also have in mind the way in which Paul writes to his Churches. The main aim of these ancient preachers, it must be remembered, was not to investigate new truth; it was to awaken sinners to the error of their ways; and to compel them to see truths, which they knew but deliberately neglected

32

or had forgotten. Their aim was to confront men with the good life in the midst of the looseness of their living and their forgetfulness of the gods.

(i) They frequently carried on imaginary conversations with imaginary opponents. Frequently they spoke in what has been called a kind of " truncated dialogue." James also uses that method in 2: 18f and 5: 13f.

(ii) They habitually effected their transition from one part of the sermon to another, and from one subject to another, by way of a question which introduced the new subject. Again James does that in 2: 14 and 4: I.

(iii) They were very fond of imperatives in which they commanded their hearers to right action and to the abandoning of their errors. In *James's* 108 verses there are almost 60 imperatives.

(iv) They were very fond of the rhetorical question flung out at their audience. James frequently employs such questions (cp. *James* 2: 4, 5; 2: 14-16; 3: II, 12; 4: 4).

(v) They frequently dealt in apostrophes, vivid direct addresses to particular sections of the audience. So James apostrophises the merchants out for gain, and the arrogant rich (4: 13; 5: 6).

(vi) They were fond of personifying virtues and vices, sins and graces. So James personifies sin (I: I5); mercy (2: I3); rust (5: 3).

(vii) They sought to awaken the interest of their audience by pictures and figures from everyday life. The figure of the bridle, the rudder and the forest fire are standard figures in the ancient sermons (cp. *James* 3: 3-6). Amongst many others James vividly uses the picture of the farmer and his patience (5: 7).

(viii) They frequently used the example of famous men and women to point their moral. So James uses the examples of

Abraham (2: 21-23); Rahab (2: 25); Job (5: 11); Elijah (5: 17).

(ix) It was the custom of the ancient preachers to begin their sermon with a paradox which would arrest the attention of their hearers, with a surprising statement which would make men listen. James does that when he begins by telling a man to think it all joy when he is involved in all kinds of trials (1: 2). In the same way the ancient preachers often pointed out how true goodness meant the reversal of all popular verdicts on life. So James insists that the happiness of the rich lies in their being brought low (1: 10). They used the weapon of irony as James does (2: 14-19; 5: 1-6).

(x) The ancient preachers could and did speak with harshness and with sternness. So James addresses his reader as: " Vain man! " and calls those who listen to him spiritual adulterers (2: 20; 4: 4). The ancient preachers used the lash, and so does James.

(xi) The ancient preachers had certain standard ways of constructing their sermons.

(a) They often concluded a section with a vivid antithesis, setting the right beside the wrong way. James follows the same custom (cp. 2: 13; 2: 26).

(b) They often made their point by means of a searching question fired at the hearer; and so does James (4: 12).

(c) They often used quotations in their preaching and drove home an argument by a final quotation. This also James does (5: 20; 1: 11, 17; 4: 6; 5: 11).

It is true that we do not find in James the bitterness, the scolding, the frivolous and often broad humour that the Greek preachers used; but it is plain to see that James uses all the other methods which the wandering Hellenistic preachers used to win their way into the minds and hearts of men.

2. The Jewish world also had its tradition of preaching. That preaching was done mainly by the Rabbis at the services of the Synagogue. It had many of the characteristics of the preaching of the Greek wandering philosophers. It had its rhetorical questions and its imperatives and its pictures and figures taken from life, and its quotations and its citations of the example of the heroes of the faith. But Jewish preaching had one curious characteristic. It was deliberately disconnected. The Jewish masters instructed their pupils never to linger for any length of time on any one subject, but to move quickly from one subject to another, in order to maintain the interest of the listener. Hence one of the names for preaching was *charaz*, which literally means *stringing beads*. The Jewish sermon was frequently a string of moral truths and moral exhortations coming one after another. This is exactly what *James* is. It is difficult, if not impossible, to extract from *James* a continuous and coherent plan or scheme. Its sections follow each other with a certain disconnectedness. Goodspeed writes: " The work has been compared to a chain, each link related to the one before and the one after it. Others have compared its contents to beads on a string. . . . And, perhaps, *James* is not so much a chain of thoughts or beads as it is a handful of pearls dropped one by one into the hearer's mind." So, then, we see that *James*, whether looked at from the Hellenistic or from the Jewish point of view, is a good example of an ancient sermon. And therein we may find the clue we need to its authorship. With all this in our minds let us now turn to ask who the author is.

The Author of James

There are five possibilities.

(i) We begin with a theory, worked out in detail by Meyer about forty years ago, and revived by Easton in the new *Interpreter's Bible*. One of the commonest things in the ancient world was for books to be published in the name of some great figure of the past. Jewish literature between the Testaments is full of writings like that. There are writings which are put into the mouth of Moses, the Twelve Patriarchs, Baruch, Enoch, Isaiah, and many others. Devout men wrote books to encourage their contemporaries when they were going through hard times, and put what they had to say into the mouth of the great men of the past. This among the Jews was an accepted practice. One of the best-known books in the Apocrypha is the *Wisdom of Solomon*, in which the later Sage attributes new wisdom to the wisest of the kings. Now let us remember three things about *James*. (*a*) There is nothing in it which an orthodox Jew could not accept, if the two references to Jesus in 1: 1 and 2: 1 be removed, as they easily can be. (*b*) The Greek for James is in fact *Iakōbos*, which of course is *Jacob*. In the New Testament *Iakōbos* is translated *James*, but in the Old Testament it is *Jacob*. (c) The book is addressed to " the twelve tribes who are scattered abroad." This theory holds that *James* is nothing other than a Jewish writing, written under the name of Jacob, and meant for the Jews who were exiles from Palestine and scattered throughout the world, meant to confirm and encourage them in faith and belief amidst the trials through which they might be passing in Gentile lands.

This theory is further elaborated in this way. In *Genesis* 49 we have Jacob's last address to his sons. The address consists of a series of short descriptions in which each of his sons is in turn characterized; it is like a series of short character studies. Meyer professed to be able to find in our letter of *James* repetitions and allusions which lead the mind back to the descriptions of each of the patriarchs, and, therefore, of each of the twelve tribes, in Jacob's address. Here are some of his identifications with the reference in *James*, and the passage in *Genesis* to which it is supposed to be an allusion.

36

Asher is the worldly rich man; *James* I: 9-11; *Genesis* 49: 20.

Issachar is the doer of good deeds; *James* I: 12; *Genesis* 49: 14, 15.

Reuben is the first fruits; *James* I: 18; *Genesis* 49: 3.

Simeon stands for anger; *James* I: 19, 20; *Genesis* 49: 5-7.

Levi is the tribe which is specially connected with religion and is alluded to in *James* I: 26, 27.

Naphtali is characterized by peace; *James* 3: 18; *Genesis* 49: 21.

Gad stands for wars and fightings; *James* 4: I, 2; *Genesis* 47: 19.

Dan represents waiting for salvation; *James* 5: 7; *Genesis* 49: 18.

Joseph represents prayer; *James* 5: 14-18; *Genesis* 49: 22-26.

Benjamin stands for birth and death; *James* 5: 20; *Genesis* 48: 27.

That is a most ingenious theory. No one can either finally prove it or disprove it; and it certainly would explain the reference to the twelve tribes scattered abroad in I: I in the most natural way. This theory would hold that some Christian came upon this Jewish tract, written under the name of Jacob to all the exiled Jews, and was so impressed with its moral worth and value, that he made certain adjustments and additions to it and issued it as a Christian book. There is no doubt that this is an attractive theory—but it is possible for a theory to be too ingenious.

(ii) Just as the Jews did, the Christians also wrote many books under the names of the great figures of the Christian faith. There are gospels issued under the name of Peter and Thomas and James himself; there is a letter under the name of Barnabas; there are gospels of Nicodemus and Bartholomew; and there are Acts of John, Paul, Andrew, Peter, Thomas, Philip and others. It was common practice for the Christian to write books under the names of the great figures of the Church. The technical title for these books is *pseudonymous*, that is, written under a *false name*. It has been suggested that this is a letter written by someone else under the name of James the Lord's brother. That is apparently what Jerome thought when he said that this letter " was issued by someone under James's name." But, whatever else this work is, it cannot be that, because, when anyone wrote such a book, he was very careful to make quite clear who was supposed to be writing it, and the name of the great figure of the past, in whose name it was being issued, was very prominently displayed. If this had been pseudonymous no possible doubt would have been left that the author was supposed to be James *the brother of our Lord*. That supposed fact would have been heavily stressed; but, in fact, it is not mentioned at all. The theory of pseudonymity is ruled out.

(iii) Moffatt inclined to the theory that this book was written by a teacher called James, about whom we know nothing at all. He inclined to believe that the writer indeed was called James, but that he was not the brother of our Lord, or any other well-known James, but simply a teacher called James of whose life and story we have no information whatever. That is by no means impossible for the name James was just as common then as it is now; but it would be rather difficult to understand how such a book gained entry into the New Testament, and how it came to be connected with the name of James, the Lord's brother.

(iv) The traditional view is that the book was written by James, the Lord's brother. We have already seen that it seems strange that such a book should have only two incidental references to Jesus, and none at all to the Resurrection, or to Jesus as the Messiah. And a further and most serious difficulty is this. The book is written in Greek; further, it is written in good Greek. Ropes says that Greek must have been the mother tongue of the man who wrote it; and Mayor, himself one of the greatest of Greek scholars, says, " I should be inclined to rate the Greek of this epistle as approaching more nearly to the standard of classical purity than that of any other book in the New Testament with the exception perhaps of the Epistle to the Hebrews." Now, quite certainly, James's mother tongue was Aramaic and not Greek. Quite certainly if he wrote, it would be in Aramaic; and quite certainly he would not be a master of classical Greek. His whole orthodox Jewish upbringing would make him despise and avoid Greek, as a Gentile and accursed tongue. It is next door to impossible to think of James actually penning this letter.

(v) So we come to the fifth possibility. Let us remember how closely *James* resembles a sermon. Surely it is possible that this is, in fact, in substance a sermon preached by James, and taken down by someone else, translated into Greek, added to and decorated a little, and then issued to the Church at large so that all men should possess it and benefit from it. That explains its form; it explains how it ever came to be attached to the name of James; it even explains the scarcity of the references to Jesus, to the Resurrection, and to the Messiahship of Jesus; for in one single sermon James could not go through the whole gamut of orthodoxy, and is, in fact, engaged in pressing moral duty upon men, and not in talking about theology at all. It seems to us that the one theory which explains the facts is that this indeed goes back to a sermon of James, which someone took down, knew, loved and remembered, which was edited with skill and loving care, which was judiciously added to, and which was then issued to the Church at large. One thing is certain—we may approach this little letter feeling that it is one of the lesser books of the New Testament; if we study it faithfully, we will lay it down thanking God that it was preserved for our edification and our inspiration.

JAMES

GREETINGS

James 1 : 1

> James, the slave of God and of the Lord Jesus Christ, sends greetings to the twelve tribes who are scattered throughout the world.

AT the very beginning of his letter James describes himself by the title wherein lies his only honour and his only glory. He describes himself as *the slave of God and of the Lord Jesus Christ*. With the exception of Jude he is the only New Testament writer to describe himself by that term (*doulos*, slave) without any qualification. Paul describes himself as the slave of Jesus Christ, and His apostle (*Romans* 1 : 1; *Philippians* 1 : 1). To the title of slave he adds the title of apostle. But James will go no further than to call himself the slave of God and of the Lord Jesus Christ. There are at least four implications in this title.

(i) It implies *absolute obedience*. The slave knows no law but his master's word; the slave has no rights whatever of his own. The slave is the absolute possession of his master, and is bound to give his master an absolute and unquestioning obedience.

(ii) It implies *absolute humility*. It is the word of a man who thinks not of his privileges but of his duties; not of his rights but of his obligations. It is the word of the man who has lost his self in the service of God. It is the word of the man who has literally denied himself, who has said No to himself that he may ever say Yes to God.

(iii) It implies *absolute loyalty*. It is the word of the man who has no interests of his own, because he is utterly pledged to God. What he does, he does for God. His own profit and his own preference do not enter into his calculations. His loyalty is to God.

(iv) Yet, at the back of it, this word implies a certain *pride*. So far from being a title of dishonour it was the title by which the greatest ones of the Old Testament were known. Moses was the *doulos* of God (I *Kings* 8: 53; *Daniel* 9: 11; *Malachi* 4: 4); so were Joshua and Caleb (*Joshua* 2: 8; *Numbers* 14: 24); so were the great patriarchs, Abraham, Isaac and Jacob (*Deuteronomy* 9: 27); so was Job (*Job* 1: 8); so was Isaiah (*Isaiah* 20: 3); and *doulos* is distinctively the title by which the prophets were known (*Amos* 3: 7; *Zechariah* 1: 6; *Jeremiah* 7: 25). By taking the title *doulos* James sets himself in the great succession of those who found their freedom and their peace and their glory in perfect submission to the will of God. The only greatness to which the Christian can ever aspire is the greatness of being the slave of God.

There is one unusual thing about this opening salutation. James sends greetings to his readers; the word used is *chairein*. *Chairein* is the regular opening word of salutation in ordinary secular Greek letters. Paul never uses it. He always uses the distinctively Christian greeting, " Grace and peace " (*Romans* 1: 5; I *Corinthians* 1: 3; 2 *Corinthians* 1: 2; *Galatians* 1: 3; *Ephesians* 1: 2; *Philippians* 1: 2; *Colossians* 1: 2; I *Thessalonians* 1: 1; 2 *Thessalonians* 1: 2; *Philemon* 3). In every case Paul avoids the usual secular greeting and uses the distinctively Christian greeting. James on the other hand uses the ordinary secular greeting. This greeting occurs only twice in the rest of the New Testament, in the letter which Claudius Lysias, the Roman officer, wrote to Felix to ensure the safe journeying of Paul (*Acts* 23: 26), and in the general letter issued after the decision of the Council of Jerusalem to allow the Gentiles into the Church (*Acts* 15: 23). This is interesting, because it was James who presided over that Council (*Acts* 15: 13). It may be that James used the most general greeting that he could find, because his letter was going out to the widest public.

THE JEWS THROUGHOUT THE WORLD

James I : I (continued)

THE letter is addressed to *the twelve tribes who are scattered abroad*. Here we have a technical word at which we must stop and look. Literally the greeting is to the twelve tribes in the *Diaspora*. The word *Diaspora* is the technical word for the Jews who lived outside Palestine. All the millions of Jews who were, for one reason or another, outside the Promised Land were the *Diaspora*. It is worth while to stop and to see how the Jews were scattered all over the world, and the numbers of them who lived in every country. This dispersal of the Jews throughout the world was of the very greatest importance for the spread of Christianity, because it meant that all over the world there were synagogues, and from these synagogues the Christian preachers could take their start; it meant that all over the world there were groups of men and women who themselves already knew the Old Testament, and who had persuaded others among the Gentiles at least to be interested in their faith. The dispersal of the Jews was part of the providential working of God, for it gave the Christian preachers a point of contact in almost every city and town in the world. Let us then see how this dispersal took place.

Sometimes—and the process began in this way—the Jews were forcibly taken out of their own land, and were compelled to live as exiles in foreign lands. There were three such great movements.

(i) The first compulsory removal came when the people of the Northern Kingdom, who had their capital in Samaria, were conquered by the Assyrians and were carried away into captivity in Assyria (2 *Kings* 17: 23; I *Chronicles* 5: 26). These are the lost ten tribes who never returned. The Jews themselves believed that at the end of all things all Jews would be gathered together in Jerusalem, but until the end of the world these ten tribes, they believed, would never return. The Jews founded this belief on a rather fanciful interpretation of an Old Testament text. The Rabbis argued like this: " The ten tribes never return for it is said of them, ' He will cast them into another land, as it is this day ' (*Deuteronomy* 29: 27). As then this day departs and never returns, so too are they to depart and never return. As this day becomes dark, and then again light, so too will it one day be light again for the ten tribes for whom it was dark." So then the first dispersal by compulsion was to Assyria.

(ii) The second compulsory removal was about 580 B.C. At that time the Babylonians conquered the Southern Kingdom whose capital was at Jerusalem, and carried the best of the people away to Babylon (2 *Kings* 24 :14-16; *Psalm* 137). In Babylon the Jews behaved very differently; they stubbornly refused to be assimilated and to lose their nationality. They were said to be congregated mainly in the cities of Nehardea and Nisibis. It was actually in Babylon that Jewish scholarship reached its finest flower, for there there was produced the Babylonian *Talmud*, the immense sixty volume exposition of the Jewish law. When Josephus wrote his book on the *Wars of the Jews* the first edition was not in Greek, but in Aramaic, and was designed for the scholarly Jews in Babylon. He tells us that the Jews rose to such power in Babylon that at one time the province of Mesopotamia was under Jewish rule. Its two Jewish rulers were Asidaeus and Anilaeus; and on the death of Anilaeus it was said that no fewer than 50,000 Jews were massacred. The dispersal took the Jews to Babylon, and raised them to eminence there.

(iii) The third compulsory transplantation took place much later. When Pompey conquered the Jews, and took Jerusalem in 63 B.C., he took back to Rome many Jews as slaves. Their rigid adherence to their own ceremonial law, and their stubborn observance of the Sabbath, made them difficult as slaves; and most of them were freed. They took up residence in a kind of quarter of their own on the far side of the Tiber. But before long they were to be found flourishing all over the city. Dio Cassius says of them, "They were often suppressed, but they nevertheless mightily increased, so that they achieved even the free exercise of their customs." Julius Caesar was their great protector, and we read of them mourning all night long at his bier. We read of them present in large numbers when Cicero was defending Flaccus. In A.D. 19 the whole Jewish community was banished from Rome on the charge that they had robbed a wealthy female proselyte on pretence of sending the money to the Temple; and at that time 4,000 of them were conscripted to fight against the brigands in Sardinia; but they were soon received back. When the Jews of Palestine sent their deputation to Rome to complain of the rule of Archelaus, we read that the deputation was joined by 8,000 Jews resident in the city. Roman literature is full of contemptuous references to the Jews, for anti-Semitism is no new thing; and the very number of the references is proof of the part that the Jews played in the life of the city.

So, then, we see that compulsory transplantation took the Jews by the thousand to Babylon and to Rome. But far greater numbers left Palestine of their own free-will for more comfortable and more profitable lands. Two lands in particular received thousands of Jews. Palestine was sandwiched between the two great powers, Syria and Egypt. Palestine was, therefore, liable at any time to become a battleground. For that reason many Jews left Palestine to take up residence either in Egypt or in Syria.

During the time of Nebuchadnezzar there was a voluntary exodus of many Jews to Egypt (2 *Kings* 25: 26). As far back as 650 B.C. the Egyptian king Psammetichus was said to have had Jewish mercenaries in his armies. When Alexander the Great founded Alexandria special privileges were offered to settlers there, and the Jews came in large numbers. Alexandria was divided into five administrative sections; and two of them were inhabited by Jews. In Alexandria alone there were more than 1,000,000 Jews.

The settlement of the Jews in Egypt went so far that about 50 B.C. a temple, modelled on the temple of Jerusalem, was built at Leontopolis for the Egyptian Jews.

To Syria the Jews also went. The highest concentration of them was in Antioch, where the gospel was first preached to the Gentiles, and where the Christians were first called Christians. In Damascus we read of 10,000 of them being massacred at one time in an attack upon them.

So, then, Egypt and Syria had very large Jewish populations. But they had spread far beyond that. In Cyrene in North Africa we read that the population was divided into citizens, agriculturists, resident aliens, and Jews. Mommsen, the Roman historian, writes: " The inhabitants of Palestine were only a portion, and not the most important portion, of the Jews; the Jewish communities of Babylonia, Syria, Asia Minor and Egypt were far superior to those of Palestine." That mention of Asia Minor leads us to another sphere in which the Jews were numerous. When Alexander's empire broke up on his death Egypt fell to the Ptolemies, and Syria and the surrounding districts fell to Seleucus and his successors, who are known as the Seleucids. The Seleucids had two great characteristics. They followed a deliberate policy of the fusion of populations; they hoped to gain security by banishing nationalism. And they were inveterate founders of cities. These cities needed citizens, and special attractions and privileges were offered to those who would settle in them. The Jews accepted citizenship of these cities by the thousand. All over Asia Minor, in the great cities of the Mediterranean sea coast, in the great commercial centres, Jews were numerous and prosperous. Even there there were compulsory transplantations. Antiochus the Great took 2,000 Jewish families from Babylon and settled them in Lydia and Phrygia. In fact, so great was the drift out from Palestine that the Jews of Palestine complained against their brethren who left the austerities of Palestine for the baths and feasts of Asia and

Phrygia; and Aristotle tells of meeting a Jew in Asia Minor who was "not only Greek in his language but in his very soul."

It is quite clear that everywhere in the world there were Jews. Strabo, the Greek geographer, writes: "It is hard to find a spot in the whole world which is not occupied and dominated by Jews." Josephus, the Jewish historian writes: "There is no city, no tribe, whether Greek or barbarian, in which Jewish law and Jewish customs have not taken root." The Sibylline Oracles, written about 140 B.C., say that every land and every sea is filled with the Jews. There is a letter, said to be from Agrippa to Caligula, which Philo quotes. In it he says that Jerusalem is the capital not only of Judaea, but of most countries, by reason of the colonies it has sent out on fitting occasions into the neighbouring lands of Egypt, Phoenicia, Syria, Coelesyria, and the still more remote Pamphylia and Cilicia, into most parts of Asia as far as Bithynia, and into the most distant corners of Pontus; also to Europe, Thessaly, Boeotia, Macedonia, Aetolia, Attica, Argos, Corinth, and the most and best parts of the Peloponnese. And not only is the continent full of Jewish settlements, but also the more important islands—Euboea, Cyprus, Crete—to say nothing of the lands beyond the Euphrates, for all have Jewish inhabitants.

The fact is that the Jewish Diaspora was coextensive with the world; and the importance of that fact is that there was no greater factor in the spread of Christianity.

THE RECIPIENTS OF THE LETTER

James I : I (*continued*)

So, then, James writes to the *twelve tribes in the Diaspora,* the twelve tribes who are scattered abroad throughout the world. Who then has he in his mind's eye as he writes? To

whom is the letter addressed, and for whom is it meant?
The twelve tribes in the Diaspora could equally well mean
any of three things.

(i) It could stand for all the Jews outside of Palestine.
We have seen that such Jews were numbered by the
million. There were actually far more Jews scattered
throughout Syria and Egypt and Greece and Rome and
Asia Minor and all the Mediterranean lands and far off
Babylon than there were in Palestine. Under the conditions of the ancient world it would be quite impossible to
send out a message to such a huge and scattered constitu-
ency. With the resources of modern printing and modern
broadcasting it might be done; but it certainly could not
have been done in the time of James.

(ii) It could mean Christian Jews outside Palestine. For
James, if it means that, it would mean the Jews in the lands
closely surrounding Palestine, perhaps particularly the
Jews in Syria and in Babylon. That is a perfectly possible
meaning; and if anyone was going to write a letter to such
Jews, it would be James, for James was the acknowledged
leader of Jewish Christianity.

(iii) But the phrase can have a third meaning. To the
Christians the Christian Church was the real and the true
Israel. At the end of *Galatians* Paul sends his blessing to the
Israel of God (*Galatians* 6: 16). One of the commonest of
all Christian conceptions was the conception of the Church
as the new Israel. The nation Israel had been the specially
chosen people of God; but they had failed, and refused to
accept their place and their responsibility and their task.
When the Son of God came they had rejected him. Therefore all the privileges which had once belonged to them
passed over to the Church, for the Church was in truth the
chosen people of God. Paul (cp. *Romans* 9: 7, 8) had fully
worked out the idea. It was his conviction that the true
descendants of Abraham, the true Israel, were not those
who could trace their physical descent from Abraham, but
those who had made the same venture of faith as Abraham

had made. The true Israel was not composed of any nation or race; it was composed of those who accepted Jesus Christ in faith. So, then, this phrase may well mean *the Christian Church at large.*

We may choose between the second and the third meanings, each of which gives excellent sense. James may be writing to the Christian Jews scattered amidst the surrounding nations; or he may be writing to the true Israel, the new Israel, the whole Church of God.

TESTED AND TRIUMPHANT

James 1: 2-4

> My brothers, reckon it all joy whenever you become involved in all kinds of testings, for you are well aware that the testing of your faith produces unswerving constancy. And let constancy go on to work out its perfect work that you may be perfect and complete, deficient in nothing.

JAMES never suggested to the Christians to whom he wrote that Christianity would be for them an easy way. He warns them that they would find themselves involved in what the Authorised Version calls *divers temptations.* The word which the Authorised Version translates temptations is the word *peirasmos.* This is a word whose meaning we must fully understand, if we are to see the very essence of the Christian life.

Peirasmos is not *temptation* in the English modern sense of the term; *peirasmos* is *testing.* *Peirasmos* is trial, testing, temptation *directed towards an end,* and the end is that he who is tested should emerge stronger and purer from the testing. The corresponding verb *peirazein,* which the Authorised Version usually translates *to tempt,* has the same meaning. The idea is not that of seduction into sin; the idea is that of strengthening and purifying and proving and testing. For instance, a young bird is said to test (*peirazein*) its wings. The Queen of Sheba was said to come to test (*peirazein*) the wisdom of Solomon. God is said to test (*peirazein*) Abraham, when He appeared to be demanding the sacrifice of Isaac (*Genesis* 22: 1). When Israel came into the Promised Land, God did not remove the people who were already there. He left them so that Israel might be tested (*peirazein*) in the struggle against them (*Judges* 2: 22; 3: 1, 4). The experiences in Israel were tests which went to the making of the people of Israel (*Deuteronomy* 4: 34; 7: 19).

Here is a great and an uplifting thought. Hort writes: " The Christian must expect to be jostled by trials on the Christian way." All kinds of experiences will come to us. There will be the test of the sorrows and the disappointments which seek to take our faith away. There will be the test of the seductions which seek to lure us from the right way. There will be the tests of the dangers, the sacrifices, the unpopularity which the Christian way must so often involve. But the whole point of them is that they are not sent to make us fall; they are sent to make us soar. They are not sent to defeat us; they are sent that we may defeat them. They are not sent to make us weaker; they are sent to make us stronger. And therefore we cannot bemoan them; we must exult in them and rejoice in them. The Christian is like the athlete. The heavier the burden the athlete's trainer lays upon him, the more the course of training is intensified, the more the athlete is glad, because he knows that it is all fitting him more and more for strenuous and victorious effort. As Browning said, we must " welcome each rebuff that turns earth's smoothness rough," for every hard thing is another step on the upward way.

THE RESULT OF TESTING

James 1: 2-4 (*continued*)

JAMES describes this process of testing by the word *dokimion*. This is an interesting word. It is the word for *sterling coinage,* for money which is genuine and unalloyed. The aim of testing is to purge us of all impurity, to burn out the dross of the human character, to leave us cleansed and purified.

If we meet this testing in the right way, it will produce *unswerving constancy.* The word is *hupomonē.* The Authorized Version translates this word *patience;* but *patience* is far too passive a word for it. *Hupomonē* is not simply the ability to bear things; it is the ability to turn them to greatness and glory. The thing which amazed the heathen in the centuries of persecution was that the martyrs did not die grimly, they died singing. One smiled in the flames; they asked him what he found to smile at there. " I saw the glory of God," he said, " and was glad." *Hupomonē* is the quality which makes a man able, not simply to suffer things, but to welcome them, and to vanquish them. The effect of testing rightly borne is strength to bear still more and to conquer in still harder battles.

This unswerving constancy in the end makes a man three things.

(i) It makes him *perfect.* The word is *teleios,* and in Greek *teleios* most usually has the meaning of *perfection towards a given end, and for a given purpose.* A sacrificial animal is *teleios* if it is fit to offer to God. A scholar is *teleios,* if he is past the initial stages of learning, and is mature. A person is *teleios,* if he is past the age of bodily undevelopment, and if full grown. So, then, this constancy, born of testing well met, makes a man *teleios,* that is to say, it makes him fit for the task in the world which he was sent into the world to do, and which God meant him to do. Here, then, is a great thought. By the way in which we meet every experience in life we are either fitting or unfitting ourselves for the task which God meant us to do.

(ii) It makes him *complete.* The word is *holoklēros. Holoklēros* means *entire, perfect in every part.* It is used of the animal which is fit to be offered to God, and of the priest who is fit to serve God. It means that the animal or the person has no disfiguring and disqualifying blemishes. Bit by bit this unswerving constancy removes the weaknesses and the imperfections from a man's character. Daily it enables him to conquer old sins, to shed old blemishes and to gain new virtues, until in the end he becomes entirely fit for the service of God and the service of his fellow-men.

(iii) It makes him *deficient in nothing*. The verb used is *leipesthai*. The word is used of the defeat of an army, of the giving up of a struggle, of the failure to reach a standard that should have been reached. If a man meets his testing in the right way, if day by day he develops this unswerving constancy, then day by day he will live more victoriously, and day by day he will reach nearer to the standard of Jesus Christ Himself.

GOD'S GIVING AND MAN'S ASKING

James I : 5-8

> If any of you is deficient in wisdom, let him ask it from God, who gives generously to all men, and never casts up the gift, and it will be given to him. Let him ask in faith, with no doubts in his mind; for he who oscillates between doubts is like a surge of the sea, wind-driven and blown hither and thither. Let not that man think that he will receive anything from the Lord, a man with a divided mind, inconstant in all his ways.

THERE is a close connection between this passage and what has gone before. James has just told his readers that, if they use all the testing experiences of life in the right way, they will emerge from them with that unswerving constancy which is the basis of all the virtues. But immediately the question arises, " How can I so use these testing experiences? Where can I find the wisdom and the understanding to use them in the right way? " James's answer is, " If any man feels that he has not the wisdom to use aright the experiences of this life—and no man in himself possesses that wisdom—let him ask it from God."

One thing stands out here. For James, the Christian teacher with the Jewish background, wisdom is a practical thing. Wisdom is not philosophic speculation and intellectual knowledge. Wisdom is wisdom for life. The Stoics defined wisdom as " knowledge of things human and divine." But Ropes defines this Christian wisdom as " the supreme and divine quality of the soul whereby man knows and practises righteousness." Hort defines it as " that endowment of heart and mind which is needed for the right conduct of life." In the Christian wisdom there is, of course, knowledge of the deep things of God; there is, of course, the seeking and the goal of the questing mind; but Christian wisdom is essentially practical; it is such knowledge turned into action in all the decisions and the personal relationships of everyday life. When a man asks God for that wisdom, he must remember two things.

(i) He must remember *how God gives*. God gives generously and God never casts up the gift. " All Wisdom," said Jesus the son of Sirach, " cometh from the Lord and is with Him for ever " (*Ecclesiasticus* 1: 1). But the Jewish wise men were well aware how the best gift in the world can be spoiled by the manner of the giving. They have much to say about how the fool gives. " My son, blemish not thy good deeds, neither use uncomfortable words when thou givest anything . . . Lo, is not a word better than a gift? But both are with a gracious man. A fool will upbraid churlishly, and a gift of the envious consumeth the eyes " (*i.e.*, " brings tears ") (*Ecclesiasticus* 18: 15-18). " The gift of a fool shall do thee no good when thou hast it; neither yet of the envious for his necessity; for he looketh to receive many things for one. He giveth little, and upbraideth much; he openeth his mouth like a crier; today he lendeth, and tomorrow will he ask it again; such an one is to be hated of God and man " (*Ecclesiasticus* 20: 14, 15). The same writer warns against " upbraiding speeches before friends " (*Ecclesiasticus* 41: 22). There is a kind of giver who gives only with a view to getting more than he has given; who gives only to gratify his vanity and his sense of power by putting the recipient under an obligation which he will never be allowed to forget; who gives and who then continuously casts up the gift that he has given. But God gives with generosity. Philemon, the Greek poet, called God " the lover of gifts," not in the sense of loving to receive gifts, but in the sense of loving to give gifts. Nor does God cast up the gift; He gives with all the splendour of His love, because it is His nature to give.

(ii) We must remember *how the asker must ask.* The asker must ask without doubts. He must be sure of both the power and the desire of God to give. He must not ask in doubts. If he asks in doubts, his mind is like the broken water of the sea, driven hither and thither by any chance wind. Mayor says that he is like a cork carried by the waves, now near the shore, now far away. Such a man is unstable in his ways. Hort suggests that the picture is the picture of a man who is drunk, staggering from side to side on the road, and getting nowhere. James uses a vivid word of such a man. He says that he is *dipsuchos*, which literally means a man with two souls, or two minds, inside him. One mind believes, the other mind disbelieves; and the man is a walking civil war in which trust and distrust of God wage a continual battle against each other.

If we are to use aright the experiences of life to beget a sterling character, we must ask wisdom from God. And when we ask we must remember the absolute generosity of God, and we must see to it that we ask believing that we shall receive that which God knows that it is good and right for us to have.

AS EACH MAN NEEDS

James I: 9-11

Let the lowly brother be proud of his exaltation; and let the rich brother be proud of his humiliation; for he will pass away like a flower of the field. The sun rises

with the scorching wind and withers the grass, and the
flower wilts, and the beauty of its form is destroyed.
So the rich will wither away in all his ways.

As James saw it, Christianity brings to every man what
every man needs. As Mayor put it " As the despised poor
learns self-respect, so the proud rich learns self-abasement."

(i) Christianity brings to the poor man a new sense of his
own value. He is lifted out of the valuelessness in which he
lives into a new sense of worth and importance. (*a*) He
learns that he matters *in the Church*. In the Early Church
there were not class distinctions. It could, and did happen,
that it was the slave who was the minister of the congregation, who preached and who dispensed the sacrament,
while it was the master who was no more than a humble
member. In the Church the social distinctions which divide
men in the world are obliterated, and there is none who
matters more than any other. (*b*) He learns that he matters
in the world. It is the teaching of Christianity that every
man in this world has a task to do, that so long as God
leaves him in the world God has a purpose for him. No
man is useless, for every man is of use to God. Even if he
be confined to a bed of helplessness and pain, the power of
his prayers can still act on the world of men. (*c*) He learns
that he matters *to God*. As Muretus said long ago, " Call no
man worthless for whom Christ died." Every man is dear
to God.

(ii) Christianity brings to the rich man a new sense of
self-abasement. The great peril of riches is that they tend
to bring to a man a false sense of security. He feels that he
is safe; he feels that he has the resources to cope with
anything; he feels that he can buy anything he wants, and
buy himself out of any situation which he may wish to
escape or to avoid.

James draws a vivid picture, very familiar to the people
of Palestine. In the desert places, if there is a shower of
rain, the thin green shoots of grass will sprout; but one
day's burning sunshine will make them vanish as if they

had never been. The *scorching heat* is the *kausōn*. The *kausōn* was the south-east wind, the Simoon. It came straight from the deserts, and it burst on Palestine like a blast of hot air when an oven door is opened. In an hour it could wipe out all vegetation with its fiery heat.

All that is a picture of what a life which depends on riches can be like. A man who puts his trust in riches is trusting in things which the chances and changes of life can take from him at any moment. Life itself is an uncertain thing. At the back of James's mind there is Isaiah's picture: " All flesh is grass, and all the goodliness thereof is as the flower of the field. The grass withereth, the flower fadeth, because the Spirit of the Lord bloweth upon it; surely the people is grass " (*Isaiah* 40: 6, 7; cp. *Psalm* 103 : 15).

Now James's point is this. If life is so uncertain, if man is so vulnerable, if the externals of life are so perishable, then calamity and disaster may come at any moment. Since that is so, a man is a fool to put all his trust in things —like wealth—which he may lose at any moment. He is only wise if he puts his trust in things which he cannot lose.

So, then, James urges the rich to cease to put their trust in that which their own power can amass. He urges them to realize and to admit their own essential human helplessness, and humbly to put their trust in God, who alone can give us the things which abide for ever. He is pleading with men to glory in that new humility which realizes its utter dependence on God.

THE CROWN OF LIFE

James 1: 12

> Happy is the man who meets trial with steadfast constancy, because, when he has shown himself of sterling worth, he will receive the crown of life which He has promised to those who love Him.

To the man who meets trials and testings in the right way there is joy here and hereafter.

(i) In this life he becomes a man of sterling worth. He is *dokimos*; he is like metal which is cleansed and purified of all alloy. The weaknesses of his character are eradicated; the faults are cleansed away; and he emerges strong and pure.

(ii) In the life to come he receives *the crown of life*. There is far more than one thought here. In the ancient world the crown (*stephanos*) had at least four great associations.

(a) The crown of flowers was worn at times of joy, at weddings and at feasts (cp. *Isaiah* 28: 1, 2; *Song of Solomon* 3: 11). The crown was the sign of happy and of festive joy.

(b) The crown was the mark of royalty. It was worn by kings and by those in authority. Sometimes this was the sign of the crown of gold; sometimes it was the linen band, or fillet, worn around the brows (cp. *Psalm* 21: 3; *Jeremiah* 13: 18).

(c) The crown of laurel leaves was the victor's crown in the games, the prize which the athlete coveted above all (cp. 2 *Timothy* 4: 8).

(d) The crown was the mark of honour and of dignity. The instructions of parents can bring a crown of grace to those who listen to them (*Proverbs* 1: 9); Wisdom provides a man with a crown of glory (*Proverbs* 4: 9); in a time of disaster and dishonour it can be said, " The crown is fallen from our heads " (*Lamentations* 5: 16).

We do not need to choose between these meanings. They are all included. The Christian has a *joy* that no other man can ever have. Life for him is like life for ever at a feast. The Christian has a *royalty* that other men have never realized, for, however humble his earthly circumstances, he is nothing less than the child of God. The Christian has a *victory* which others cannot win, for he meets life and all its demands in the conquering power of the presence and the company of Jesus Christ. It is God Himself who gives us the victory. The Christian has a new dignity, for he is ever conscious that God thought him worth the life and death of Jesus Christ. No man can ever be worthless, if Christ died for him.

What is the crown? It is the *crown of life*; and that phrase means that it is *the crown which consists of life*; the crown is life itself. The crown of the Christian, the possession of the Christian, is a new kind of life which is life indeed; through Jesus Christ he has entered into life and life more abundant.

So, then, James says that if the Christian meets the trials and the testings and the temptations of life in the steadfast and unswerving constancy which Christ can give, then life becomes an infinitely more splendid thing than ever it was before. The struggle is the way to glory, and the very struggle itself is a glory.

PUTTING THE BLAME ON GOD

James I: 13-15

> Let no man say when he is tempted, " My temptation comes from God." For God Himself is untemptable by evil, and tempts no man. But temptation comes to every man, because he is lured on and seduced by his own desire; then desire conceives and begets sin; and, when sin has reached its full development, it spawns death.

AT the back of this passage there lies a Jewish way of belief which is also a universal way of belief of which all of us are to some extent guilty. James is here rebuking the man who puts the blame for temptation on to God.

Jewish thought was haunted by the inner division that is in every man. It was the problem which haunted Paul: " I delight in the law of God after the inward man; but I see another law in my members, warring against the law of my mind, and bringing me into captivity to the law of sin which is in my members " (*Romans* 7: 22, 23). Every man is a walking civil war; and every man is pulled in two directions. Purely as an interpretation of experience the Jews arrived at the doctrine that in every man there are two tendencies or two natures. They called them the *Yetser Hatob*, which means *the good tendency*, and the *Yetser Hara*, which means *the evil tendency*. Now this simply states the problem; it does not explain it. In particular, it does not say where the evil tendency comes from. So Jewish thought set out to try to explain where the evil tendency came from.

The writer of *Ecclesiasticus* is deeply impressed with the havoc that the evil tendency causes. " O evil tendency, O *Yetser Hara*, why wast thou made to fill the earth with thy deceit? " (*Ecclesiasticus* 37: 3). In his view the evil tendency came from Satan, and man's defence against it was man's own will. " God made man from the beginning and He delivered him into the hand of him who took him for a prey. He left him in the power of his will. If thou willest, thou wilt observe the commandments, and faithfulness is a matter of thy good pleasure " (*Ecclesiasticus* 15: 14, 15). On this view, it was Satan who put the evil tendency into a man; and a man can defeat it by the exercise of his own will.

There were Jewish writers who traced this evil tendency right back to the Garden of Eden. In the apocryphal work, *The Life of Adam and Eve*, the story is told. Satan took the form of an angel, and, speaking through the serpent, put into Eve the desire for the forbidden fruit, and made her swear that she would give the fruit to Adam as well. " When he had made me swear," says Eve, " he ascended up into the tree. But in the fruit he gave me to eat *he placed the poison of his malice*, that is, of his lust. For lust is the beginning of all sin. And he bent down the bough to the earth, and I took of the fruit and ate it." In this conception it was Satan himself who succeeded in inserting the evil tendency into man; and that evil tendency is identified with the lust of the flesh. A later development of this story was that the beginning of all sin was in fact Satan's lust for Eve.

The Book of Enoch has two theories. One is that the fallen angels are responsible for sin (85). The other is that man himself is responsible for the evil tendency and for sin. " Sin has not been sent upon the earth, but man himself created it " (98: 4).

But every one of these theories simply pushes the problem one step further back. Where did the evil tendency *ultimately* come from? Satan may have put it into man; the fallen angels may have put it into man; man may have put it into himself. But where did it ultimately come from?

To meet this problem certain of the Rabbis took a bold and a very dangerous step. They argued that, since God has created everything, He must have created the evil tendency also. So we get Rabbinic sayings such as the following. " God said, It repents me that I created the evil tendency in man; for had I not done so, he would not have rebelled against me. I created the evil tendency; I created the law as a means of healing. If you occupy yourself with the law, you will not fall into the power of it. God placed the good tendency on a man's right hand, and the evil on his left." The danger of all this is obvious. It means that in the last analysis a man can blame God for his own sin. He can say, as Paul said, " It is no more I that do it, but sin that dwelleth in me " (*Romans* 7: 15-24). Of all strange doctrines surely the strangest is that God is directly and ultimately responsible for sin.

THE EVASION OF RESPONSIBILITY

James I: 13-15 (continued)

IT remains true that from the beginning of time it has been man's first instinct to blame others for his own sin. The ancient writer who wrote the story of the first sin in the Garden of Eden was a first-rate psychologist with a deep knowledge of the human heart. When God challenged Adam with his sin, Adam's reply was, " The woman whom Thou gavest to be with me, she gave me of the tree, and I did eat." And when God challenged Eve with her action, her answer was, " The serpent beguiled me, and I did eat." Adam said, " Don't blame me; blame Eve." Eve said, " Don't blame me; blame the serpent " (*Genesis* 3: 12, 13). Man has always been an expert in evasion.

Robert Burns wrote:

> Thou knowest Thou hast formed me
> With passions wild and strong;
> And listening to their witching voice
> Has often led me wrong.

In effect, he is saying that his conduct was as it was because God made him as he was. The blame is laid on God. So men blame their fellow-men; they blame their circumstances; they blame the way in which they are made for the sin of which they are guilty.

James sternly rebukes that view. To him that which is responsible for sin is man's own evil desire. Sin would be helpless, if there was nothing in man to which it could appeal. If temptation struck no answering chord, then temptation would not be temptation. Now desire is something which can be nourished or stifled. A man can check and control his discipline, and even, by the grace of God, eliminate desire if he faces it and deals with it at once. But a man can allow his thoughts to follow certain tracks, he can allow his steps to take him into certain places and certain company, he can encourage his eyes to linger on certain forbidden things, he can spend his life fomenting desire. He can use mind and heart and eyes and feet and lips to nourish desire. He can so hand himself over to Christ and to the Spirit of Christ that he is cleansed of evil desire. He can be so engaged on good things that there is no time or place left for desire. It is idle hands for which Satan finds mischief to do; and it is an unexercised mind which plays with desire, and an uncommitted heart which is vulnerable to the appeal of lust.

If a man nourishes and encourages desire long enough, there is an inevitable consequence. *Desire becomes action.* If a man thinks about anything long enough, if he allows himself to desire it long enough, all the chances are that in the end he will do it. Desire in the heart in the end begets sin in the action.

Further, it was the Jewish teaching that sin begat death. The old life of Adam and Eve, that we have already quoted, says that the moment Eve ate of the fruit she caught a glimpse of death. The word which James uses in verse 15, and which the Authorized Version translates *bringeth forth* death, is not a human word at all; it is an animal word for birth; and it means that sin *spawns* death. Mastered by desire, man becomes less than a man and sinks to the level of the brute creation.

The great value of this passage is that it urges upon man man's personal responsibility for sin. No man was ever born without desire for some wrong thing. Desire goes far beyond mere sexual desire, for there are all kinds of desire. But some wrong thing fascinates every man. And, if a man deliberately foments and encourages and nourishes that desire, until it becomes full-grown and monstrously strong, then it will inevitably issue in the action which is sin—and that is the way to death. And such a thought—and it is a thought which all human experience admits to be true—must drive us to that grace of God which alone can make us clean and keep us clean, and which is available to all.

GOD'S CONSTANCY FOR GOOD

James 1: 16-18

> My dear brothers, do not be deceived. Every good gift and every perfect boon comes down from the Father of lights, with whom there is none of that changeableness which comes from changing shadows. Of His own purpose he has begotten us by the word of truth, so that we might be, as it were, the first-fruits of His created things.

ONCE again James stresses the great truth that every gift that God sends is good. Verse 17 might well be translated: " All giving is good." That is to say, there is nothing which comes from God which is not good. There is a strange phenomenon here in the Greek. The phrase which we have translated, " Every good gift and every perfect boon," is, in fact, a perfect hexametre line of poetry. Either James had a rhythmic ear for a fine cadence, or else he is quoting from some work which we do not know.

What James is stressing here is the unchangeableness of God. To do so he uses two astronomical terms. The word he uses for changeableness is the word *parallagē*, and the word he uses for the turn of the shadow is *tropē*. Both these words have to do with the variation which the heavenly bodies show, the variation in the length of the day and of the night, the apparent variation in the course of the sun, the phases of waxing and waning, the different brilliance at different times of the stars and the planets. Variability, change is characteristic of all created things. God is the creator of the lights of heaven—the sun, the moon, the stars. The Jewish morning prayer says, " Blessed be the Lord God who hath formed the lights." The lights change and vary, but He who created them never changes. Nothing that ever comes from Him can be anything but good.

Further, His purpose is altogether gracious. *The word of truth* is the gospel; and by the sending of that gospel it is God's purpose that man should be reborn into a new life. When the gospel enters into life, it is as if life begins anew. The shadows are ended, and the certain word of truth has come.

And that rebirth is a rebirth into the family and the possession of God. In the ancient world it was the law that all first-fruits were sacred to God. The first-fruits were taken and offered in grateful sacrifice to God, because they belonged to God. So, when we are reborn by the true word of the gospel, we become the property of God, even as the first-fruits of the harvest did.

So James insists that, so far from ever tempting man, God's gifts are invariably good. In all the changes and the changes of a changing world they never vary. And God's supreme object is to re-create life through the truth of the gospel, so that men should know that they belong by right to Him.

WHEN TO BE QUICK AND WHEN TO BE SLOW

James 1: 19, 20

> All this, my dear brothers, you already know. Let every man be quick to hear, slow to speak, slow to anger; for the anger of man does not produce the righteousness which God desires.

THERE are few wise men who have not been impressed by the dangers of being too quick to speak and too unwilling to listen. A most interesting list could be compiled of the things in which it is well to be quick, and the things in which it is well to be slow. In the Sayings of the Jewish Fathers we read: " There are four characters in scholars. Quick to hear and quick to forget; his gain is cancelled by his loss. Slow to hear and slow to forget; his loss is cancelled by his gain. Quick to hear and slow to forget; he is wise. Slow to hear and quick to forget; this is an evil lot." Ovid bids men to be slow to punish, but swift to reward. Philo bids a man to be swift to benefit others, and slow to harm them. In particular the wise men were impressed by the necessity of being slow to speak. Rabbi Simeon said, " All my days I have grown up among the wise, and have not found aught good for a man but silence . . . Whoso multiplies words occasions sin." Jesus, the son of Sirach, writes, " Be swift to hear the word that thou mayest understand . . . If thou hast understanding, answer thy neighbour; if not, lay thy hand upon thy mouth, lest thou be surprised in an unskilful word, and be confounded "

(*Ecclesiasticus* 5: 11, 12). *Proverbs* is full of the perils to too hasty speech. " In the multitude of words there wanteth not sin; but he that refraineth his lips is wise " (*Proverbs* 10: 19). " He that keepeth his mouth keepeth his life; but he that openeth wide his lips shall have destruction " (*Proverbs* 13: 3). " Even a fool when he holdeth his speech is counted wise " (*Proverbs* 17: 28). " Seest thou a man that is hasty in his words? There is more hope of a fool than of him " (*Proverbs* 29: 20).

Hort says that the really good man will be much more anxious to listen to God than arrogantly, garrulously and stridently to shout his own opinions. The classical writers had the same idea. Zeno said, " We have two ears, but only one mouth, that we may hear more and speak less." When Demonax was asked how a man might rule best, he answered, " Without anger, speaking little, and listening much." Bias said, " If you hate quick speaking, you will not fall into error." The tribute was once paid to a great linguist that he could be silent in seven different languages. Many of us would do well to wait and listen more, and to rush in and speak less.

It is James's advice that we should also be *slow to anger*. He is probably meeting the arguments of some people that there is a place in life for the blazing anger of rebuke. That is undoubtedly true; the world would be a poorer place without those who blazed in pure white anger against the abuses and the tyrannies of sin. But too often this is made an excuse, not for real and righteous anger, but for petulant and self-centred irritation.

The *teacher* will be tempted to be angry with the slow and the backward, and still more with the lazy scholar. But, except on the rarest occasions, he will achieve more by encouragement than by the lash of the tongue. The *preacher* will be tempted to anger. But " don't scold " is always a good advice to the preacher; and the preacher loses his power whenever he does not make it clear by every word and gesture that he loves his people. When anger gives the impression in the pulpit of hatred, dislike, contempt, then it has no power to convert the souls of men. The *parent* will be tempted to anger. But a parent's anger is much more likely to produce a still more stubborn resistance than it is to control and direct. The accent of love always has more power than the accent of anger; and when anger becomes constant irritability, petulant annoyance, carping nagging, then it always does more harm than good.

To be slow to speak, to be slow to anger, to be quick to listen is always good advice for life.

THE TEACHABLE SPIRIT

James 1:21

> So then strip yourself of all filthiness and of the excrescence of vice, and in gentleness receive the inborn word which is able to save your souls.

HERE James uses a series of vivid words and pictures.

He tells his readers to strip themselves of all vice and filthiness. The word which he uses for *to strip* is the word which is used literally for *stripping off one's clothes*. He bids his hearers get rid of all defilement as a man strips off soiled garments, or as a snake sloughs off its skin.

Both the words he uses for *defilement* are vivid. The word we have translated *filthiness* is *ruparia*; and it can be used for the filth which soils clothes or which soils the body. But it has one very interesting connection. It is a derivative of the word *rupos*, and, when *rupos* is used in a medical sense it means *wax in the ear*. It is just possible that it still retains that meaning here; and that James is telling his readers to get rid of everything which would stop their ears to the true word of God. When wax gathers in the ear, it can make a man deaf; and a man's own sins can make him deaf to God. Further, James talks of the *excrescence* (*perisseia*) of vice. He thinks of vice as a tangled

THE LETTER OF JAMES

undergrowth which must be cut away; or, as a cancerous growth on the body or on a tree. Vice is an ugly, cancerous, defiling growth on the soul, and it must be cut away.

He bids them receive the *inborn word* in gentleness. The word for inborn is *emphutos*, and it is capable of two general meanings. (i) It can mean *inborn* in the sense of *innate* as opposed to acquired. If James uses it in that way he is thinking of much the same thing as Paul was thinking of when he spoke of the Gentiles doing the works of the law by nature because they have a kind of law in their hearts (*Romans* 2: 14, 15); it is the same picture as the Old Testament picture of the law " very nigh to thee in thy mouth, and in thy heart " (*Deuteronomy* 30: 14). It would be practically equal to our word *conscience*. If James means this, he means that there is an instinctive knowledge of good and evil in a man's heart, and the guidance of that knowledge we should at all times obey. (ii) It can mean *inborn* in the sense of *implanted*, as a seed is planted in the ground. In 4 *Ezra* 9: 31 we read of God saying: " Behold, I sow my law in you, and ye shall be glorified in it for ever." If James is using the word in this sense, the idea may well go back to the Parable of the Sower (*Matthew* 13: 1-8), which tells how the seed of the word is sown into the hearts of men. Through His prophets and His preachers, and above all through Jesus Christ, God sows His truth into the hearts of men, and implants it there, and the man who is wise will receive it and welcome it. It may well be that we are not required to make a choice between these two meanings. It may well be that James is implying that knowledge of the true word of God comes to us from *two* sources; it comes from the depths of our own being, and it comes from the Spirit of God and the teaching of Christ and the preaching of men. From inside of us and from outside of us there come voices telling us the right way; and the wise man will listen and obey.

He will receive the word with *gentleness*. *Gentleness* is an attempt to translate the untranslatable word *prautēs*.

67

which James uses. *Prautēs* is a great Greek word which has no precise English equivalent. Aristotle defined it as the mean between excessive anger and excessive angerlessness; it is the quality of the man whose feelings and emotions and impulses are under perfect control. Andronicus Rhodius, commenting on Aristotle, writes, " *Prautēs* is moderation in regard to anger . . . You might define *prautēs* as serenity and the power, not to be lead away by emotion, but to control emotion as right reason dictates." The Platonic *definitions* say that *prautēs* is the regulation of the movement of the soul which is caused by anger. It is the temperament (*krasis*) of a soul in which everything is mixed in the right proportions. No one can ever find one word to translate all this, but it is a one word summary of the truly teachable spirit. The teachable spirit is *docile* and *tractable*, and therefore humble enough to learn. The teachable spirit is *without resentment* and *without anger*, and is, therefore, able to face the truth, even when the truth hurts and condemns. The teachable spirit is not blinded by its own overmastering *prejudices*, but is clear-eyed to the truth. The teachable spirit is not seduced by *laziness*, but is so self-controlled that it can willingly and faithfully accept the discipline of learning. *Prautēs* describes the perfect conquest and control of everything in a man's nature which would be a hindrance to his seeing, learning and obeying the truth.

HEARING AND DOING

James 1: 22-24

Prove yourselves to be doers of the word, and not only hearers, for those who think that hearing is enough deceive themselves. For, if a man is a hearer of the word, and not a doer of it, he is like a man who looks in a mirror at the face which nature gave him. A glance, and he is gone; and he immediately forgets what kind of man he is.

HERE again James presents us with two of these vivid pictures of which he is such a master. First of all, he speaks of the man who goes to the church meeting, and who listens to the reading of the word, and the expounding of it, and who thinks that that listening has made him a Christian. He deceives himself by thinking that his attendance at public worship, and his hearing of what is read and said there, is enough. He has shut his eyes to the fact that what is read and heard in Church must then be lived and done in life. It is still possible to identify Church attendance and Bible reading with Christianity, and to believe that the man who faithfully attends Church, and who diligently studies His Bible, is a good Christian. Those who act like that have come less than half the way, because they have failed to see that the really important thing is to turn that to which they have listened into action and deeds.

A man who does that is like a man who in the Church service has seen the ideal of what he ought to be and has promptly forgotten it. Then James presents us with a second picture. He is like a man who looks in a mirror — ancient mirrors were made, not of glass, but of highly polished metal—and who sees the smuts which disfigure his face, and the dishevelment of his hair, and who goes away, and forgets what he looks like, and so omits to do anything about it. In his listening to the true word a man has revealed to him that which he is and that which he ought to be. He sees what is wrong, and he sees what must be done to put it right; but, if he is only a hearer, then he remains just as he is, and all his hearing has gone for nothing.

James does well to remind us that that which is heard in the holy place must be lived in the market place—or there is no point in hearing at all.

THE TRUE LAW

James I: 25

> He who looks into the perfect law, which is the law
> in the observance of which a man finds freedom, and
> who abides in it, and who shows himself not a forgetful
> hearer but an active doer of the word, will be blessed
> in all his action.

THIS is just the kind of passage in *James* which Luther so
much disliked. Luther disliked the idea of law altogether,
for with Paul he would have said, "Christ is the end of
the law" (*Romans* 10: 4). "James," said Luther, "drives
us to law and works." And yet beyond all doubt there is a
sense in which James is right. There is in Christianity
an ethical demand; there is a law of life and a law of
living which the Christian must realize and accept and seek
to put into action. That law is to be found first in the
Ten Commandments, and then in all ethical teaching
of Jesus.

James calls that law two things.

(i) He calls it the *perfect law*. There are three reasons
why the law is perfect. (*a*) It is God's law, given and
revealed by God. The way of life which Jesus laid down
for His followers is the way of life which is in accordance
with the will of God. (*b*) It is perfect in that it cannot be
bettered. The Christian law is the law of love; and the
demand of love can never be satisfied. We know well,
when we love some one, that even though we gave them
all the world, and even though we served them for a life-
time, we still could not satisfy or deserve their love. The
Christian law is perfect in that there can be no higher law
than the law of love. (*c*) But there is still another sense in
which the Christian law is perfect. The word perfect is
teleios. *Teleios* nearly always describes perfection towards
some given end. It is perfection for some given purpose
and some given use. Now, if a man obeys the law of Christ,
he will realize the purpose of his own manhood; he will
fulfil the purpose for which God sent him into the world;

he will be the person he ought to be, and he will make the contribution to the world he ought to make. He will be perfect in the sense that he will, by obeying the law of God, realize the purpose for which he was sent into the world.

(ii) He calls it the *law of liberty*; that is, it is the law in the keeping of which a man finds his true liberty. All the great men have agreed that it is only in obeying the law of God that a man becomes truly free. " To obey God," said Seneca, " is liberty." " The wise man alone is free," said the Stoics, " and every foolish man is a slave." Philo said " All who are under the tyranny of anger or desire or any other passion are altogether slaves; all who live with the law are free." So long as a man has to obey his own passions and emotions and desires, he is nothing less than a slave. It is when a man accepts the will of God that he becomes really free—for then he is free to be good, and free to be what he ought to be. His service is perfect freedom, and in doing His will is our peace.

TRUE WORSHIP

James 1: 26, 27

> If anyone thinks that he is a worshipper of God, and yet does not bridle his tongue, his worship is an empty thing. This is pure and undefiled worship, as God the Father sees it, to visit the orphans and the widows, and to keep oneself unspotted from the world.

WE must be careful to understand what James is saying here. The Authorized Version translates the phrases at the beginning of verse 27: " Pure *religion* and undefiled is . . ." The word translated relation is *thrēskeia,* and its meaning is not so much *religion* as the outward expression of religion in ritual and liturgy and ceremony. It is *worship* in the sense of which we speak of the *worship* part of the service; it is *worship* in the sense in which we speak of the different kinds of *worship* that are found in different

71

Churches. What James is saying is, " The finest ritual and the finest liturgy you can offer to God is service of the poor and personal purity." To James real worship did not lie in elaborate vestments, or in a noble liturgy, or in magnificent music, or in a carefully wrought service; it lay in the practical service of mankind and in the purity of one's own personal life. James was insisting that the most beautiful forms of worship in the world could never take the place of Christian charity. It is perfectly possible for a Church to be so taken up with the beauty of its buildings and the splendour of its liturgy that it has neither the time nor the money for practical Christian service; and that is what James is condemning.

In point of fact James was only condemning what the prophets had always condemned long ago. " God," said the Psalmist, " is a father of the fatherless, and a judge of the widows " (*Psalm* 68: 5). It was Zechariah's complaint that the people pulled away their shoulders and made their hearts as adamant as stone, at the demand to execute true justice, to show mercy and compassion every man to his brother, to oppress not the widow, the fatherless, the stranger and the poor, and not to entertain evil thoughts against another within the heart (*Zecharaiah* 7: 6-10). It was Micah's complaint that all ritual sacrifices were useless, if a man did not do justice and love mercy and walk humbly before God (*Micah* 6: 6-8).

All through history men have tried to make ritual and liturgy a substitute for sacrifice and service. They have made religion splendid *within* the Church at the expense of neglecting it *outside* the Church. This is by no means to say that it is wrong to seek to offer the noblest and the most splendid worship to God within God's house; but it is to say that all such worship is an empty and an idle thing unless it sends a man out to love God by loving his fellow-men, and to walk more purely in the tempting ways of the world.

THE LETTER OF JAMES

RESPECT OF PERSONS

James 2: 1

My brothers, you cannot really believe that you have faith in our glorious Lord Jesus Christ, and yet continue to have respect of persons.

RESPECT of persons is the New Testament phrase for undue and unfair partiality; respect of persons means truckling or pandering or paying special attention to someone, because he is a rich or influential or powerful or popular person. It is a fault which the New Testament consistently condemns. It was a fault of which the orthodox Jewish leaders completely acquitted Jesus. Even they were bound to see and to admit that there was no respect of persons with him, and that he treated no man with snobbish respect or prejudiced favouritism (*Luke* 20: 21; *Mark* 12: 14; *Matthew* 22: 16). After his vision of the sheet with the clean and unclean animals upon it, the lesson that Peter learned was that with God there is no respect of persons (*Acts* 10: 34). It was Paul's conviction that Gentile and Jew stand under a like judgment in the sight of God, for with God there is no respect of persons, no favouritism (*Romans* 2: 11). This is a truth which Paul urges on his people again and again (*Ephesians* 6: 9; *Colossians* 3: 25).

The word itself is a curious word—*prosōpolēmpsia*. The noun comes from the expression *prosōpon lambanein*. *Prosōpon* is the *face*, the *countenance*; and *lambanein* here means *to lift up*. The expression in Greek is a literal translation of a Hebrew original phrase. To lift up a person's countenance was to regard him with favour, in contradistinction perhaps with *casting down his countenance*.

Originally the word was not a bad word at all; it simply meant *to accept a person with favour*, with no bad sense. Malachi asks if the governor will be pleased with the people and *will accept their persons*, if they bring him blemished offerings (*Malachi* 1: 8, 9). But the word rapidly

73

acquired a bad sense. It soon began to mean, not so much to favour a person, as to show favouritism, to allow oneself to be unduly influenced by a person's social status, or his prestige and power and influence, or his wealth and eminence. In that sense it is unsparingly condemned. Malachi goes on to condemn that very sin when God accuses the people of not keeping his ways, and of being *partial in their judgments* (*Malachi* 2:9). The great characteristic of God is His fairness, His justice, His complete impartiality. In the Law it was written, " Ye shall do no unrighteousness in judgment; thou shalt not respect the person of the poor, nor honour the person of the mighty; but in righteousness shalt thou judge thy neighbour " (*Leviticus* 19:15). In point of fact there is a necessary emphasis there. A person may be unjust and a respecter of persons because of the snobbery which truckles to the rich; and he can be equally unjust because of the inverted snobbery which glorifies the poor. " The Lord," said Ben Sirach, " is judge and with him is no respect of persons " (*Ecclesiasticus* 35:12).

The Old and the New Testaments unite in condemning that partiality of judgment and that favouritism of treatment which comes of giving undue weight to a man's social standing, wealth or worldly influence. And it is a fault to which every one is more or less liable. " The rich and poor meet together," says *Proverbs*, " the Lord is the maker of them all " (*Proverbs* 22:2). " It is not meet," says Ben Sirach, " to despise the poor man that hath understanding; neither is it fitting to magnify a sinful man that is rich " (*Ecclesiasticus* 10:23). And we do well to remember that it is just as much respect of persons to truckle to the mob as it is to pander to a tyrant.

THE PERIL OF SNOBBERY WITHIN THE CHURCH
James 2:2-4

For, if a man comes into your assembly with his fingers covered with gold rings, and dressed in elegant

> clothes, and, if a poor man comes in dressed in shabby
> clothes, and, if you pay special attention to the man
> who is dressed in elegant clothes, and, if you say to
> him: " Will you sit here, please? " and, if you say to
> the poor man, " You stand there! " or, " Squat on
> the floor beside my footstool! " have you not drawn
> distinctions within your minds, and have you not
> become judges whose thoughts are evil? "

IT is James's fear that snobbery may invade the Church.
He draws a picture of two men entering the Christian
assembly. The one is well-dressed; his fingers are covered
with gold rings. The more ostentatious of the ancients
wore rings on every finger except the middle finger, and
wore far more than one on each finger. They even hired
rings to wear when they wished to give an impression of
special wealth. " We adorn our fingers with rings," said
Seneca, " and we distribute gems over every joint."
Clement of Alexandria indeed recommends that a
Christian should wear only one ring, and that he should
wear it on his little finger. It ought to have on it a religious
emblem, such as a dove, a fish or an anchor; and the
justification for wearing it was that it might be used as a
seal. So, then, into the Christian assembly comes an
elegantly dressed and much beringed man of wealth. The
other man is a poor man, dressed in poor clothes because
he has no other clothes to wear, and unadorned by any
jewels. Then, in James's picture, the rich man is ushered
to a special seat with all due ceremony and respect; while
the poor man is bidden to stand, or to squat on the floor,
beside the footstool of the well-to-do.

That the picture is not overdrawn is seen from certain
of the instructions in some of the early service order books.
Ropes quotes a typical passage from the Ethiopic *Statutes
of the Apostles:* " If any other man or woman enters in
fine clothes, either a man of the district or from other
districts, being brethren, thou, presbyter, while thou
speakest the word which is concerning God, or while thou
hearest or readest, thou shalt not respect persons, nor

leave thy ministering to command places for them, but remain quiet, for the brethren shall receive them, and if they have no place for them, the lover of brothers and sisters, will rise, and leave a place for them . . . And if a poor man or woman of the district or of other districts should come in and there is no place for them, thou, presbyter, make place for such with all thy heart, even if thou wilt sit on the ground, that there should not be the respecting of the person of man but of God." Here is the same picture. It is even suggested that the leader of the service might be liable, when a rich man entered, to stop the service and to conduct the rich worshipper to a special seat.

There is no doubt that there must have been social problems in the Early Church. The Church was the only place in the ancient world where social distinctions did not exist. There must have been a certain initial awkwardness when a master found himself sitting next his slave, or, when a master arrived at a service in which his slave was actually the leader and the dispenser of the Sacrament. The gap between the slave, who in law was nothing more than a living tool, and the master must have been so wide as to cause problems of approach on either side. Further, in its early days the Church was predominantly poor and humble; and therefore if a rich man was converted, and did come to the Christian fellowship, there must have been a very real temptation to make a fuss of him, and to treat him as a special trophy for Christ.

But the Church must be the one place where all distinctions are wiped out. There can be no distinctions of rank and place and prestige, when men meet in the presence of the God who is the King of glory. There can be no distinctions of merit and worth, when men meet in the presence of the supreme holiness of God. In the presence of that glory all earthly distinctions are less than the dust, and all earthly righteousness are as filthy rags. In the presence of God all men are one.

In verse 4 there is one problem of translation. In that verse the word *diekrithēte* can have two meanings. (i) It can mean, " You are wavering, vacillating, hesitating in your judgments, if you act like that." That is to say, " If you pay special honour to the rich, you are torn between the standards of the world and the standards of God, and you can't make up your mind which you are going to apply." (ii) It may mean, " You are guilty of making class distinctions. You are guilty of setting up distinctions between man and man which in the Christian fellowship should not exist." We prefer the second meaning, because James goes on to say, " If you do that, you are judges whose thoughts are evil." That is to say, " You are breaking the commandment of Him who said, ' Judge not that he be not judged ' " (*Matthew* 7: 1).

THE RICHES OF POVERTY AND THE POVERTY OF RICHES

James 2: 5-7

> Listen, my dear brothers. Did God not choose those who are poor by the world's valuation to be rich because of their faith, and to be heirs of the Kingdom which He has promised to those who love Him? But you dishonour the poor man. Do not the rich oppress you, and is it not they who drag you to the law-courts? And is it not they who abuse the fair name by which you have been called?

" GOD," said Abraham Lincoln, " must love the common people because He made so many of them." Christianity had always had a special message for the poor. In Jesus' first sermon in the Synagogue at Nazareth His claim was: " He hath anointed me to preach the gospel to the poor " (*Luke* 4: 18). His answer to John's puzzled inquiries, as to whether or not He was God's Chosen One, culminated in the claim: " The poor have the gospel preached to them " (*Matthew* 11: 5). The first of the Beatitudes was indeed

the Beatitude of the promise: " Blessed are the poor in
spirit, for theirs is the Kingdom of Heaven " (*Matthew*
5: 3). And Luke is even more definite: " Blessed be ye
poor; for yours is the Kingdom of God (*Luke* 6: 20).
During the ministry of Jesus, when He was banished from
the synagogues, and when he took to the open road and
to the hillside and to the seaside, in the very nature of
things it was the ordinary crowds of common men and
women to whom His message came. In the days of the
Early Church it was to the crowds that the street preachers
preached. In point of fact the message of Christianity was
that those who mattered to no one else mattered intensely
to God. " You see your calling, brethren," wrote Paul to
the Corinthians, " how that not many wise men after the
flesh, not many mighty, not many noble, are called "
(I *Corinthians* I: 26). It is not that Christ and the Church
do not want the great and the rich and the wise and the
mighty; we must beware of an inverted snobbery, as we
have already seen. But it was the simple fact that the
gospel offered so much to the poor, and demanded so much
from the rich, that it was the poor who were swept into the
Church. It was, in fact, the common people who heard
Jesus gladly, and the rich young ruler who went sorrow-
fully away because he had great possessions. James is not
shutting the door on the rich—far from that. He is only
saying that the gospel of Christ is specially dear to the
poor, and that in it there is a welcome for the man who has
none to welcome him, and through it there is a value set
on the man whom the world regards as valueless.

In any event in the society which James inhabited
the rich oppressed the poor. They dragged them to the law-
courts. No doubt this was for debt. At the bottom end of
the social scale men were so poor that they could hardly
live, and moneylenders were plentiful and extortionate.
In the ancient world there was a custom of summary
arrest. If a creditor met a debtor on the street, he could
seize him by the neck of his robe, nearly throttling him

and literally drag him to the law courts. That is what the rich did to the poor. They had no sympathy; all they wanted was the uttermost farthing. It is not riches that James is condemning. It is the conduct of riches without sympathy.

It is the rich who abuse the name by which the Christians are called. The name may be the name *Christian* by which the heathen first called the followers of Christ at Antioch, and which was given at first as a jest and a nickname. The name may be the name of Christ, which was pronounced over a Christian on the day of his baptism. The word James uses for *called* is interesting (*epikaleisthai*). It is the word which is used for a wife taking her husband's name in marriage, or for a child being called after his father. The Christian takes the name of Christ; he is called after Christ. It is as if he was married to Christ, or born and christened into the family of Christ.

The rich and the masters would have many a reason for insulting the name Christian. A slave who became a Christian would have a new *independence*; the Christian slave would no longer cringe at his master's power; punishment would cease to terrorize him; he would meet his master clad in a new manhood. He would have a new *honesty*. That would make him a better slave, but it would also mean he could no longer be his master's instrument in sharp practice and petty dishonesty as once he had been. He would have a new *sense of worship*; and on the Lord's Day he would insist on leaving work aside in order that he might worship with the people of God. There would be ample opportunity for a master to find reasons for insulting the name of Christian and cursing the name of Christ.

THE ROYAL LAW

James 2: 8-12

If you perfectly keep the royal law, as the Scripture has it: " You must love your neighbour as yourself," you do well. But, if you treat people with respect of persons, such conduct is sin, and you stand convicted by the law as transgressors. For, if a man keeps the whole law, and yet fails to keep it in one point, he becomes guilty of transgressing the law as a whole. For He who said, " Do not commit adultery," also said, " Do not kill." If you do not commit adultery, but if you kill, you become a transgressor of the law.

THE connection of thought between this and the previous passage is this. James has been condemning the man who paid special attention to the rich man who enters the Church. " But," the man might answer, " the law tells me to love my neighbour as myself. Therefore I am under duty to welcome the man when he comes to Church." " Very well," answers James, " If you are really welcoming the man because you love him as you do yourself, and you wish to give him the welcome you yourself would wish to receive, that is fine. But, if you are giving him this special welcome because he is a rich man, that is respect of persons and that is wrong—and so far from keeping the law, you are in fact breaking it. You don't love your neighbour, or you would not neglect the poor man. What you do love is wealth—and that is not what the law commands."

James calls the great injunction to love our neighbour as ourselves the *royal law*. There can be various meanings of that phrase. It may mean the law which is of *supreme excellence*, the highest part of the law. It may mean *the law which is given by the King of the kings*, that which is uniquely the law of the king. It may mean that that great injunction is *the king of all laws*, that it in fact is the law in the light of which all other laws must be used and judged and applied. It could just possibly mean *the law that makes kings and is fit for kings*. Christians are a royal priesthood belonging to God (*Revelation* 1: 6). To keep that greatest law is to become king of oneself and a king among men. It is a law fit for those who are royal, and able to make men royal.

James goes on to lay down a great principle about the
law of God. To break any part of it is to become a law-
breaker. The Jew was very apt to regard the law as **a**
series of detached injunctions. To keep one of these
injunctions was to gain credit; to break one was to incur
debt. Therefore, a man could add up the ones he kept and
subtract the ones he broke, and, as it were emerge with a
credit or a debit balance. There was a Rabbinic saying,
" Whoever fulfils only one law, good is appointed to him ;
his days are prolonged and he will inherit the land." Again
many of the Rabbis held that " the Sabbath weighs against
all precepts," and to keep it is to keep the whole law. In
this way a man could keep some laws and break others,
and still emerge with a credit balance.

But as James saw it, the *whole* law is the will of God; to
break any part of it is to infringe the will of God, and
therefore to be guilty of sin. That is perfectly true. To
break any part of the law is to become a law breaker in
principle. Even under earthly law a man becomes **a**
criminal when he has broken one law. So James argues:
" No matter how good you may be in other directions, if
you treat people with respect of persons, you have acted
against the will of God; you have broken God's law; and
you are a transgressor."

There is a great truth here, a truth which is relevant and
practical. We may put it much more simply. A man may
be in many respects, in nearly all respects, a good man;
and yet he may spoil it all by one fault. He may be moral
in his action, pure in his speech, meticulous in his devotion.
But he may be hard and self-righteous; he may be rigid
and unsympathetic; and, if so, all the goodness is spoiled
by the infecting fault.

We do well to remember that, though we may claim to
have done many a good thing and to have resisted many
an evil thing, there may well be something in us by which
everything is spoiled—and all the goodness goes for nothing.

THE LETTER OF JAMES

THE LAW OF LIBERTY AND THE LIFE OF MERCY

James 2: 13

> So speak and so act as those who are going to be
> judged under the law of liberty. For he who acts
> without mercy will have judgment without mercy.
> Mercy triumphs over judgment.

HERE, as he comes to the end of a section, James reminds
his readers of two great facts of the Christian life.

(i) The Christian lives under the law of liberty, and it is
by the law of liberty he will be judged. What James means
is this. Unlike the Pharisee and the orthodox Jew, the
Christian is not a man whose life is governed by the external
pressure of a whole series of rules and regulations, which
are imposed on him from without. He is, in fact, governed
by the inner compulsion of love. That is to say, the
Christian is self-governed and self-directed by the love
which resides within his heart. He follows the right way,
the way of love to God and love to men, not because any
external law compels him to do so, and not because any
threat of punishment frightens him into doing so, but
because the love of Christ which is within his heart makes
him desire to do so. The Christian is not governed by a
man-made law, but by a God-given love.

(ii) The Christian must ever remember that it is only he
who shows mercy who will find mercy. This is a principle
which runs through all Scripture. The Psalmist said,
" With the merciful Thou wilt show Thyself merciful "
(*Psalm* 18: 25). Ben Sirach wrote, " Forgive thy neighbour
the hurt that he hath done thee, so shall thy sins also be
forgiven. One man beareth hatred against another, and
doth he seek pardon from the Lord? He showeth no mercy
to a man who is like himself; and doth he ask forgiveness
for his own sins?" (*Ecclesiasticus* 28: 2-5). Jesus said,
" Blessed are the merciful for they shall obtain mercy "
(*Matthew* 5: 7). " If ye forgive men their trespasses, your
heavenly Father will also forgive you; but if ye forgive

not men their trespasses, neither will your heavenly Father forgive your trespasses " (*Matthew* 6: 14, 15). " Judge not that ye be not judged, for with what judgment ye judge, ye shall be judged " (*Matthew* 7: 1, 2). He tells of the condemnation which fell upon the unforgiving servant, and ends the parable by saying, " So, also, likewise shall my heavenly Father do unto you, if ye from your hearts forgive not everyone his brother their trespasses " (*Matthew* 18: 22-35).

All Scripture teaching is agreed that he who would find mercy must himself be merciful. And James goes even further, for in the end he says that mercy triumphs over judgment, by which he means that in the day of judgment the man who has shown mercy will find that his mercy has even blotted out his own sin.

FAITH AND WORKS

James 2: 14-26

My brothers, what use is it if a man claims to have faith, and has no deeds to show? Are you going to claim that his faith is able to save him? If a brother or sister has nothing to wear, and if they have not enough for their daily food, and if one of you says to them, " Go in peace! Be warmed and fed! " and yet does not give them the essentials of bodily existence, what use is that? So, if faith too has no deeds to show, by itself it is dead.

But someone may well say, " Have you faith? " My answer is, " I have deeds. Show me your faith apart from your deeds, and I will show you my faith by means of my deeds." You say that you believe that there is one God. Excellent! The demons also believe the same thing—and shudder in terror.

Do you wish for proof, you empty creature, that faith without deeds is ineffective? Was not our father Abraham proved righteous in virtue of deeds, when he was ready to offer Isaac his own son upon the altar? You see how his faith co-operated with his deeds, and how his faith was completed by his deeds, and so there was fulfilled the passage of Scripture which says, " Abraham believed in God, and it was reckoned to him for righteousness, for he was the friend of God." You see that it is by deeds that a man is proved righteous, and not only by faith.

In the same way was Rahab the harlot not also proved righteous by deeds, when she received the messengers and sent them away by another way? For just as the body without breath is dead, so faith without works is dead.

THIS is a passage which we must take as a whole before we look at it in parts, for this is the passage which is so often used to seek to show that James and Paul were completely at variance. It is apparently Paul's stress and emphasis that a man is saved by faith and by faith alone, and that deeds do not come into the process at all. " Therefore, we conclude that a man is justified by faith without the deeds of the law " (*Romans* 3: 28). " A man is not justified by works of the law, but by faith in Jesus Christ . . . for by the works of the law shall no flesh be justified " (*Galatians* 2: 16). It is often argued that not only is James differing from Paul, but that he is even flatly contradicting him. This is a matter which we must investigate.

(i) We may begin by noting that the emphasis of James is in fact a universal New Testament emphasis. It was the preaching of John the Baptist that men should bring forth fruits meet for repentance (*Matthew* 3: 8; *Luke* 3: 8), that, in fact, they should prove the reality of their repentance by the excellence of their deeds. It was Jesus' preaching that men should so live that the world might see their good works and give the glory to God (*Matthew* 5: 16). He insisted that it was by their fruits that men must be known, and that a faith which expressed itself in words could never take the place of a faith which expressed itself in the actual doing of the will of God (*Matthew* 7: 15-21).

Nor is this emphasis missing from Paul himself. Apart from anything else there can be few teachers who have ever so stressed the ethical effect of Christianity as Paul does. However doctrinal and theological his letters may be they never fail to end with an ethical section in which the expression of Christianity in deeds is insisted upon. Apart from that general custom Paul repeatedly makes clear the importance he attaches to deeds. He speaks of God who will render to every man according to his deeds (*Romans* 2: 6). He insists that every one of us shall give account of himself to God (*Romans* 14: 12). He urges men to put off the works of darkness and to put on the armour of light (*Romans* 13: 12). Every man, he says, shall receive his own reward according to his labour (I *Corinthians* 3: 8). We must all, he warns men, appear before the judgment seat of Christ, that every one may receive the things done in his body, according to that he hath done, whether it be good or bad (2 *Corinthians* 5: 10). The Christian has to put off the old man and all his deeds (*Colossians* 3: 9). No one can read the letters of Paul without seeing at once the importance he attaches to deeds as part of the Christian life. The fact that Christianity must be ethically demonstrated is an essential part of the Christian faith throughout the whole New Testament.

(ii) That is undoubtedly so, and yet the fact remains that James reads as if he were at variance with Paul; for in spite of all that we have said the main emphasis of Paul is upon grace and faith, and the main emphasis of James is upon action and works. But this must be said—that which James is condemning is not Paulinism; it is, in fact, a perversion of Paulinism. The essential Pauline position, when it had to be summed up in one sentence was: " Believe in the Lord Jesus Christ and thou shalt be saved " (*Acts* 16: 31). But clearly the significance we attach to this demand will entirely depend on the meaning we attach to the word *believe*. There are two kinds of belief. There is belief which is purely intellectual, and which consists in the acceptance of a fact with the mind. For instance, I believe that the square on the hypotenuse of a right-angled triangle equals the sum of the squares on the other two sides. I have no doubt that that is true. If I had to, I could prove it—but it makes no difference at all to my life and my living. I accept it, but it has no effect upon me. On the other hand, I believe that six and six make twelve, and, therefore, I will resolutely refuse to pay more than a shilling for two sixpenny bars of chocolate. I accept that fact—and I direct my life by it. I take that fact, not only into my mind, but into every part of my life and action. What James is arguing against is, in fact, the first kind of belief, the acceptance of a fact without allowing the fact to have any influence upon life. The devils are intellectually convinced of the existence of God; they, in fact, tremble before God; but for all that they are none the less devils; their belief has not in the least altered them. What, in fact, Paul held is the second kind of belief. To believe in Jesus was to take that belief into every part and section of life, and to live by it.

It is easy to pervert Paulinism, and to emasculate the word *believe* of all effective meaning; and it is not real Paulinism, but misunderstood or perverted Paulinism which James condemns. He is condemning profession without practice; he is condemning an intellectual acceptance of Christianity as opposed to an acceptance by the whole personality—and with that condemnation Paul would have entirely agreed.

(iii) But, even allowing for that, there is still a difference between James and Paul. And the main difference is this —*they begin at different times in the Christian life*. Paul begins *at the very beginning*. He insists that no man can ever win or earn the forgiveness of God; no man can ever put himself into a right relationship with God. That initial step must come from the free grace of God; a man can only accept the forgiveness which God offers him in Jesus Christ; he can only accept the offer of God that the way to God is open. That initial step *must* come solely from the action and the initiative of God.

James begins much later; James begins *with the professing Christian*, the man who already claims to have been forgiven, the man who already claims to be in this right relationship with God. Such a man, James rightly says, must live a new life for he is a new creature. He has been *justified*; he must now go on to show that he is *sanctified*. And with that Paul would have entirely agreed.

The fact is that no man can be saved by works; but equally no man can be saved without producing works. By far the best analogy is the analogy of a great human love. He who is loved is quite certain that he does not deserve to be loved; there is nothing in him to merit this great privilege. But he is also quite certain that he must spend the rest of his life trying to be worthy of that love, and seeking to make himself the kind of person who is worthy to be loved. He cannot *earn* love, but he is bound to try to *deserve* love—or he does not know what love is.

So the difference between James and Paul is a difference of the starting-point. Paul starts with the great basic fact of the forgiveness of God which no man can earn or win or deserve; James starts with the professing Christian, and insists that unless a man proves his Christianity by his deeds he is not a Christian at all. We are not saved *by* deeds; we are saved *for* deeds; these are the twin truths of the Christian life. And Paul's whole emphasis is on the first truth, and James's whole emphasis is on the second truth. In point of fact James and Paul do not contradict each other; they complement each other; and the message of both is essential to the Christian faith in its fullest form. As the paraphrase has it:

> Let all who hold this faith and hope
> In holy deeds abound;
> Thus faith approves itself sincere,
> By active virtue crown'd.

THE LETTER OF JAMES

PROFESSION AND PRACTICE

James 2: 14-17

> My brothers, what use is it, if a man claims to have
> faith, and has no deeds to show? Are you going to
> claim that his faith is able to save him? If a brother
> or sister has nothing to wear, and, if they have not
> enough for their daily food, and if one of you says to
> them, " Go in peace! Be warmed and fed! " and yet
> does not give them the essentials of bodily existence,
> what use is that? So, if faith too has no deeds to show,
> by itself it is dead.

THE one thing that James cannot stand is profession
without practice, words without deeds. He chooses a vivid
illustration of what he means. Suppose a man to have
neither clothes to protect him or food to feed him; and
suppose his so-called friend to express the sincerest
sympathy for his sad plight; and suppose that sympathy
stops with words, and no effort is made to alleviate the
plight of the unfortunate man, what use is that that? What
use is sympathy without some attempt to turn that
sympathy into practical effect? So, says James, faith
without deeds is dead. This is a passage which would
appeal specially to a Jew.

(i) To a Jew almsgiving was of paramount importance.
So much so was this the case that righteousness and almsgiving can, for a Jew, mean one and the same thing
Almsgiving was considered to be a man's one defence when
he was judged by God. " Water will quench a flaming
fire," writes Ben Sirach, " and alms maketh an atonement
for sin " (*Ecclesiasticus* 3: 30). In *Tobit* it is written, " Everyone who occupieth himself in alms shall behold the face of
God, as it is written, I will behold thy face by almsgiving "
(*Tobit* 4: 8-10). When the leaders of the Jerusalem Church
agreed that Paul should go to the Gentiles the one injunction
that was laid upon him was not to forget the poor
(*Galatians* 2: 9). This stress on practical help is one of the
great and lovely marks of Jewish piety.

(ii) There was a strain of Greek religion to which this stress on sympathy, pity and almsgiving was quite alien. The Stoics aimed at *apatheia*. *Apatheia* is the complete absence of all feeling and all emotion. The aim of life was serenity. Emotion disturbs serenity. The way to perfect calm is to annihilate all feeling and all emotion. Pity is a mere disturbance of the detached philosophic calm in which a man should aim to live. So Epictetus lays it down that only he who disobeys the divine command will ever feel grief or pity (*Discourses* 3: 24, 43). When Virgil in the *Georgics* (2: 498) draws the picture of the perfectly happy man, the happy man is marked by the absence of pity in his heart. He has no pity for the poor and no grief for the sorrowing, for such emotions would only upset his own serenity. Here is the very opposite of the Jewish point of view. For the Stoic, blessedness meant being wrapped up in his own philosophic detachment and calm; for the Jew blessedness meant actively sharing in the misfortunes of others.

(iii) In his approach to this subject James is profoundly right. There is nothing more dangerous than the repeated experiencing of a fine emotion with no attempt to put that emotion into action. It is a fact of experience that every time a man experiences a fine emotion without putting it into action, he is less likely ever to put it into action. In a sense it is true to say that a man has no right to feel pity and sympathy unless he at least tries to put that pity and sympathy into action. An emotion is not something in which to luxuriate; it is something which at the cost of effort and of toil and of discipline and of sacrifice must be turned into the stuff of life.

NOT EITHER OR, BUT BOTH AND

James 2: 18, 19

But some one may well say, " Have you faith? " My answer is, " I have deeds. Show me your faith apart from your deeds, and I will show you my faith by means of my deeds." You say that you believe there is one God. Excellent! The demons also believe the same thing—and shudder in terror.

HERE James is meeting a possible objection. He is thinking of an objector who says, " Faith is a fine thing; and works are fine things. They are both perfectly real and genuine manifestations of real religion. But the one man does not necessarily possess both. One man will have faith and another man will have works. Well, then, you carry on with your works, and I will carry on with my faith; and we are both being truly religious, each in our own way." It is the objector's view that you can have *either* faith *or* works, that faith and works are alternative expressions of the Christian religion. But James will have none of that. It is not, as he sees it, a case of *either* faith *or* works; it is necessarily a case of *both* faith *and* works. It is all too true that people have a habit of presenting religion as an *either or*, but in every case it must be a *both and*.

(i) In the well-proportioned life there must be *thought* and *action*. It is tempting and it is common to think that a man may be either a *man of thought* or a *man of action*. The man of thought will sit in his study thinking great thoughts; the man of action will be out in the world doing great deeds. But that is wrong. The thinker is but half a man, unless he turns his thoughts into deeds. He will not even inspire men to action unless he comes down into the battle and shares the arena with them. As Kipling had it:

O England is a garden and such gardens are not made
By saying, " O how beautiful," and sitting in the shade;
While better men than we began their working lives
By digging weeds from garden paths with broken
    dinner knives.

Nor can the man of action be a real man of action unless he has thought out the great eternal principles on which his action is founded, and which are the moving cause of all his deeds.

(ii) In the well-proportioned life there must be *prayer*

and *effort*. Again it is tempting to divide men into two classes—the saints who spend life secluded on their knees in constant devotion, and the toilers who labour in the dust and the heat of the day. But it will not do. It is said that Martin Luther was close friends with another monk. The other monk was as fully persuaded of the necessity of the Reformation as Luther was. So they made an arrangement. Luther would go down into the world and fight the battle there; the other monk would remain in his cell praying all the time for the success of Luther's labours. But one night the monk had a dream. In it he saw a single reaper engaged on the impossible task of reaping an immense field unaided and alone. The lonely reaper turned his head and the monk saw his face, and it was the face of Martin Luther; and he knew that he must leave his cell and leave his prayers and go to help. It is, of course, true that there are some who, because of age or bodily weakness, can do nothing other than pray; and their prayers are indeed a strength and a support. But if any normal person thinks that prayer can be a substitute for effort, then his prayers are merely a way of escape. Prayer and effort must go hand in hand.

(iii) In any well-proportioned life there must be *faith* and *deeds*. It is only through deeds that faith can prove and demonstrate itself; and it is only through faith that deeds will be attempted and done. Faith is bound to overflow into action; and action only begins when a man has faith in some great cause or some great principle which God has presented to him.

If life is to be well-proportioned and fully effective in service and devotion, we must never think of it in terms of *either or*, but always in terms of *both and*.

THE PROOF OF FAITH

James 2: 20-26

> Do you wish for proof, you empty creature, that faith without deeds is ineffective? Our father Abraham was proved righteous in consequence of deeds, when he

was ready to offer Isaac his son upon the altar. You
see how his faith co-operated with his deeds, and how
his faith was completed by his deeds, and so there was
fulfilled the passage of Scripture which says,
" Abraham believed in God, and it was reckoned to
him for righteousness, and he was called the friend of
God." You see that it is by deeds that a man is proved
righteous, and not only by faith. In the same way was
Rahab the harlot not also proved righteous by deeds,
when she received the messengers and sent them away
by another way? For just as the body without the
breath is dead, so faith without deeds is dead.

JAMES offers two illustrations of the point of view on
which he is insisting. Abraham is the great example of
faith; but Abraham's faith was proved by his willingness
to sacrifice Isaac at the apparent demand of God. Rahab
was a famous figure in Jewish legend. She had sheltered
the spies who had been sent to spy out the Promised Land
(*Joshua* 2: 1-21). Later legend said that she became a
proselyte to the Jewish faith, that she married Joshua, and
that she was a direct ancestress of many priests and
prophets, including Ezekiel and Jeremiah. It was her
treatment of the spies which proved that she indeed had
faith.

Paul and James are both right here. Unless Abraham
had had faith he would never have answered the call and
the summons of God at all. Unless Rahab had had faith,
she would never have taken the risk of identifying her
future with the fortunes of Israel. Faith was indeed the
moving cause of the action of Abraham and of Rahab.
And yet, unless Abraham had been prepared to obey God
to the uttermost his faith would have been an unreal
thing; and unless Rahab had been prepared to risk all to
help the spies her faith would have been a useless thing.

These two examples show fully and finally that faith
and deeds are not opposites; they are, in fact, inseparables.
No man will ever be moved to action without faith; and
no man's faith is real until it moves him to action. Faith
and deeds are opposite sides of a man's experience of God.

THE LETTER OF JAMES

THE TEACHER'S PERIL

James 3: 1

> My brothers, it is a mistake for many of you to become teachers, for you must be well aware that those of us who teach will receive a greater condemnation.

IN the Early Church the teachers were of first rate importance. Wherever they are mentioned they are mentioned with honour. In the Church at Antioch they are ranked with the prophets who sent out Paul and Barnabas on the first missionary journey (*Acts* 13: 1). In Paul's list of those who hold great gifts within the Church the teachers come second only to the apostles and to the prophets (I *Corinthians* 12: 28; cp. *Ephesians* 4: 11). The apostles and the prophets were for ever on the move. Their field was the whole Church; and they did not stay long in any one congregation. But the teachers worked within a congregation, and their supreme importance was that it must have been to them that the converts to Christianity were handed over for instruction in the facts of the Christian gospel, and for edification in the Christian faith. It was the teacher's awe-inspiring responsibility that he could put the stamp of his own faith and knowledge on to those who were entering the Church for the first time.

In the New Testament itself we get glimpses of teachers who failed in their responsibility and their task, and who became false teachers. There were teachers who tried to turn Christianity into another kind of Judaism, and who tried to introduce circumcision and the keeping of the law (*Acts* 15: 24). There were teachers who taught others, but who themselves lived out nothing of the truth which they taught, teachers whose whole life was a contradiction of their instruction, and who did nothing but bring dishonour on the faith they represented (*Romans* 2: 17-29). There were some who tried to teach before they themselves knew anything (I *Timothy* 1: 6, 7). There were false teachers who would pander to the false desires of the crowd (2 *Timothy* 4: 3).

But, apart altogether from the false teachers, it is James's conviction that teaching is a dangerous occupation for any man. His instrument is speech and his agent the tongue. And, as Ropes puts it, James was concerned to point out, " the responsibility of teachers and the dangerous character of the instrument they have to use."

The Christian teacher entered into a perilous heritage. In the Christian Church he took the place of the Rabbi in the Jewish Church. There were many great and saintly Rabbis, but the Rabbi was treated in a way that was liable to ruin the character of any man. His very name means, " My great one." Everywhere he went he was treated with the greatest respect. It was actually held that a man's duty to his Rabbi exceeded his duty to his parents, because his parents only brought him into the life of this world, but his teacher brought him into the life of the world to come. It was actually said that if a man's parents and a man's teacher were captured by an enemy, the Rabbi must be ransomed first. If Rabbi and parents needed help, it was a duty to help the Rabbi first. It was true that a Rabbi was not allowed to take money for teaching, and that he was supposed to support his bodily needs by working at a trade; but it was held that it was a specially pious and meritorious work to take a Rabbi into the household and to support him with every care. It was desperately easy for a Rabbi to become the kind of person whom Jesus depicted, a spiritual tyrant, an ostentatious ornament of piety, a lover of the highest place at any function, a person who gloried in the almost subservient respect which others showed to him in public (*Matthew* 23: 4-7). Any teacher runs the risk of becoming " Sir Oracle." No profession is more liable to beget spiritual and intellectual pride.

There are two dangers which every teacher must avoid. In virtue of his office he will either be teaching those who

94

are young in years or those who are children in the faith.
He must, therefore, all his life struggle to avoid two things.
He must always have every care that he is teaching the
truth, and not his own opinions, or even his own prejudices.
It is fatally easy for any teacher to distort the truth, to
teach, not God's version, but his version of the truth.
He must have every care that he does not contradict
his teaching by his life, and that he does not continually
in effect have to be saying, not, " Do as I do," but, " Do
as I say." The teacher must never get into the position
when his scholars and students cannot hear what he says
for listening to what he is. As the Jewish Rabbis themselves
said, " Not learning but doing is the foundation, and he
who multiplies words multiplies sin " (*Sayings of the
Fathers* I: 18).

It is James's warning that the teacher has of his own
choice entered into a special office; and is, therefore,
under a special responsibility; and is, therefore, under the
greater condemnation, if he fails in it. The people to
whom James was writing coveted the prestige and the
place and the honour of the teacher; James demanded
that they should never forget the responsibility of being
a teacher.

THE UNIVERSAL DANGER

James 3: 2

> There are many things in which we all slip up; but if
> a man never slips up in his speech, he is a perfect
> man, able to keep the whole body also on the rein.

HERE James sets down two ideas which were woven into
Jewish thought and literature.

(i) There is no man in this world who does not sin in
something. The word which James uses means *to slip up*.

" Life," said Lord Fisher, the great sailor, " is strewn with orange peel." Sin is so often not deliberate, but the result of a slip up when we are off our guard. This universality of sin runs all through the Bible. " There is none righteous, no not one," quotes Paul. " For all have sinned and come short of the glory of God " (*Romans* 3: 10, 23). " If we say that we have no sin," says John, " we deceive ourselves, and the truth is not in us " (I *John* I: 8). " There is not a just man upon the earth that doeth good and sinneth not," said the preacher (*Ecclesiastes* 7: 20). " There is no man," says the Jewish sage, " among them that be born, but he hath dealt wickedly; and among the faithful there is none who hath not done amiss " (2 *Esdras* 8: 35). There is no room for pride in human life, for there is not a man upon earth who has not some blot of which to be ashamed. Even the pagan writers have the same conviction of sin. " It is the nature of man to sin both in private and in public life," said Thucydides (3: 45). " We all sin," said Seneca, " some more grievously, some more lightly " (*On Clemency* I: 6). All men are involved in sin.

(ii) There is no sin into which it is easier to fall, and no sin which has graver consequences, than the sin of the tongue. Again this is woven into Jewish thought. Jesus Himself warned men that they would give account for every word they spoke. " By thy words thou shalt be justified; and by thy words thou shalt be condemned" (*Matthew* 12: 36, 37). " A soft answer turneth away wrath; but grievous words stir up anger. . . . A wholesome tongue is a tree of life; but perverseness therein is a breach of the spirit " (*Proverbs* 15: 1-4). Of all Jewish writers, Jesus ben Sirach, the writer of *Ecclesiasticus*, was most impressed with the terror of the evil potentialities of the tongue. " Honour and shame is in talk; and the tongue of man is his fall. Be not called a whisperer, and lie not in wait with the tongue; for a foul shame is upon the thief, and an evil condemnation upon the double tongue. . . .

Instead of a friend become not an enemy; for thereby thou shalt inherit an ill name, shame and reproach; even so shall a sinner that hath a double tongue " (*Ecclesiasticus* 5: 13—6: 1). " Blessed is the man who has not slipped with his mouth " (14: 1). " Who is he that hath not offended with his tongue? " (19: 15). " Who shall set a watch before my mouth, and a seal of wisdom upon my lips, that I shall not suddenly fall by them, and that my tongue destroy me not? " (22: 27). He has a lengthy passage which is so nobly and passionately said that it is worth quoting in full:

> Curst the whisperer and the double-tongued; for such have destroyed many that were at peace. A backbiting tongue hath disquieted many, and driven them from nation to nation; strong cities hath it pulled down, and overthrown the houses of great men. It hath cut in pieces the forces of people, and undone strong nations. A backbiting tongue hath cast out virtuous women, and deprived them of their labours. Whoso hearkeneth unto it shall never find rest, and never dwell quietly, neither shall he have a friend in whom he may repose. The stroke of the whip maketh marks in the flesh: but the stroke of the tongue breaketh the bones. Many have fallen by the edge of the sword; but not so many as have fallen by the tongue. Well is he that is defended from it, and has not passed through the venom thereof; who hath not drawn the yoke thereof, nor hath been bound in her bands. For the yoke thereof is a yoke of iron, and the bands thereof are bands of brass. The death thereof is an evil death, the grave were better than it. . . . Look that thou hedge thy possession about with thorns, and bind up thy silver and gold, and weigh thy words in a balance, and make a bridle for thy lips, and make a door and bar for thy mouth. Beware thou slide not by it, lest thou fall before him that lieth in wait, and thy fall be incurable unto death (28: 13-26).

No man can say that he has not been warned of the dangers of the tongue, and no man can say that he has entirely avoided them.

LITTLE BUT POWERFUL

James 3: 3-5a

> If we put bits into horses' mouths to make them obedient to us, we can control the direction of their whole body as well. Look at ships, too. See how large they are, and how they are driven by rough winds, and see how their course is altered by a very small rudder, wherever the pressure of the steersman desires. So, too, the tongue is a little member of the body, but it makes arrogant claims for itself.

IT might be argued against James's terror of the tongue that the tongue is a very small part of the body to make such a fuss about and to which to attach so much importance. To combat that argument James uses two pictures.

(i) We put a bit into the mouths of horses, for we know that if we can control the horse's mouth, we can control its whole body. So James says that if we can control the tongue, we can control the whole body, but if the tongue is uncontrolled the whole life is set on the wrong way.

(ii) Suppose the tongue is so small a part of the body—a rudder is very small in comparison with the great size and bulk and weight of a ship; and yet, by exerting pressure on that little rudder, the steersman can alter the course of the ship, and direct it to safety. Long before this Aristotle had used this very same picture when he was talking about the science of mechanics: " A rudder is small, and it is attached to the very end of the ship, but it has such power that by this little rudder, and by the power of one man—and that a power gently exerted—the great bulk of ships can be moved." The rudder is small, yet it can direct the course of the whole ship; the tongue is small, yet it can direct the course of the whole body and life of a man.

Philo had called the mind the charioteer and steersman of man's life; it is when the mind controls every word and emotion, and when the mind is itself controlled by Christ, that life is safe.

It is to be noted that James is not for a moment saying that silence is better than speech. He is not pleading for a Trappist life, where speech is forbidden. What he is pleading for is the control of the tongue. Aristippus the Greek had a wise saying, " The conqueror of pleasure is not the man who never uses pleasure. He is the man who uses pleasure as a rider guides a horse or a steersman directs a ship, and so directs them wherever he wishes." Abstention from anything is never a complete substitute for control in the use of it. And James is not pleading for a cowardly silence, but for a wise use of speech.

A DESTRUCTIVE FIRE

James 3: 5b-6

See how great a forest how little a fire can set alight. And the tongue is a fire; in the midst of our members the tongue stands for the whole wicked world, for it defiles the whole body, and sets on fire the ever-recurring cycle of creation, and is itself set on fire by hell.

THE damage the tongue can cause is like the damage caused by a forest fire. The picture of the forest fire is common in the Bible. It is the prayer of the Psalmist that God may make the wicked like the stubble before the wind; and that God's tempest may destroy them as the fire burneth a wood, and as the flame setteth the mountains on fire (*Psalm* 83: 13, 14). Isaiah sees the picture of " wickedness burning as the fire; it shall devour the briars and the thorns, and kindle in the thickets of the forest " (*Isaiah* 9: 18). Zechariah speaks of " a hearth of fire among the wood, and a torch of fire in a sheaf " (*Zechariah* 12: 6). The picture was a picture the Jews of Palestine knew. In the dry season the scanty grass and the lowgrowing thorn bushes and scrub were as dry as tinder. If they were set on fire, the flames would spread like a wave which there was no stopping.

The picture of the tongue as a fire is also a Jewish picture. " An ungodly man diggeth up evil," says the writer of the *Proverbs*, " and in his lips there is a burning fire " (*Proverbs* 16: 27). " As pitch and tow, so a hasty contention kindleth fire " (*Ecclesiasticus* 28: 11). There are two reasons why the damage which the tongue can do is like a fire.

(i) It is wide-ranging. The danger of the tongue is that it can damage at a distance. A chance word dropped in one end of the country or the town can finish up by bringing damage and grief and hurt and heartbreak at the other. The Jewish Rabbis had this picture: " Life and death are in the hand of the tongue. Has the tongue a hand? No, but as the hand kills, so the tongue. The hand kills only at close quarters; the tongue is called an arrow because it kills at a distance. An arrow kills at forty or fifty paces, but of the tongue it is said (*Psalm* 63: 9), ' They have set their mouth in heaven and their tongue goeth through the earth.' It ranges over the whole earth and reaches to heaven." That, indeed, is the peril of the tongue. A man can ward off a blow with the hand, for the striker must be in his presence to strike him. But a man can drop a malicious word, or repeat a scandalous and untrue story, about someone whom he does not even know, and about someone who stays hundreds of miles away, and cause infinite damage and harm. The very range the tongue can reach is the tongue's greatest peril.

(ii) It is quite uncontrollable. In the tinder-dry wood and scrub of Palestine, a forest fire was almost immediately out of control. No man can control the damage of the tongue. " Three things come not back—the spent arrow, the spoken word, and the lost opportunity." Once a word is spoken there is no getting it back. There is nothing which it is so impossible to kill as a rumour; there is nothing which it is so impossible to obliterate as an idle and a malignant story. Let a man, before he speaks, remember that once a word is spoken it is gone from his control; and let him think before he speaks, because, although he cannot get it back, he will most certainly answer for it.

THE CORRUPTION WITHIN

James 3: 5b-6 (continued)

WE must spend a little longer on this passage, because in it there are two specially difficult phrases.

(i) The tongue, says the Authorized Version, is *a world of iniquity*. That is a mistranslation; it ought to be *the world of iniquity*, which most likely means *the wicked world*. In our bodies, that is to say, the tongue stands for the whole wicked world. In Greek the phrase is *ho kosmos tēs adikias*. And we shall best get at its meaning by remembering the meaning of this word *kosmos*. *Kosmos* can have two meanings. (*a*) *Kosmos* can mean *adornment*, although this is its less usual meaning. The phrase, therefore, could mean that the tongue is *the adornment of evil*. That would mean that the tongue is the organ which can fatally and fascinatingly make evil attractive. It is by the tongue that men can make the worse appear the better reason; it is by the tongue that men can excuse and defend and gloss over and seek to justify their own wicked ways; it is by the tongue that men can persuade and seduce and lure others into sin. There is no doubt that that meaning gives excellent sense; but it is not altogether sure that the phrase really can mean that. (*b*) *Kosmos* can mean *world*. Now in almost every part of the New Testament the word *kosmos* means the world with more than a suggestion of *the evil world*. The world cannot receive the Spirit (*John* 14: 17). Jesus manifests Himself to the disciples, but not to the world (*John* 14: 22). The world hates Him, and therefore hates His disciples (*John* 15: 18, 19). Jesus' Kingdom is not of this world (*John* 18: 36). Paul condemns the wisdom of this world (*I Corinthians* 1: 20). The Christian must not be conformed to this world (*Romans* 12: 2). When *kosmos* is used in this sense it means *the world without God*, the world in its ignorance of, and often its hostility to, God. Therefore, if we call the tongue the evil *kosmos*, it means that the tongue is that part of the body which is without God. An uncontrolled tongue is like a world hostile to, and ignorant of, God. It is the part of us which disobeys, defies, and rebels against God.

(ii) The second difficult phrase is the phrase which the Authorized Version translates *the course of nature* (*trochos geneseōs*). The phrase literally means *the wheel of being*.

The ancients used the picture of the wheel to describe life in four different ways.

(i) The wheel is a circle, a rounded and complete whole, and, therefore, the wheel of life can mean *the totality of life*, everything that is contained in life and living.

(ii) The wheel is always moving; any particular point in it is always moving up and down. Therefore, the wheel of life can stand for *the ups and downs of life*, the chances and the changes. In this sense the phrase very nearly means the wheel of fortune, always changing and always variable.

(iii) The wheel is circular; it is always turning back upon itself in exactly the same circle; therefore, the wheel came to stand for *the cyclical repetition of life*, the unvarying coming and going of the generations, the weary round of an existence which is ever repeating itself without becoming any further on.

(iv) The phrase had one particular technical use. The Orphic religion believed in birth and rebirth. It believed that the human soul was always being born and dying and being reborn again. And the aim of life was to escape from this treadmill of death and birth and death and death again into endless and infinite being. So the Orphic devotee who has achieved can say, " I have flown out of the sorrowful, weary wheel." In this sense the wheel of life can stand for *the weary treadmill of constant reincarnation*.

It is entirely unlikely that James knew anything about Orphic reincarnation. It is not at all likely that any Christian would think in terms of a circular and cyclical life which was not going anywhere. It is not likely that a Christian would be afraid of the chances and changes of life. Therefore, the phrase most probably means *the whole of life and living*. Therefore, what James is saying is that the tongue can kindle a destructive fire which can destroy all life; and the tongue itself is kindled with the very fire of hell. Here indeed is the terror of the tongue.

BEYOND ALL TAMING

James 3: 7, 8

> Every kind of beasts and birds, and reptiles and fishes, is, and has been, tamed for the service of mankind; but no man can tame the tongue. It is a restless evil, full of deadly poison.

THE idea of the taming of the animal creation in the service of mankind is an idea which often occurs in Jewish literature. We get it in the creation story. God said of man, " Let them have dominion over the fish of the sea, and over the fowl of the air, and over the cattle and over all the earth, and over every creeping thing that creepeth upon the earth " (*Genesis* I: 28). It is, in fact, to that verse that James is very likely looking back. The same promise is repeated to Noah: " And the fear of you and the dread of you shall be upon every beast of the earth, and upon every fowl of the air, upon all that moveth upon the earth, and upon all the fishes of the sea; into your hand they are delivered (*Genesis* 9: 2). The writer of *Ecclesiasticus* repeats the same idea: " God put the fear of man upon all flesh, and gave him dominion over beasts and fowls " (*Ecclesiasticus* 17: 4). The Psalmist also thought on the same lines: " Thou madest him to have dominion over the works of Thy hands; Thou hast put all things under his feet; all sheep and oxen, yea, and the beasts of the field; the fowl of the air, and the fish of the sea, and whatsoever passeth through the paths of the sea " (*Psalm* 8: 6-8). The Roman world knew of tame fish in the fish-ponds which were in the open central hall or *atrium* of a Roman house. The serpent was the emblem of Aesculapius, and in his temples tame serpents glided about, and were supposed to be incarnations of the god. People who were ill slept in the temples of Aesculapius at night, and if one of these tame serpents glided over them, that was supposed to be the healing touch of the god.

Man's ingenuity, as James sees it, has tamed every wild creature, the tongue alone is beyond taming. To tame means to control, and to render useful and beneficial; that, says James, is what no man by his own unaided efforts has ever been able to do with the tongue.

BLESSING AND CURSING

James 3: 9-12

> With it we bless the Lord and Father, and with it we curse the men who have been made in the likeness of God. From the same mouth there emerge blessing and cursing. These things should not be so, my brothers. Surely the one stream from the same cleft in the rock does not gush forth fresh and salt water? Surely, brothers, a fig-tree cannot produce olives, nor a vine figs, nor can salt water produce fresh water?

WE know only too well from experience that there is a cleavage in human nature. In man there is something of the ape and something of the angel, something of the hero and something of the villain, something of the saint and much of the sinner. It is James's conviction that nowhere is this contradiction more evident than in the tongue.

With it, he says, we bless God. This was specially relevant to a Jew. Whenever the name of God was mentioned, a Jew must respond: " Blessed be He! " Three times a day the devout Jew had to repeat the *Shemoneh Esreh*, the famous eighteen prayers called *Eulogies*, everyone of which begins, " Blessed be Thou, O God." God was indeed *eulogētos*, which literally means *The Blessed One*, the One who is continually blessed. And yet that very same mouth and that very same tongue which has frequently and so piously blessed God, are the very same mouth and tongue which can curse and swear at a fellow-man. To James there is something unnatural about this; it is as unnatural as for a stream to gush out both fresh and salt water, or as for a bush to bear opposite kinds of fruit. Unnatural and wrong such things may be, but they are none the less tragically common.

Peter could say, " Though I should die with Thee, yet will I not deny Thee " (*Matthew* 26: 33), and that very same tongue of his could deny Jesus with oaths and curses (*Matthew* 26: 69-75). The same John who said, " Little children, love one another," was the John who had once wished to call down fire from heaven in order to blast a Samaritan village out of existence (*Luke* 9: 51-56). Even the tongues of the saints and the apostles could say very different things.

John Bunyan tells us of Talkative: " He was a saint abroad and a devil at home." Many a man speaks with perfect courtesy to strangers and even preaches love and gentleness, and yet snaps with ungracious and impatient anger and irritability at his own family at home. It has not been unknown for a man to speak with piety on the Sunday, and to curse a squad of workmen on the Monday. It has not been unknown for a man to utter the most pious sentiments one day, and to repeat the most questionable stories the next. It has not been unknown for a woman to speak with sweet graciousness at a religious meeting, and then to go outside to murder someone's reputation with a malicious and a gossiping tongue.

These things, said James, should not be. There are some drugs, for instance strychnine and opium, which are at once poisons and cures; but they are benefits to men when they are wisely controlled by the doctors who use them. The tongue can bless or curse; the tongue can wound or soothe; the tongue can speak the fairest things, and the tongue can speak the foulest things. It is one of life's hardest duties, and it is one of life's plainest duties, to see to it that the tongue does not contradict itself, but that it ever speaks only such words as we would wish God to hear.

THE MAN WHO OUGHT NEVER TO BE A TEACHER

James 3: 13, 14

> Who among you is a man of wisdom and of understanding? Let him show by the loveliness of his behaviour that all he does is done with gentleness. If in your hearts you have a zeal that is bitter, and selfish ambition, do not be arrogantly boastful about your attainments, for you are false to the truth.

HERE James goes back, as it were, to the beginning of the chapter. His argument runs like this: " Is there any of you who wishes to be a real sage and a real teacher? Then let him live a life of such beautiful graciousness that he will prove to all that gentleness is enthroned as the controlling power within his heart. For, if he has a fanatical bitterness, and if he is obviously controlled by selfish and personal ambition, then, whatever claims he in his arrogance may make, all he does is to be false to the truth which he claims to teach." In this passage James uses two interesting words. The word he uses for zeal is *zēlos*. In Greek *zēlos* is a most significant word. It need not be a bad word at all. It can, and often does, mean the noble emulation which a man feels when he is confronted with some picture of greatness and goodness. But there is a very narrow dividing line between noble emulation and ignoble envy and jealousy. The word James uses for *selfish ambition* is *eritheia*. *Eritheia* was also a word with no necessarily bad meaning. It originally meant *spinning for hire,* and was used of serving women. Then it came to mean any work that is done for pay. Then it came to mean the kind of work that is done simply and solely for what can be got out of it. Then it entered politics and came to mean that selfish ambition which is out for self and for nothing else, and which is ready to intrigue and to plot and to use any means to gain its ends.

A scholar and a teacher is always under a double temptation.

(i) He is under the temptation to *arrogance.* Arrogance was the besetting sin of the Rabbis. The greatest of the Jewish teachers were well aware of that. In *The Sayings of the Fathers* we read, " He that is arrogant in decision is foolish, wicked, puffed up in spirit." It was the wise advice of one of the wise men: " It rests with thy colleagues to choose whether they will adopt thy opinion: it is not for thee to force it upon them." There are few who are in such constant spiritual peril as the teacher and the preacher. They are used to being listened to; they are used to having their words accepted. They are used to telling people rather than listening to people. All unconsciously they tend, as Shakespeare had it, to say,

> " I am Sir Oracle,
> And when I ope my lips let no dog bark! "

It is very difficult to be a teacher or a preacher and to remain humble; but however difficult it is, it is absolutely necessary.

(ii) He is under the temptation to *bitterness.* We know how easily " learned discussion can produce passion." The *odium theologicum* is notorious. Sir Thomas Browne has a passage on the savagery of scholars to each other: " Scholars are men of peace, they bear no arms, but their tongues are sharper than Actius' razor; their pens carry farther, and give a louder report than thunder: I had rather stand the shock of a basilisco, than the fury of a merciless pen." Philip Lilley reminds us of how Dr. H. F. Stewart described the arguments of Pascal with the Jesuits. Dr. Stewart said that these arguments reminded him of Alan Breck's fight with the crew of the *Covenant* as he drove them before him along the deck in Stevenson's *Kidnapped*: " The sword in his hand flashed like quicksilver into the middle of our flying enemies, and at every flash came the scream of a man hurt." One of the most difficult things in the world is to argue without passion, and to meet arguments without wounding. To be utterly convinced of one's own beliefs without at the same time being bitter to those of others is no easy thing, and yet it is a first necessity of the Christian teacher and scholar.

We may find in this passage four characteristics of the wrong kind of teaching.

(i) It is *fanatical*. The truth it holds is held with unbalanced violence rather than with reasoned conviction.

(ii) It is *bitter*. It regards its opponents as enemies to be annihilated rather than as friends to be persuaded.

(iii) It is *selfishly ambitious*. It is, in the end, more eager to display itself than to display the truth, and it is interested more in the victory of its own opinions than in the victory of the truth.

(iv) It is *arrogant*. Its whole attitude is pride in its own knowledge rather than humility in its own ignorance. The real scholar will be far more aware of what he does not know than of what he knows.

THE WRONG KIND OF WISDOM

James 3: 15, 16

> Such wisdom is not the wisdom which comes down from above, but is earthly, characteristic of the natural man, inspired by the devil. For where there is envy and selfish ambition, there there is disorder and every evil thing.

THIS bitter and arrogant wisdom, so-called, is very different from the wisdom which is the real wisdom. James first of all describes it in itself, and then he describes it in its effects. In itself it is three things.

(i) It is earthly. Its standards are earthly standards; its sources are earthly sources. It measures success in worldly terms; and its aims are worldly aims.

(ii) It is characteristic of the natural man. The word which James uses is difficult to translate. The word is *psuchikos*, which comes from the word *psuchē*. The ancients divided man into three parts—body, soul and spirit. The body (*sōma*) is our physical flesh and blood and constitution; the soul (*psuchē*) is the physical life which we share with the beasts; it is no more than animal life; the spirit (*pneuma*) is that which man alone possesses, that which differentiates him from the beasts, that which makes him a rational creature and kin to God. This is a little confusing for us, because we are in the habit of using the word *soul* in the same sense as the ancient people used the word *spirit*, whereas to them the word *soul* meant the physical life which is not peculiar to man, but which is shared by all the animal creation which has life. So then, what James is saying is that this wrong kind of wisdom is no more than an animal kind of thing; it is the kind of wisdom which makes an animal snap and snarl with no other thought than that of prey or personal survival. The wrong kind of wisdom is the wisdom which a man shares with the animals and which is part of his lower nature.

(iii) Finally James says the wrong kind of wisdom is devilish. Its source is not God, but the devil. It produces, not the kind of people or the kind of situation which God delights in, but the kind of situation in which the devil delights.

James then describes this arrogant and bitter wisdom in its effects. The most notable thing about it is that it issues in disorder. That is to say, instead of bringing people together, it drives them apart. Instead of producing peace, it produces strife. Instead of producing a fellowship, it produces a disruption in personal relationships. There is a kind of person who is undoubtedly clever; he has an acute brain and a skilful tongue; but his effect in any committee, in any Church, in any group, is to cause trouble, to drive people apart, to foment strife, to make trouble, to disturb personal relationships. It is a sobering thing to remember that the wisdom that that man possesses is devilish rather than divine, and that such a man is engaged on Satan's work and not on God's work. It may well be said that all forces which make for division are forces which are against the will of God, and which advance the cause of the devil.

THE TRUE WISDOM (I)

James 3: 17, 18

> The wisdom which comes from above is first pure, then peaceable, considerate, willing to yield, full of mercy and of good fruits, undivided in mind, without hypocrisy. For the seed which one day produces the reward which righteousness brings can only be sown when personal relationships are right, and by those whose conduct produces such relationships.

THE Jewish sages were always agreed that the true wisdom comes from above. It was not the attainment of man; it was the gift of God. *Wisdom* describes this wisdom as " the breath of the power of God, and a pure influence flowing from the glory of the Almighty " (*Wisdom of Solomon* 7: 25). The same book prays, " Give me the wisdom that sitteth by Thy throne " (*Wisdom* 9: 4); and again, " O send her from Thy holy heavens, and from the throne of Thy glory " (*Wisdom* 9: 8). Ben Sirach began his book with the sentence, " All wisdom cometh from the Lord, and is with Him for ever " (*Ecclesiasticus* 1: 1); and he makes Wisdom say, " I came out of the mouth of the Most High" (*Ecclesiasticus* 24: 3). With one voice the Jewish sages agreed that wisdom came to men from above, from God.

James uses eight words to describe this wisdom, and every one of them has a great picture in it.

(i) The true wisdom is *pure*. The Greek word is *hagnos*. The root meaning of the word *hagnos* is *pure enough to approach the gods*. At first it had only a ceremonial meaning, and it meant nothing more than that a man had gone through the right ritual cleansings. So, for instance, Euripides can make one of his characters say, " My hands are pure, but my heart is not." At this stage *hagnos* describes ritual, but not necessarily moral purity. But as time went on the word came to describe the moral purity which alone can approach the gods. On the Temple of Aesculapius at Epidaurus there was the inscription at the entrance: " He who would enter the divine temple must be pure (*hagnos*); and purity is to have a mind which thinks holy thoughts." The true wisdom is the wisdom which is so cleansed of all ulterior motives, so cleansed of self, that it has become pure enough to see God. Worldly wisdom might well wish to escape God's sight. The true wisdom is able to bear the very scrutiny of God.

(ii) The true wisdom is *eirēnikos*; we have translated this *peaceable*; but it has a very special meaning. *Eirēnē* means peace, and when *eirēnē* is used of men its basic meaning is *right relationships between man and man, and between man and God*. The true wisdom is the wisdom which produces right relationships. There is a kind of clever and arrogant wisdom which separates man from man, and which makes a man look with a superior contempt on his fellow-men. There is a kind of cruel wisdom which takes a delight in hurting others with clever, but cutting, words. There is a kind of depraved and wicked wisdom which seduces men away from purity and from their loyalty to God. But the true wisdom is the wisdom which at all times brings men closer to one another and closer to God.

(iii) The true wisdom is *epieikēs*. Of all Greek words in the New Testament this is the most untranslatable. Aristotle defined it as that " which is just beyond the written law." He defined it as " justice and better than justice." He defined it as that " which steps in to correct things when the law itself becomes unjust." The man who is *epieikēs* is the man who knows when it is actually wrong to apply the strict letter of the law. He is the man who knows how to forgive, when strict justice gives him a perfect right to condemn. He is the man who knows how to make allowances, the man who knows when not to stand upon his rights, the man who knows how to temper justice with mercy, the man who always remembers that there are greater things in the world than rules and regulations. It is impossible to find an English word to translate this quality. Matthew Arnold called it " sweet reasonableness." It is the ability to extend to others the kindly consideration which we would wish to receive ourselves.

THE TRUE WISDOM (2)

James 3: 17, 18 (*continued*)

(iv) The true wisdom is *eupeithēs*. Here we must make a choice between two meanings. (*a*) *Eupeithēs* can mean *ever ready to obey*. The first of William Law's rules for life was, " To fix it deep in my mind that I have but one business upon my hands, to seek for eternal happiness by doing the will of God." If we take the word in this sense, it means that the truly wise man is for ever ready and willing to obey God, whenever God's voice comes to him. (*b*) *Eupeithēs* can mean *easy to persuade*, not in the sense of being pliable and weak, but in the sense of not being stubborn, and of being willing to listen to reason and to appeal. Coming as it does after *epieikēs*, it probably bears this second meaning here. The true wisdom is not rigid and austere and beyond all appeal. It is willing to listen, willing to be persuaded, skilled in knowing when to wisely yield.

(v) We take the next two terms together. The true wisdom is *full of mercy (eleos) and good fruits. Eleos, mercy,* is a word which acquired a quite new meaning in Christian thought. The Greeks defined *eleos* as *pity for the man who is suffering unjustly.* But Christianity means far more than that by *eleos.* (a) In Christian thought *eleos* means mercy for the man who is in trouble, even if the trouble is his own fault. The Christian pity is the reflection of the pity of God; and the pity of God went out to men, not when they were suffering unjustly, but when they were suffering for their own sins and through their own fault. We are so apt to say of someone who is in trouble, "It is his own fault; he brought it on himself," and, therefore, to feel that we have no responsibility for him. But Christian mercy is mercy for any man who is in trouble, even if he has brought that trouble on himself. (b) In Christian thought *eleos* means mercy which issues in good fruits, that is, mercy which issues in practical help. Christian pity is not merely an emotion; Christian pity is action. Christian pity is not merely feeling sorry for someone; Christian pity is turning sorrow and sympathy and pity into deeds. We can never say that we have truly pitied anyone until we have helped him.

(vi) The true wisdom is *adiakritos, undivided.* This means that the true wisdom is not wavering and hesitant and vacillating; it means that it knows its own mind, chooses its course, and abides by it. It means that it has certain convictions which it will not change. There are those who think that it is clever never to make one's mind up about anything. They speak about having an open mind; they speak about suspending judgment. But the Christian wisdom is based on the Christian certainties which come to us from God through Jesus Christ.

(vii) The true wisdom is *anupokritos, without hypocrisy.* That is to say, the Christian wisdom is not a pose, and never acts a part. It does not deal in deception for its own ends. It is not the wisdom which is clever at putting on disguises and concealing its real aims and motives. The Christian wisdom is honest; it never claims or prétends to be what it is not; and it never acts a part to gain its own ends.

Finally, James says something which every Christian Church and every Christian group and fellowship should remember and have written on its heart. The Authorized Version correctly translates the Greek in a literal translation: " The fruit of righteousness is sown in peace of them that make peace." This is a highly compressed sentence. Let us begin by remembering one thing. Peace, *eirēnē*, means *right relationships between man and man*, it means a state in which men are in uninterrupted friendship and fellowship with one another. So, then, what James is saying is this, " We are all trying to reap the fruit and the reward and the results which a good life brings. But the seeds which bring the rich harvest can never flourish in any other atmosphere than in an atmosphere of right relationships between man and man. Right relationships are the soil in which the reward of righteousness alone can grow. And the only people who can sow these seeds, and who will reap the reward, are those whose life work it has been to produce such right relationships." That is to say, nothing good can ever grow in an atmosphere where men are at variance with each other. A group, a Church, any body of men where there is bitterness and strife is a barren and a sterile soil in which the seeds of righteousness can never grow, and out of which no reward can ever come. The man who disturbs personal relationships, the man who is responsible for strife and bitterness has cut himself off from the reward which God gives to those who live His life. Without right relationships between man and man righteousness cannot exist, and all man's striving for righteousness is rendered ineffective and without reward.

THE LETTER OF JAMES

MAN'S PLEASURE OR GOD'S WILL?

James 4: 1-3

> Whence come feuds and whence come fights among you? Is this not their source—do they not arise because of these desires for pleasures which carry on their constant warring compaign within your members? You desire, but you do not possess; you murder; you covet, but you cannot obtain. You fight and war, but you do not possess, because you do not ask. You ask, but you do not receive, because you ask wrongly, because your only desire is to spend what you receive on your own pleasures.

JAMES is here setting before his people a basic question— Whether is your aim in life to submit to the will of God, or to gratify your own desires for the pleasures of this world? And his warning is that, if pleasure is the policy of life, then nothing but strife and hatred and division can possibly follow. He says that the result of the over-mastering search for pleasure is *polemoi* and *machai*. *Polemos* is *war* and *machē* is a *battle*; and he means that the overmastering desire for pleasure, and the feverish search for it, issue in long-drawn-out resentments which are like wars, and sudden explosions and collisions of enmity which are like battles. The ancient moralists would have thoroughly agreed with James.

When we look at human society we so often see a seething mass of competitive hatred and warring strife. Philo writes, " Consider the continual war which prevails among men even in times of peace, and which exists not only between nations and countries and cities, but also between private houses, or, I might rather say, is present with every individual man; observe the unspeakable raging storm in men's souls that is excited by the violent rush of the affairs of life; and you may well wonder whether anyone can enjoy tranquility in such a storm, and maintain calm amidst the surge of this billowing sea."

The root cause of this unceasing and bitter conflict is nothing other than desire. Philo points out that the Ten Commandments culminate in the forbidding of covetousness which is desire, for desire is the worst of all the passions of the soul. " Is it not because of this passion that relations are broken, and this natural goodwill changed into desperate enmity? that great and populous countries are desolated by domestic dissensions? and land and sea filled with ever new disasters by naval battles and land campaigns? For the wars famous in tragedy . . . have all flowed from one source—desire either for money, or glory or pleasure. Over these things the human race goes mad." Lucian writes, " All the evils which come upon man—revolutions and wars, strategems and slaughters—spring from desire. All these things have as their fountain-head the desire for more." Plato writes, " The sole cause of wars and revolutions and battles is nothing other than the body and its desires." Cicero writes, " It is insatiable desires which overturn not only individual men, but whole families, and which even bring down the state. From desires there spring hatred, schisms, discords, seditions and wars." Desire is at the root of all the evils which ruin life and which divide men.

The New Testament is clear that this overmastering desire for the pleasures of this world is always a threatening danger to the spiritual life. It is the cares and riches and pleasures of this life which combine to choke the good seed (*Luke* 8: 14). A man can become a slave to lusts and pleasures, and, when he does, malice and envy and hatred enter into life (*Titus* 3: 3).

The ultimate choice in life lies between pleasing oneself and pleasing God; and a world in which men's first aim is to please themselves is a world which is a battleground of savagery and division.

THE CONSEQUENCES OF THE PLEASURE-
DOMINATED LIFE

James 4: 1-3 (continued)

THIS pleasure-dominated life has certain inevitable consequences.

(i) It sets men at each other's throats. Desires, as James sees it, are characteristically and inherently warring powers. He does not mean that they war within a man—although that is also true—he means that they set men warring against each other. The basic desires are for the same things—for money, for power, for prestige, for worldly possessions, for the gratification of bodily lusts. When all men are striving, each one to possess all for himself the same thing, life inevitably becomes a competitive arena. Men trample each other down in the rush to grasp the same things. Men will do anything to eliminate a rival for the thing or for the person they are on fire to possess. Obedience to the will of God draws men together, for it is the will of God that men should love and serve one another; obedience to the craving for pleasure drives men apart, for pleasure drives men to an internecine rivalry and competition and warfare for the same things. To obey the will of God is to be essentially selfless; to serve the will of pleasure is to be essentially selfish.

(ii) The craving for pleasure drives men to shameful deeds. It drives them to envy and to jealousy and to enmity; and it can even drive them to murder. Before a man can arrive at a deed there must be a certain driving power of emotion in his heart. A man may restrain himself from the things that the desire for pleasure incites him to do; but the fact remains that so long as that desire for pleasure is in his heart he is never safe. It may at any time explode into ruinous action. The steps of the process are very simple and very terrible. A man allows himself to desire something. That thing begins to dominate his thoughts; he finds himself involuntarily thinking about it in his waking hours, and dreaming of it when he sleeps. It begins to be what is aptly called a *ruling passion*. He then begins to form imaginary plans and schemes of how he may obtain it; and these plans and schemes may well involve imaginary ways of eliminating those who stand in his way. For long enough all this may go on in a man's mind and thoughts and heart. But then one day the imaginings may blaze into action; and he may find himself taking the necessary and the terrible steps to obtain his desire. Every crime in this world has come from desire, desire which was first only a feeling in the heart, but which, being nourished long enough, came in the end to action.

(iii) The craving for pleasure in the end shuts the door of prayer. If a man's prayers are simply for the things which will gratify his desires, then his prayers are essentially selfish, and, therefore, it is not possible for God to answer them, for to answer them would be to do nothing other than to provide the man with ways of sinning. The true end of prayer is to say to God, " Thy will be done." The prayer of the man who is pleasure-dominated is: " My desires be satisfied." If, when a man prays, his prayer is only for things which may help him to satisfy his own desires, then he has sent to God a prayer which God cannot answer. It is one of the grim facts of life that a selfish man can hardly ever pray aright. We can never pray aright until we remove self from the centre of life, and put God into the centre of life.

In this life we have to choose whether to make our main object our own desires or the will of God. And, if we choose to make our own desires our main object, we have thereby separated ourselves from our fellow-men and from God.

INFIDELITY TO GOD

James 4: 4-7

> Renegades to your vows, do you not know that love for this world is enmity to God? Whoever makes it his aim to be the friend of this world thereby becomes the enemy of God. Do you think that the saying of Scripture is only an idle saying: " God jealously yearns for the spirit which He has made to dwell within us "? But God gives the more grace. That is why Scripture says, " God sets Himself against the haughty, but gives grace to the humble." So, then, submit yourselves to God. Resist the devil, and he will flee from you; draw near to God, and He will draw near to you.

THE Authorized Version makes this passage even more difficult than it is. In it the warning is addressed to *adulterers* and *adulteresses*. In the true text the word only occurs in the feminine, and the masculine *adulterers* should not be there. Further, the word is not intended to be taken literally at all. The reference is not to physical adultery, but to spiritual adultery; and the whole conception is based on the Old Testament idea of Jahweh as the husband of Israel and Israel as the bride of God. That picture is common in the Old Testament. " Thy Maker is thy husband; the Lord of hosts is His name " (*Isaiah* 54: 5). " Surely as a wife treacherously departeth from her husband, so have ye dealt treacherously with me, O house of Israel, saith the Lord " (*Jeremiah* 3: 20). This idea of Jahweh as the husband and the nation of Israel as the wife, explains the way in which the Old Testament constantly expresses spiritual infidelity in terms of physical adultery. To make a covenant with the gods of a strange land and to sacrifice to them, and to intermarry with their people is " to go awhoring after strange gods " (*Exodus* 34: 15, 16). It is God's forewarning to Moses, that the day will come when the people " will go awhoring after the gods of the strangers of the land, whither they go to be among them," and that they will forsake the true God (*Deuteronomy* 31: 16). It is the threat of the

Psalmist that God has destroyed all those who go awhoring from Him (*Psalm* 73: 27). It is Hosea's complaint that the people have gone awhoring from God (*Hosea* 9: 1). It is in this spiritual sense that the New Testament speaks of " an evil and *adulterous* generation " (*Matthew* 13: 39; 16: 4; *Mark* 8: 38). And the whole picture came into Christian thought in the conception of the Church as the Bride of Christ (2 *Corinthians* 11: 1, 2; *Ephesians* 5: 24-28; *Revelation* 19: 7; 21: 9).

This form of expression may offend the delicacy of modern ears; but this picture of Israel as the bride of God, and of God as the husband of Israel has something very precious in it. It means that to disobey God is like breaking the marriage vow. It means that all sin is sin against love. It means that our relationship to God is not like the distant relationship of king and subject, or master and slave, but that it is like the intimate relationship of husband and of wife. It means that sin is infidelity to love, and that when we sin we break God's heart, as the heart of one partner in a marriage is broken when the other callously and deliberately deserts him or her.

FRIENDSHIP WITH THE WORLD AND ENMITY WITH GOD

James 4: 4-7 (*continued*)

IN this passage James says that love of the world is enmity with God, and that he who is the friend of the world thereby becomes the enemy of God. It is important to understand what James means.

(i) This is not spoken out of hatred and contempt for the world. It is not spoken out of the point of view which regards earth as a desert drear and which denigrates everything in the natural world. There is a story of a Puritan who was out for a walk in the country with a friend. The friend noticed a very lovely flower at the roadside, and said, " That is a lovely flower." The Puritan replied, " I have learned to call nothing lovely in this lost and sinful world." That is not James's point of view; James would have agreed that this world is the creation of God; and like Jesus he would have rejoiced in the beauty and the loveliness of it. This must not be read as a contemptuous indictment of all created things.

(ii) We have already seen that the New Testament often uses the word *kosmos*, which ordinarily means *world*, in the sense *of the world apart from God*, the godlessness of the world, the world's disregard of God, the world's resentment of the standards of God, the world's intentness on its own ways and its refusal of the ways of God. There are two New Testament passages which well illustrate what James means. Paul writes, " The carnal mind is enmity against God. . . . So, then, they that are in the flesh cannot please God " (*Romans* 8: 7, 8). What he means is that those who insist on assessing everything by purely human standards, those whose interests are purely human interests, are necessarily at variance with God. The second passage is one of the most poignantly tragic epitaphs on the Christian life in all literature: " Demas hath forsaken me, having loved this present world " (2 *Timothy* 4: 10). The idea here is that of *worldliness*. If a man is worldly, he cannot be godly. If material things are the things to which he dedicates his life, then clearly he cannot dedicate his life to God. In that sense the man who has dedicated his life to the world is at enmity with God.

(iii) The best commentary on this saying is the saying of Jesus: " No man can serve two masters " (*Matthew* 6: 24). There are two attitudes to the things of this world, and the things of time. We may be so dedicated to them, so immersed in them, so dominated by them, that the world becomes our master. Or, we may so use the things of the world as to serve our fellow-men and prepare ourselves for eternity, in which case the world is not our master, but our servant. A man may either use the world, or be used by the world. He may make the world his servant, or he may accept the world as his tyrant. To use the world to serve God and to serve men is, in fact, to be the friend of God, for that is what God meant the world to be. To use the world as the controller and the dictator of life is to be at enmity with God, for that is precisely what God never meant the world to be.

GOD THE JEALOUS LOVER

James 4: 4-7 (continued)

VERSE 5 is an exceedingly difficult verse. To begin with, it is cited as a quotation from Scripture, but there is no part of Scripture of which it is, in fact, anything like a recognizable quotation. We may either assume that James is quoting from some book which is now lost, and which he regarded as Scripture; or, that he is summing up in one sentence that which is often in the Old Testament the eternal sense of the whole view of Scripture, and that he is not meaning to quote any definite and particular passage.

Further, the translation of the Authorized Version is difficult: " The spirit that dwelleth in us lusteth to envy." Taken that way, the sentence seems to be a condemnation of the human spirit, but that translation is hardly possible. There are two possible translations, which in the end give much the same sense. " He (that is, God) jealously yearns for the devotion of the spirit which He has made to dwell within us," or, " The Spirit which God has made to dwell within us jealously yearns for the full devotion of our hearts."

In either case the meaning is that God is the jealous lover, who will brook no rival, and who will share the human heart with no other love. The Old Testament was never afraid to apply the word *jealous* to God. Moses says of God to the people: " They provoked Him to jealousy with strange gods " (*Deuteronomy* 32: 16). He hears God say, " They have moved me to jealousy with that which is not God " (*Deuteronomy* 32: 21). In the insistence on his sole right to worship, God in the Ten Commandments says, " I the Lord am a jealous God " (*Exodus* 20: 5). " Thou shalt worship no other god, for the Lord whose name is Jealous is a jealous God " (*Exodus* 34: 14). Zechariah hears God say, " Thus saith the Lord of hosts, I was jealous for Zion with great jealousy " (*Zechariah* 8: 2). *Jealous* comes from the Greek word *zēlos*, and *zēlos* has in it the idea of hot and burning heat. The idea is that God loves men with such a passion that He cannot bear any rival love within the hearts of men.

It may be that the word *jealous* is a word which nowadays we find it difficult to connect with God, for it is certainly true that the word has acquired a lower significance; but behind it there is the great and precious and amazing truth that God is the lover of the souls of men. There is a sense in which love must be diffused among all men and over all God's children; but there is also a sense in which love gives and demands an exclusive devotion to one person. It is profoundly true that a man can only be in love with one person at the same time; if he thinks otherwise, he does not know the meaning of love. What James means is that God is the jealous lover, who will brook no rival in the human heart, and that He must receive from us a love which is beyond all earthly devotion.

THE GLORY OF HUMILITY AND THE TRAGEDY OF PRIDE

James 4: 4-7 (*continued*)

JAMES now goes on to meet an almost inevitable reaction to this picture of God as the jealous lover. If God is like that, how can any man give to God the devotion which

God demands? James's answer is that, if God makes a great demand, he gives a great grace to fulfil it, and the greater the demand, the greater the grace God gives. Only the grace of God can enable us to respond to the love of God.

But grace has a constant characteristic—a man cannot receive grace until he has realized his need of grace, and has come to God humbly pleading for help. Therefore, it must always remain true that God sets Himself against the proud, and that He gives lavishly of His grace to the humble. " God sets Himself against the proud, but gives grace to the humble." This is a quotation from *Proverbs* 3: 34; and it is quoted again in I *Peter* 5: 5.

What then is this destructive *pride*? The word for *proud* is *huperēphanos*. This word literally means *one who shows himself above other people*. Even the Greeks hated this pride. Theophrastus described it as " a certain contempt for all other people." Theophylact, the Christian writer, called it, " the citadel and summit of all evils." The real terror of this pride is that it is a thing of the heart. It certainly means *haughtiness*, but the man who suffers from it might well appear to be walking in downcast humility, while all the time there was in his heart a vast contempt for all his fellow-men. This pride shuts itself off from God for three reasons. (i) *It does not know its own need*. It so admires itself that it recognizes no need to be supplied. It walks in proud self-sufficiency. (ii) *It cherishes its own independence*. It will be beholden to no man; it will not even be beholden to God. It will admit dependence on nothing and on no one, human or divine. (iii) *It does not recognize its own sin*. It is occupied with thinking of its own goodness, and it never realizes that it has any sin from which it needs to be saved. A pride like that cannot receive help, because it does not know that it needs help, and, therefore, it cannot ask. It loves, not God, but itself.

But this humility for which James pleads is no cringing thing. It has two great characteristics.

(i) It knows that if a man takes a resolute stand against the devil, the devil is ultimately a coward. " The devil," as Hermas puts it, " can wrestle against the Christian, but he cannot throw him." This is a truth of which the Christians were fond, for Peter says the same thing (1 *Peter* 5: 8, 9). The great example and the great inspiration is the example of Jesus in His own temptations. In them Jesus showed that the devil is vulnerable; the devil is not invincible; when he is confronted with the word of God, as Jesus confronted him with that word, he, in the end, can be put to flight. The Christian has humility, but it is the humility which knows that it can fight its battles with the tempter, not in its own power, but in the power of God.

(ii) It knows that it has the greatest privilege of all, the privilege of access to God. The Christian knows that he can approach God, knowing that all the time God is approaching him. This is a tremendous thing, for this right of approach to God under the old order of things belonged only to the priests. The priests alone are those who come near to God (*Exodus* 19: 22). The office of the priest was to come near to God for sin-stained people (*Ezekiel* 44: 13). But through the work of Jesus Christ any man can come boldly before the throne of God, certain that he will find mercy and grace to help in time of need (*Hebrews* 4: 19). There was a time when only the High Priest might enter the Holy of Holies, but we have a new and a living way, a better hope by which we draw nigh to God (*Hebrews* 7: 19).

Certainly the Christian must have humility, but it is a humility which gives him dauntless courage, and it is a humility which humbly knows that the way to God is open to the most fearful and the most trembling saint.

GODLY PURITY

James 4: 8-10

> Cleanse your hands, you sinners, and purify your
> hearts, you double-minded. Be afflicted and mourn
> and weep. Let your laughter be turned to sorrow,
> and your joy to gloom. Humble yourself before God,
> and then He will exalt you.

IN James's thought the ethical demand of Christianity
is never far away. He has talked about grace, the grace
which God gives to the humble, the grace which God
supplies to enable a man to meet His great demands.
But James is sure that there is something needed beyond
asking and passive receiving. He is sure that moral effort
is a prime necessity.

His appeal is addressed to *sinners*; the word is *hamartōlos*,
which means the hardened sinner, the bad man, the man
whose sin is open, obvious and notorious. Suidas defines
hamartōloi as " those who choose to live in company
with disobedience to the law, and who love a corrupt life."
From such people James demands moral reform, a reform
which will embrace both their outward conduct and their
inner desires. He demands both clean hands and a pure
heart (*Psalm* 24: 4).

The phrase *cleanse your hands* is interesting. Originally
it denoted nothing more than ceremonial cleansing, the
ritual, outward washing with water which made a man
ceremonially clean to approach the worship of God. The
priests must wash and bathe themselves before they
entered on their service (*Exodus* 30: 19-21; *Leviticus*
16: 4). The orthodox Jew must ceremonially wash his
hands before he ate (*Mark* 7: 3). But men came to see
that God requires much more than an outward washing;
and so the phrase came to stand for moral purity. " I will
wash mine hands in innocence," says the Psalmist (*Psalm*
26: 6). It is Isaiah's demand that men should " wash
themselves and make themselves clean," and that is
equated with ceasing to do evil (*Isaiah* 1: 16). In the

letter to Timothy men are urged to lift holy hands to God in prayer (I *Timothy* 2: 8). The very history of the phrase shows a deepening consciousness of what God demands. Men began by thinking in terms of an outward washing, a ritual and ceremonial thing; and ended by seeing that the demand of God is a moral, and not a ritual, demand.

Biblical thought demands a fourfold cleansing. It demands a cleansing of the *lips* (*Isaiah* 6: 5, 6). It demands a cleansing of the *hands* (*Psalm* 24: 4). It demands a cleansing of the *heart* (*Psalm* 73: 13). It demands a cleansing of the *mind* (*James* 4: 8). That is to say, the ethical demand of the Bible is that a man's words and deeds and emotions and thoughts should all be cleansed. Inwardly and outwardly a man must be clean, for only the pure in heart shall see God (*Matthew* 5: 8).

THE GODLY SORROW

James 4: 8-10 (*continued*)

IN his demand for a godly sorrow James is going back to the fact that Jesus had said, " Blessed are they that mourn for they shall be comforted " (*Matthew* 5: 4; *Luke* 6: 20-26). We must not read into this passage that which James did not mean. He is not denying the joy of the Christian life. He is not demanding that men should live a gloom-encompassed life in a dark and shadowed world. He is doing two things. He is pleading for sobriety in place of frivolousness, and he is doing so with all the intensity of one whose natural instincts were puritan. And he is describing, not the *end*, but the *beginning* of the Christian life. He demands three things.

(i) He demands what he calls *affliction*. The verb is *talaipōrein*, and it can describe—Thucydides so uses it— the experiences of an army whose food has gone done and who have no shelter from the stormy weather. What James is demanding is a voluntary abstinence from lavish luxury and effeminate comfort. He is talking to people who are in love with the world; and he is pleading with them not to make luxury and comfort the standards by which they judge all life. It is discipline which produces the scholar; it is rigorous training which creates the athlete; and it is a wise abstinence which produces the Christian who knows how to use the world and its gifts aright.

(ii) He demands that they should mourn, that their laughter should be turned to sorrow, and their joy to gloom. Here, indeed, James is describing the *first* step of the Christian life. The Christian life begins when a man is confronted with God and with his own sin. And that indeed is a daunting and a grievous experience. When Wesley preached to the miners of Kingswood, they were moved to tears so that the tears made runnels as they ran down the grime of their faces. But that is by no means the end of the Christian life. The terrible sorrow of the realization of sin moves on to the thrilling joy of sins forgiven. But to get to the second a man must go through the first. What James is demanding is that these self-satisfied, easy-going, luxury-loving, complacent, unworried hearers of his, should be confronted with their sins and should be ashamed, grief-stricken and afraid; for only then could they reach out for grace and go on to a joy far greater than their earthbound pleasures.

(iii) He demands that they should weep. It is perhaps not reading too much into this to say that James here may well have been thinking of *tears of sympathy*. Up to this time these wealthy and luxury-loving people had lived in utter selfishness. They had been quite unaware of, and quite insensitive to, what the poet called " the world's rain of tears." James is insisting that they must become aware of the tears of things, that the sorrows and the tears and the griefs and the needs of others should pierce the armour of their own pleasure and comfort, that they should develop a new sensitiveness to the needs of their fellow-men. A man is not a Christian until he becomes aware of the poignant need and cry of that humanity for which Christ died.

So, then, in words deliberately chosen to waken the sleeping soul, James demands that his hearers should substitute the way of abstinence for the way of luxury, that they should become aware of their own sins and mourn for them, that they should become conscious of the world's sorrow and need and weep for it.

THE GODLY HUMILITY

James 4: 8-10 (continued)

JAMES concludes with the demand for a godly humility. All through the Bible there runs the conviction that it is only the humble who can know the blessings of God. God will save the humble person (*Job* 22: 29). A man's pride will bring him low; but honour shall uphold the humble in spirit (*Proverbs* 29: 33). God dwells on high, but he is also with him that is of a humble and a contrite spirit (*Isaiah* 57: 15). They that fear the Lord will humble their souls in his sight, and the greater a man is the more he ought to humble himself, if he is to find favour in the sight of God (*Ecclesiasticus* 2: 17; 3: 17). And Jesus Himself repeatedly declared that it was the man who humbled himself who alone would be exalted (*Matthew* 23: 12; *Luke* 14: 11).

Only when a man realizes his own ignorance can he ask the guidance of God. Only when a man realizes his own poverty in the things that matter will he pray for the riches of God's grace. Only when a man realizes his weakness in necessary things will he come to draw upon the strength of God. Only when a man realizes that he cannot cope with life by himself will he kneel before the Lord of all good life. Only when a man realizes his own sin will he realize his need of a Saviour and of the forgiveness of God.

In life there is one basic sin which can be said to be the basis of all other sins; and that is the sin of forgetting that we are creatures and that God is creator. When a man realizes his essential creatureliness then he realizes his essential helplessness, and he goes to the source in which that helplessness can alone be supplied.

And such a dependence begets the only real independence, for then a man faces life, not in his own strength, but in God's strength, and life is exalted to victory. But so long as a man regards himself as independent of God he is on the way sooner or later to collapse and to defeat.

THE SIN OF JUDGING OTHERS

James 4: 11, 12

Stop talking harshly about each other. He who speaks harshly of his brother, or who judges his brother, speaks harshly of the law, and judges the law; and, if you judge the law, you are not a doer of the law, but a judge of it. One is law-giver and judge, He who is able to save and to destroy. Who are you to judge your neighbour?

THE word that James uses for *to speak harshly of,* or, *to speak evil of,* is the verb *katalalein.* Usually this verb means to speak evil of someone else in that person's absence, to criticize, to insult, to slander someone when he is not there to defend himself. This sin of slander and of insult and of evil-speaking is condemned all through the Bible. It is the Psalmist's accusation against the wicked man: " Thou sittest and speakest evil against thy brother; thou slanderest thine own mother's son " (*Psalm* 50: 20). The Psalmist hears God saying, " Whoso privily slandereth his neighbour, him will I cut off " (*Psalm* 101: 5). In the Pauline letters *katalalia,* the noun, is translated *back-biting.* Paul lists it among the sins which are characteristic of the unredeemed evil of the pagan world (*Romans* 1: 30); and it is one of the sins which he fears to find in the warring

Church of Corinth (2 *Corinthians* 12: 20). It is significant to note that in both these passages *katalalia* comes in immediate connection with *whisperings*. *Katalalia* is the sin of those who meet in corners and gather in little groups and pass on confidential titbits of whispered information which destroy the reputation and good name of those who are not there to defend themselves. The same sin, in this case translated *evil-speaking*, is condemned by Peter (I *Peter* 2: I). So, then, this is a sin which is universally condemned. There is great necessity for this warning. People are slow to realize that there are few sins which the Bible so unsparingly condemns as the sin of irresponsible and malicious gossip. There are few activities in which the average person finds more delight than spicy gossip; to tell and to listen to the slanderous story—especially about some distinguished person—is for all people a fascinating activity. We do well to remember what God thinks of this. James condemns this for two fundamental reasons.

(i) It is a breach of the royal law. The royal law is that we should love our neighbour as ourselves (*James* 2: 8; *Leviticus* 19: 18). Obviously a man cannot love his neighbour as himself and speak slanderous evil about him. Now, if a man breaks a law, knowing that he is breaking it, he sets himself above the law. That is to say, he has made himself a judge of the law. He has sat in judgment on the law, and has made his own will more binding than the law. But a man's duty is not to judge the law, but to obey the law. So the man who speaks evil of his neighbour has appointed himself a judge of the law, and has taken to himself the right to break the law, and therefore stands condemned.

(ii) It is an infringement of the prerogative of God. To speak evil of our neighbour, to criticize, slander and insult our neighbour, is, in fact, to pass judgment upon him. And no human being has any right to judge any other human being; the right of judgment belongs to God and to God alone.

It is God alone who is able to save and to destroy. This great prerogative of God runs all through Scripture. " I kill and I make alive," says God (*Deuteronomy* 32: 39). " The Lord killeth and maketh alive," says Hannah in her prayer (1 *Samuel* 2: 6). " Am I God to kill and make alive?" is the shocked question of the Israelite king to whom Naaman came with a demand for a cure for his leprosy (2 *Kings* 5: 7). It is Jesus' warning that we should not fear men, who at the worst can only kill the body, but that we should fear Him who can destroy both body and soul (*Matthew* 10: 28). As the Psalmist had it, it is to God alone that the issues of life and of death belong (*Psalm* 68: 20). To judge another is to take to ourselves a right to do that which God alone has the right to do; and he is a reckless man who deliberately infringes the prerogatives of God.

We might very probably say that to speak evil of our neighbour is not a very serious sin. But Scripture would say that it is one of the worst of all sins, because it is a breach of the royal law and it is an infringement of the rights of God.

THE MISTAKEN CONFIDENCE

James 4: 13-17

> Come now, you who say, " Today, or tomorrow, we will go into this city, and we will spend a year there, and we will trade and make a profit." People like you do not know what will happen tomorrow. What is your life like? You are like a mist which appears for a little time, and then disappears. And yet you talk like that instead of saying, " If the Lord wills, we shall live, and we shall do this or that." As it is you make your arrogant claims in your braggart ways. All such arrogant claims are evil. So then, if a man knows what is good and does not do it, that to him is sin.

HERE again is a contemporary picture which James's readers would recognize, and in which they might well see their own portrait. The Jews were the great traders of the ancient world; and in many ways the ancient world gave them every opportunity to practise their commercial abilities. This was an age of the founding of cities; and often when cities were founded, and when their founders were looking for citizens to occupy them, citizenship was offered freely to the Jews, for where the Jews came there came money and trade. So the picture is the picture of a man looking at a map. He points at a certain spot on it, and says, " Here is a new city where there are great trade chances. I'll go there; and I'll get in on the ground floor: and I'll trade for a year or so; and I'll make my fortune, and come back rich." James's answer is that no man has a right to make constant and confident plans for the future, for no man knows what even a day may bring forth. Man may propose, but it is God who disposes, for the future is in the hands of God.

The essential uncertainty of the future is a fact which was deeply impressed on the minds of men of all nations. The Hebrew sage wrote, " Boast not thyself of tomorrow, for thou knowest not what a day may bring forth " (*Proverbs* 27: 1). Jesus told his story of the rich, but foolish, man who made his fortune, and built up his plans for the future, and forgot that that night his soul might be required of him (*Luke* 12: 16-21). Ben Sirach wrote, " There is that waxeth rich by his wariness and pinching, and this is the portion of his reward: whereas, he saith, ' I have found rest, and now will eat continually of my goods '; and yet he knoweth not what time shall come upon him, and that death approacheth; and that he must leave these things to others, and die " (*Ecclesiasticus* 11: 18, 19). Seneca said: " How foolish it is for a man to make plans for his life, when not even tomorrow is in his control." And again: " No man has such rich friends that he can promise himself tomorrow." The Rabbis had a proverb: " Care not for the morrow, for ye know not what a day may bring forth. Perhaps you may not find tomorrow."

Dennis Mackail was the friend of Sir James Barrie. He tells that, as Barrie grew older, he would never make any arrangement for even a social engagement at any distant date. " Short notice now! " he would always say.

But James goes on. This uncertainty of life is not a cause either for fear or for inaction because of the insecurity of the future. It is a reason for accepting and realizing our complete dependence on God. It has always been the mark of a serious-minded man that he made his plans in dependence on God. Paul writes to the Corinthians: " I will come to you shortly, if the Lord will " (I *Corinthians* 4: 19). " I trust to tarry a while with you, if the Lord will permit " (I *Corinthians* 16: 7). Xenophon writes, " May all these things be, if the gods so will. If anyone wonders that we often find the phrase written, ' if the gods will,' I would have him to know that, once he has experienced the risks of life, he will not wonder nearly so much." Plato relates a conversation between Socrates and Alcibiades. Alcibiades says: " I will do so if you wish, Socrates." Socrates answers, " Alcibiades, that is not the way to talk. And how ought you to speak? You ought to say, ' If *God* so wishes.' " Minucius Felix writes, " ' God grant it '—it comes instinctively to the ordinary man to speak like that." Constantly among the Arabs there is heard the expressions: " Inshallah—If Allah wills." The curious thing is that there seems to have been no such corresponding phrase which the Jews themselves used. In this the Jews had to learn.

The true Christian way is not to be terrorized into fear, and not to be paralysed into inaction, by the uncertainty of the future, but to commit the future and all our plans into the hands of God, and always to remember that our plans may not be within the purpose of God.

The man who does not remember that, is guilty of arrogant boasting. The word is *alazoneia*. *Alazoneia* was originally the characteristic of the wandering quack. He offered cures which were not cures, and boasted of things that he was not able to do. *Alazoneia* is the characteristic of the man who lays claim to that which he does not possess, and who boasts of that which he cannot do. The future is not within the hands of men, and no man can arrogantly claim that he has power to decide it.

So James ends with a threat. If a man knows that a thing is wrong and still continues to do it, that to him is sin. James is in effect saying, " You have been warned. Now the truth has been placed before your eyes." To continue now in the self-confident habit of seeking to dispose of one's own life is sin for the man who has been forcibly reminded that the future is not in his hands, but in God's.

THE WORTHLESSNESS OF RICHES

James 5: 1-3

> Come now, you rich, weep and wail at the miseries which are coming upon you. Your wealth is rotten, and your garments are food for moths. Your gold and silver are corroded clean through with rust; and the rust of them is proof to you of how worthless they are. It is a rust which will eat into your very flesh like fire. It is a treasure indeed that you have amassed for yourselves in the last days!

In the first six verses of this chapter James has two aims. First, he aims to show the ultimate worthlessness of all earthly riches; and second, he aims to show the detestable character of those who possess riches. By doing this his aim is to prevent his readers from placing all their hopes and aims and desires on earthly things.

If you knew what you were doing, he says to the rich, you would weep and wail for the terror of the judgment that is coming upon you when the Day of the Lord comes. The vividness of the picture is increased by the word which James uses for *to wail*; it is the verb *ololuzein*, which is an onomatopoetic word, a word which carries its meaning in its very sound. It means even more than to wail; it means *to shriek*, and in the Old Testament it is often translated *to howl*; and it depicts the frantic terror of those on whom the judgment of God has come (*Isaiah* 13: 6; 14: 31; 15: 2, 3; 16: 7; 23: 1, 14; 65: 14; *Amos* 8: 3). We might well say that it is the word which describes those who are going through the tortures of the damned.

All through this passage the words are vivid and pictorial and carefully chosen. In the east there were three main sources of wealth, and James has a word for the decay of each one of them. There was corn and grain; that is the wealth which grows rotten (*sēpein*). There are garments. In the east garments were wealth. Joseph gave changes of raiment to his brothers (*Genesis* 45: 22). It was for a goodly Babylonish garment that Achan brought disaster on the nation and death on himself and his family (*Joshua* 7: 21). It was changes of garments that Samson promised to anyone who would solve his riddle (*Judges* 14: 12). It was garments that Naaman brought as a gift to the prophet of Israel, and to obtain which Gehazi sinned his soul (*2 Kings* 5: 5, 22). It was Paul's claim that he had coveted no man's money or apparel (*Acts* 20: 33). These garments, which are so splendid, will be food for moths (*sētobrōtos*, cp. *Matthew* 6: 19). The climax of the world's inevitable decay comes at the end. Even their gold and silver will be so corroded with rust that it will be rusted clean through (*katiasthai*). Now the point is that gold and silver do not actually rust; so James in the most vivid way is warning men that even the most precious and even the most apparently indestructible things are doomed to decay and to dissolution. This rust is a proof of the impermanence and the ultimate valuelessness of all earthly things. More, it is a dread warning. The desire of these things is like a dread rust, a terrible cancer, which eats into men's bodies and souls. And then there comes a grim and terrible sarcasm. It is a fine treasure indeed that any man who concentrates on these things is heaping up for himself at the last. The only treasure that he will possess is a consuming fire which will wipe him out.

It is James's conviction that to concentrate on material things is not only to concentrate on a decaying and corpse-like delusion; it is to concentrate on self-produced destruction and disaster.

THE SOCIAL PASSION OF THE BIBLE

James 5: 1-3 (continued)

NOT even the most cursory reader of the Bible can fail to be impressed with the social passion which blazes through its pages. Plato said that every city is an unending civil war, the eternal warfare between the rich and the poor, between the haves and the have-nots. There is no book which condemns dishonest and selfish wealth with such searing passion as the Bible does. The book of prophet Amos was called by J. E. McFadyen " The Cry for Social Justice." Amos condemns those who store up violence and robbery in their palaces (*Amos* 3: 10). He condemns those who tread on the poor, and who themselves have houses of hewn stone and pleasant vineyards—which in the wrath of God they will never enjoy (*Amos* 5: 11). He lets loose the vials of his wrath on those who give short weight and short measure, who buy the poor for silver and the needy for a pair of shoes, and who palm off on the poor the refuse of their wheat. " I will never forget any of their works," says God (*Amos* 8: 4-7). Isaiah warns those who build up great estates by adding house to house and field to field (*Isaiah* 5: 8). The sage insisted that he that trusts in riches shall fall (*Proverbs* 11: 28). In the New Testament Luke quotes Jesus as saying, " Woe unto you who are rich! " (*Luke* 6: 24). It is only with difficulty that those who have riches can enter into the Kingdom of God (*Luke* 18: 24). Riches are a temptation and snare; the rich are liable to foolish and hurtful lusts, which end in ruin, for the love of money is the root of all evil (I *Timothy* 6: 9, 10).

In the inter-testamental literature there is the same note. " Woe to you who acquire silver and gold in unrighteousness. . . . They shall perish with their possessions, and in shame will their spirits be cast into the furnace of fire " (*Enoch* 97: 8). In the *Wisdom of Solomon* there is a savage passage in which the sage makes the selfish rich speak of their own way of life as compared with that of the righteous. " Come on, therefore, let us enjoy the good things that are present; and let us speedily use created things like as in youth. Let us fill ourselves with costly wine and ointments: and let no flower of the spring pass by us. Let us crown ourselves with rosebuds before they be withered; let there be no meadow but our luxury shall pass through it. Let none of us go without his part of our voluptuousness; let us leave tokens of our joyfulness in every place; for this is our portion, and our lot is this. Let us oppress the poor righteous man, let us not spare the widow, nor reverence the ancient gray hairs of the aged. . . . Therefore, let us lie in wait for the righteous; because he is not for our turn, and is clean contrary to our doings: he upbraideth us with our offending of the law, and objecteth to our infamy, the sins of our way of life " (*Wisdom of Solomon* 2: 6-12).

One of the mysteries of social thought is how religion, at least the Christian religion, ever came to be regarded as " the opiate of the people," or how it ever came to seem an other-worldly affair, which neglected this world to concentrate on some world to come. There is no book in any literature with such a burning social passion as the Bible. There is no book which speaks so explosively and dynamically of social wrongs and social injustice. There is no book so burningly conscious that the great gap between riches and poverty is an active and terrible transgression of the law of God and the will of God. There is no book which has, in fact, proved so powerful a social dynamic as the Bible has. The Bible does not condemn wealth as such, but there is no book which more strenuously insists on the responsibility of wealth, and on the perils which surround a man, who is abundantly blessed with this world's goods.

THE WAY OF SELFISHNESS AND ITS END

James 5: 4-6

> Look you, the pay of the reapers, who reaped your estates, the pay kept back from them by you, cries against you, and the cries of those who reaped have come to the ears of the Lord of Hosts. On the earth you have lived in soft luxury and played the wanton; you have fattened your hearts for the day of slaughter. You condemned, you killed the righteous man, and he does not resist you.

HERE is the condemnation of the way of life of selfish riches, and here is the warning of where that way must end.

(i) The selfish rich have gained their wealth by injustice. The Bible is always sure that the labourer is worthy of his hire (*Luke* 10: 7; I *Timothy* 5: 18). The day labourer in Palestine always lived on the very verge of starvation. His wage was small; it was impossible for him to save anything; and if the wage was withheld from him, even for a day, then literally he and his family would not eat. That is why the merciful laws of Scripture again and again insist on the prompt payment of wages to the hired labourer. " Thou shalt not oppress a hired servant that is poor and needy. . . . At his day shalt thou give him his hire, neither shall the sun go down upon it; for he is poor and setteth his heart upon it; lest he cry against thee unto the Lord, and it be sin unto thee " (*Deuteronomy* 24: 14, 15). " The wages of him that is hired shall not abide with thee all night until the morning " (*Leviticus* 19: 13). " Say not to thy neighbour, Go, and come again, and tomorrow I will give; when thou hast it by thee " (*Proverbs* 3: 27, 28). " Woe unto him that buildeth his house by unrighteousness and his chambers by wrong; that useth his neighbour's service without wages, and giveth him not for his work " (*Jeremiah* 22: 13). " Those that oppress the hireling in his wages " are under the judgment of God (*Malachi* 3: 5). " He that taketh away his neighbour's living, the bread gotten by sweat, slayeth him; and he that defraudeth the labourer of his hire, defraudeth his Maker, and shall receive a bitter reward, for he is brother to him that is a bloodshedder " (*Ecclesiasticus* 34: 22). " Let not the wages of any man, which hath wrought for thee, tarry with thee, but give it him out of hand " (*Tobit* 4: 14).

The law of the Bible is nothing less than the charter of the labouring man. The social concern of the Bible speaks in the words of the Law, in the words of the Prophets, and in the words of the Sages alike. Here in the Authorized Version it is said that the cries of the man who has been defrauded have reached the ears of the Lord of *Sabaoth*. The Lord of Sabaoth means the Lord of Hosts; and the hosts are the hosts of heaven, the stars and the heavenly powers. It is the teaching of the Bible in every part of it that the Lord of the universe, who holds the stars in His hand, and who commands the angels, is concerned for the rights of the labouring man.

(ii) The selfish rich have used their wealth selfishly. They have lived in soft luxury, and have played the wanton. The word translated *to live in soft luxury* is *truphein*. *Truphein* comes from a root which means *to break down*; and it describes the soft living which in the end saps and destroys a man's moral fibre; it describes that enervating luxury which ends by destroying strength of body and strength of soul alike. The word translated *to play the wanton* is *spatalan*; it is a much worse word; it means to live in lewdness and lasciviousness and wanton riotousness. It is the condemnation of the selfish rich that they have used their possessions to gratify their own love of comfort, and to satisfy their own lusts, and they have forgotten all duty to their fellow-men.

(iii) But anyone who chooses this pathway has also chosen the end of it. The end of specially fattened cattle is that they will be slaughtered for some feast; and those who have sought this easy luxury and this selfish wantonness are like men who have fattened themselves for the day of judgment. The end of their pleasure is grief, and the goal of their luxury is death. Selfishness always leads to the death of the soul.

(iv) Finally, James says of them that they have slain the unresisting righteous man. It is doubtful to whom this refers. It could be a reference to Jesus. " Ye denied the Holy One and the Just (*dikaios*; the same word as *righteous*), and desired a murderer to be granted unto you " (*Acts* 3: 14). It is Stephen's charge that the Jews always slew God's messengers even before the coming of the Just One (*Acts* 7: 52). It is Paul's declaration that God chose the Jews to see the Just One although they rejected Him (*Acts* 22: 14). Peter says that Christ suffered for our sins, the just for the unjust (I *Peter* 3: 18). The suffering servant of the Lord offered no resistance. He opened not his mouth, and like a sheep before his shearers he was dumb (*Isaiah* 53: 7), a passage which Peter quotes in his picture of Jesus (I *Peter* 2: 23). It may well be that James is saying that in their oppression of the poor and the righteous man, the selfish rich have crucified Christ again, that every wound inflicted on Christ's people is another wound on Christ. To live selfishly is to pierce Christ again.

It may be that James is not specially thinking of Jesus when he speaks about the righteous man; but that he is thinking of the evil man's instinctive hatred of the good man. We have already quoted the passage in *The Wisdom of Solomon* which describes the conduct of the rich. That passage goes on: " He (the righteous man) professeth to have the knowledge of God, and he calleth himself the child of the Lord. He was made to reprove our thoughts. He is grievous unto us even to behold: for his life is not like other men's, his ways are of another fashion. We are

esteemed of him as counterfeits: he abstaineth from our
ways as from filthiness: he pronounceth the end of the
just to be blessed, and maketh his boast that God is his
Father. Let us see if his words be true: and let us prove
what shall happen in the end of him. For if the just man
be the son of God, He will help him, and deliver him from
the hand of his enemies. Let us examine him with despite-
fulness and torture, that we may know his meekness, and
prove his patience. Let us condemn him with a shameful
death: for by his own saying he shall be respected "
(*The Wisdom of Solomon* 2: 13-30). These, says the Sage,
are the words of men whose wickedness has blinded them.

Alcibiades was the friend of Socrates, and Alcibiades for
all his great talents often lived a riotous and reckless and
debauched life. And there were times when he used to say
to Socrates: " Socrates, I hate you; for every time I see
you, you show me what I am." The evil man would gladly
eliminate the good man, for the good man reminds him
of what he is and of what he ought to be.

WAITING FOR THE COMING OF THE LORD

James 5: 7-9

> Brothers, have patience until the coming of the Lord.
> Look you, the farmer waits for the precious fruit of the
> earth, patiently waiting for it, until it receives the
> early and the late rains. So do you too be patient.
> Make firm your hearts for the coming of the Lord is
> near. Brothers, do not complain against each other,
> that you may not be condemned. Look you, the
> judge stands at the door.

THE early Church lived in the expectation of the immediate
Second Coming of Jesus Christ; and James exhorts his
people to wait with patience for the few years which remain.
The farmer has to wait for his crops until the early and the
late rains have come. The early and the late rains are
often spoken of in Scripture, for they were all-important

to the farmer of Palestine (*Deuteronomy* 11: 14; *Jeremiah* 5: 24; *Joel* 2: 23). The early rain was the rain in late October and early November; without it the seed which had been sown would not germinate at all. The late rain was the rain of April and May, without which the grain would not mature. The farmer needs patience to wait until nature does her work; and the Christian needs patience to wait until Christ comes.

During that waiting they must confirm their faith. They must not blame one another for the troubles of the situation in which they find themselves, for, if they do, they will be breaking the commandment which forbids Christians to judge one another (*Matthew* 7: 1), and if they break that commandment, they will be condemned. James has no doubt of the nearness of the coming of Christ. The judge is at the door, he says, using a phrase which Jesus Himself had used (*Mark* 13: 29; *Matthew* 24: 33).

It so happened that the early Church was mistaken; and Jesus Christ did not return within a generation of men. But it will be of interest to gather up the teaching of the New Testament about the Second Coming that we may see the essential truth at the heart of it.

We may first note that the New Testament uses three different words to describe the Second Coming of Jesus Christ.

(i) The commonest word is the word *parousia*, a word which has come into English as it stands. It is used in *Matthew* 24: 3, 27, 37, 39; 1 *Thessalonians* 2: 19; 3: 13; 4: 15; 5: 23; 2 *Thessalonians* 2: 1; 1 *Corinthians* 15: 23; 1 *John* 2: 28; 2 *Peter* 1: 16; 3: 4). In ordinary secular Greek this is the ordinary word for someone's presence or arrival. But it has two other usages, one of which became quite technical. It is used of the invasion of a country by an army; and specially it is used of the visit of a king or a governor to a province of his empire. So, then, when this word is used of Jesus, it means that the *parousia*, the Second Coming of Jesus, is the final invasion of earth by heaven, and the coming of the King to receive the final submission and adoration of his subjects.

(ii) The New Testament also uses the word *epiphaneia* of the Second Coming of Jesus (*Titus* 2: 13; 2 *Timothy* 4: 1; 2 *Thessalonians* 2: 9). In ordinary Greek this word has two special usages. It is used of the appearance of a god to his worshipper; and it is used of the accession of an emperor to the imperial power of Rome. So when this word is used of Jesus, it means that His *epiphaneia*, His Second Coming, is God appearing to His people, to both those who are waiting for Him, and to those who are rebelling against Him and disregarding Him; it is God at last mounting the throne of the universe with His last enemy subdued.

(iii) Finally the New Testament uses the word *apoka-lupsis* of the Second Coming of Jesus (1 *Peter* 1: 7, 13). The word *apokalupsis* in ordinary Greek means an *unveiling* or a *laying bare*; and when this word is used of the Second Coming of Jesus, it means that that Coming is the laying bare, the full displaying, the unveiling of the power and glory of God come upon men.

Here, then, we have a series of great pictures. The Second Coming of Jesus Christ is the arrival of the King; it is God appearing to His people and mounting His eternal throne; it is God directing on the world the full blaze of His heavenly glory.

THE COMING OF THE KING

James 5: 7-9 (*continued*)

WE may now gather up briefly the teaching of the New Testament about the Second Coming, and the various uses it makes of the whole idea of it.

(i) The New Testament is clear that no man knows the day or the hour when Christ comes again. So secret, in fact, is that time that Jesus Himself did not know it; it is known to God and to God alone (*Matthew* 24: 36; *Mark* 13: 32). From this basic fact one thing is clear. Human speculation about the time of the Second Coming is not only useless, it is actively blasphemous; for surely no man may seek to gain a knowledge which is hidden from Jesus Christ Himself, a knowledge which resides only in the mind of God.

(ii) The one thing that the New Testament does say about the Second Coming is that it will be as sudden as the lightning and as unexpected as a thief in the night (*Matthew* 24: 27, 37, 39; *I Thessalonians* 5: 2; *2 Peter* 3: 10). It is not something for which one can get ready when it comes; one must be ready for its coming.

Because of that, the New Testament in view of the Second Coming urges certain duties upon men.

(i) They must be for ever on the watch (*I Peter* 4: 7). They are like servants whose master has gone away, and who do not know when he will return, but must have everything ready for his return, whether he come at morning, at midday, or at evening (*Matthew* 24: 36-51).

(ii) Long delay must not beget despair or forgetfulness (*2 Peter* 3: 4). God does not see time as men see time; to Him a thousand years are as a watch in the night. Even if the years pass on, God has neither changed nor abandoned His design.

(iii) Men must use the time given to them to prepare themselves for the coming of the King. They must be sober (*I Peter* 4: 7). They must get to themselves holiness (*I Thessalonians* 3: 13). By the grace of God they must become blameless in body and in spirit (*I Thessalonians* 5: 23). They must put off the works of darkness and put on the armour of light, now that the day is far spent

(*Romans* 13: 11-14). Men must use the time that is given to them to make themselves such that they can greet the coming of the King with joy, and without shame.

(iv) When that time comes, they must be found in fellowship. Peter uses the thought of the Second Coming to urge men to love and mutual hospitality (I *Peter* 4: 8, 9). Paul commands that all things be done in charity—*Maran atha*—the Lord is at hand (I *Corinthians* 16: 14, 22). He says that our *moderation* must be known unto all men because the Lord is at hand (*Philippians* 4: 5). The word which the Authorized Version translates *moderation* is the Greek word *epieikes*, which means the spirit which is more ready to offer forgiveness than it is to demand justice. The writer to the Hebrews demands mutual help, mutual Christian fellowship, mutual encouragement because the day is coming near (*Hebrews* 10: 24, 25). The New Testament is sure that in view of the Coming of Christ we must have our personal relationships right with our fellow-men. The New Testament would urge that no man ought to go to sleep, or end a day, with an unhealed breach between himself and a fellow-man, lest in the night Christ should come.

(v) John uses the Second Coming as a reason for urging men to abide in Christ (I *John* 2: 28). Surely the best preparation for meeting Christ is to live close to Christ every day in life.

We know well that much of the imagery which is attached to the Second Coming is Jewish imagery, and is part of the traditional apparatus of the last things in the ancient Jewish mind. We know that there are many things which we cannot, and are not meant to, take literally. But the great truth behind all the temporary pictures of the Second Coming is the truth that this world is not purposeless and aimless and planless, but that it is going somewhere, that there is one divine far-off event to which the whole creation moves.

THE TRIUMPHANT PATIENCE

James 5: 10, 11

> Brothers, take as an example of patience in hardship the prophets who spoke in the name of the Lord. Look you, we count those who endure blessed. You have heard of Job's steadfast endurance, and you have seen the conclusion of his troubles which the Lord gave to him, and you have proof that the Lord is very kind and merciful.

IT is always a comfort to feel that others have gone through that which we have to go through. James reminds his readers that the prophets and the men of God could never have done their work and borne their witness had they not patiently endured. He reminds them that Jesus Himself had said that the man who endured to the end was blessed, for he would be saved (*Matthew* 24: 13).

And then he quotes the example of Job, of whom in the Synagogue discourses they had often heard. We generally speak of the *patience* of Job, and that indeed is the word which the Authorized Version uses. But patience is far too passive a word. There is a sense in which Job was anything but patient. As we read the tremendous drama of his life we see him passionately resenting what has come upon him, passionately questioning the conventional and orthodox arguments of his so-called friends, passionately agonizing over the terrible thought that God might have forgotten and forsaken him. There are few men who have spoken such passionate words as Job spoke. But the great fact about Job is that in spite of all his torrent of questionings, and in spite of the agonizing questionings which tore at his heart, he never lost his faith in God. " Though he slay me, yet will I trust Him " (*Job* 13: 15). " My witness is in heaven, and my record is on high " (*Job* 16: 19). " I know that my redeemer liveth " (*Job* 19: 25). The very greatness of Job lies in the fact that in spite of everything which tore at his heart, he never lost his grip on faith and his grip on God. Job's is no grovelling, passive, unquestioning submission; Job struggled and questioned, and sometimes even defied, but the flame of faith was never extinguished in his heart.

The word used of him is that great New Testament word *hupomonē*, the word which describes, not a passive patience, but that gallant spirit which can breast the tides of doubt and sorrow and disaster, and still hold on, and come out with faith still stronger on the other side. There may be a faith which never in its life complained or questioned; but a still greater faith is the faith which exploded in complaints and was tortured by questions—and which still believed. It was that faith which held even grimly on which came out on the other side, for " the Lord blessed the latter end of Job more than his beginning " (*Job* 42: 12).

There will be moments in life when we think that God has forgotten, but if we cling to the remnants of faith, at the end of life we too shall see that God is very kind and very merciful.

THE NEEDLESSNESS AND THE FOLLY OF OATHS

James 5: 12

> Above all things, my brothers, do not swear, neither by heaven, nor by earth, nor by any other oath. Let your yes be a simple yes, and your no a simple no, lest you fall under judgment.

HERE James is repeating the teaching of Jesus Himself in the Sermon on the Mount (*Matthew* 6: 33-37). And it was a teaching which was very necessary in the days of the early Church. James is not thinking of what we call bad language, and of swearing in the modern sense of the term; he is thinking of what we call taking oaths, and confirming a statement or a promise or an undertaking by an oath. In the ancient world, there were two evil practices.

(i) There was a distinction—especially in the Jewish world—between oaths which were binding and oaths which were not binding. The distinction was this: any oath in which the name of God was directly used was considered to be definitely binding; but any oath in which direct mention of the name of God was not made was held not to be binding. The idea was that, once God's name was definitely used, God became an active partner in the transaction, but He did not become a partner unless His name was so introduced. The result of this was that men became experts in evasive swearing; and it became a matter of skill and sharp practice to find an oath which was not binding. Obviously this made a mockery of the whole practice of confirming anything by an oath.

(ii) There was in this age an extraordinary amount of oath-taking. This in itself was quite wrong. For one thing, the value of an oath depends to a large extent on the fact that it is very seldom necessary to take one. Its impressiveness lies in its exceptional character; and when oaths became a commonplace, they cease to be respected as they ought to be. And for another thing, the practice of taking frequent oaths was nothing other than a proof of the prevalence of lying and cheating and falsehood and swindling. In an honest society no oath is needed; it is only when men cannot be trusted to tell the truth that they have to be put upon oath. And the prevalence of oath-taking was in itself a proof of the prevalence of falsehood.

In this the ancient writers on morals most thoroughly agreed with Jesus. Philo says, " Frequent swearing is bound to beget perjury and impiety." The more frequent oath-taking is, the more lightly men regard their oaths. The Jewish Rabbis said, " Accustom not thyself to vows, for sooner or later thou wilt swear false oaths." The Essenes forbade all oaths. They held that if a man required an oath to make him tell the truth, he was already branded as untrustworthy, and was already under condemnation.

The great Greeks held that the best guarantee of any statement was not an oath, but the character of the man who made it; and that the ideal was to make ourselves such that no one would ever think of demanding an oath from us, but would be certain that we would always speak the truth.

The New Testament view is that every word is spoken in the presence of God, and that, therefore, every word must be true; and the New Testament would agree that the Christian must be known to be a man of such honour that it is quite unnecessary ever to put him upon oath. The New Testament would not entirely condemn oaths, but it would deplore the human tendency to falsehood, which on occasion makes oaths necessary.

A SINGING CHURCH

James 5: 13-15

> Is any among you in trouble? Let him pray. Is any in good spirits? Let him sing a hymn. Is any among you sick? Let him call in the elders of the Church; and let them anoint him with oil in the name of the Lord, and pray over him; and the believing prayer will restore to health the ailing person, and the Lord will enable him to rise from his bed; and even if he has committed sin, he will receive forgiveness.

HERE we have set out before us certain great dominant characteristics of the early Church.

The early Church was a *singing Church*; it was characteristic of the early Christians that they were always ready to burst into song. In Paul's description of the meetings of the Church at Corinth, we find singing as an integral part (I *Corinthians* 14: 15, 26). When Paul thinks of the grace of God going out to the Gentiles, it reminds him of the joyous saying of the Psalmist: " I will confess to Thee among the Gentiles, and sing unto Thy name "

(*Romans* 15: 9; cp. *Psalm* 18: 49). It is characteristic of the Christians that they speak to each other in psalms and hymns and spiritual songs, singing and making melody in their hearts to the Lord (*Ephesians* 5: 19). For very gratitude they are compelled to sing. The word of Christ dwells in them, and they teach and admonish each other in psalms and hymns and spiritual songs, singing with grace in their hearts to the Lord (*Colossians* 3: 16). There was a joy in the heart of the Christians which issued from their lips in songs of praise for the mercy and the grace of God.

The fact is that the heathen world has always been a sad and a weary and a frightened world. Matthew Arnold wrote his poem describing the bored weariness of the pagan world:

> " On that hard Pagan world disgust
>   And secret loathing fell;
> Deep weariness and sated lust
>   Made human life a hell.
> In his cool hall, with haggard eyes,
>   The Roman noble lay;
> He drove abroad in furious guise
>   Along the Appian Way;
> He made a feast, drank fierce and fast,
>   And crowned his hair with flowers—
> No easier nor no quicker past
>   The impracticable hours."

There is the mood of paganism. And in contrast with that weary mood the accent of the Christian is singing joy. That was what impressed John Bunyan when he heard the four poor old women talking, as they sat at a door in the sun: " Methought they spake, as if joy did make them speak." When Bilney the martyr grasped the wonder of the redeeming grace, he said, " It was as if dawn suddenly broke on a dark night." Archibald Lang Fleming, the first Bishop of the Arctic, that great modern missionary pioneer, tells of the saying of an Eskimo hunter: " Before you came the road was dark and we were afraid. Now we are not afraid, for the darkness has gone away and all is light as we walk the Jesus way."

Always the Church has been a singing Church. When Pliny, the governor of Bithynia, wrote to Trajan, the Roman Emperor, in A.D. III to tell him of this new sect of Christians, he said that his information was, " that they were in the habit of meeting on a certain fixed day before it was light, when they sang in alternate verses a hymn to Christ as God." In the orthodox Jewish Synagogue, since the Fall of Jerusalem in A.D. 70, there has been no music, for, when they worship, they remember a tragedy; but in the Christian Church, from the beginning until now, there has been the music of songs of praise, for the Christian remembers an infinite love and enjoys a present glory.

A HEALING CHURCH

James 5: 13-15 (continued)

BUT another great characteristic of the early Church meets us here; the early Church was a *healing* Church. Here the Church inherited its tradition from Judaism. When a Jew was ill, it was to the Rabbi he went rather than to the doctor. And the Rabbi anointed him with oil—which Galen the Greek doctor called " the best of all medicines "— and prayed over him. There can have been few Churches so devotedly attentive to their sick as the early Church was. Justin Martyr writes that numberless demoniacs are healed by the Christians, when all other exorcists have been helpless to cure them, and when all drugs have been unavailing. Irenaeus, writing far down the second century, tells us that the sick were still healed by having hands laid on them, and were made whole. Tertullian, writing midway through the third century, says that no less a person that the Roman Emperor, Alexander Severus, was healed by anointing at the hands of a Christian called

Torpacion, and that in his gratitude he kept Torpacion as a guest in his palace until the day of his death.

One of the earliest books concerning Church administration is the *Canons of Hippolytus*, which go back to the end of the second century or the beginning of the third. It is there laid down that men who have the gift of healing are to be ordained as presbyters, when investigation has been made to ensure that they really do possess the gift, and that it comes from God. That same book gives the noble prayer used at the consecration of the local bishops, and part of that prayer runs: " Grant unto him, O Lord, . . . the power to break all the chains of the evil power of the demons, to cure all the sick, and speedily to subdue Satan beneath his feet." In the *Clementine Letters* the duties of the deacons are laid down; and they include the rule: " Let the deacons of the Church move about intelligently and act as eyes for the bishop. . . . Let them find out those who are sick in the flesh, and bring such to the notice of the main body who know nothing of them, that they may visit them, and supply their wants." In the *First Epistle of Clement* the prayer of the Church is: " Heal the sick; raise up the weak; cheer the faint-hearted." A very early Church code lays it down that each congregation must appoint at least one widow to take care of women who are sick. For many centuries the Church consistently used anointing as a means of healing the sick. In fact it is important to note that the sacrament of unction, or anointing, was in the early centuries always designed as a means of cure, and not as a preparation for death, as it now is in the Roman Catholic Church. It was not until A.D. 852 that the sacrament of unction did, in fact, become the Sacrament of Extreme Unction, administered to prepare for death.

The Church has always cared for her sick; and in the Church there has always resided the gift of healing. The social gospel is not an appendix to Christianity; it is the very essence of the Christian faith and life.

THE LETTER OF JAMES

A PRAYING CHURCH

James 5: 16-18

> Confess your sins to each other, and pray for each other, that you may be healed. The prayer of a good man, when it is set to work, is very powerful. Elijah was a man with the same emotions as ourselves, and he prayed earnestly that it should not rain, and for three years and six months no rain fell upon the earth. And he prayed again and the heaven gave rain; and the earth put forth her fruit.

THERE are in this passage three basic ideas of Jewish religion.

(i) There is the idea that all sickness is due to sin. It was a deeply-rooted Jewish belief that where there were sickness and suffering, there must have been sin. " There is no death without guilt," said the Rabbis, " and no suffering without sin." The Rabbis, therefore, believed and taught that before a man could be healed of his sickness his sins must be forgiven by God. Rabbi Alexandrai said, " No man gets up from his sickness until God has forgiven him all his sins." That is why Jesus began His healing of the man with the palsy by saying, " Son, thy sins be forgiven thee " (*Mark* 2: 5). The Jew always identified suffering and sin. Nowadays we cannot make this mechanical identification; but this remains true—that no man can know any health of either soul, or mind, or body until he is right with God. A right relationship with God is a pre-requisite of health in every part of a man's life and being.

(ii) There is the idea that, to be effective, confession of sin has to be made to men, and especially to the person wronged, as well as to God. In a very real sense it is easier to confess sins to God than it is to confess them to men; and yet in sin there are two barriers to be removed—the barrier which sin sets up between us and God, and the barrier which sin sets up between us and our fellow-men. And if both these barriers are to be removed, then both kinds of confession must be made. This was, in fact, the

154

custom of the Moravian Church, and it was a custom which Wesley took over from the Moravian Church for his earliest Methodist classes: they used to meet two or three times a week " to confess their faults to one another and to pray for one another that they might be healed." This principle is clearly a principle which must be used with wisdom. It is quite true that there may well be cases where confession of sin to each other may do infinitely more harm than good; but where a barrier has been erected because of some wrong which has been done, then a man must put himself right both with God and his fellow-man.

(iii) Above all, this passage enables us to see that the Jews set no limits to the power of prayer. They had a saying that he who prays surrounds his house with a wall that is stronger than iron. They said, " Penitence can do something; but prayer can do everything." To them prayer was nothing less than contacting the power of God; prayer is the channel through which the strength and grace of God are brought to bear on the troubles and problems and ills of life. If that was so for a Jew, how much more must it be so for a Christian?

Tennyson wrote:

> " More things are wrought by prayer
> Than this world dreams of. Wherefore, let thy voice
> Rise like a fountain for me night and day.
> For what are men better than sheep or goats
> That nourish a blind life within the brain,
> If, knowing God, they lift not hands of prayer
> Both for themselves and those who call them friend?
> For so the whole round earth is every way
> Bound by gold chains about the feet of God."

As the Jew saw it, and as indeed it is, to cure the ills of life we need to be right with God, and right with men, and we need to bring to bear upon them through prayer the mercy and the might of God.

Before we leave this passage there is one interesting technical fact that we must note. It quotes Elijah as an

example of the power of prayer. It says that he prayed
earnestly and the rain was withheld for three years and
six months; and that he prayed again and the rain came.
Now this is an excellent example of how Jewish rabbinic
exegesis developed the meaning of Scripture. The full
story is in I *Kings* 17 and 18. The *three years and six months*
—a period also quoted in *Luke* 4: 25—is a deduction from
I *Kings* 18: 1. Further, the Old Testament narrative
does not say in so many words that Elijah himself *brought*
the drought; it only says that he *prophesied* the drought.
The Old Testament narrative does not say that either the
coming or the cessation of the drought was due to the
prayers of Elijah; he was merely the prophet who announced
its coming and its going. But the Rabbis always studied
Scripture under the microscope. In I *Kings* 17: 1 we
read the words of Elijah: " As the Lord God of Israel
liveth, *before whom I stand,* there shall not be dew nor
rain these years, but according to my word." Now the
Jewish attitude of prayer was *standing before God*; and so
in this phrase the Rabbis found what was to them an
indication that the drought was the result of the prayers
of Elijah. In I *Kings* 18: 42 we read that Elijah went up
to Carmel, and *cast himself down upon the earth,* and put
his face between his knees. Once again the Rabbis saw
here the attitude of agonizing prayer; and so found what
was to them an indication that it was the prayer of Elijah
which brought the drought to an end. Here we see the
Rabbis finding lessons in Scripture, not only from its
direct words, but also from what could be read into them.

THE TRUTH WHICH MUST BE DONE

James 5: 19, 20

> My brothers, if any among you wanders from the
> truth, and if anyone turns him again to the right way,
> let him know that he who has turned a sinner from
> his wandering way will save his brother's soul from
> death, and will hide a multitude of his own sins.

HERE in this passage there is set down the great differen-
tiating characteristic of Christian truth. Christian truth
is something from which a man can *wander*. Christian
truth is not only intellectual, philosophical, speculative,
abstract; Christian truth is always moral truth. Christian
truth is, therefore, not something about which a man may
merely be mistaken in opinion; it is something from which
he can wander in action.

This comes out very clearly when we go to the New
Testament to see the expressions which are used in connection with truth. Truth is something which a man must
love (2 *Thessalonians* 2: 10); it is something which a man
must *obey* (*Galatians* 5: 7); it is something which a man
must *display in life* (2 *Corinthians* 4: 2); it is something
which must be *spoken in love* (*Ephesians* 4: 14); it is
something which must be *witnessed to* (*John* 18: 37); it is
something which must be *manifested in a life of love* (1 *John*
3: 19); it is something which liberates (*John* 8: 32);
and it is something which is the gift of the Holy Spirit,
sent by Jesus Christ (*John* 16: 14).

Clearest of all is the reference in *John* 3: 21; in that
verse there is the phrase *he that doeth the truth*. That is to
say, *Christian truth is something which must be done*. Christian
truth is not only an intellectual exercise; it is not only
something which is the object of the search of the mind;
it is not an academic affair; it is not a matter of knowledge
and of opinion, of argument and of debate. Christian truth
is always moral truth; it is always truth which issues in
action; it is not only a process of the mind, it is also a
way of life. It is not something to be studied, it is something to be done. Christian truth is not something to
which a man must submit only his mind; it is something
to which he has to submit his whole life. It is not only
something by which he thinks, it is also, and even more,
something by which he lives. Christian truth is not the
affair only of the study circle and the discussion group;
Christian truth is the affair of life.

THE SUPREME HUMAN ACHIEVEMENT

James 5: 19, 20 (*continued*)

JAMES finishes his letter with one of the greatest and most uplifting thoughts in the New Testament, and yet a thought which occurs more than once in the Bible. Suppose a man goes wrong, and strays away; and suppose a fellow-Christian rescues that man from the error of his ways, and brings him back to the right path. Then the man who has rescued his brother, has not only saved his brother's soul, he has covered a multitude of his own sins. In other words, to save another's soul is the surest way to save one's own.

Mayor points out that Origen has a wonderful passage in one of his Homiles in which he points out six ways in which a man may gain forgiveness of his sins. He may gain remission of his sins, by baptism, by martyrdom, by almsgiving (*Luke* 11: 41), by the forgiveness of others (*Matthew* 6: 14), by love (*Luke* 7: 47), and by converting a sinner from the evil of his ways. God will forgive much to the man who has been the means of leading another brother back to Him.

This is a thought which shines forth every now and then from the pages of Scripture. Jeremiah says, " If thou take forth the precious from the vile, thou shalt be as my mouth " (*Jeremiah* 15: 19). Daniel writes: " They that be wise shall shine as the brightness of the firmament; and they that turn many to righteousness as the stars for ever and ever " (*Daniel* 12: 3). The advice to the young Timothy is: " Take heed to thyself, and unto thy teaching; for in doing this thou shalt both save thyself, and them that hear thee " (I *Timothy* 4: 16).

There is a saying of the Jewish Fathers: " Whosoever makes a man righteous, sin prevails not over him." Clement of Alexandria says that the true Christian reckons that which benefits his neighbour his own salvation. It is told that an ultra-evangelical lady once asked Wilberforce, who gained their freedom for the slaves, if his soul was saved. "Madame," he answered, " I have been so busy trying to save the souls of others that I have had no time to think of my own." It has been said that those who bring sunshine into the lives of others cannot keep it from their own; and very certainly those who bring the lives of others to God cannot keep God out of their own lives. The highest honour God can give is given to him who leads another to God, for the man who does that does nothing less than share in the work of Jesus Christ, the Saviour of men.

THE LETTERS OF PETER

THE LETTERS OF PETER

INTRODUCTION TO FIRST PETER

The Catholic or General Epistles

First Peter belongs to that group of New Testament letters which are known as the *Catholic* or the *General* Epistles. Two explanations of that title have been offered.

(i) It is suggested that these letters were called *Catholic* or *General* because they were addressed to the Church at large, in contradistinction to the letters of Paul which were addressed to single, individual Churches. But that is not so. *James* is addressed to a quite definite, though widely scattered, community. It is written to the twelve tribes who are scattered abroad (*James* I: I). It needs no argument that 2 and 3 *John* are addressed to very definite communities; and, although I *John* has no definite address, it is quite clearly written with the needs and perils of a definite community in mind. I *Peter* itself is written to the strangers scattered abroad throughout Pontus, Galatia, Cappadocia, Asia and Bithynia (I *Peter* I: I). It is true that these General Epistles have a wider range than the letters of Paul; but it is not true to say that they were addressed to the whole Church at large, for, as we can see, they all have a quite definite community in mind.

(ii) So we must turn to the second explanation of the title. It is suggested that these letters were called *Catholic* or *General* because they were accepted as Scripture by the whole Church in contradistinction to a large number of letters which enjoyed a local and a temporary authority, but which never universally ranked as Scripture. At the time when these letters were being written there was an outbreak of letter-writing in the Church. We still possess many of the letters which were then written—the letter of Clement of Rome to Corinth, the letter of Barnabas, the letters of Ignatius, and the letters of Polycarp. All these letters were regarded as very precious in the Churches to which they were written, but they were never regarded as having authority throughout the whole Church; on the other hand these *Catholic* or *General* Epistles gradually won for themselves a place in Scripture and were accepted throughout the whole Church. Here, then, is the true explanation of the title by which they are called.

The Lovely Letter

Of all these General Epistles it is probably true to say that *First Peter* is the best known and loved, and the most read. No one has ever been in any doubt about its attractiveness and its charm. Moffatt writes of it: " The beautiful spirit of the pastoral shines through any translation of the Greek text. ' Affectionate, loving, lowly, humble,' are Isaak Walton's quaternion of adjectives for the Epistles of James, John and Peter, but it is *First Peter* which deserves them pre-eminently." It is written out of the love of a pastor's heart to help people who were going through it and on whom worse things were still to come. " The key-note," says Moffatt, " is steady encouragement to endurance in conduct, and innocence in character." It has been said that the distinctive characteristic of *First Peter* is *warmth*. E. J. Goodspeed wrote: " *First Peter* is one of the most moving pieces of persecution literature." To this day *First Peter* is one of the easiest letters in the New Testament to read, for it has never lost its winsome appeal to the human heart.

The Modern Doubt

Until a comparatively short time ago few would have raised any doubts about the genuineness and authenticity of *First Peter*. Renan, who was by no means a conservative critic, wrote of it: " The First Epistle is one of the writings of the New Testament which are most anciently and most unanimously cited as genuine." But in recent times the Petrine authorship of the letter has been very widely questioned. The most recent commentary in English, that of F. W. Beare, published in 1947, goes the length of saying, " There can be no possible doubt that ' Peter ' is a pseudonym." That is to say, Beare has no doubt that someone else wrote this letter under the name of Peter. We shall go on in fairness to investigate that view, although we do not ourselves accept it. But first we shall set out the traditional view—which we ourselves unhesitatingly accept—of the date and authorship of this letter. That view is that *First Peter* was written from Rome by Peter himself, about the year A.D. 67, in the days immediately following the first persecution of the Christians by Nero, to the Christians in those parts of Asia Minor which are named in the address. What, then, is the evidence for this early date, and, therefore, for the Petrine authorship?

The Second Coming

When we go to the letter itself we find that it is keenly and intensely interested in the second coming. The expectation of the second coming of Christ is in the very forefront of its thought. Christians are being kept for the salvation which is to be revealed at the last time (1: 5), Those who keep the faith will be saved from the coming judgment (1: 7). Christians are to hope for the grace which will come at the revelation of Jesus Christ (1: 13). The day of visitation is expected (2: 12). The end of all things is at hand (4: 17). Those who suffer with Christ will also rejoice with Christ when His glory is revealed (4: 13). Judgment is to begin at the house of God (4: 17). The writer himself is sure that he will be a sharer in the glory to come (5: 1). When the Chief Shepherd shall appear the faithful Christian will receive a crown of glory (5: 4). From the beginning to the end of the letter the second coming is in the forefront of the writer's mind. It is the motive for steadfastness in the faith, for the loyal living of the Christian life, and for gallant endurance amidst the sufferings, which have come, and which will come upon them. Now, it would be untrue to say that the second coming ever dropped out of Christian belief, but it is true to say that it tended to recede from the forefront of Christian belief, as the years passed on and Christ did not return. It is, for instance, significant that in *Ephesians*, which is one of Paul's latest letters, there is no mention of the second coming. On this ground it is, therefore, reasonable to suppose that *First Peter* is early, and comes from the days when the Christians vividly expected the return of their Lord at any moment.

Simplicity of Organization

It is further clear that *First Peter* comes from a time when the organization of the Church was very simple. There is no mention of deacons. Still less is there any mention of the *episkopos*, the bishop, who begins to emerge in the Pastoral Epistles, and who becomes prominent in Ignatius' letters in the first half of the second century. The only Church officials who are mentioned are the elders. " The elders who are among you I exhort, who am also an elder " (5: 1). On this ground also it is reasonable to suppose that *First Peter* comes from an early date.

The Theology of the Early Church

What is most significant of all is that the theology of *First Peter* is the theology of the very early Church. E. G. Selwyn has made a detailed study of this; and he has proved beyond all question that the theological ideas of *First Peter* are precisely and exactly the same as the theological ideas which we meet in the recorded sermons of Peter in the early chapters of *Acts*.

The preaching of the early Church was based on five mains ideas. One of the greatest contributions of C. H. Dodd to New Testament scholarship was his formulation of these five main ideas. These are the ideas which form the framework of all the sermons of the early Church, as they are recorded in *Acts*; and these ideas are the basic foundation of the thought of all the New Testament writers. To the summary of these basic ideas there has been given the name the *Kērugma*, which means the announcement or the proclamation of a herald. These are the fundamental ideas which the Church in its first days heralded forth. We shall take these ideas one by one, and we shall set down after each of them, first, the references to them in the early chapters of *Acts*, and second, the references to them in *First Peter*; and we will make the significant discovery that the basic ideas of the sermons of the early Church, many of which Peter preached, and the theology of *First Peter* are precisely the same. It may be well to make it clear that we are not claiming that the sermons in *Acts* are, as it were verbatim, short-hand reports of the sermons as they were preached; but we do believe that these sermons in *Acts* do correctly give the *substance* of the message of the first preachers.

    (i) The age of fulfilment has dawned; the Messianic age has begun. This is God's last word. A new order is being inaugurated, and the elect are summoned to join the new community. *Acts* 2: 14-16; 3: 12-26; 4: 8-12; 10: 34-43; I *Peter* 1: 3, 10-12; 4: 7.

    (ii) This new age has come through the life, the death, and the resurrection of Jesus Christ, all of which are in direct fulfilment of the prophecies of the Old Testament, and are, therefore, the result of the determinate counsel and foreknowledge of God. *Acts* 2: 20-31; 3: 13, 14; 10: 43; I *Peter* 1: 20, 21.

    (iii) By virtue of the resurrection Jesus has been exalted to the right hand of God, and is the Messianic head of the new Israel. *Acts* 2: 22-26; 3: 13; 4: 11; 5: 30, 31; 10: 39-42; I *Peter* 1: 21; 2: 7; 2: 24; 3: 22.

    (iv) These Messianic events will shortly reach their consummation in the return of Christ in glory, and the judgment of the living and the dead. *Acts* 3: 19-23; 10: 42; I *Peter* 1: 5, 7, 13; 4: 5, 13, 17, 18; 5: 1, 4.

    (v) These facts are made the grounds for an appeal for repentance, and offer of forgiveness and of the Holy Spirit, and the promise of eternal life. *Acts* 2: 38, 39; 3: 19; 5: 31; 10: 43; I *Peter* 1: 13-25; 2: 1-3; 4: 1-5.

These five declarations are the five main planks in the edifice of early Christian preaching, as it is recorded for us in the sermons of Peter in the early chapters of *Acts*; they are also the dominant ideas in *First Peter*. The correspondence is so close and so consistent that we can with entire probability see the same hand and the same mind in both.

Quotations from the Fathers

We may add still another point to our evidence that *First Peter* is a very early book. Very early the fathers and teachers of the Church begin to quote *First Peter*. The first person to quote *First Peter* by name is Irenaeus who lived from A.D. 130 until well on the next century. He twice quotes I *Peter* 1: 8: " Whom, having not seen, ye love; in whom, though now ye see Him not, ye rejoice with joy unspeakable." And he once quotes I *Peter* 2: 16 with its command not to use liberty as a cloak for maliciousness. But even before this the fathers of the Church were quoting Peter without mentioning his name. Clement of Rome, writing about A.D. 95, speaks of " the precious blood of Christ," an unusual phrase which may well come from Peter's statement that we are redeemed by the precious blood of Christ (1: 19). Polycarp, who was martyred in A.D. 155, continuously quotes Peter, although he does not mention him by name. We may select three passages to show how closely Polycarp gives the words of Peter.

> Wherefore, girding up your loins, serve God in fear . . . believing on Him who raised up our Lord Jesus Christ from the dead, and gave Him glory (Polycarp; *To the Philippians* 2: 1).
> Wherefore, gird up the loins of your mind . . . who by Him do believe in God that raised Him from the dead and gave Him glory (I *Peter* 1: 13, 21).

Christ Jesus who bare our sins in His own body on the tree, who did no sin, neither was guile found in His mouth (Polycarp 8: 1).

Who did no sin, neither was guile found in His mouth . . . who His own self bare our sins in His own body on the tree (I *Peter* 2: 22, 24).

Having your conversation blameless among the Gentiles (Polycarp 10: 2).

Having your conversation honest among the Gentiles (I Peter 2: 12).

There can be no doubt that Polycarp is quoting Peter, although he does not name him. Now it takes some time for a book to acquire such an authority and such a familiarity that it can be quoted almost unconsciously, that its language is woven into the language of the Church. Therefore, once again we see that we may regard I *Peter* as a very early book.

We have dealt with this matter at some length, and in some detail, because we think it important that we should be able to meet the arguments of those who hold that Peter has nothing to do with the letter which bears his name.

The Excellence of the Greek

But, if we are defending the Petrine authorship of this letter, there is one question which we must face—and that is the excellence of the Greek. The Greek is of such distinguished excellence that it seems impossible that it should be the work of a Galilaean fisherman. New Testament scholars are at one in praising the Greek of this letter. F. W. Beare writes: " The epistle is quite obviously the work of a man of letters, skilled in all the devices of rhetoric, and able to draw on an extensive, and even learned, vocabulary. He is a stylist of no ordinary capacity, and he writes some of the best Greek in the whole New Testament, far smoother and more literary than that of the highly-trained Paul." Moffatt speaks of this letter's " plastic language and love of metaphor." Mayor says that *First*

Peter has no equal in the New Testament for " sustained stateliness of rhythm." Bigg has likened certain of *First Peter's* phrases to the writing of Thucydides. Selwyn has spoken of *First Peter's* " Euripidean tenderness," and of its ability to coin and use compound words as Aeschylus might have done. The Greek of *First Peter* is not entirely unworthy to be set beside the Greek of the masters of the Greek language. Here there is a real difficulty. It is difficult, if not impossible, to imagine Peter using the Greek language like that.

But the letter itself supplies its own solution to this problem. In the concluding short section Peter himself says, " By Silvanus . . . I have written briefly " (I *Peter* 5: 12). *By Silvanus*—in Greek *dia Silouanou*—is an unusual phrase. The Greek means that Silvanus was Peter's agent or instrument in the writing of this letter. It certainly means that Silvanus was more than merely Peter's secretary or stenographer or amanuensis. It means that Silvanus had much more to do with the writing of the epistle than that.

Let us approach this from two angles. First, let us enquire what we know about Silvanus. (The evidence is set out more fully in our study section on I *Peter* 5: 12). The Silvanus of *First Peter* is in all probability the same person as the Silvanus of the letters of Paul, and the Silas of the story of *Acts*, for Silas is a shortened and more familiar form of Silvanus. Let us then examine these passages. When we do so, we find that Silas or Silvanus was no ordinary person, but a leading figure in the life and counsels of the early Church.

Silvanus was a prophet (*Acts* 15: 32); he was one of the " chief among the brethren " at the council of Jerusalem, and he was one of the two chosen to deliver the decisions of the council to the Church at Antioch (*Acts* 15: 22, 27). He was Paul's chosen companion in the second missionary journey, and was with Paul both in Philippi and in Corinth (*Acts* 15: 37-40; 16: 19, 25, 29;

18: 5; 2 *Corinthians* 1: 19). He is associated with Paul in the initial greetings of 1 and 2 *Thessalonians* (1 *Thessalonians* 1: 1; 2 *Thessalonians* 1: 1). And finally we find that Silvanus was a Roman citizen (*Acts* 16: 37). Silvanus, then, was a notable man in the early Church; he was not so much the assistant as the colleague of Paul in Paul's work; and, since he was a Roman citizen, there is at least a possibility that Silvanus was a man of an education and a culture such as Peter could never have enjoyed.

Now let us add our second line of thought. In the missionary situation, when a missionary can speak a language well enough, but cannot write it very well, it is quite common for him to do one of two things, if he wishes to send a message to his people. He either writes it out in as good a style as he can, and then gets a native speaker of the language to correct his mistakes and to polish his style; or, if he has a native colleague and adviser whom he can fully trust, he tells him what he wishes said, leaves him to put the message into written form, and then vets, and finally approves, the result.

We can well imagine that that was the part that Silvanus played in the writing of *First Peter*. Either, he corrected and polished Peter's necessarily inadequate Greek; or, since Silvanus was a man of such eminence, it may well have been that Peter told him what he wanted said, and left him to say it, and then approved the result, and added the last personal paragraph to it.

When Peter says that Silvanus was his instrument or agent in the writing of this letter, it gives us the solution to the excellence of the Greek. The thought is the thought of Peter; but the style is the style of Silvanus. And so, although the Greek is so excellent, there is no necessity to deny that the letter comes from Peter himself.

The Recipients of the Letter

The recipients of the letter are the strangers (a Christian is always a stranger and a sojourner on the earth) scattered abroad throughout Pontus, Galatia, Cappadocia, Asia and Bithynia.

It is true that almost all of these words had a double significance. They stood for ancient kingdoms; and they stood for Roman provinces to which the ancient names had been given; and the ancient kingdoms and the new provinces did not always cover the same territory. Pontus was never a province. It had originally been the kingdom of Mithradates, and part of it was incorporated in Bithynia and part of it in Galatia. Galatia had originally been the kingdom of the Gauls in the area of the three cities Ancyra, Pessinus, and Tavium, but the Romans had expanded it into a much larger unit of administration, including sections of Phrygia, Pisidia, Lycaonia, and Isauria. The kingdom of Cappadocia had become a Roman province in A.D. 17 in practically its original form. Asia is not the continent of Asia as we use the term. It had been an independent kingdom, whose last king, Attalus the Third, had bequeathed it as a gift to Rome in 133 B.C. It embraced the centre of Asia Minor and was bounded on the north by Bithynia, on the south by Lycia, and on the east by Phrygia and Galatia. In popular language Asia was that part of Asia Minor which lay along the shores of the Aegean Sea.

We do not know why these particular districts are picked out; but this much is certain—they embraced a large area, and an area with a very large population; and the fact that they are all mentioned is one of the greatest proofs of the immense missionary activity of the early Church, apart altogether from the missionary activities of Paul.

All these districts lie in the north-east corner of Asia Minor. Why they are named as a group, and why they are named in the order in which they are named, we do not know. But a glance at the map will show that if the bearer of this letter—who may very probably also have been Silvanus—sailed from Italy and landed at Sinope in north-east Asia Minor, a tour through these provinces would be a circular tour which would take him back to where he started at Sinope. From Sinope in Bithynia he would go south to Galatia, still further south to Cappadocia; he would then turn west to Asia, and north again to Bithynia; and then, if he bore east, he would arrive back in Sinope.

It is clear from the letter itself that its recipients were mainly Gentiles. There is no mention of any question of the law, a question which always arose when there was a Jewish background. Their previous condition had been one of fleshly and lustful sin (1: 14; 4: 3, 4) which fits Gentiles far better than Jews. Previously they had been no people—Gentiles outside the covenant—but now they are the people of God (2: 9, 10).

The form of his name which Peter uses also shows that this letter was intended for Gentiles. Peter is a Greek name. When Paul speaks of Peter he calls him Cephas (1 *Corinthians* 1: 12; 3: 22; 9: 5; 15: 5; *Galatians* 1: 18; 2: 9, 11, 14). Among his fellow Jews, Peter was known as Simeon (*Acts* 15: 14), which is the name by which he is called in *Second Peter* (1: 1). Since he uses his Greek name, it is likely that Peter was writing to Greek people.

The Circumstances behind the Letter

That this letter was written in a time when persecution threatened, and when the Christians were in danger, is abundantly clear. They are in the midst of manifold trials (1: 6). They are likely to be falsely accused as evil-doers (3: 16). A fiery trial is going to try them (4: 12). When they suffer, they are to commit themselves to God (4: 19). They may well have to suffer for righteousness' sake (3: 14). They are sharing in the afflictions which the Christian brotherhood throughout the world is called upon to endure (5: 9). At the back of this letter there are fiery trial, a campaign of slander, and suffering for the sake of Christ. Can we then identify this situation?

There was a time when the Christians had little to fear from the Roman government. In *Acts* it is repeatedly the

Roman magistrates and the Roman soldiers and officials who saved Paul from the fury of the Jews and of the pagans alike. As Gibbon had it, the tribunal of the pagan magistrate proved the most assured refuge against the fury of the synagogue. The reason for this was that in the early days the Roman government was not able to distinguish between Jews and Christians. And within the empire Judaism, was what was called a *religio licita*, a permitted religion, and the Jews had full liberty to worship in their own way. It was not that the Jews did not try to enlighten the Romans to the true facts of the situation; they did so in Corinth, for example (*Acts* 17: 12-17). But for some time the Romans simply regarded the Christians a Jewish sect, and, therefore, did not molest them.

But then the change came in the days of Nero, and we can trace almost every detail of the story. On 19th July, A.D. 64, the great fire of Rome broke out. Rome was a city of narrow streets, and of high wooden tenements, and it was in real danger of being wiped out. The fire burned for three days and three nights; it was checked; and then it broke out again with redoubled violence. The Roman populace had no doubt who was responsible for it. They put the blame fairly and squarely on Nero, the Emperor. Nero had a passion for building; and they believed that he had deliberately taken steps to obliterate Rome that he might build it again. Nero's responsibility must remain for ever in doubt; but it is certain that he watched the raging inferno from the tower of Maecenas, and expressed himself as charmed with the flower and loveliness of the flames. It was freely said that those who tried to extinguish the fire were deliberately hindered, and that men were seen to rekindle it again, when it was likely to subside. The people were overwhelmed. The ancient landmarks and the ancestral shrines were gone. The Temple of Luna, the Ara Maxima, the great altar, the Temple of Jupiter Stator, the shrine of Vesta, the very household gods of the Roman people were gone. The people were homeless, and, in

Farrar's phrase, there was "a hopeless brotherhood of wretchedness."

The resentment of the people was bitter; Nero had to divert suspicion from himself; a scapegoat had to be found. The Christians were made the scapegoat. Tacitus, the Roman historian, tells the story:

> Neither human assistance in the shape of imperial gifts, nor attempts to appease the gods, could remove the sinister report that the fire was due to Nero's own orders. And, so, in the hope of dissipating the rumour, he falsely diverted the charge on to a set of people to whom the vulgar gave the name of Chrestians, and who were detested for the abominations they perpetrated. The founder of the sect, one Christus by name, had been executed by Pontius Pilate in the reign of Tiberius; and the dangerous superstition, though put down for the moment, broke out again, not only in Judaea, the original home of the pest, but even in Rome, where everything shameful and horrible collects and is practised (Tacitus, *Annals* 15: 44).

Clearly Tacitus had no doubt that the Christians were not to blame for the fire, and that Nero was simply choosing them to be the scapegoats for his own crime.

But the question arises, why did Nero pick on the Christians, and how was it possible even to suggest that they were responsible for the fire of Rome? There are two possible answers to that question.

(i) The Christians were already the victims of certain associationships and of certain slanders.

(a) The Christians were in the popular mind connected with the Jews. Antisemitism is no new thing. The Jews have always been hated; and it was easy for the Roman mob to attach any crime to the Jews, and, therefore, to the Christians.

(b) The Lord's Supper was secret, at least in a sense. It was open only to the members of the Church. And there were certain phrases connected with it which were fruitful sources of pagan slanders. There were phrases about eating someone's body and drinking someone's blood.

That was enough for a rumour to arise that the Christians were cannibals. In time the rumour grew until it became a story that the Christians killed and ate a Gentile or a newly born child. At the Lord's Table the Christians gave each other the kiss of peace (I Peter 5: 14). Their meeting was called the *Agapē*, the Love Feast. That was enough for stories to spread that the Christian meetings were orgies of vice and of unbridled lust. It was not difficult for slanders to arise.

(c) It was always a charge against the Christians that they " tampered with family relationships." There was this much truth in such a charge that Christianity did indeed become a sword to split families, when some members of the family became Christian, and some did not. A religion which split homes was bound to be an unpopular religion.

(d) It was indeed the truth that the Christians did speak of a coming day when the world would dissolve in flames. Many a Christian preacher must have been heard preaching of the second coming and the fiery dissolution of all things (Acts 2: 19, 20). It would not be difficult to put the blame for the fire on to people who spoke like that.

There was abundant material which could be twisted and perverted into false charges against the Christians by anyone maliciously disposed to injure them and to victimise them.

(ii) The Jewish faith had always appealed, especially to women, because of its moral standards in a world where chastity did not exist. There were, therefore, many well-born women who had embraced the Jewish faith. Now the Jews did not hesitate to work upon these women to influence their husbands against the Christians. We get a definite example of that in what happened to Paul and his company in Antioch of Pisidia. There it was through such women that the Jews stirred up action against Paul (Acts 13: 50). Two of Nero's court favourites were Jewish proselytes. There was Aliturus, his favourite actor; and there was

Poppaea, his mistress. It is very likely that the Jews through them influenced Nero to take action against the Christians.

In any event, the blame for the fire was attached to the Christians, and a savage outbreak of persecution blazed up. Nor was it simply persecution by legal means. What Tacitus called an *ingens multitudo*, a huge multitude of Christians, perished, and perished in the most sadistic ways. Nero rolled the Christians in pitch, and then set light to them, while they were still alive, and used them as living torches of flame to light his gardens. He sewed them up in the skins of wild animals, and then set his hunting-dogs upon them, to tear them limb from limb, while they still lived.

Tacitus writes:

> Mockery of every sort was added to their deaths. Covered with the skins of beasts, they were torn by dogs and perished, or were nailed to crosses, or were doomed to the flames and burned, to serve as a nightly illumination, when daylight had expired. Nero offered his gardens for the spectacle, and was exhibiting a show in the circus, while he mingled with the people in the dress of a charioteer, or stood aloft on a car. Hence, even for criminals who deserve extreme and exemplary punishment, there arose a feeling of compassion; for, it was not, as it seemed, for the public good, but to glut one man's cruelty that they were being destroyed (Tacitus, *Annals* 15: 44).

The same terrible story is told by the later Christian historian, Sulipicius Severus, in his *Chronicle*:

> In the meantime, the number of Christians being now very large, it happened that Rome was destroyed by fire, while Nero was stationed at Antium. But the opinion of all cast the odium of causing the fire upon the emperor, and he was believed in this way to have sought for the glory of building a new city. And, in fact, Nero could not, by any means he tried, escape from the charge that the fire had been caused by his orders. He, therefore, turned the accusation against the Christians, and the most cruel tortures

were accordingly inflicted upon the innocent. Nay, even new kinds of death were invented, so that, being covered in the skins of wild beasts, they perished by being devoured by dogs, while many were crucified, or slain by fire, and not a few were set apart for this purpose, that, when the day came to a close, they should be consumed to serve for light during the night. In this way, cruelty first began to be manifested against the Christians. Afterwards, too, their religion was prohibited by laws which were enacted; and by edicts openly set forth it was proclaimed unlawful to be a Christian.

The Christians perished, and they perished in a delirium of savagery.

Now it is true that this persecution was confined originally to Rome; but the gateway to persecution had been opened. The Christians had been, so to speak, discovered, and in every place they were ready victims for the mob.

Moffatt writes:

After the Neronic wave had passed over the capital, the wash of it was felt on the far shores of the provinces; the dramatic publicity of the punishment must have spread the name of Christian *urbi et orbi*, far and wide, over the entire empire; the provincials would soon hear of it, and when they desired a similar outburst at the expense of the loyal Christians, all that they needed was a proconsul to gratify their wishes, and some outstanding disciple to serve as a victim.

For ever after the Christians were to live under threat. The mobs of the Roman cities knew what had happened in Rome. There were always these slanderous stories against the Christians. There were times when the mob loved blood, and revelled in a lynching. There were governors who were ready to pander to the mob by gratifying their outbreaks of blood-lust. It was not Roman law but lynch law which threatened the Christians.

From now on the Christian was in peril of his life. For years nothing might happen; then some spark might set off the explosion; and the terror would break out. That is the situation at the back of *First Peter*; and it is in face of that that Peter calls his people to hope and to courage and to that lovely Christian living which alone could defeat, and to give the lie to, the slanders with which they were attacked, and which were the grounds for the outbreaks against them. *First Peter* was written to meet no theological heresy; it was written to strengthen men and women who were in jeopardy of their lives.

The Doubts

We have now set out in full the arguments which go to prove that Peter is really the author of the first letter which bears his name. But, as we have said, in recent times there have been not a few first-class scholars who have felt that this letter cannot have been the work of Peter. We ourselves fully accept the view that Peter is the author of the letter; but in fairness we must set out the other side. Even if we do not agree with another point of view, it is a duty to know what that other point of view is, and how it is supported, if for no other reason than that we may be able to meet it with our own arguments. The version of the other point of view which we here set down is largely taken from the chapter on *First Peter* in *The Primitive Church* by B. H. Streeter.

Strange Silences

Bigg writes in his introduction: " There is no book in the New Testament which has earlier, better, or stronger attestation (than *First Peter*)." It is true that Eusebius, the great fourth century scholar and historian of the Church and of the New Testament, classes *First Peter* among the books about which there is not, and never was, any dispute, and which was universally accepted in the early Church as part of scripture (Eusebius, *Ecclesiastical History* 3.25.2). But certain things are to be noted.

(a) Eusebius in point of fact adduces certain quotations from earlier writers to prove his contention that *First Peter* was universally accepted. This he never does in connection with the gospels or the letters of Paul; and the very fact that Eusebius feels called upon to produce his evidence in the cast of *First Peter* might possibly be held to indicate that in the case of it he felt some necessity to prove his case, a necessity which did not exist in the case of the other books. Was there a doubt in Eusebius' own mind? Or, were there people who had doubts, and who had to be convinced? Was the universal acceptance of *First Peter* not quite so universal and unanimous after all?

(b) In his book on *The Canon of the New Testament*, Westcott had already noted that, although no one in the early Church questions the right of *First Peter* to be part of the New Testament, yet surprisingly few of the early fathers quote it, and, still more surprising, very few of the early fathers in the west and in Rome quote it. Tertullian is an immense quoter of scripture. In his writings there are 7,258 quotations from the New Testament, and only 2 of them are from *First Peter*. This is very surprising. If Peter wrote this letter, and, if he wrote it in Rome, we would expect it to be very well known, and very largely used, in the Church of the west.

(c) The earliest known official list of New Testament books is known as the Muratorian Canon, so called after Cardinal Muratori who discovered it. It is the official list of New Testament books as accepted in the Church at Rome about the year A.D. 170. It is an extraordinary fact that *First Peter* does not appear in that list at all. Now it can be fairly argued that the Muratorian Canon, as we possess it, is in fact defective, and there may have been a reference to *First Peter* in it originally. But that argument is seriously weakened by the next argument.

(d) It is a fact that *First Peter* was not in the New Testament of the Syrian Church as late as A.D. 373. It did not get into the Syrian New Testament, until the Syriac version of the New Testament, known as the Peshitto was made about A.D. 400. It is, indeed, true that the Peshitto did become the official Syriac New Testament, but before that *First Peter* was not part of the Syriac New Testament. Now we know that it was Tatian who brought the New Testament books to the Syriac-speaking Church; and he brought them to Syria from Rome when he went to Edessa, and founded the Church there in A.D. 172. It could, therefore, be argued that the Muratorian Canon is correct as we possess it, and that *First Peter* was not part of the Roman Church's New Testament as late as A.D. 170. This would be a very surprising fact if Peter wrote it—and actually wrote it at Rome.

When all these facts are put together, it does indeed seem that there are some strange silences in regard to *First Peter*, and that its attestation is not as strong as is usually assumed.

First Peter and Ephesians

Still further, there is definitely some connection between *First Peter* and *Ephesians*. There are many close parallels of thought and expression between the two. We select the following parallels as specimens of this similarity.

> Blessed be the God and Father of our Lord Jesus Christ, who according to His abundant mercy, hath begotten us again unto a lovely hope by the resurrection of Jesus Christ from the dead (I *Peter* I: 3).
>
> Blessed be the God and Father of our Lord Jesus Christ, who hath blessed us with spiritual blessings in heavenly places in Christ (*Ephesians* I: 3).
>
> Wherefore, gird up the loins of your mind, be sober and hope to the end for the grace that is to be brought unto you at the revelation of Jesus Christ (I *Peter* I: 13).
>
> Stand, therefore, having your loins girt about with truth (*Ephesians* 6: 14).
>
> Jesus Christ, who verily was ordained before the foundation of the world, but was manifest in these last times for you (I *Peter* I: 20).
>
> According as He hath chosen us in Him, before the foundation of the world (*Ephesians* I: 4).

> Jesus Christ, who is gone into heaven, and is on the right hand of God, angels and authorities and powers being made subject unto Him (I *Peter* 3: 22).

> God hath set Him at His own right hand in the heavenly places, far above all principality, and power and might and dominion (*Ephesians* 1: 20, 21).

Further, the injunctions to slaves, husbands and wives in *First Peter* and *Ephesians* are very similar. The argument is that *First Peter* is quoting *Ephesians*. Now, although *Ephesians* must have been written somewhere about A.D. 64, the letters of Paul were not collected and edited until about A.D. 90; and if Peter was also writing in A.D. 64, how did he know *Ephesians*?

This is one of the arguments to which there is more than one reply. (*a*) The injunctions to slaves, husbands and wives are part of the standardized ethical teaching of the Church, given to all converts in all Churches. Peter was not borrowing from Paul; both were using common stock. (*b*) All the similarities quoted are similarities which can well be explained from the fact that there were certain phrases and certain lines of thought which were universal in the early Church. For instance, " Blessed be the God and Father of our Lord Jesus Christ," was part of the universal devotional language of the early Church, which both Peter and Paul would know, and delight in, and use without any borrowing from each other. (*c*) Even if there is mutual borrowing, it is by no means certain that *First Peter* borrows from *Ephesians*; the borrowing might well be the other way round, and indeed probably is the other way round, for *First Peter* is much simpler than *Ephesians*. (*d*) Lastly, even if *First Peter* borrows from *Ephesians*, if Peter and Paul were in Rome at the same time, it is perfectly possible that Peter should have seen a copy of *Ephesians*, before it was sent to Asia Minor, and he might well have discussed its ideas with Paul.

The argument that *First Peter* must be late because it quotes from *Ephesians* seems to us very uncertain and very insecure and very precarious, and possibly quite mistaken.

Your Fellow-Elder

It is objected that Peter could not well have written the sentence: " The elders who are among you I exhort, who am also an elder " (I *Peter* 5: 1). It is maintained that Peter was not in fact an elder, and that he could not have called himself an elder. Peter was an apostle, and the function of the apostle was quite different from the function of the elder. The apostle was characteristically a man whose work and whose authority were not confined to any one congregation, but whose writ ran throughout the whole Church at large; on the other hand the elder was the governing official of the local congregation. The apostle was attached to no congregation, and moved everywhere throughout the Church; the very essence of the eldership was that the elder was attached to one congregation, and that his work lay there.

That is perfectly true. But it must be remembered that amongst the Jews there was no office more universally honoured than the office of elder. The elder was the man who had the respect of the whole community, and to whom the community looked for guidance in their problems, and justice in their disputes. Peter, as a Jew, would feel nothing out of place in calling himself an elder; and in so doing he avoided the conscious claim of authority that the title of apostle might have implied, and graciously and courteously identified himself with the people to whom he spoke.

A Witness of the Sufferings of Christ

It is objected that Peter could not honestly have called himself a witness of the sufferings of Christ, for after the arrest in the garden all the disciples forsook Jesus and fled (*Matthew* 26: 56), and, apart from the beloved disciple, none of the disciples was a witness of the Cross (*John* 19: 26, 27). A witness of the *resurrection*, Peter could call himself, and indeed to be such was the function of an apostle (*Acts* 1: 22), but a witness of the Cross he was not. In a sense that is undeniable. And yet Peter is not here claiming to be a witness of the crucifixion, but to be a witness of the sufferings of Christ. Indeed he did see Christ suffer in His continual rejection by men, in the poignant moments of the Last Supper, in the agony in the garden, and in that moment, when, after he had denied Him, Jesus turned and looked on him (*Luke* 22: 61). It may well be said that in that look after the denial there were gathered up all the sufferings of a broken heart. It is a prosaic, insensitive and pedestrian criticism which would deny to Peter the right to say that he had been a witness of the sufferings of Christ.

Persecution for the Name

But the main argument for a late date for *First Peter* is drawn from its references to persecution. It is argued that by the time of *First Peter* the implication is that it was a crime to be a Christian as such; that Christians were brought before the courts, not for any crime, and not for any fault, but for the bare fact that they were Christians. *First Peter* speaks about being reproached for the name of Christ (4: 14); it speaks of sufferings as a Christian (4: 16). Now it is argued that that stage of persecution was not reached until after A.D. 100. It is argued that early on in the history of the Church Christians were punished and persecuted as evil-doers, as Nero persecuted them for allegedly setting fire to Rome; that early on Christians were accused of acting and behaving criminally; that it was not until later that they were liable to punishment and persecution for no other reason than that they were Christians. There is no doubt that that was the law by A.D. 112. At that time Pliny was governor of Bithynia. Pliny was a personal friend of the Emperor Trajan, and he had a way of referring all his difficulties to Trajan for solution. In Bithynia the problem of the Christians had arisen. Pliny was well aware that the Christians were harmless and law-abiding citizens to whose practices no crimes were attached. They told him that " they had been accustomed to assemble on a fixed day before daylight, and sing by turns a hymn to Christ as God; that they had bound themselves with an oath, not for any crime, but to commit neither theft, nor robbery, nor adultery, nor to break their word, and not to deny a deposit when demanded." Pliny accepted all this; but, when they were brought before him, he asked only one question. " I have asked them whether they were Christians. Those who confessed I asked a second and a third time, threatening punishment Those who persisted I ordered to be led away to execution." Their sole crime was the crime of being a Christian. Trajan's answer is that this is the correct proceeding, and that anyone who denies being a Christian, and who proves that he is not by sacrificing to the gods is immediately to be set free. From the letters it is clear that there was a good deal of information against the Christians going on; and Trajan lays it down that no anonymous letters of information are to be accepted or acted upon (Pliny, *Letters* 96 and 97). Now it is argued that this stage of persecution did not emerge until the time of Trajan; and it is argued that *First Peter* implies a situation in which the mere fact of being a Christian is a crime, and that, therefore, it must be as late as Trajan's time.

The only way in which we can settle this is to sketch the progress of persecution, and the reason for it, in the Roman Empire. We may do so by setting out one basic fact, and three developments from it.

(i) Under the Roman system, religions were divided into two kinds. There were those which were *religiones licitae*, permitted religions; these were recognized by the state and it was open to any man to hold and to practise them. There were *religiones illicitae*; these were forbidden by the state and it was illegal for any man to practise them. If he did practise them, his prosecution was an automatic police affair. Anyone who practised a *religio illicita* was as much a criminal as a burglar or a murderer. He was automatically an outlaw, and automatically under condemnation. It is to be noted that Roman toleration was very wide; and that any religion which did not affect public morality and civil order was certain to be permitted. The Romans were not characteristically persecutors, and were instinctively tolerant.

(ii) Judaism was a *religio licita*; in the very early days the Romans, not unnaturally, did not know the difference between Judaism and Christianity. Christianity, as far as they were concerned, was merely a sect of Judaism, and if there was tension and hostility between Judaism and Christianity, that was a private religious quarrel and no concern of the Roman government. Now because of that in the very early days Christianity was under no danger of persecution. It enjoyed the same freedom of worship as Judaism enjoyed. It was assumed to be a *religio licita*, a permitted religion.

(iii) The action of Nero changed the whole situation. However it came about, and most likely it came about by the deliberate action of the Jews, the Roman government discovered that Judaism and Christianity were quite different. It is true that Nero first persecuted the Christians, not for being Christians, but for burning Rome. But the fact remains that Christianity had been discovered by the government as a separate religion.

(iv) The consequence was immediate and inevitable. Christianity was at once a *religio illicita*, a prohibited religion; and immediately, *ipso facto*, every Christian became an outlaw, and every Christian became a criminal, not for any crimes, but simply because he was a Christian. In point of fact in the Roman historian, Suetonius, we have direct evidence that that was precisely what happened. Suetonius gives a kind of list of the legislative reforms initiated by Nero:

During his reign many abuses were severely punished and put down, and not a few new laws were made; a limit was set to expenditures; the public banquets were confined to a distribution of food; the sale of any kind of cooked viands in the taverns was forbidden, with the exception of pulse and vegetables, whereas, before, every kind of dainty was exposed for sale. Punishment was inflicted on the Christians, a class of men given to a new and mischievous superstition. He put an end to the diversions of the chariot-drivers, who from immunity of long standing claimed the right of ranging at large and amusing themselves by cheating and robbing the people. The pantomimic actors and their partisans were banished from the city.

We have quoted that passage in full because it is the proof that by the time of Nero the punishment of Christians had become nothing more or less than an ordinary police affair. It is abundantly clear that we do not need to wait for the time of Trajan for the bare fact of being a Christian to be a crime. Any time after Nero any Christian was liable to punishment and death simply for the name of Christian.

This does not mean that persecution was constant, continuous, and consistent; but it does mean that any Christian was liable to execution at any time, purely as a police matter. In one area a Christian might live half a life-time or even a whole life-time at peace; in another area there might be outbreaks of persecution every few months. It depended very largely on two things. It depended on the governor himself. The governor might leave the Christian unmolested, or equally he might set the processes of the law in action against them. It depended on informers. The governor might not wish to act against the Christians, but if information was laid against a Christian he had to act; and there were times when the mob were out for blood, when information was laid, and when the Christians were butchered to make a Roman holiday.

To compare small things with great, the legal position of the Christians and the attitude of the Roman law can be parallelled in Britain today. There are certain actions which are illegal—to take a very small example, parking one's car all night outside one's house without lights—but which for long enough may be permitted. But if the police authorities decide to institute a drive against such an action, or if it develops into too blatant a breaking of the law, or if someone lays a complaint and an information, then the law will go into action, and due penalty and punishment will be exacted. That was the position of the Christians in the empire. Technically they were outlaws; in actual fact no action might be taken against them; but a kind of sword of Damocles was for ever suspended over them. None knew when information would be laid against them; none knew when a governor would take action; none knew when he might have to die. And it must be clearly understood that that situation obtained consistently after the action of Nero. Up to that time the Roman authorities had not realized that Christianity was a new religion; after that time they knew it was; and from that time the Christian was automatically an outlaw.

Let us, then, look at the situation as it is depicted in *First Peter*. Peter's people are undergoing manifold trials (I: 6). Their faith is liable to be tried as metal is tested with fire (I: 7). Clearly they are undergoing a campaign of slander in which ignorant and baseless charges are being maliciously directed against them (2: 12; 2: 15; 3: 16; 4: 4). At that very moment they are in the midst of an outbreak of persecution because they are Christians (4: 12, 14, 16; 5: 9). Such suffering is only to be expected, and they must not be surprised at it (4: 12). And in any event it gives them the happiness of suffering for right-eousness' sake (3: 14, 17), and of being sharers in the suffering of Christ (4: 13). There is no need to come down to the time of Trajan for this situation. It is a situation in which the Christians daily found themselves in every part of the empire at any time after their existence had been disclosed by the action of Nero. The persecution situation in *First Peter* does not in any way compel us to date it after the life time of Peter himself.

Honour the King

But we must proceed with the arguments of those who cannot hold the Petrine authorship of this letter. It is argued that in the situation which obtained in the time of Nero, Peter could never have written: " Submit yourselves to every ordinance of man for the Lord's sake, whether it be as unto the king, as supreme, or unto governors that are sent by him for the punishment of evil-doers, and for the praise of them that do well. . . . Fear God. Honour the king " (2: 13-17). It is argued that Peter could never have written that when Nero was Emperor. But the fact is that this is precisely the same point of view as is expressed in *Romans* 13: 1-7 by Paul. The whole teaching of the New Testament, except only in the *Revelation* in which Rome is doomed and damned, is that the Christian must be a loyal citizen, and must demonstrate the falsity of the charges made against him by the excellence of his behaviour as a citizen (I *Peter* 2: 15). Even in times of persecution the Christian fully acknowledged the obligation to be a good citizen; and his only defence against persecution was to show by the excellence of his citizenship that he did not deserve such treatment. It is by no means impossible that Peter should have written like that.

A Sermon and a Pastoral

What then is the view of those who cannot believe that *First Peter* is the actual work of Peter himself?

First of all, it is suggested that the initial address (I: I, 2), and the closing greetings and salutations (5: I2-I4) are later additions, and were no part of the original letter.

It is then suggested that *First Peter* as it stands is composed of two separate and quite different works. In

4: 11 we find a doxology. The natural place for a doxology is at the end; and it is suggested that 1: 3—4: 11 is the first of the two works of which the letter is composed. It is further suggested that this part of *First Peter* was originally a baptismal sermon. There is indeed in it a reference to the baptism which saves us (3: 21); and the advice to slaves, wives and husbands (2: 18—3: 7) would be entirely relevant to those who were entering the Christian Church from paganism, and who were setting out on the newness of the Christian life. It is argued that the doxology in 4: 11 concludes this separate work.

It is then suggested that the second part of the letter, 4: 12—5: 11, is a separate work altogether and contains the substance of a pastoral letter, written to strengthen and comfort during a time of persecution (4: 12-19). At such a time the elders were very important; on them the resistance power of the Church depended. The writer of this pastoral fears that greed and arrogance are creeping in (5: 1-3), and he urges them faithfully to perform their high task (5: 4).

So, then, on this view *First Peter* is composed of two separate works—a baptism sermon, and a pastoral letter written in time of persecution, and neither of them has anything to do with Peter.

Asia Minor, not Rome

Let us continue to trace out these speculations. If *First Peter* is a baptismal sermon and a pastoral letter in time of persecution, where, then, is its place of origin? If the letter is not Peter's, then there is no necessity to connect it with Rome; and, in any event, it appears that the Roman Church did not know or use *First Peter* Where, then, was the letter written? Let us put together certain facts.

(*a*) Pontus, Galatia, Cappadocia, Asia and Bithynia (1: 1) are a group of provinces all in *Asia Minor*, and all centred in Sinope.

THE LETTERS OF PETER

(b) The first extensive quoter of *First Peter* is Polycarp who was bishop of Smyrna, and Smyrna is in *Asia Minor*.

(c) There are certain phrases in *First Peter* which immediately turn our thoughts to parallel phrases in other parts of the New Testament. In I *Peter* 5: 13 the Church is called " she that is elect," and in 2 *John* 13 the Church is also described as an " elect lady." I *Peter* I: 8 speaks of Jesus Christ, " whom having not seen, ye love; in whom, though now ye see Him not, yet believing, ye rejoice with joy unspeakable and full of glory." This turns our thoughts very naturally to Jesus' saying to Thomas in the Fourth Gospel: " Blessed are they that have not seen, and have yet believed " (*John* 20: 29). *First Peter* urges the elders to tend, that is, to shepherd, the flock of God (I *Peter* 5: 2). That turns our thoughts to Jesus' injunction to Peter to feed His lambs and his sheep (*John* 21: 15-17), and to Paul's farewell injunction to the elders of Ephesus to take heed to the flock over which the Holy Spirit has made them overseers (*Acts* 20: 28). All this is to say, that the memories which *First Peter* awakens are of the Fourth Gospel, the Letters of John, and of Paul at Ephesus. The Fourth Gospel and the Letters of John were most probably written at Ephesus, and Ephesus is in *Asia Minor*.

It does seem as we study the question that in the case of *First Peter* all roads lead to Asia Minor.

The Occasion of the Publication of First Peter

Assuming, then, that *First Peter* has its origin in Asia Minor, can we suggest an occasion when it was written? It was written at a time of persecution. Now we know from Pliny's letters that in Bithynia, about A.D. 112, there was a very serious persecution of the Christians. Bithynia is actually one of the provinces named in the address of *First Peter*; and we may well conjecture that it was to give courage to the Christians at that time that *First Peter* was issued. It may be that at that time someone in a Church in Asia Minor came upon these two documents, a rousing and challenging baptismal sermon and a word of encouragement in time of trouble, and sent them out under the name of Peter. It has to be said that at that time this would not have been looked upon as forgery. Both in Jewish and in Greek practice it was the regular custom to attach books to the name of the great writers of the past. In the ancient world that was a quite normal and blameless proceeding.

The Author of First Peter

If Peter did not write *First Peter*, is it possible to conjecture who is the author? Let us see if we can reconstruct some of the essential qualifications of such an author. On our previous assumption he must come from Asia Minor. On the basis of *First Peter* itself, he must be an *elder*, and he must be an *eye-witness* of the sufferings of Christ (I Peter 5: 1). Is there anyone who fits these requirements? Papias, the Bishop of Hierapolis about A.D. 170, who spent his life collecting all the information he could acquire about the early days of the Church, tells us of his methods and his sources: " Nor shall I hesitate, along with my own interpretations, to set down for thee whatsoever I learned with care and remembered with care from the elders, guaranteeing its truth. . . . Furthermore, if anyone chanced to arrive who had been really a follower of the elders, I would enquire as to the sayings of the elders—as to what Andrew or Peter said, or Philip, or Thomas or James, or John or Matthew, or any other of the Lord's disciples, also as to what Aristion or the Presbyter John, the Lord's disciples say. For I supposed that things out of books would not be of such use to me as the utterances of a living voice which was still with us." Here we have an elder called Aristion. Aristion was an elder, and he was a disciple of the Lord, and, therefore, a witness of the sufferings of the Lord. Is there anything to connect him with *First Peter*?

THE LETTERS OF PETER

Aristion of Smyrna

When we turn to the *Apostolic Constitutions* we find that one of the first bishops of Smyrna was called Ariston—which is the same name as Aristion. Now who is the great quoter of *First Peter*? None other than Polycarp, a later Bishop of Smyrna. What more natural than that Polycarp should quote what might well have been the devotional classic of the Church at Smyrna? Can it be that *First Peter* is actually a baptismal sermon and a pastoral letter of Aristion of Smyrna?

Let us take one more step. Let us turn to the letters to the Seven Churches in the *Revelation*, and let us read the letter to Smyrna: " Fear not the things which thou art about to suffer. Behold, the devil is about to cast some of you into prison that you may be tried; and you shall have tribulation for ten days. Be ye faithful unto death, and I will give you a crown of life " (*Revelation* 2: 10). Can this be the very same persecution as that which originally lay behind *First Peter*? And was it for this persecution that Aristion, the Bishop of Smyrna, first wrote the pastoral letter, which was afterwards to become a part of *First Peter*?

Such, then, is the suggestion of B. H. Streeter. He thinks that *First Peter* is composed of a baptismal sermon and a pastoral letter written by Aristion, Bishop of Smyrna. Originally that pastoral letter was written to comfort and strengthen the people of Smyrna in A.D. 90 when the persecution mentioned in the *Revelation* threatened the Church. These writings of Aristion became the devotional classics and the cherished possessions of the Church at Smyrna. Rather more than twenty years later a much wider and much more far-reaching persecution broke out in Bithynia and spread throughout northern Asia Minor. Then someone remembered the letter and the sermon of Aristion, felt that they were the very thing the Church needed in her time of trial, and sent them out under the name of Peter, the great apostle.

THE LETTERS OF PETER

An Apostle's Letter

We have stated in full both views of the origin, the date and the authorship of *First Peter*. There is no doubt of the interest and the ingenuity of the theory which B. H. Streeter has produced, and there is no doubt that those who feel that a later date for *First Peter* is necessary have produced arguments which have to be met and considered; but for our own part we see no reason to doubt that the letter is indeed the letter of Peter himself, and that it was written not long after the great fire of Rome and the first persecution of the Christians, and that its object is to encourage the Christians of Asia Minor to stand fast when the onrushing tide of persecution seeks to engulf them and to take their faith away.

PETER

THE GREAT INHERITANCE

I Peter I: I, 2

> Peter, an apostle of Jesus Christ, to God's Chosen
> People, who are scattered as exiles throughout Pontus,
> Galatia, Cappadocia, Asia and Bithynia. I am an
> apostle, and you are chosen, according to the fore-
> knowledge of God, through the consecration of the
> Spirit, for obedience and to be sprinkled by the blood
> of Jesus Christ. May grace and peace be multiplied
> to you.

IT happens again and again in the New Testament that the
true greatness and wonder of a passage lies not only on the
surface, and in that which is actually said, but in the ideas
and the convictions which lie behind it, and out of which
it is written. That is particularly so of this passage.

It is quite clear that this letter was written to people
who were Gentiles. They have been released from the
futile way of life which they had learned from their fathers
(1: 18). Those who were once not a people had become
nothing less than the people of God (2: 10). In previous
times they had walked after the will and the lusts of the
Gentiles (4: 3). But the outstanding thing about this
passage is that it takes words and conceptions which had
originally applied only to the Jews, the Chosen Nation,
and applies them to the Gentiles, who had once been
believed to be outside the mercy of God. Once it had been
said that " God created the Gentiles to be fuel for the
fires of Hell." Once it had been said that, just as the best
of the snakes must be crushed, so even the best of the
Gentiles must be destroyed. Once it had been said that God
loved only Israel of all nations upon the earth. But now
the mercy, the privileges, and the grace of God have gone
out to all the earth and to all men, even to those who
could never have expected them.

(i) Peter calls the people to whom he writes *the elect,
God's Chosen People.* Once that had been a title which

belonged to Israel and to Israel alone: " Thou art an holy people unto the Lord thy God; the Lord thy God hath chosen thee to be a special people unto Himself, above all people that are upon the face of the earth " (*Deuteronomy* 7: 6; cp. 14: 2). The prophet speaks of " Israel, mine elect " (*Isaiah* 45: 4). The Psalmist speaks of " the children of Jacob His chosen " (*Psalm* 105: 6, 43). There was a time when it was possible to speak of Israel as the Chosen People, to the exclusion of all other nations.

But the nation of Israel failed in the purposes of God, for, when God sent His Son into the world, they rejected Him, and crucified Him. When Jesus spoke the Parable of the Wicked Husbandmen, He Himself said that the inheritance of Israel was to be taken from them, and given to others (*Matthew* 21: 41; *Mark* 12: 9; *Luke* 20: 16). The Master would give the vineyard to others. That is the basis of a great New Testament conception, the conception of the Christian Church as the true Israel, the new Israel, the Israel of God (cp. *Galatians* 6: 16). All the privileges which had once belonged to Israel now belonged to the Christian Church. The Church with its members taken from every nation in the world is the Chosen People; the mercy of God has gone out to the ends of the earth, and all nations have seen the glory, and experienced the grace, of God.

(ii) But there is another word here which once belonged exclusively to Israel. The address literally reads: " To the elect strangers of the Diaspora, the dispersion, throughout Pontus, Galatia, Cappadocia, Asia and Bithynia." The word *Diaspora*, literally the *dispersion*, was the technical name for the Jews scattered in exile in all the countries outside the bounds of Palestine. Sometimes in their troubled history the Jews had been forcibly deported from their native land; sometimes they had gone out of their own free will to work, and often to prosper, in other lands. Those exiled Jews were called the *Diaspora*, the dispersion. But now the real Diaspora is not the Jewish nation; the real Diaspora is the Christian Church scattered abroad throughout the provinces of the Roman Empire and the nations of the world. Once the people who had been different from other peoples was the Jews; now the people who are different are the Christians. They are the people whose King is God, and whose home is eternity, and who are strangers, sojourners, and exiles in the world.

THE CHOSEN OF GOD AND THE EXILES OF ETERNITY

I Peter I: I, 2 (*continued*)

WHAT we have just been saying means that the two great titles of which we have just been thinking belong to us who are Christians.

(i) We are *the Chosen People of God*. There is *uplift* here. Surely there can be no greater compliment and privilege in all the world than to be chosen by God. The word *eklektos* can describe anything that is specially chosen; it can describe specially chosen fruit, articles specially chosen because they are so outstandingly well made, picked troops specially chosen for some great duty and for some great exploit. We have the honour of being specially chosen by God. But there is also *challenge* and *responsibility* here. God always chooses for service. The honour which God gives a man is the honour of being used for His plans and for His purposes. The fact that we are chosen means that the honour and the work of God are delivered into our hands. It was precisely there that the Jews failed, and we have to see to it that the tragedy of a like failure does not mark our lives.

(ii) We are *the exiles of eternity*. This is never to say that we must withdraw from the world, but it is to say that we must be in the world in the realest sense, and at the same time not of the world in the realest sense. It has been wisely said that the Christian must be *apart* from the world, although he must never be *aloof* from the world. Wherever the exiled Jew settled, his eyes were towards Jerusalem. In foreign countries his synagogues were so built that, when the worshipper entered to worship, he was facing towards Jerusalem. However useful a citizen of his adopted country the Jew was, his greatest loyalty was to Jerusalem.

The Greek word for such a sojourner in a strange land is *paroikos*. A *paroikos* was a man who was away from home in a strange land, and whose thoughts ever turned home. Such a sojourning was called a *paroikia*; and *paroikia* is the direct derivation of the English word *parish*. The Christians in any place, the parish in any place, are a group of people whose eyes are turned to God, and whose loyalty is beyond. " Here," said the writer to the Hebrews, " we have no continuing city, but we seek one to come " (*Hebrews* 13: 14).

We must repeat that this does not mean withdrawal from the world; but it does mean that the Christian sees all things in the light of eternity, and he sees life as a journey towards God. It is this which decides the value and the importance which he attached to anything; it is this which dictates his conduct. This is the touchstone and the dynamic of his life.

There is a famous unwritten saying of Jesus: " The world is a bridge. The wise man will pass over it, but he will not build his house upon it." This is the thought which is behind the famous passage in *The Epistle to Diognetus*, one of the best-known works of the post-apostolic age: " Christians are not marked out from the rest of mankind by their country or their speech or their customs. . . . They dwell in cities both Greek and barbarian, each as his lot is cast, following the customs of the region in clothing and in food and in the outward things of life generally; yet they manifest the wonderful and openly paradoxical character of their own state. They inhabit the lands of their birth, but as temporary residents thereof; they take their share of all responsibilities as citizens, and endure all disabilities as aliens. Every foreign land is their native land, and every native land a foreign land. . . . They pass their days upon earth, but their citizenship is in heaven."

It would be quite wrong to think that this makes the Christian a bad citizen of the land in which he lives. It is because he sees all things in the light of eternity that he is the best of all citizens, for it is only in the light of eternity that the true values of all things can be seen.

We, as Christians, are the Chosen People of God; we are the exiles of eternity. Therein lie both our priceless privilege and our inescapable responsibility.

THE THREE GREAT FACTS OF THE CHRISTIAN LIFE

I *Peter* I: I, 2 (*continued*)

In verse 2 we are confronted with the three great facts of the Christian life.

(i) The Christian is *chosen according to the foreknowledge of God*. C. E. B. Cranfield has a fine comment on this phrase: " If all our attention is concentrated on the hostility or indifference of the world or the exiguousness of our own progress in the Christian life, we may well be discouraged. At such times we need to be reminded that our election is *according to the foreknowledge of God the Father*. The Church is not just a human organisation— though, of course, it is that. Its origin lies, not in the will of the flesh, in the idealism of men, in human aspirations and plans, but in the eternal purpose of God." When we are discouraged we may well remind ourselves that the Christian Church came into being according to the purpose and the plan of God, and, if the Church is true to God and obedient to God, she can never ultimately fail.

(ii) The Christian is chosen *to be consecrated by the Spirit.*

Luther said: " I believe that I cannot by my own reason or strength believe in Jesus Christ my Lord, or come to Him." For the Christian the Holy Spirit is essential to every part of the Christian life and every step in it. It is the Holy Spirit who awakens within us the first faint desires and longings for God and goodness. It is the Holy Spirit who convicts us of our sin, and who leads us to the Cross where that sin is forgiven. It is the Holy Spirit who enables us to walk the way to holiness, to be freed from the sins which have us in their grip, and to gain the virtues which are the fruit of the Spirit. It is the Holy Spirit who gives us the assurance that our sins are forgiven and that Jesus Christ is Lord. The beginning, the middle and the end of the Christian life are all the work of the Holy Spirit.

(iii) The Christian is chosen *for obedience and for sprinkling by the blood of Jesus Christ*. In the Old Testament there are three occasions when sprinkling with blood is mentioned. It may well be that all three were present in Peter's mind, and that all three have something to contribute to the thought behind these words.

(*a*) When a leper had been healed, he was sprinkled with the blood of a bird (*Leviticus* 14: 1-7). Sprinkling with blood is, therefore, the symbol of *cleansing*. By the sacrifice of Christ the Christian is cleansed from sin.

(*b*) Sprinkling with blood was part of the ritual of the setting apart of Aaron and the priests (*Exodus* 29: 20-22; *Leviticus* 8: 30). Sprinkling was the sign of *setting apart* for the service of God. The Christian is specially set apart for the service of God, not only within the Temple, but also within the world.

(*c*) But the great picture of the sprinkling comes from the covenant relationship between Israel and God. In the covenant God, of His own gracious free will, approached Israel that they might be His people, and that He might be their God. But that relationship depended on the Israelites accepting the conditions of the covenant and obeying the law. Obedience was a necessary condition of the covenant, and failure in obedience meant failure of the covenant relationship between God and Israel. So the book of the covenant was read to Israel, and the people pledged themselves: " All the words which the Lord hath said we will do." As a token of this relationship of obedience between the people and God, Moses took half the blood of the sacrifice and sprinkled it on the altar, and half the blood of the sacrifice and sprinkled it on the people (*Exodus* 24: 1-8). Sprinkling was sprinkling for *obedience*. Through the sacrifice of Jesus Christ the Christian is called into a new relationship with God, in which the sins of the past are forgiven, and he is pledged to obedience in the time to come. Through Christ the Christian is cleansed, set apart, pledged to obedience for all his days.

It is in the purpose of God that the Christian is called. It is by the work of the Holy Spirit that his life is hallowed towards God. It is by the sprinkling of the blood of Christ that he is cleansed from past sin and dedicated to future obedience to God.

THE REBIRTH OF THE CHRISTIAN

1 *Peter* 1: 3-5

> Blessed be the God and Father of our Lord Jesus Christ, who, according to His great mercy, has brought about in us that rebirth which leads to a living hope through the resurrection of Jesus Christ from the dead, an inheritance imperishable, undefilable, and unfading, kept safe in heaven for us, who are protected by the power of God through faith, until there comes that deliverance which is ready to be revealed at the last time.

IT will take us a long time to appropriate the riches of this passage, for there are few passages in the New Testament where more of the great fundamental Christian ideas and conceptions meet and come together.

It begins with a doxology to God—but a doxology with a difference. For a Jew the commonest of all beginnings to prayer was, " Blessed art Thou, O God." " Blessed art Thou, O God, who quickenest the dead," is the typical form of a Jewish prayer. The Christian takes over that prayer—but he takes it over with a difference. His prayer begins, " Blessed be the God and Father of our Lord Jesus Christ." The Christian is not praying to a distant, remote, unknown God; he is praying to the God who is the God and Father of our Lord Jesus Christ; he is praying to the God who is like Jesus, and to whom, through Jesus Christ, we may come with childlike confidence and boldness.

This passage begins with the idea of *rebirth*; the Christian is a man who has been reborn; he has been begotten again by God to a new and a different kind of life. Whatever else this means, it means that, when a man becomes a Christian, there comes into his life a change so radical and so decisive that he can only be said to be born again. He has become so different and life has become so different that everything is so new that the only thing that can be said is that life has begun all over again. This idea of rebirth runs all through the New Testament. Let us try to collect what the New Testament says about it.

(i) The Christian rebirth happens by the will and by the act of God (*John* I: 13; *James* I: 18). It is not something which a man achieves any more than he achieves his natural physical birth; it is something which happens to him by the will and the grace and the power of God.

(ii) Another way to put that is to say that this rebirth is the work of the Spirit (*John* 3: 1-15). It happens to a man, not by his own effort, but when he yields himself to be possessed and occupied and recreated by the Spirit within him.

(iii) It happens by the word of truth (*James* I: 18; I *Peter* I: 23). In the beginning it was the word of God which created heaven and earth, and all that is in them;

THE LETTERS OF PETER

God spoke and the chaos became a world, and the world was equipped with and for life. It is the creative word of God in Jesus Christ and in God's book which brings about this rebirth in a man's life.

(iv) The result of this rebirth is that the man who is reborn becomes the first fruits of a new creation (*James* 1: 18). This rebirth lifts a man out of this world of space and time, out of this world of change and decay, out of this world of sin and defeat, and brings him here and now into living touch with eternity and with eternal life.

(v) When a man is reborn, he is reborn to a living hope (I *Peter* 1: 3). Paul describes the heathen world as being without hope (*Ephesians* 2: 12). Sophocles wrote: " Not to be born at all—that is by far the best fortune; the second best is as soon as one is born with all speed to return thither whence one has come." To the heathen the world was a world where all things faded and decayed, a world which might be pleasant enough in itself, but which was going out into nothing but an endless dark. To the ancient world the Christian characteristic was hope. That hope came from two things. (*a*) The Christian felt that he had been born, not of corruptible, but of incorruptible seed (I *Peter* 1: 23). He had something of the very seed of God in him, and he, therefore, had in him a life which neither time nor eternity could destroy. (*b*) It came from the resurrection of Jesus Christ (I *Peter* 1: 3). The Christian had for ever beside him, even more, the Christian was one with, this Jesus Christ who had conquered even death, and, therefore, there was nothing left of which he could be afraid.

(vi) The rebirth of the Christian is a rebirth to righteousness (I *John* 2: 29; 3: 9; 5: 18). In this rebirth he is cleansed from himself, from the sins which shackle him and the habits which bind him; he is emancipated from sin; and he is given a power which enables him to walk in righteousness. That is not to say that the man who is reborn will never sin; but it is to say that he will be given the power and the grace every time he falls to rise again.

(vii) The rebirth of the Christian is a rebirth to love (I John 4: 7). Because the life of God is in him, he is cleansed from the essential selfishness of the Christless life, from the essential unforgiving bitterness of the self-centred life, and there is in him something of the forgiving and the sacrificial love and life of God.

(viii) Finally, the rebirth of the Christian is rebirth to victory (I John 5: 4). Life ceases to be defeat, and life begins to be victory, victory over self and sin and Satan and circumstances. Because the life of God is in him, the Christian has learned the secret and the power of victorious living.

THE GREAT INHERITANCE

I Peter I: 3-5 (*continued*)

STILL further, the Christian has entered into a great *inheritance*. The word for *inheritance* is *klēronomia*. Here is a word with a great history; for it is the word which is regularly used in the Greek Old Testament for the inheritance of Canaan, the Promised Land. Again and again the Old Testament speaks of the land which God had given his people *for an inheritance to possess it* (*Deuteronomy* 15: 4; 19: 10). To us the word *inheritance* tends to mean something into which we shall one day enter, and which in the future we shall possess; as the Bible uses the word, it rather means a settled and secure possession. To the Jew the great inheritance, the great settled possession, the great inheritance of God was the Promised Land.

But the Christian inheritance is even greater. Peter uses three great words with three great pictures behind them to describe this Christian inheritance. It is *imperishable*. The word is *aphthartos*; that word does mean *imperishable* and *incorruptible*; but it can have another meaning. It can mean *unravaged by any invading army*. Many and many a time the land of Palestine had been ravaged by

the armies of the aliens; it had been fought over and
blasted and destroyed; but the Christian possesses a
peace, a joy, a safety, a serenity which no invading army
can ravage and destroy. It is *undefilable*. The word is
amiantos, and the verb *miainein*, from which this adjective
comes, means to *defile* or *pollute* with impious impurity.
Many and many a time the land of Palestine had been
defiled and rendered impure by false worship of false gods
(*Jeremiah* 2: 7, 23; 3: 2; *Ezekiel* 20: 43). The defiling
things had often left their touch even on the Promised
Land; but the Christian has a purity and a holiness which
the sin of the world cannot infect. It is *unfading*. The
word is *amarantos*. In the Promised Land, and in any
land, even the loveliest flower fades, and the loveliest
blossom dies. But the Christian is lifted into a world
where there is no change and decay, where his peace and
joy and serenity are untouched by the chances and the
changes of life.

What, then, is this wonderful inheritance which the
reborn Christian possesses? There may be many secondary
answers to that question, but there is only one ultimate
answer—the inheritance of the Christian is nothing other
than God Himself. The Psalmist had said, " The Lord is
the portion of mine inheritance " (*Psalm* 16: 5). God
is his portion for ever (*Psalm* 73: 23-26). " The Lord,"
said the prophet, " is my portion; therefore will I hope in
Him " (*Lamentations* 3: 24).

It is because the Christian possesses God and is possessed
by God that he has the inheritance which is imperishable,
undefilable, and which can never fade away.

PROTECTED IN TIME AND SAFE IN ETERNITY

I *Peter* I: 3-5 (*continued*)

THE inheritance of the Christian, the full joy of God, is
waiting for the Christian in heaven; and of that Peter has
two great things to say.

(i) On our journey through this world to eternity we are protected by the power of God through faith. The word which Peter uses for to *protect* (*phrourein*) is a military word. It means that our life is garrisoned by God, that God stands sentinel over us all our days. The man who has faith never doubts, even when he cannot see Him, that God is standing within the shadows keeping watch upon His own. It is not that God saves us from the troubles and the sorrows and the problems of life; it is that he enables us to encounter them, to bear them, and to conquer them, and to march on.

(ii) The final salvation, the final deliverance will be revealed at the last time. Here we have two conceptions which are at the very basis of New Testament thought.

The New Testament frequently speaks of the last day, or the last days, or the last time. At the back of this there is the Jewish idea of time. The Jew divided all time into two ages. There was this present age, which is wholly bad and wholly under the domination of evil; and there was the age to come, which will be the golden age of God. In between there was the day of the Lord during which the world would be destroyed and remade, and when judgment would come. It is this in between time which is the last days, or the last time. It is simplest to say that when the New Testament speaks of the last days and the last time, it is speaking of that time when time and the world as we know them will come to an end.

We must always remember that it is not given to us to know when that time will come, nor what will happen then. But we can gather together what the New Testament does say about these last times.

(i) The Christians believed that they were already living in these last days. " It is the last time," said John to his people (1 *John* 2: 18). The writer to the Hebrews speaks of the fulness of the revelation which has come to men in Christ in these last days (*Hebrews* 1: 2). As the first

Christians saw it, God had already invaded time, and the end was hastening on.

(ii) The last times were to be times of the pouring out of God's Spirit upon men (*Acts* 2: 17). Once again the early Christians saw that being fulfilled in Pentecost and in the Spirit-filled Church.

(iii) It is the regular conviction of the early Christians that before the end the powers of evil would make a kind of final assault, and that all kinds of false and deceiving teachers would arise (2 *Timothy* 3: 1; 1 *John* 2: 18; *Jude* 18). There would be a kind of final flare up of evil and of falsehood.

(iv) The dead would be resurrected. It is Jesus' promise that at the last time He will raise up His own (*John* 6: 39, 40, 44, 54; 11: 24).

(v) Inevitably it would be a time of judgment when God's justice would be exercised, and God's enemies would find their just condemnation and punishment (*John* 12: 48; *James* 5: 3).

Such are the ideas which are in the minds of the New Testament writers, when they actually use this phrase *the last times* or *the last days*.

Clearly for many a man such a time would be a time of terror; but it is at that time that for the Christian there is, not terror, but salvation and deliverance. For the Christian it is not terror but salvation that is to be revealed. We must always remember that the word *sōzein* means *to save* in far more than what we might call the theological sense of the term. It is the regular word for *to rescue from danger*, and *to heal in sickness*. Charles Bigg in his commentary points out that in the New Testament the word *sōzein*, to save, and *sōtēria*, salvation, have four different, but closely related spheres of meaning. (*a*) They describe deliverance from danger (*Matthew* 8: 25). (*b*) They describe deliverance from disease (*Matthew* 9: 21). (*c*) They describe deliverance from the condemnation of God (*Matthew* 10: 23; 24: 13). (*d*) They describe deliverance from

the disease and from the power of sin (*Matthew* 1: 21).
Salvation is a many-sided thing. In it there is deliverance
from danger, deliverance from disease, deliverance from
condemnation, and deliverance from sin. And it is that,
and nothing less than that, to which the Christian can
look forward at the end.

THE SECRET OF ENDURANCE

1 *Peter* 1: 6, 7

> Herein you rejoice, even if it is at present necessary
> that for a brief time you should be grieved by all
> kinds of trials, for the object of these trials is that
> your tried and tested faith, more precious than gold
> which perishes though it is tested by the fire, may
> win praise and glory and honour when Jesus Christ
> shall appear.

IT is now that Peter comes to the actual situation in life
in which his readers found themselves. Their Christianity
had always made them unpopular, but now they were
facing the threat of almost certain persecution. It was
certain that soon the storm was going to break, and that
life was going to be an agonizing thing. Here in face of
that threatening situation Peter in effect reminds them of
three reasons why they can stand anything that may come
upon them.

(i) They can stand anything because of what they are
able to look forward to. At the end of things there is for
them the magnificent and splendid inheritance. At the end
of things there is for them life and joy with God. At the
end of things there is for them rescue, salvation, deliverance.
In point of fact this is how Westcott understands the
phrase *in the last time* (*en kairō eschatō*). We have taken
the phrase to mean *in the time when the world as we know it
will come to an end*; but the Greek phrase can mean *when
the worst comes to the worst*, when the crisis comes, when
the limit of endurance is reached. It is then, says Westcott,

when things have reached their limit, that the saving power of Christ will be displayed. In any event the ultimate meaning is the same. For the Christian persecution, trouble, affliction is not the end; beyond there, there lies the glory; and in the hope of that glory the Christian can endure anything that life brings to him. It sometimes happens that a man who is ill has to undergo a painful operation or course of treatment; but he gladly and willingly accepts the pain and the discomfort because of the renewed health and strength which lie beyond. It is one of the basic facts of life that a man can accept and endure anything so long as he has something to look forward to—and the Christian can look forward to the ultimate joy.

(ii) They can stand anything that comes, if they remember that every trial is, in fact, a test. Before gold is pure it has to be tried and tested and purified in the fire. The trials which come to a man are tests of his faith, and out of them his faith can emerge stronger and clearer and firmer than ever it was before. The rigours which the athlete has to undergo are not meant to make him collapse; they are meant to make him able to develop more and more strength and staying-power. In this world trial and affliction are not meant to take the strength out of us, but to put the strength into us.

In this connection there is a most suggestive fact in the language which Peter uses. He says that the Christian for the moment may well have to undergo, as the Authorized Version has it, *manifold* trials. In the Greek the word for manifold is *poikilos*, which literally means *many-coloured*. Now Peter uses that word once again and only once again, and the one other time he uses it is to describe the grace of God (I *Peter* 4: 10). Our troubles may be many-coloured, but so is the grace of God. There is no colour in the human situation which the grace of God cannot match. Whatever life is doing to us there is that in the grace of God which will enable us to meet it and to overcome it. There is a grace to match every trial, and there is no trial without its grace.

(iii) They can stand anything, because at the end of it, when Jesus Christ appears, they will receive from Him praise and glory and honour. They can face anything in the knowledge that some day they will hear Jesus Christ's " Well done! " Again and again in this life we make our biggest efforts and we do our best work, not for pay and not for profit, but in order to see the light in someone's eyes, and to hear someone's word of praise. These things mean more to us than anything else in all the world. So, then, the Christian knows that, if he endures, he will in the end hear the Master's " Well done! "

Here, then, is the recipe for endurance when life is hard and faith is difficult. We can stand up to things because of the greatness to which we can look forward, because every trial is another test to strengthen and to purify our faith, because at the end of it Jesus Christ is waiting to say, " Well done! " to all His faithful servants.

UNSEEN BUT NOT UNKNOWN

I *Peter* I: 8, 9

> Although you never knew Him, you love Him; although you do not see Him, you believe in Him. And you rejoice with unspeakable and glorious joy because you are receiving that which faith must end in—the salvation of your souls.

PETER here is drawing an implicit contrast between himself and his readers. It was his great privilege to have known and walked with Jesus in the days of His flesh. His readers had not had that joy; but, although they never knew Jesus in the flesh, they love Him; and although they do not see Him with the bodily eye, they nonetheless see Him with the eye of faith and believe. And that belief brings to them a joy beyond speech and clad with glory, for even here and now this faith makes them certain of the ultimate welfare of their souls.

E. G. Selwyn in his commentary distinguishes four stages in man's apprehension of Christ.

(i) The first is the stage of hope and desire, the stage of those who throughout the ages hoped for, and dreamed of, the coming of the King. As Jesus Himself said to His disciples, " Many prophets and kings desired to see the things which you have seen and have not seen them " (*Luke* 10: 23, 24). There were the days of hopes and dreams and longings and expectations which were never fully realized.

(ii) The second stage came to those who knew Christ in the flesh. That is what Peter is thinking about here. That is what he was thinking about when he said to Cornelius, " We were witnesses of all things which He did, both in the land of the Jews and in Jerusalem " (*Acts* 10: 39). There were those who walked with Jesus, and on whose witness our knowledge of the life and the words of Jesus depend.

(iii) There are those in every nation and land and time who see Jesus with the eye of faith. Jesus said to Thomas, " Thomas, because thou hast seen me, thou hast believed; blessed are they that have not seen, and believed " (*John* 20: 29). This way of seeing Jesus is possible only because Jesus is not someone who lived and died and who exists only as a figure in a book; He is someone who lived and died and who is alive for evermore. It has been said that " no apostle ever *remembered* Jesus." That is to say, Jesus is not only a memory; He is a person whose presence we can experience, and whom we can meet.

(iv) There is the beatific vision. It was John's confidence that we shall see Him as He is (I *John* 3: 2). " Now," said Paul, " we see through a glass darkly, but then face to face " (I *Corinthians* 13: 12). If the eye of faith endures, the day will come when it will be the eye of sight, and we shall see face to face, and know even as we are known.

Jesus, these eyes have never seen
  That radiant form of Thine;
The veil of sense hangs dark between
  Thy blessed face and mine.

I see Thee not, I hear Thee not,
  Yet art Thou oft with me;
And earth hath ne'er so dear a spot
  As where I meet with Thee.

Yet, though I have not seen, and still
  Must rest in faith alone,
I love Thee, dearest Lord, and will,
  Unseen but not unknown.

When death these mortal eyes shall seal,
  And still this throbbing heart,
The rending veil shall Thee reveal
  All glorious as Thou art.

THE FORETELLING OF THE GLORY

1 Peter I: 10-12

> Prophets, who prophesied about the grace which was
> to come to you, enquired and searched concerning
> that salvation, seeking to find out when and how
> the Spirit of Christ within them, testifying in advance
> to the sufferings destined for Christ and to the glories
> which must follow them, was telling them that it
> would come. It was revealed to them that the ministry
> which they were exercising in these things was not
> for themselves but for you, things which have now
> been proclaimed to you through those who preached
> the gospel to you through the power of the Holy
> Spirit sent down from heaven, things of which the
> angels long to catch a glimpse.

HERE again we have a rich passage. The wonder of the
salvation which was to come to men in Christ was such
that the prophets searched and enquired about it; it
was such that even the angels were eager to catch a glimpse
of it. This passage has a great deal to tell us about how
the prophets received their message, and about how they
wrote and spoke; there are few passages which have more

to tell us about how men of God wrote and about how they were inspired.

(i) We are told two things about the prophets. First, they searched and enquired about the salvation which was to come. Second, the Spirit of Christ told them the truth of Christ. Here we have the great truth that inspiration depends on two things—the searching mind of man, and the revealing Spirit of God. It used sometimes to be said that the men who wrote Scripture had no more to do with what they wrote than the pen which a man uses has to do with what he writes. They were said to be pens in the hands of God; they were said to be flutes into which the Spirit of God breathed, or lyres across which the Spirit of God moved. That is to say, the writers of Scripture were held to be nothing more than almost unconscious instruments in the hands of God. But this passage tells us the great truth that God's truth comes only to the man who searches for it, that inspiration comes when the revelation of the Spirit of God meets the searching of the mind of man. In all inspiration there is an element which is human and an element which is divine; it is the product at one and the same time of the search of the mind of man and the revelation of the Spirit of God.

Further, this passage tells us that the Holy Spirit, the Spirit of Christ, was always operative in this world. Wherever men have glimpsed beauty, wherever men have laid hold on truth, wherever men have had longings for God or true thoughts about God, the Spirit of Christ was there. Never has there been any time in any nation when the Spirit of Christ was not moving men to seek, and guiding men to find, God. Sometimes men were blind and deaf, sometimes men misinterpreted that guidance, sometimes they grasped but fragments of it, because they could take in no more, but always that revealing Spirit has been there to meet and to guide the searching mind.

(ii) This passage tells us what the prophets told. They told of the sufferings and the glory of Christ. Such passages

as *Psalm* 22 and *Isaiah* 52: 13—53: 12 found their consummation and fulfilment in the sufferings of Christ.
Such passages as *Psalm* 2, *Psalm* 16: 8-11, *Psalm* 110,
found their fulfilment in the glory and the triumph of
Christ. We need not think that the prophets foresaw the
actual physical man Jesus. What they did foresee was
that one would some day come in which their dreams
and visions would all be fulfilled.

(iii) This passage tells for whom the prophets spoke. It
was the message of the glorious deliverance of God that
they brought to men. That was a deliverance which they
themselves never saw and never experienced. Sometimes
God gives a man a vision, but says to the man himself,
" Not yet! " God took Moses to Pisgah and showed him
the Promised Land and said to him, " I have caused thee
to see it with thine eyes, but thou shalt not go over thither "
(*Deuteronomy* 34: 1-4). Someone tells of watching one night
at dusk a lamplighter, who was himself blind, lighting the
lamps. He tapped his way from lamp-post to lamp-post
bringing to others a light which he himself would never see.
As the prophets knew, it is a great gift to receive the
vision, even if the fulfilment and the consummation of the
vision is for others who are still to come.

THE MESSAGE OF THE PREACHER

I Peter I: 10-12 (*continued*)

BUT, further, this passage tells us not only of the visions
of the prophets, it tells us also of the message of the preacher.
It was the preachers who brought the message of salvation
to the readers of Peter's letter.

(i) It tells us that preaching is the announcement of
salvation; it is the bringing of the gospel, the good news.
Preaching may at different times have many notes and
many aspects, but fundamentally it is the proclamation
of the gospel. The preacher may at times have to warn,
to threaten and to condemn; he may have to remind

men of the judgment of God and the wrath of God; but basically, beyond all else, the message of the preacher is the announcement of salvation.

(ii) It tells us that preaching is through the Holy Spirit sent down from heaven. The preacher's message is not his own; it is given to him. He brings, not his own opinions and views and even prejudices; he brings the truth as given to him by the Holy Spirit. Like the prophet he will have to search and enquire; he will have to study and to learn; but having searched and enquired, having studied and learned, he must then wait, for the voice and the guidance of the Spirit to come to him.

(iii) It tells us that the preacher's message is of things of which the angels long to catch a glimpse. There is no excuse for triviality in preaching. There is no excuse for an earth-bound and unlovely message without interest and without thrill. The salvation of God is such a tremendous thing that even the angels long to see it.

It is with the message of salvation and the inspiration of the Spirit of Christ that the preacher must ever appear before men.

THE NECESSARY VIRILITY OF THE CHRISTIAN FAITH

I *Peter* I: 13

> So, then, gird up the loins of your mind; be sober; come to a final decision to place your hope on the grace which is going to be brought to you at the revealing of Jesus Christ.

PETER has been talking about the greatness and the glory to which the Christian may look forward; but the Christian can never be lost in dreams of the future; he must always be virile in the battle of the present. So Peter sends out three challenges to his people.

(i) He tells them *to gird up the loins of their mind.* This is a deliberately vivid phrase. In the east men wore long flowing robes which hindered fast progress or strenuous action. Round the waist they wore a broad belt or girdle; and when strenuous action was necessary they shortened the long flowing robe by pulling it up within the belt in order to give them freedom of movement. The English equivalent of the phrase would be to roll up one's sleeves, or to take off one's jacket to the task. Here, then, Peter is telling his people that they must be ready for the most strenuous mental endeavour. They must never be content with a flabby and unexamined faith; they must set to and think things out and think them through. They must never be content with an easy and superficial acceptance of the faith. They must think it out. It may be that they will have to discard some things. It may be that they will make mistakes. But that with which they are left will be theirs in such a way that nothing and nobody can ever take it away from them.

(ii) He tells them *to be sober*. The Greek word, like the English word, can have two meanings. It can mean that they must refrain from drunkenness in the literal sense of the term; and it can also mean that they must be steady, steadfast, solid in their minds. They must neither become intoxicated with intoxicating liquor or with intoxicating thoughts; they must preserve a sound, solid, balanced judgment. It is easy for the Christian to be carried away with this, that, and the next sudden enthusiasm, to have a mind which becomes readily intoxicated with the latest fashion and the newest craze. Peter is appealing to them to maintain the essential steadiness of the man who knows what he believes.

(iii) He tells them *to set their hope on the grace which is going to be given to them when Jesus Christ comes*. It is the great characteristic of the Christian that he lives in hope; and because he lives in hope he can endure the trials of the present. Any man can endure present struggle, and present effort, and present toil, if he is certain that it is all leading somewhere. That is the way in which the athlete accepts his training and the student his study. The effort and the discipline and the toil become meaningful because of that to which they lead. So, for the Christian the best is always still to come. The Christian can live with gratitude for all the mercies of the past, with resolution to meet the challenge of the present, and with the certain hope that in Christ the best is yet to be.

THE CHRISTLESS LIFE AND THE CHRIST-FILLED LIFE

I Peter I: 14-25

Be obedient children. Do not continue to live a life which matches the desires of the days of your former ignorance, but show yourselves holy in all your conduct of life, as He who called you is holy, because it stands written: " You must be holy, because I am holy." If you address as Father Him who judges each man according to his work with complete impartiality, conduct yourselves with reverence throughout the time of your sojourn in this world; for you know that it was not by perishable things, by silver or gold, that you were rescued from the futile way of life which you learned from your fathers, but it was by the precious blood of Christ, as of a lamb without blemish and without spot. It was before the creation of the world that He was predestined to His work; it is at the end of the ages that He has appeared, for the sake of you who through Him believe in God, who raised Him from the dead and gave Him glory, so that your faith and hope might be in God. Now that you have purified your souls by obedience to the truth—a purification that must issue in a brotherly love that is sincere—love each other heartily and steadfastly, for you have been reborn, not of mortal but of immortal seed, through the living and abiding word of God, for, " All flesh is like grass, and its glory is like the flower of the grass. The grass withers and its flower fades; but the word of the Lord lasts for ever." And that is the word, the good news of which was brought to you.

THERE are three great lines of approach in this passage, and we shall look at them one by one.

I.—JESUS CHRIST REDEEMER AND LORD

This passage has great things to say about Jesus Christ as Redeemer and Lord.

(i) Jesus Christ is the Emancipator, through whom men are delivered from the bondage of sin and death. He is the Lamb without blemish and without spot (verse 19). When Peter spoke like that of Jesus, his mind was going back to two Old Testament pictures. He was going back to *Isaiah* 53, with its picture of the Suffering Servant, through whose suffering the people were saved and healed. And above all he was going back to the picture of the Passover Lamb (*Exodus* 12: 5). On that for ever memorable night when they left the slavery of Egypt, the children of Israel were bidden to take a lamb and to slay it and to mark their doorposts with its blood; and, when the angel of death saw the blood of the lamb on that door post as he went throughout the land slaying the first-born sons of the Egyptians, he would pass over that house and it would be safe. In that picture of the Passover Lamb there are the twin thoughts of emancipation from slavery and deliverance from death. No matter how we interpret it, the basic fact remains that it cost the life and death of Jesus Christ to liberate men from their bondage to sin and to death, and to give them life and to bring them back to God.

(ii) Jesus Christ is the eternal purpose of God. It was before the creation of the world that He was predestined for the work which was given Him to do (verse 20). Here is a great thought. It is a thought which is repeated in *Revelation* 13: 8, where we read of " the lamb slain from the foundation of the world." There is a thought of infinite preciousness here. Sometimes we tend to think of God as first Creator and then Redeemer. We think of God as having created the world, and then, when things went wrong, finding a way to rescue the world through Jesus Christ. But here we have the tremendous vision of a God who was Redeemer *before* He was Creator. God's redeeming power and purpose, God's redeeming love is not an emergency measure to which God was compelled when things went wrong. God's redeeming purpose goes back before creation. God is Redeemer as eternally as He is Creator. His love is as timeless as His power.

(iii) But Peter here has a connection of thought which is universal in the New Testament. Jesus Christ is not only the Lamb who was slain; He is the resurrected and triumphant one to whom God gave glory. The New Testament thinkers seldom separate the Cross and the Resurrection; they seldom think of the *sacrifice* of Christ without thinking of the *triumph* of Christ. Edward Rogers, in his book *That they might have Life*, tells us that on one occasion he went very carefully through the whole story of the Passion and the Resurrection in order to find a way to represent it dramatically, and after that detailed study he began to have a certain conviction. " I began to feel," he writes, " that there was something subtly and tragically wrong in any emphasis on the agony of the Cross which dimmed the brightness of the Resurrection, any suggestion that it was endured pain rather than overcoming love which secured man's salvation." He asks where the eyes of the Christian turn at the beginning of the season of Lent. What do we dominantly see? " Is it the darkness that covered the earth at noon, swirling round the pain and anguish of the Cross? Or is it the dazzling, mysterious early-morning brightness that shone from an empty tomb? " He then goes on to say, " There are forms of most earnest and devoted evangelical preaching and theological writing which convey the impression that somehow the Crucifixion has overshadowed the Resurrection and that the whole purpose of God in Christ was completed on Calvary. The truth, which is obscured only at grave spiritual peril, is that the Crucifixion cannot be interpreted and understood save in the light of the Resurrection."

Through His death Jesus emancipated men from the bondage to slavery and death; but through His Resurrection He gives to men a life which is as glorious and indestructible as His own life. Through this triumphant Resurrection we have faith and hope in God (verse 21).

Here in this passage we see Jesus the great liberator and emancipator, at the cost of the sacrifice of His life, and at the price of the Cross on Calvary. Here we see Jesus the eternal redeeming purpose of God, a redeeming purpose which is older than time. Here we see Jesus the triumphant victor over death and the glorious Lord of life, the giver of life which death cannot touch, and the bringer of hope which nothing can take away.

2.—THE CHRISTLESS LIFE

In this passage Peter picks out three characteristics of the Christless life, three characteristics of life within the world, before Christ enters into life.

(i) It is the life of *ignorance* (verse 14). The pagan world was always haunted by the unknowability of God; at best men could but guess and grope after the mystery of God. " It is hard," said Plato, " to investigate and to find the framer and the father of the universe; and, if one did find him, it would be impossible to express him in terms which all could understand." Even for the philosopher to find God is difficult; and for the ordinary man to understand Him is impossible. Aristotle spoke of God as the supreme cause, by all men dreamed of, and by no man known. The ancient world did not so much doubt that there was a God or gods as it believed that such gods as there were were quite unknowable, and were totally uninterested in the men and in the universe. In a world without Christ God was mystery and power, but never love. There was no one to whom men could raise their hands for help or their eyes for hope.

(ii) It is the life which is *dominated by desire* (verse 14).
As we read the records of the social history of that world
into which Christianity came we cannot but be astonished
and appalled at the sheer fleshliness of life within it. It
was a world in which there was desperate poverty at the
lower end of the social scale; but at the top end of the
scale we read of banquets which cost literally thousands
of pounds, where peacocks' brains and nightingales' tongues
were served, where the Emperor Vitellius set on the table
at one banquet two thousand fish and seven thousand
birds. Chastity was forgotten. Martial speaks of a woman
who had reached her tenth husband; Juvenal of a woman
who had eight husbands in five years; and Jerome tells
us that in Rome there was one woman who was married
to her twenty-third husband, she herself being his twenty-
first wife. And both in Greece and in Rome homosexuality
was so common that unnatural vice had come to be looked
on as natural. It was a world which was mastered by desire.
Its aim was to find newer and wilder ways of gratifying
its own lusts. It was a desire-dominated civilization.

(iii) It was a life which was characterized by *futility*.
The basic trouble of ancient life was that it was not going
anywhere. Catullus writes to his Lesbia pleading for the
delights of love. He pleads with her to seize the moment
with its fleeting joys. " Suns can rise and set again; but
once our brief light is dead, there is nothing left but one
long night from which we never shall awake." If a man
was to die like a dog, why should he not live like a dog?
Life was a futile business with no pleasures to offer but the
pleasures of the moment, with a few brief years in the
light of the sun—and then an eternal nothingness. There
was nothing for which to live, and nothing for which to die.
The present must always be futile when there is no future
beyond it, and earth is always meaningless when there is
nothing on the other side of death.

As Peter sees it, the Christless life is the life of ignorance,
the life of desire, the life of futility, the life which is drained

of meaning and which has nothing left but the fleeting pleasure of the passing moment.

3.—THE CHRIST-FILLED LIFE

In this passage Peter finds three characteristics of the Christ-filled life, and for each characteristic he finds certain compelling reasons.

(i) The Christ-filled life is the life of *obedience and of holiness* (verses 14-16). To be chosen by God is to enter, not only into great privilege, but also into great responsibility. Peter remembers the ancient command which is at the very heart of all Hebrew religion. It was God's insistence to His people that they must be holy, because He, their God, is holy (*Leviticus* 11: 44; 19: 2; 20: 7, 26). The word for *holy* is *hagios*; and the root meaning of *hagios* is *different*. That which is *hagios* is *different* from ordinary things. The Temple is *hagios* because it is different from other buildings; the Sabbath is *hagios* because it is different from other days; the Christian is *hagios* because he is different from other men. The Christian is God's man by God's choice. He is chosen for a task in the world, and for a destiny in eternity. He is chosen to live for God in time, and with God in eternity. In the world he must obey the law of God, and reproduce the life of God. The Christian has been chosen by God, and, therefore, in his life there must be something of the purity of God and in his action there must be something of the love of God. There is laid on the Christian the task of being different.

(ii) The Christ-filled life is the life of *reverence* (verses 17-21). Reverence is the attitude of mind of the man who is always aware that he is in the presence of God. It is the attitude of the man who speaks every word and who performs every action and who lives every moment conscious of God. In these four verses Peter picks out four reasons for this Christian reverence. (*a*) The Christian is a sojourner in this world. Life for him is lived in the shadow of eternity; he thinks all the time, not only of where he is, but also of where he is going. His judgments are made, not in the light of the moment, but in the light of eternity. (b) He is going to God; true, he can call God Father, but that very God whom he calls Father is also the God who judges ever man with strict impartiality. The Christian is a man for whom there is a day of reckoning. He is a man with a destiny to win or to lose. Life in this world becomes of tremendous importance because it is leading to the life beyond. (c) The Christian must live life in reverence, because life cost so much. It cost nothing less than the life and death of Jesus Christ. Since, then, life is a thing of such surpassing value, it cannot be wasted, or thrown away; it must be used as a precious thing. No honourable man squanders that which is of infinite human worth. (d) The Christian cannot squander a life which was bought at the price of the death of the Son of God. There is an incalculable obligation upon a man whose life cost so much.

(iii) The Christ-filled life is the life of *brotherly love*. It must issue in a love for the brethren which is sincere and hearty and steadfast. The Christian is a man who is reborn, not of mortal, but of immortal seed. That may mean either of two things. It may mean that the remaking of the Christian is due to no human agency, but to the agency of God. It may be another way of saying what John said when he spoke of those " who were born, not of blood, nor of the will of the flesh, but of God " (*John* 1: 13). More likely it means that the Christian is remade by the entry into him of the seed of the word, and the picture is the picture of the Parable of the Sower and the seed which is the word (*Matthew* 13: 1-9). The quotation which Peter makes is from *Isaiah* 40: 6-8, and it is the second meaning which fits that better. However we take it, the meaning is that the Christian is reborn and remade. Because he is reborn, the life of God is in him. The great characteristic of the life of God is love, and the Christian in his life must show that love of God for men.

The Christian is the man who lives the Christ-filled life, lives the life that is different; the life that never forgets the infinity of its obligation; the life which is made beautiful by the love of the God who gave it birth.

WHAT TO LOSE AND WHAT TO YEARN FOR

1 *Peter* 2: 1-3

Strip off, therefore, all the evil of the heathen world and all deceitfulness, acts of hypocrisy and feelings of envy, and all gossiping disparagements of other people, and, like newly-born babes, yearn for the unadulterated milk of the word, so that by it you may grow up until you reach salvation. You are bound to do this, if you have tasted that the Lord is kind.

No Christian can stay the way he is; and here Peter urges his people to have done with the evil things, and to set their hearts on that which alone can nourish life.

There are things which must be *stripped off*. The word (*apothesthai*) is a vivid word; it is the word for *stripping off* one's clothes. There are things of which the Christian must divest himself, as he would strip off a soiled and polluted garment.

He must strip off *all the evil of the heathen world;* the word is *kakia;* it is the most general word for evil and wickedness; it includes all the wicked ways of the heathen and the Christless world. The other words are illustrations and manifestations of this *kakia;* and it is to be noted that they are all sins and faults of character which would hurt and injure the great characteristic Christian virtue of brotherly love. There can be no brotherly love so long as these evil things exist.

There is *deceitfulness* (*dolos*). *Dolos* is the two-facedness, the trickery, the conscious deception of the man who is out to deceive others to attain his own ends. *Dolos* is the vice of the man whose motives are always adulterated and never pure.

There is *hypocrisy (hupokrisis)*. In Greek the word for *hypocrite* is *hupokritēs*. It is a word with a curious history. It is the noun from the verb *hupokrinesthai* which means *to answer*; a *hupokritēs* began by being an *answerer*. The next move that the word makes is that it comes to mean an *actor*, the man who takes part in the question and answer of the stage. It then comes to mean a *hypocrite* in the bad sense of the word, a man who all the time is acting a part, a man who all the time is concealing his real motives, a man who meets you with a face which is very different from his heart, and with words which are very different from his real feelings. The hypocrite is the man who may well enter the Church from the wrong motives, and whose alleged Christian profession is for his own profit and prestige, and not for the service and for the glory of Christ.

There is *envy (phthonos)*. It may well be said that envy is the last sin to die. It reared its ugly head even in the apostolic band. The other ten were envious of James and John, when these two had seemed to steal a march upon them in the matter of precedence in the coming Kingdom (*Mark* 10: 41). Even at the last supper the disciples were disputing about who should occupy the seats of greatest honour (*Luke* 22: 24). So long as self remains active within a man's heart there will be envy in his life. E. G. Selwyn calls envy " the constant plague of all voluntary organisations, not least religious organisations." C. E. B. Cranfield says that " we do not have to be engaged in what is called ' church work ' very long to discover what a perennial source of trouble envy is." Envy can only die when self dies.

There is *gossiping disparagement (katalalia)*. *Katalalia* is a word with a quite definite flavour. It means *evil-speaking*; it is almost always the fruit of envy in the heart; and it usually takes place when the victim of it is not there to defend himself. There is nothing so attractive as listening to spicy gossip, unless it be repeating the slanderous and the malicious tale. Disparaging gossip is something which everyone deplores, and which everyone admits to be wrong, and which at the same time almost everyone enjoys; and yet there is nothing more productive of trouble and of heartbreak, and nothing which is so destructive of brotherly love and Christian unity.

These, then, are the things which the reborn man must strip off, for, if he continues to allow them to have a grip upon his life, the unity of the brethren cannot but be injured and destroyed.

THAT ON WHICH TO SET THE HEART

I Peter 2: 1-3 (continued)

BUT there is something on which the Christian must set his heart. He must yearn for *the unadulterated milk of the word*. This is a phrase about the meaning of which there is some difficulty. The difficulty is with the word *logikos* which with the Authorized Version we have translated *of the word*. The Revised Version translates it *spiritual*, and in the margin gives the alternative translation *reasonable*. Moffatt has *spiritual*, as has the American Revised Standard Version.

The word, as we have said, is *logikos*. This is the Greek adjective from the noun *logos*. The difficulty is that there are three perfectly possible translations of this.

(a) *Logos* is the great Stoic word for the reason which guides the universe, the God who is behind and in and through all things. *Logikos* is a favourite Stoic word and it describes that which has to do with this divine reason which is the ruler and the governor of all things. If we think that the word comes from this connection, then clearly *spiritual* is the meaning.

(b) *Logos* is the normal Greek word for *mind* or *reason*; therefore, the adjective *logikos* does often mean *reasonable or intelligent*. It is in that way that the Authorized Version translates the word in *Romans* 12: 1, where it speaks of our *reasonable* service.

(c) *Logos* is the Greek for *word*, and *logikos* means *belonging to the word*. This is the sense in which the Authorized Version takes the word, and we think that it is entirely correct. Peter has just been talking about the word of God which lives and abides for ever (I *Peter* 1: 23-25). It is the word of God which is in his mind; and we think that what Peter means here is that the Christian must desire with his whole heart the nourishment which comes from the word of God, for by that nourishment he can thrive and grow up until he reaches salvation itself. In face of all the evil of the heathen world the Christian must strengthen his soul and his life with the pure food of the word of God.

This food of the word is *unadulterated* (*adolos*). That is to say, there is not the slightest admixture of anything evil in it. The word *adolos* is an almost technical word to describe corn that is entirely free from any chaff or dust or useless or harmful matter. In all human wisdom there is some admixture of that which is either useless or harmful; the word of God alone is altogether good.

The Christian is to yearn for this milk of the word; the word for *yearn* is *epipothein*, and it is a strong word; it is the word which is used for the hart *panting after* the waterbrooks (*Psalm* 42: 1), and for the Psalmist *longing* for the salvation of the Lord (*Psalm* 119: 174). For the sincere Christian, to study God's word is not a labour but a delight, for he knows that therein his heart will find the nourishment for which it longs.

The metaphor of the Christian as a babe, and the word of God as the milk whereby he is nourished, is common in the New Testament. Paul thinks of himself as the nurse who cares for the infant Christians of Thessalonica (I *Thessalonians* 2: 7). He thinks of himself as feeding the Corinthians with milk for they are not yet at the stage of meat (I *Corinthians* 3: 2); and the writer of the Letter to the Hebrews blames his people that they are still at the infant stage of milk when they should have gone on to maturity (*Hebrews* 5: 12; 6: 2). To symbolize the rebirth of baptism, in the early Church the newly baptized Christian was clothed in white robes, and sometimes he was fed with milk as if he was a little child. It is this nourishment with the milk of the word which makes a Christian grow up and grow on until he reaches salvation.

Peter finishes this introduction with an allusion from *Psalm* 34: 8. " You are bound to do this," he writes, " if you have tasted the kindness of God." Here is something of the greatest significance. The fact that God is gracious and kind is not an excuse for us to do as we like and to trust to God to overlook it; it is an obligation to toil upwards and onwards to deserve that graciousness and that love which have been so kind to us. The kindness of God is not an excuse for laziness in the Christian life; it is the greatest of all incentives to effort.

THE NATURE AND FUNCTION OF THE CHURCH

I *Peter* 2: 4-10

Come to Him, the living stone, rejected by men, but chosen and precious with God, and, be yourselves, like living stones, built into a spiritual house, until you become a holy priesthood, to offer spiritual sacrifices, which are well-pleasing to God through Jesus Christ; for there is a passage in Scripture which says, " Behold, I place in Sion a stone, chosen, a cornerstone, precious, and he who believes in Him shall not be put to shame." So, then, there is preciousness in that stone to you who believe; but, to those who disbelieve, the stone which the builders rejected has become the headstone of the corner, and a stone over which they will stumble, and a rock over which they will trip. They stumble because they disobey the word—a fate for which they were appointed. But you are a chosen race, a royal priesthood, a people dedicated to God, a nation for Him specially to possess,

that you might tell forth the excellencies of Him,
who called you out of darkness into His glorious light,
you, who were once not a people, and who are now the
people of the Lord, you who were once without
mercy, and have now found mercy.

IN this passage Peter sets before us the nature and the
function of the Church. There is so much in it that we
propose to divide it into four sections.

I.—THE STONE WHICH THE BUILDERS REJECTED

This passage makes much of the idea of the *stone*. In it
three Old Testament passages are symbolically used. Let
us look at them one by one.

(i) The beginning of the whole matter goes back to the
words of Jesus Himself. One of the most revealing and
illuminating parables which Jesus ever told is the Parable
of the Wicked Husbandmen. In that parable Jesus told
how the wicked husbandmen killed servant after servant
and in the end even murdered the son. He was showing
men how the nation of Israel had again and again refused
to listen to the prophets, and had persecuted them, and
how this refusal was to reach its climax with His own death.
But beyond the death He saw the triumph, and He told
of that triumph in words taken from the *Psalms*: " The
stone which the builders rejected is become the head of the
corner; this was the Lord's doing and it is marvellous
in our eyes (*Matthew* 21: 42; *Mark* 12: 10; *Luke* 20: 17).
That is a quotation from *Psalm* 118: 22. In the original
it is a reference to the nation of Israel itself. A. K. Kirk-
patrick writes of it: " Israel is ' the head corner-stone.'
The powers of the world flung it aside as useless, but God
destined it for the most honourable and important place in
the building of His kingdom in the world. The words
express Israel's consciousness of its mission and destiny
in the purpose of God." So Jesus took these words and
applied them to Himself. It looked as if He was utterly
rejected by men; but in the purpose of God He was the

corner-stone of the edifice of the Kingdom, honoured above all.

(ii) In the Old Testament there are other references to this symbolic stone; and the early Christian writers discovered them and used them for their purposes. The first of these other references is in *Isaiah* 28: 16. In the Authorized Version that passage reads: " Therefore, thus saith the Lord God, Behold I lay in Sion for a foundation a stone, a tried stone, a precious stone, a sure foundation; he that believeth shall not make haste. " Again the reference is to the nation of Israel. The sure and certain and precious stone is God's own unfailing relationship to His people, a relationship which was to end in the coming of the Messiah. So once again the early Christian writers took this passage, and applied it to Jesus Christ, and thought of Him as this precious and immovable foundation stone of God.

(iii) The second of the other passages is also from *Isaiah*. In the Authorized Version it reads: " Sanctify the Lord of Hosts Himself; and let Him be your fear and let Him be your dread. And He shall be for a sanctuary; but for a stone of stumbling and a rock of offence to both the houses of Israel, for a gin and for a snare to the inhabitants of Jerusalem " (*Isaiah* 8: 13, 14). The meaning of this passage is that God was offering His lordship to the people of Israel; and that to those who accepted Him He would become a sanctuary and a salvation, but to those who rejected Him He would become a terror and a destruction. So again the early Christian writers took this passage and applied it to Jesus. To those who accept Him Jesus is Saviour and Friend; to those who reject Him He is judgment and condemnation.

(iv) For the understanding of the thought of this passage, we have to add a New Testament passage to these Old Testament passages. It is hardly possible that Peter could speak and think in terms of Jesus as the corner-stone and of Christians as being built into a spiritual house, united in Him, without thinking of Jesus' own words to Himself. When Peter made his great confession of faith at Caesarea Philippi, Jesus said to him, " Thou art Peter, and on this rock I will build my Church " (*Matthew* 16: 18). It is on the faith of the loyal believer that the Church is built; the believer is like a brick in the edifice of the Church, built by faith into Jesus Christ.

These, then, are the origins of the pictures in this passage.

2.—THE NATURE OF THE CHURCH

From this passage we learn three things about the very nature of the Church.

(i) The Christian is likened to a living stone, and the Church is likened unto a living edifice into which he is built (verse 5). Clearly that means that *Christianity is community*. The individual Christian only finds his true place when he is built into the edifice of the Church. " Solitary religion " is ruled out as an impossibility. C. E. B. Cranfield writes: " The free-lance Christian, who would be a Christian but is too superior to belong to the visible Church upon earth in one of its forms, is simply a contradiction in terms."

There is a famous story from Sparta. A Spartan king boasted to a visiting monarch about the walls of Sparta. The visiting monarch looked around and he could see no walls. He said to the Spartan king, " Where are these walls about which you speak and boast so much? " The Spartan king pointed at his bodyguard of magnificent Spartan troops. " These," he said, " are the walls of Sparta, and every man of them a brick."

Now, the point is quite clear. So long as a brick lies by itself it is useless. It only becomes of use when it is built into a building. That is why it was made; and it is in being built into a building that it realizes its function and the reason for its existence. It is so with the individual Christian. To realize his destiny he must not remain alone, but must be built into the fabric and edifice of the Church.

Suppose that in time of war a man says, " I wish to serve my country and to defend her from her enemies." If he tries to carry out that resolution alone, he can do nothing. He can only do so by entering into the forces and the army of his country. If a man is going to defend or support any great cause, he must associate himself with those who are like-minded with himself. It is so with the Church. Individualistic Christianity is not Christianity; Christianity is community within the fellowship of the Church.

(ii) Christians are a holy priesthood (verse 5). There are two great characteristics of the priest.

(a) The priest is the man who himself has access to God and whose task it is to bring others to God. In the ancient world this access to God was the privilege of the few, the professional priests, and in particular of the High Priest. He alone could enter into the Holy of Holies and into the nearer presence of God. But, through Jesus Christ the new and living way, that access of God is the privilege of every Christian, however simple and unlettered he may be. Further, the Latin word for priest is *pontifex*, which means a *bridge-builder*; the priest is the man who builds the bridge for others to come to God; and the Christian has the duty and the privilege of bringing others to that Saviour whom he himself has found and loves.

(b) The priest is the man who brings an offering to God. The Christian also must continuously bring his offerings to God. Under the old dispensation the offerings which were brought were animal sacrifices; but the sacrifices of the Christian are *spiritual* sacrifices. The Christian makes his *work* an offering to God. Everything he does is done for God; and, when that is so, even the meanest task is clad with glory. The Christian makes his *worship* an offering to God; and, when that happens, the worship of God's house becomes, not a burden and a weariness, but a joy and a privilege. It is not something to be pushed through, but something in which the best must be brought to God.

The Christian makes *himself* an offering to God. " Present your bodies," said Paul, " a living sacrifice to God " (*Romans* 12: 1). That which God desires most of all is the love of our hearts and the service of our lives. That is the perfect Christian sacrifice which every Christian must make.

(iii) The function of the Church is *to tell forth the excellencies* of God. That is to say, the function of the Church is to witness to men concerning the mighty acts of God. To put that much more simply and much more personally, the function of the Christian is to tell others about what God has done for his soul. By his very life, even more than by his words, the Christian is a witness of what God in Christ has done for him.

3.—THE GLORY OF THE CHURCH

In verse 10 we read of the things to which the Christian is a witness, the things which God has done for his soul.

(i) God has called the Christian out of darkness into His glorious light. *The Christian is called out of darkness into light.* When a man comes to know Jesus Christ, he comes to know *God*. No longer does he need to guess and to grope. No longer does he need to think of God as the distant, the remote and the unknowable. " He who has seen me," said Jesus, " has seen the Father " (*John* 14: 9). In Jesus is the light of the knowledge of God. When a man comes to know Jesus Christ, he comes to know *goodness*. In Christ he has a standard by which all actions and motives may be tested. He knows what real goodness is; the perfect pattern and the perfect ideal are disclosed to him in Jesus Christ. When a man comes to know Jesus Christ, he comes to know the *way*. Life is no longer a trackless road without a star to guide. Life is no longer a bewildering maze in which he does not know where to go and what to do. In Christ the way becomes clear and plain. When a man comes to know Jesus Christ, he comes to know *power*. It would be little use to God to know God without the power to serve God. It would be little use to know goodness, and yet to be helpless to attain to it. It would be little use to see the right way, and to be quite unable to take it. In Jesus Christ there is the vision *and* the power.

(ii) God has made the people who were not a people into the people of God. Here Peter is quoting from *Hosea* I: 6, 9, 10; 2: I, 23). This means that *the Christian is called out of insignificance into significance*. It continually happens in this world that a man's greatness lies not in himself but in that which has been given him to do. His greatness is in his task. The Christian's greatness lies in the fact that God has chosen him to be his man and to do his work in the world. No Christian can be ordinary, for every Christian is a man of God.

(iii) *The Christian is called out of no mercy into mercy.* The great characteristic of non-Christian religion is the fear of God. The Christian is the man who in Jesus Christ has discovered the love of God, and who knows that he need no longer fear God, because it is well with his soul.

4.—THE FUNCTION OF THE CHURCH

In verse 9 Peter uses a whole series of phrases which are a summary of the functions of the Church. He calls the Christians " a chosen race, a royal priesthood, a people dedicated to God, a nation for Him specially to possess." Peter is steeped in the Old Testament, and these phrases are all great description of the people of Israel. They come from two main sources. In *Isaiah* 43: 21 Isaiah hears God say, " This people have I formed for myself." But, even more, in *Exodus* 19: 5, 6, the voice of God is heard: " Now, therefore, if ye will obey my voice indeed, and keep my covenant, then ye shall be a peculiar treasure unto me above all people; for all the earth is mine: and ye shall be unto me a kingdom of priests, and an holy nation." The great promises which God made to His people Israel are being fulfilled to the Church, which is the new Israel, the Israel of God. Everyone of these titles is full of meaning.

(i) Christians are *a chosen people*. Here we are back to the covenant idea. *Exodus* 19: 5, 6 is from the passage which describes how God entered into His covenant with His people Israel. In the covenant God offered a special relationship with Himself to the people Israel. He approached them with the spontaneous offer that they should be specially His people, and that He would be uniquely their God. But that whole relation depended on the people of Israel accepting the conditions of the covenant and keeping the law. That relation would only hold, " if ye shall obey my voice, and keep my covenant " (*Exodus* 19: 5). From this, then, we learn that the Christian is chosen for three things. (*a*) He is chosen for *privilege*. In Jesus Christ there is offered to him a new and intimate relationship of fellowship with God. God has become his friend, and he has become God's friend. (*b*) He is chosen for *obedience*. That whole relationship depends on obedience. The privilege brings with it the responsibility. The Christian is chosen in order that he may become the obedient child of God. He is not chosen to do as he likes; he is chosen to do as God likes. His privilege is not to obey his own will, but to obey the will of God. (*c*) He is chosen for *service*. His honour is that he is the servant of God. His privilege is that he will be used for the purposes of God. But he can only be so used when he brings to God the obedience which God desires. Chosen for privilege, chosen for obedience, chosen for service—the three great facts go hand, in hand.

(ii) Christians are *a royal priesthood*. We have already seen that that means that every Christian has the right of access and of approach to God; and that every Christian must offer his work, his worship and himself to God.

(iii) Christians are what the Authorized Version calls *a holy nation*. The word for *holy* is *hagios*, and, we have already seen that the basic meaning of this word *hagios* is *different*. The Christian has been chosen that he may be different from other men. That difference lies in the fact that he is dedicated to God's will and to God's service. Other people may follow the standards of the world, but for him the only law is the standard of God and the will of God. A man need not even start on the Christian way unless he realizes that it will compel him to be different from other people.

(iv) Christians are *a people for God specially to possess*. It frequently happens that the value of a thing lies in the fact that some one has possessed it. A very ordinary thing acquires a new value, if it has been possessed by some famous person. In any museum we will find quite ordinary things—clothes, a walking-stick, a pen, books, pieces of furniture—which are only of value because they were once possessed and used by some great person. It is the ownership which gives them worth. It is so with the Christian. The Christian may be a very ordinary person, but he acquires a new value and dignity and greatness because he belongs to God. The greatness of the Christian lies in the fact that he is God's.

REASONS FOR RIGHT LIVING

I *Peter* 2: II, I2

> Beloved, I urge you, as strangers and sojourners, to abstain from the fleshly desires which carry on their campaign against the soul. Make your conduct amongst the Gentiles fine, so that in every matter in which they slander you as evil-doers, they may see from your fine deeds what you are really like, and glorify God on the day when He will visit the earth.

THE basic commandment in this passage is that the Christian should *abstain from fleshly lusts*. It is of the greatest importance that we should see what Peter means by this. The phrases *sins of the flesh*, and *fleshly lusts* have become much narrowed in their meaning in modern usage. When we speak of *sins of the flesh* we usually mean sexual sin; but in the New Testament *sins of the flesh* are much wider than that. Paul gives us his list of the sins of the flesh in *Galatians* 5: 19-21, and the list includes " adultery, fornication, uncleanness, lasciviousness, idolatry, witchcraft, hatred, variance, emulations, wrath, strife, seditions, heresies, envyings, murders, drunkenness, revellings and such like." Clearly, there are far more than *bodily* sins here; the sins of the flesh include far more than the grosser sins of sex and of the body and the appetites of the body. In the New Testament the word *flesh* stands for far more than the body and the physical nature of man; it stands for *human nature apart from God*; it means unredeemed and unregenerate human nature; it means Christless human nature; it means life lived without the standards, without the help, without the grace and without the influence of Christ. *Fleshly lusts* and *sins of the flesh*, therefore, include, not only the grosser sins, but all the sins of pride and envy and malice and hatred and false and evil thinking which are characteristic of sinful and fallen human nature. From these sins and desires the Christian must abstain. As Peter sees it, there are two reasons why the Christian must abstain from these sins.

(i) The Christian must abstain from these sins because he is a stranger and a pilgrim. The words are *paroikos* and *parepidēmos*. They are quite common Greek words and they describe someone who is resident in a country which is not his own; they describe someone who is only temporarily resident in a place, and whose home is somewhere else; they describe someone who is not a citizen of the place in which at the moment he happens to be, but whose citizenship is of another country. They are used to describe the patriarchs in their wanderings, and especially to describe Abraham who went out not knowing whither he went and whose search was for the city whose maker and builder is God (*Hebrews* 11: 9, 13). They are used to describe the children of Israel when they were slaves and strangers in the land of Egypt, before they entered into the Promised Land (*Acts* 13: 7).

So, then, these words give us two great truths about the Christian. (*a*) There is a real sense in which the Christian is a stranger in the world; and, because he is a stranger in the world, he cannot accept the world's laws and the world's ways and the world's standards. Others may accept these laws and standards; but the Christian is a citizen of the Kingdom of God, and it is by the laws of that Kingdom that he must guide and direct his life. The Christian lives upon earth, and he must take his full share of responsibility for living upon earth, but his citizenship is in heaven, and it is by the laws of heaven that he must live. (*b*) The Christian is a resident upon earth, but he is not a permanent resident upon earth. He is a man who is on the way to the country which is beyond. He must therefore, do nothing which would keep him from reaching his ultimate goal. He must never become so entangled in the world that he cannot escape from its grip. He must never adopt courses of action which so affect his being and personality and character that he is unfit for his pilgrimage. He must never so soil himself as to unfit himself to enter into the presence of the holy God to whom he is going.

The Christian must abstain from fleshly lusts because his law is the law of the Kingdom, and his goal is the eternal joy which is in the presence of God.

THE GREATEST ANSWER AND DEFENCE

I *Peter* 2: 11, 12 (*continued*)

(ii) But there was for Peter another and even more practical reason why the Christian must abstain from fleshly lusts. The early Church was a Church under fire. Slanderous and untrue charges were continually being made against the Christians; and the only effective way to refute these charges was to live so lovely a life that they would be proved to be obviously untrue. To modern ears the Authorized Version can be a little misleading, although in the seventeenth century, when it was first made, it was perfectly accurate. It speaks about " having your conversation honest among the Gentiles." To modern ears that sounds as if it meant that the Christian must always speak the truth, and that in his words and in his talk with others he must never be guilty of dishonesty. The word translated *conversation* is *anastrophē*, which means a man's *whole* conduct, not simply his words and talk. That is, in fact, what *conversation* did mean in the seventeenth century; it means a man's whole conduct and his whole way of life. The word translated *honest* is *kalos*; in Greek there are two words for *good*. There is *agathos*, which simply means good in quality; and there is this word *kalos*, which means not only *good*, but also *lovely*, fine, attractive, winsome. That is what *honestus* means in Latin; it means *fine, gracious, fair to look upon*. So, what Peter is saying is that the Christian must make his whole way of life so lovely and so fair and so good to look upon that the slanders of his heathen enemies may be undeniably demonstrated to be false.

Here, then, is the great timeless truth. The best argument for Christianity is a real Christian; and, therefore, whether we like it or not, every Christian is an advertisement for Christianity. By his life he either commends Christianity to others, or he makes others think less of Christianity. The strongest missionary force in the world is a Christian life.

In the early Church this demonstration of the loveliness of the Christian life was supremely necessary, because the heathen deliberately cast their slanders on the Christian Church. Let us see what some of these slanders were.

(i) Christianity began with the initial disadvantage of being closely connected with the Jews. By race Jesus was a Jew; Paul was a Jew; Christianity was cradled in

Judaism; and inevitably many of its early converts were Jews. It was connected in the heathen mind with the Jews, and for a time it was, indeed, regarded merely as a sect and form of Judaism. Antisemitism is no new thing; the Jews have always been a hated people. Friedlander gives a selection of the slanders which were launched and repeated against the Jews in his *Roman Life and Manners under the Early Empire*. " According to Tacitus they (the Jews) taught their proselytes above all to despise the gods, to renounce their fatherland, to disregard parents, children, brothers and sisters. According to Juvenal, Moses taught the Jews not to show anyone the way, nor to guide the thirsty traveller to the spring, except he were a Jew. Apion declares that, in the reign of Antiochus Epiphanes, the Jews every year fattened a Greek, and having solemnly offered him up as a sacrifice on a fixed day in a certain forest, ate his entrails and swore eternal hostility to the Greeks. These were the things which the heathen had persuaded themselves were true about the Jews, and inevitably the Christian shared in this odium.

(ii) But, apart from these slanders which were attached to the Jews, there were slanders directed particularly against the Christians themselves. The Christians were accused of cannibalism. This accusation took its rise from a perversion of the words of the Last Supper, " This is my body," " This cup is the new covenant in my blood." So the Christians were accused of killing and eating a child at their feasts. The Christians were accused of immorality and even of incest. This accusation took its rise from the fact that the Christians called their meeting the *Agapē*, the Love Feast, and the heathen perverted that name to make it mean that the Christian feasts were sensual orgies at which nameless and shameless deeds were done.

The Christians were accused of damaging trade. Such was the charge of the silversmiths of Ephesus (*Acts* 18: 21-41). They were accused of " tampering with family relationships," because often homes were, in fact, broken up when some members of the family became Christians, and others did not. They were accused of turning slaves against their masters, and Christianity indeed did give to every man a new sense of worth and dignity. They were accused of " hatred of mankind," and indeed the Christian did speak as if the world and the Church were entirely opposed to each other. Above all they were accused of disloyalty to Caesar, for no Christian would worship the Emperor's godhead, and burn his pinch of incense, and declare that Caesar was Lord, for to him Jesus Christ and no other was Lord.

Such were the charges which were directed against the Christians. To Peter there was only one way to deny these charges; and that one way was to live in such a way that the Christian life demonstrated that these charges were untrue. When Plato was told that a certain man had been making certain slanderous charges against him, his answer was: " I will live in such a way that no one will believe what he says." That was Peter's solution.

Jesus Himself had said—and doubtless the saying was in Peter's mind: " Let your light so shine before men that they may see your good works and glorify your Father who is in heaven " (*Matthew* 5: 16). This was a line of thought which the Jews knew well. In one of the books, written between the Old and the New Testaments, it is written: " If ye work that which is good, my children, both men and angels shall bless you; and God shall be glorified among the Gentiles through you, and the devil shall flee from you " (*The Testament of Naphtali* 8: 4).

The amazing fact of history is that by their lives the Christians actually did defeat the slanders of the heathen. In the early part of the third century Celsus made the most famous and the most systematic attack of all upon the Christians in which he accused them of ignorance and foolishness and superstition and all kinds of things— *but never of immorality*. In the first half of the fourth century, Eusebius, the great Church historian, could write: " But the splendour of the catholic and only true Church, which is always the same, grew in magnitude and power, and reflected its piety and simplicity and freedom, and the modesty and purity of its inspired life and philosophy to every nation both of Greeks and barbarians. At the same time the slanderous accusations which had been brought against the whole Church also vanished, and there remained our teaching alone, which has prevailed over all, and which is acknowledged to be superior to all in dignity and temperance, and in divine and philosophical doctrines. So that none of them now ventures to affix a base calumny upon our faith, or any such slander as our ancient enemies formerly delighted to utter " (Eusebius, *The Ecclesiastical History* 4.7.15). It is true that the terrors of persecution were not even then ended, for the Christian would never admit that Caesar was Lord, but the excellence of the life of the Christians had silenced for ever the calumnies and slanders against the Church.

Here is our challenge and our inspiration. It is by the loveliness of our daily life and conduct that we must commend Christianity to those who still do not believe.

THE DUTY OF THE CHRISTIAN

I Peter 2: 13-15

Submit to every human institution for the Lord's sake, whether it be to the king, who has the first place, or to governors as sent by him for the punishment of those whose deeds are evil, and the praise of those whose deeds are good, for it is the will of God that by so doing you should muzzle the ignorance of foolish men.

I.—As a Citizen

PETER now begins to look at the duty of the Christian within the different spheres of his life; and he begins with the duty of the Christian as a citizen of the country where he happens to live.

Nothing is further from the thought of the New Testament than any kind of anarchy. Jesus had said, " Render unto Caesar the things which are Caesar's; and unto God the things that are God's " (*Matthew* 22: 21). Paul was certain that those who governed the nation were sent by God, and held their responsibility from God, and that they were no terror to the man who lived an honourable life (*Romans* 13: 1-7). In the Pastoral Epistles the Christian is instructed to pray for kings and for all that are in authority (I *Timothy* 2: 2). The instruction of the New Testament is that the Christian must be a good and useful and faithful citizen of the country in which his life is set.

It has been said that fear built the cities, and that men huddled behind a wall that they might be safe. Men join themselves together, and agree to live under certain laws, in order that the good and honourable man may have peace to live his life and to do his work and to go about his business, and in order that the evil man should be restrained and controlled and kept from his evil-doing. The idea of the New Testament is that life is meant by God to be an ordered business, and that the state is divinely appointed to provide and to maintain that order.

The view of the New Testament is perfectly logical and just. The New Testament holds that a man cannot accept the privileges with which the state provides him without also accepting the responsibilities and the duties which the state demands from him. A man cannot in honour and decency take everything and give nothing.

But how are we to translate this into modern life, and into our duty as citizens today? C. E. B. Cranfield has well pointed out that there is a fundamental difference between the state in New Testament times, and the state as we know it. In New Testament times the state was *authoritarian*. The ruler was an absolute ruler; and the sole duty of the citizen was to render absolute obedience to the state and to pay taxes as the state ordained (*Romans* 13: 6, 7). Under these conditions the keynote was bound to be *subjection to the state*. But we do not live in an *authoritarian* state; we live in a *democracy*; and in a democracy something far more than unquestioning subjection and submission becomes necessary. In a democracy government is not only government *of* the people; it is also government *for* the people and *by* the people. Now the demand of the New Testament is that the Christian should fulfil his responsibility and obligation to the state. In the authoritarian state that obligation consisted solely in submission and subjection. But what is that obligation in the very different circumstances of a democracy? To put the question in another way—if subjection is the keynote of the obligation of the citizen in the authoritarian state, what is the keynote of the obligation of the citizen in the democratic state?

It is true that in any state there must be a certain subjection. As C. E. B. Cranfield puts it, there must be " a voluntary subordination of oneself to others, putting the interest and welfare of others above one's own, preferring to give rather than to get, to serve rather than to be served." But in a democratic state the keynote must be not *subjection*, but *co-operation*, for in a democratic state the duty of the citizen is not only to submit to be ruled, but to take the necessary share in ruling. Hence, if the Christian is to fulfil his duty to the state, he must take his part in the government of the state; he must take his part in the local government of the town, the city, the county, the district where he stays; he must take his part in the life and work and administration of the trade union or association connected with his trade, craft, or profession. It is, in fact, the tragedy of the modern situation that there are so few Christians who do, in fact, fulfil their obligation to the state and the society in which they live.

The Christian must clearly see and clearly remember that it is the teaching of the New Testament that he must fulfil his obligation as a citizen of his country; and he must also clearly see that, whereas under the conditions of the authoritarian state he could fulfil that obligation by submission and obedience, under the conditions of the democratic state there is laid upon him the even greater obligation of Christian co-operation in all that affects the state and its government and its administration.

It remains to say that the Christian has a higher obligation than even his obligation to the state. While he must render to Caesar the things which are Caesar's, he must also render to God the things which are God's. He must on occasion make it quite clear that he must hearken unto God rather than unto men (*Acts* 4: 19; 5: 29). It will, then, be true that there may be times when the Christian will fulfil his highest duty and obligation to the state by refusing to obey the state, and by insisting on obeying God; for, by so doing, at least he can witness to the truth, and at best he can even compel the state to take the Christian way.

THE DUTY OF THE CHRISTIAN

I *Peter* 2: 16

> You must live as free men, yet not using your freedom as a cloak for evil, but as the slaves of God.

2.—IN SOCIETY

ANY great Christian doctrine can be perverted into an excuse for evil. The doctrine of grace can be perverted into an excuse for sinning to one's heart's content. The doctrine of the love of God can be sentimentalized into a defence for breaking the law of God. The doctrine of the life to come can be perverted into a reason for neglecting life in this world. And there is no doctrine so easy to pervert as the doctrine of Christian freedom and Christian liberty.

There are hints in the New Testament that it was frequently so perverted. Paul tells the Galatians that they have been called to liberty, but they must not use that liberty as an occasion for the flesh to do as it wills (*Galatians* 5: 13). In *2 Peter* we read of those who promise others liberty and who are themselves the servants of corruption (*2 Peter* 2: 19). Even the great pagan thinkers saw quite clearly that perfect liberty is, in fact, the product of perfect obedience. Seneca said, " No one is free who is the slave of his body," and, " Liberty consists in obeying God." Cicero said, " We are the servants of the laws that we may be able to be free." Plutarch insisted that every bad man is a slave; and Epictetus declared that no bad man can ever be free.

We may put it this way. Christian freedom is always conditioned by Christian responsibility. Christian responsibility is always conditioned by Christian love. Christian love is the reflection of God's love. And, therefore, Christian liberty can rightly be summed up in Augustine's memorable phrase: " Love God, and do what you like."

The Christian is free because he is the slave of God. In God's service is our perfect freedom. Christian freedom does not mean being free to do as we like, being free to follow the dictates and the impulses and the passions of our lower nature. Christian freedom means being free to do, not as we like, but as we ought.

In this matter we have to return to the great central truth which we have already seen. *Christianity is community.* The Christian is not an isolated unit; he is not an individual and nothing else. He is a member of a community, and within that community his freedom operates. And, therefore, Christian freedom is the freedom to serve. Only in Christ is a man freed from self and sin and passion to be as good as he ought to be. Only in Christ is a man freed from selfishness and self-seeking to be as great a servant as he ought to be. Freedom comes when a man takes the yoke of Christ upon him, and when he receives Christ as king of his heart and Lord of his life.

THE LETTERS OF PETER

A SUMMARY OF CHRISTIAN DUTY

1 *Peter* 2: 17

> Honour all men; love the brotherhood; fear God; honour the king.

HERE there is what we might call a four-point summary of Christian duty.

(i) *Honour all men.* To us this may sound something which hardly needs to be said; but when Peter wrote this letter it was something which was quite new. As we shall go on to see, there were 60,000,000 slaves in the Roman Empire. Everyone of them was considered in the eyes of the law to be, not a person, but a thing, with no rights whatever. In effect, Peter is saying, " Remember the rights of human personality; remember the dignity of every man; remember that every man in this world is a person, and not a thing." It is still possible to treat people as things. An employer may treat his employees as simply so many human machines for producing so much work. Even in a welfare state, where the aim is to do so much for the physical welfare of people, there is a very real danger that people may be regarded as numbers on a form or as cards in a card index. John Lawrence in his book, *Hard Facts, A Christian Looks at the World,* says that one of the greatest needs in the welfare state is " to see through the files and forms in triplicate to God's creatures who are at the other end of the chain of organization." In other words the danger is that we fail to see men and women as persons in their own right. This matter comes nearer home. When we regard anyone as existing simply and solely to minister to our comfort, and to further our plans, we are in effect regarding them, not as persons, but as things. And the most tragic danger of all is that we may come to regard those we live with, those who are nearest and dearest to us as existing to make things comfortable for us—and that is to treat them as things.

(ii) *Love the brotherhood.* Within the Christian community this respect for every man turns to something warmer and closer; it turns to love. The dominant atmosphere of the Church must always be love. One of the truest definitions of the Church is that the Church is " the extension of the family." The Church is the larger family of God, and its bond must be love. As the Psalmist had it (*Psalm* 133: 1):

> Behold, how good a thing it is,
> And how becoming well,
> Together such as brethren are
> In unity to dwell!

(iii) *Fear God.* The writer of the proverbs has it: " The fear of the Lord is the beginning of wisdom " (*Proverbs* 1: 7). It may well be that the translation should be, not that the fear of the Lord is the *beginning* of wisdom, but that the fear of the Lord is *the principal part,* the very *foundation* of wisdom, as the margin of the Authorized Version has it. The word *fear* here does not mean terror; it means awe and reverence. It is the simple fact of life that we will never reverence men until we reverence God. It is only when God is given His proper place in the centre of things that all other things will take their proper place

(iv) *Honour the king.* Of the four injunctions of this verse this is the most amazing, for, if it was really Peter who wrote this letter, then the king in question is none other than Nero. It is the Christian teaching of the New Testament that the ruler is sent by God to preserve order among men, and that he must be respected, even when he is a Nero.

THE DUTY OF THE CHRISTIAN AS A SERVANT

I *Peter* 2: 18-25

> Servants, be subject to your masters with all respect, not only to those who are good and equitable, but

also to those who are perverse, for it is a real sign of grace when a man bears pains in unjust suffering because of his consciousness of God. It is to live like this that you were called, because Christ too suffered for us, leaving behind Him an example that we should follow in His steps. He did no sin, nor was any guile found in His mouth. When He was insulted, He did not return insult for insult. When He suffered, He uttered no threats, but He committed Himself to Him who judges justly. He Himself bore our sins in His body on the tree, that we might depart from sins and live to righteousness. With His stripes you have been healed, for you were straying away like sheep, but now you have turned to the Shepherd and Watchman of your souls.

HERE is the passage which would be relevant to by far the greatest numbers of the readers and hearers of this letter, for here Peter writes to servants and slaves, who formed by far the greatest part of the early Church. The word which Peter uses for *servants* is not *douloi*, which is the commonest and the widest word for *slaves*; it is *oiketai*; and the *oiketai* were mainly the household and the domestic slaves.

To understand the real meaning of what Peter is saying we must understand something of the nature of slavery and servitude in the time of the early Church. In the Roman Empire there were as many as 60,000,000 slaves. In very early times there had been few slaves in Rome; slavery began with Roman conquests, for slaves were originally mainly prisoners taken in war. By New Testament times, as we have said, slaves were counted by the million. It was by no means only menial tasks which were performed by slaves. Doctors, teachers, musicians, actors, secretaries, stewards were slaves. In fact, all the work of Rome was done by slaves. By this time the Roman attitude was that there was no point in being master of the world and doing one's own work. Let the slaves do that, and let the citizens live in pampered idleness. The supply of slaves would never go done. Slaves were not allowed to marry; but they cohabited; and the children born of such a partnership were the property of the master, not of the parents, just as the lambs born to the sheep belonged to the owner of the flock, and not to the sheep.

It would be quite wrong to think that the lot of slaves was always wretched and unhappy, and that they were always treated with cruelty. Many slaves were loved and trusted members of the family; but one great inescapable fact dominated the whole situation. In Roman law a slave was not a person; he was a thing; and he had absolutely no legal rights whatsoever. However well he might be treated, he remained a thing with nothing in the world to call his own, not even himself. For that reason there could be no such thing as justice where a slave was concerned. Aristotle writes, " There can be no friendship nor justice towards inanimate things; indeed, not even towards a horse or an ox, nor yet towards a slave as a slave. For master and slave have nothing in common; a slave is a living tool, just as a tool is an inanimate slave." Varro divides the instruments of agriculture into three classes—the articulate, the inarticulate and the mute, " the articulate comprising the slaves, the inarticulate comprising the cattle, and the mute comprising the vehicles." The only difference between a slave and a beast or a farmyard cart is that a slave happens to be able to speak. Peter Chrysologus sums the matter up: " Whatever a master does to a slave, undeservedly, in anger, willingly, unwillingly, in forgetfulness, after careful thought, knowingly, unknowingly, is judgment, justice and law." That is simply to say that in regard to a slave his master's will, and even his master's caprice, was the only law.

Here, then, is the dominant fact in the life of the slave, the fact that, even if he was well treated, he remained a thing, who did not possess even the elementary rights of a person, and for whom justice did not even exist.

THE PERIL OF THE NEW SITUATION

I *Peter* 2: 18-25 (*continued*)

INTO this situation there came Christianity with its message that every man is precious in the sight of God, with the good news that God loves every man. The result of this was that within the Church the social barriers were broken down. Callistus, one of the earliest bishops of Rome, was a slave, and Perpetua, the aristocrat, and Felicitas, the slave-girl, met martyrdom hand in hand. The great majority of the early Christians were humble folk, and many of them were slaves; and it was quite possible in one of the early congregations that the slave should be the president of the congregation and the master a member of it. This was a new and a revolutionary situation. It had its glory, and it had its dangers. In this passage Peter is urging the slave to be a good slave and a faithful workman; he is telling slaves to be subject to and obedient to their masters. In his mind there were two dangers.

(i) Let us suppose that both master and servant became Christians. There then arose the danger that the slave might trade and presume upon the new relationship. He might well make the new relationship an excuse for shirking his work, and for failing in his duty, and for general slackness and inefficiency. He might well work on the principle that, now that he and his master were both Christians, he could get away with anything, that discipline and punishment were abolished, and that he could pretty well do what he liked. That is a situation which is by no means completely at an end. There are still people who trade on the goodwill and the sympathy of a Christian master, and who think that the fact that both they and their employers are Christians gives them a right to dispense with discipline and punishment. But Peter is quite clear. The relationship between Christian and Christian does not abolish the relationship between man and man. The Christian must, indeed, be a better workman than anyone else. His Christianity is not a reason for claiming exemption from discipline; it should bring him under self-discipline and should make him more conscientious than anyone else.

(ii) There was always the danger that the new dignity which Christianity brought him would make the slave rebel, and seek to abolish slavery altogether. There are some students of the New Testament who are puzzled that no New Testament writer ever pleads for the abolition of slavery, or ever even says in so many words that slavery is wrong. The reason for that was quite simple. To have encouraged the slaves to rise against their masters would have been the way to sheer and speedy disaster. There had been such revolts before and they had always been quickly and savagely crushed. And, in any event, such teaching would merely have gained for Christianity the reputation of being a subversionary and revolutionary religion. There are some things which cannot happen quickly; there are some situations in which the leaven has to work; there are some situations in which premature action can lead to nothing but complete disaster, and in which haste is the surest way to delay the desired end. The leaven of Christianity had to work in the world for many generations before the abolition of slavery became a practical possibility. Peter was concerned that Christian slaves should demonstrate to the world that their Christianity did not make them disgruntled and revolutionary rebels, but that rather it made them workmen who had no need to be ashamed and who had found a new inspiration towards doing an honest day's work. It will still often happen that, when some situation cannot at the time be changed, the Christian duty is to be a Christian within that situation, and to accept what cannot be changed until the leaven has worked.

THE NEW ATTITUDE TO WORK

I *Peter* 2: 18-25 (*continued*)

BUT Christianity did not leave the matter in that merely negative form. Christianity introduced three great new principles into a man's whole attitude as a servant and as a workman.

(i) Christianity introduced a new relationship between master and man. When Paul sent the runaway slave Onesimus back to Philemon, he did not for a moment suggest that Philemon should set Onesimus free. He did not suggest that Philemon should cease to be the master and that Onesimus should cease to be the slave. What he did say was that Philemon must receive Onesimus not now as a servant, but as a brother beloved (*Philemon* 16). Christianity did not abolish social differences; it did not abolish the difference between master and servant; but it introduced a new relationship of brotherhood in which these other differences were overpassed and transformed. Where there is real brotherhood, it does not matter if you call one man master and the other servant. There is between them a bond and a relationship which transform and transcend the necessary differences which the circumstances of life in the world make necessary. The solution of the world's problems lies in the new relationship between man and man.

(ii) Christianity introduced a new attitude to work. It is the conviction of the New Testament that all work must be done for Jesus Christ. Paul writes: " Whatsoever ye do in word or deed, do all in the name of the Lord Jesus " (*Colossians* 3: 17). " Whether ye eat or drink, or whatsoever ye do, do all to the glory of God " (I *Corinthians* 10: 31). In the Christian ideal work is not done for an earthly master; work is not done for personal prestige; work is not done to make so much money; work is done for God. It is, of course, true that a man must work in order to earn a wage, and he must work to satisfy a master; but beyond that there is for the Christian the conviction that his work must be done well enough to take it and to show it to God without shame. The Christian becomes the workman of God. However humble his task may be, if that task is contributing to the sum total of human welfare, it is being done for God.

(iii) But, when these great ideals were set against the situation in the early Church—and the situation does not entirely change—one great question arose. Suppose a man is a Christian, suppose his own attitude to men is the Christian attitude, suppose his view of work is the Christian view, and then suppose that he is treated with cruelty, injustice, insult and injury—what then? When we remember the situation of the slave in the ancient world, this is precisely what was likely to happen. Peter's answer is a great answer. His answer is that that is exactly what happened to Jesus Christ. Jesus was none other than the *Suffering Servant*. Verses 21-25 are full of reminiscences and quotations of *Isaiah* 53. *Isaiah* 53, the supreme picture of the Suffering Servant of God, came to life in Jesus Christ. Jesus was without sin; yet He was insulted and He suffered; but He accepted these insults and that suffering with serene love and bore them for the sins of mankind.

In so doing He left us an example that we should follow in His steps (verse 21). The word that Peter uses for *example* is very vivid. It is the word *hupogrammos*. It is a word which comes from the way in which children were taught to write in the ancient world. *Hupogrammos* can mean two things. It can mean an *outline sketch* which the learner had to fill up and fill in. And it can mean the *copyhead of copperplate handwriting* in a writing exercise book which the child had to copy out on the lines below. Jesus gives us the copyhead which we have to copy. He gave us the pattern which we have to follow. If we have to suffer insult and injustice and injury, we have only to go through what He has already gone through. And it may be that at the back of Peter's mind there was a glimpse of a tremendous truth. That suffering of Jesus was for the sake of the sin of man; He suffered in order to bring men back to God. And it may be that, when the Christian suffers insult and injury with uncomplaining steadfastness and unfailing love, he sets such an example and shows such a life to others, that that example and that life will lead others to God. It may be that the sufferings of the Christian also can lead men to God, and can be a real and true sharing in the redemptive sufferings of Christ.

TWO PRECIOUS NAMES FOR GOD

1.—THE SHEPHERD OF THE SOULS OF MEN

1 *Peter* 2: 18-25 (*continued*)

IN the last verse of this passage and chapter we come upon two of the great and precious names for God. As the Authorized Version has it, God is the Shepherd and Bishop of our souls. These words are so precious that we must spend some time looking at each of them.

(i) God is *the Shepherd of the souls of men*. The Greek word is *poimēn*. The word *shepherd* is one of the oldest descriptions of God. The Psalmist has it in the best-loved of all the Psalms: " The Lord is my shepherd " (*Psalm* 23: 1). Isaiah has it: " He shall feed His flock like a shepherd: He shall carry the lambs with His arm, and carry them in His bosom, and shall gently lead those that are with young " (*Isaiah* 40: 11).

The great king whom God was going to send to Israel would be the shepherd of his people. Ezekiel hears the promise of God: " And I will set up one shepherd over them, and he shall feed them, even my servant David; he shall feed them, and he shall be their shepherd " (*Ezekiel* 34: 23; 37: 24).

This was the title which Jesus took to Himself, when He called Himself the Good Shepherd and when He said that the Good Shepherd lays down His life for the sheep

(*John* 10: 1-18). To Jesus the men and women who did not know God and who were waiting for what He could give them were like sheep without a shepherd (*Mark* 6: 34). And the great privilege which is given to the servant and the minister of Christ is to feed and to shepherd the flock of God (*John* 21: 16; 1 *Peter* 5: 2).

It may be difficult for those of us who live in towns and in an industrial civilization to grasp the greatness of this picture; but in the East the picture would be very vivid and very precious. It was specially so in Judaea. In Judaea there is a narrow central tableland and plateau. On either side there is danger. On the west there lie the wastes of the Shephelah; and on the east the precipices with their jagged cliffs and crags which precipitate themselves more than a thousand feet downwards to the Dead Sea. It is on the narrow tableland that the sheep graze. Grass is sparse; there are no protecting walls; and the sheep wander. The shepherd, therefore, has to be ceaselessly and sleeplessly upon the watch lest harm should come to his flock. In *The Historical Geography of the Holy Land* Sir George Adam Smith describes the shepherd of Judaea. " With us, sheep are often left to themselves; but I do not remember ever to have seen in the East a flock of sheep without a shepherd. In such a landscape as Judaea, where a day's pasture is thinly scattered over an unfenced track of country, covered with delusive paths, still frequented by wild beasts, and rolling off into the desert, the man and his character are indispensable. On some high moor, across which at night the hyenas howl, when you meet him, sleepless, far-sighted, weather-beaten, armed, leaning upon his staff, and looking out over his scattered sheep, everyone of them on his heart, you understand why the shepherd of Judaea sprang to the front in his people's history; why they gave his name to their king, and made him the symbol of providence; why Christ took him as the type of self-sacrifice."

Indeed, this word shepherd tells us most vividly of the

ceaseless vigilance and the self-sacrificing love of God for us, who are His flock. " We are His people and the sheep of His pasture " (*Psalm* 100: 3).

TWO PRECIOUS NAMES FOR GOD

2.—THE GUARDIAN OF OUR SOULS

I *Peter* 2: 18-25 (*continued*)

(ii) The Authorized Version speaks of God as the Shepherd and *Bishop* of our souls. Nowadays the word *Bishop* is an inadequate and misleading translation. In Greek the word is *episkopos*.

Episkopos in Greek is a word with a great history. In Homer's *Iliad* Hector, the great champion of the Trojans is called the *episkopos*, who, during his lifetime, guarded the city of Troy and kept safe its noble wives and infant little ones. The word *episkopos* is used of the gods who are the guardians of the treaties which men make and of the agreements to which men come, and who are the protectors of the house and home. Justice, for instance, is the *episkopos*, the overseer, who sees to it that a man shall pay the price for the wrong that he has done.

In Plato's *Laws* the Guardians of the state are those whose duty it is to oversee the games, the feeding and the education of the children that " they may be sound of hand and foot, and may in no wise, if possible, get their natures warped by their habits." The people whom Plato calls market-stewards are the *episkopoi* who " supervise personal conduct, keeping an eye on temperate and outrageous behaviour, so as to punish him who needs punishment."

In Athenian law and administration the *episkopoi* were rulers and governors and administrators and inspectors sent out to subject states to see that law and order and loyalty are observed. In Rhodes the main magistrates were five *episkopoi* who presided over the good government and the law and order of the state.

The word *episkopos* is, therefore, a many-sided but always a noble word. It means the protector of public safety; the guardian of honour and truth and honesty; the overseer of right education and of public morals; the administrator of public law and order.

So, then, to call God the *episkopos* of our souls is to call Him our Guardian, our Protector, our Guide, and our Director.

God is the Shepherd and the Guardian of our souls. In His love He cares for us; in His power He protects us; and in His wisdom He guides and directs us in the right way.

THE SILENT PREACHING OF A LOVELY LIFE

I *Peter* 3: 1, 2

> Likewise, you wives, be submissive to your husbands, so that, if there are any who refuse to believe the word, they may be won for Christ without a word, because they have seen your pure and reverent behaviour.

PETER now turns to the domestic and family problems which Christianity inevitably produced. It was inevitable that one member of a family might be won for Christ, while the other remained untouched by the appeal of the gospel; and such a situation inevitably produced problems.

It may seem strange that Peter's advice to wives is six times as long as his advice to husbands. That was because the wife's problem was far more difficult than that of the husband. If a husband became a Christian, he would automatically bring his wife with him into the Church, and there would be no problem. But if a wife became a Christian, while her husband did not, she had taken a step which in the ancient world was unprecedented, and which produced the acutest problems. In every sphere of ancient civilization, women had no rights at all. Under Jewish law a woman was a thing; she was owned by her husband in exactly the same way as he owned his sheep and his goats; on no account could she leave him, although he could dismiss her at any moment. For a wife to change her religion while her husband did not, was unthinkable. In Greek civilization the duty of the woman was "to remain indoors and to be obedient to her husband." It was the sign of a good woman that she must see as little, hear as little, and ask as little as possible. She had no kind of independent existence and no kind of mind of her own, and her husband could divorce her almost at caprice, so long as he returned her dowry. Under Roman law a woman had no rights. In law she remained for ever a child. When she was under her father she was under the *patria potestas*, the father's power, which gave the father even the right of life and death over her; and when she married she passed equally into the power of her husband. She was entirely subject to her husband, and completely at his mercy. Cato the Censor, the typical ancient Roman, wrote: " If you were to catch your wife in an act of infidelity, you can kill her with impunity without a trial." Roman matrons were prohibited from drinking wine, and Egnatius beat his wife to death when he found her doing so. Sulpicius Gallus dismissed his wife because she had once appeared in the streets without a veil. Antistius Vetus divorced his wife because he saw her secretly speaking to a freed woman in public. Publius Sempronius Sophus divorced his wife because once she went to the public games. The whole attitude of ancient civilization was that no woman could dare to take any decision for herself. What, then, must have been the problems of the wife who became a Christian while her husband remained faithful to the ancestral gods? It is almost impossible for us to realize what life must have been for the wife who was brave enough to become a Christian.

What then is Peter's advice in such a case? We must first note what Peter did *not* advise.

He did not advise the wife to leave her husband. In

this he took exactly the same attitude as Paul took (I *Corinthians* 7: 13-16). Both Paul and Peter were quite sure that the Christian wife must remain with the heathen husband so long as the husband did not send her away. He does not tell the wife to preach, to argue and to nag. He does not tell the wife to insist that in her faith there is no difference between slave and freeman, Gentile and Jew, male and female, but that all are the same in the presence of the Christ whom she has come to know. What, then, does he tell her?

He tells her something very simple—he tells her nothing else than to be a good wife. By the silent preaching of the loveliness of her life she must break down the barriers of prejudice and hostility, and win her husband for her new Master.

She must be *submissive*. It is not a cringing and a spineless submission that is meant; it is the submission which, as someone has finely put it, is a " voluntary selflessness." It is the submission which is based on the death of pride, the abasing of self, and the instinctive desire to serve. It is not the submission of fear, but the submission of perfect love.

She must be *pure*. There must be in her life a lovely chastity and a fidelity which is founded on love.

She must be *reverent*. She must live in the conviction that the whole world is the Temple of God, and all life is lived in the presence of Christ.

The wife who became a Christian would have neither her troubles nor her sorrows to seek. Her only weapon must be the silent preaching of a lovely life.

THE TRUE ADORNMENT

I *Peter* 3: 3-6

> Let not your adornment be an outward thing of braided hair and ornaments of gold and wearing of robes, but let your adornment be an adornment of the

inward personality of the heart, wrought by the unfading loveliness of a gentle and quiet spirit, which is very precious in the sight of God. For it was thus in days of old the holy women, who placed their hopes in God, adorned themselves in submission to their husbands. It was thus that Sara obeyed Abraham calling him, " Lord." And you have become her children, if you do good, and if you do not become a prey to fluttering fears.

BENGEL, the old commentator, speaks of " the labour bestowed on dress which consumes much time." Such labour is no modern thing. We have already seen that in the ancient world women had no part in public life whatsoever; they had nothing to interest them, and nothing to pass their time; for that very reason it was sometimes argued that they must be allowed their interest in dress and adornment. Cato the Censor pled and argued for, and insisted on, simplicity; Lucius Valerius answered: " Why should men grudge women their ornaments and their dress? Women cannot hold public offices, or priesthoods, or gain triumphs; they have no public occupations. What, then, can they do but devote their time to adornment and to dress? " Undue interest in self-adornment was then, and still is, nothing other than a sign that the person who indulges in it has no greater and wider things to occupy the mind.

The ancient moralists condemned undue luxury as much as the Christian teachers did. Quintilian, the Roman master of oratory, wrote: " A tasteful and magnificent dress, as the Greek poet tells us, lends added dignity to the wearer: but effeminate and luxurious apparel fails to adorn the body, and only reveals the sordidness of the mind." Epictetus, the philosopher, thinking of the narrow life to which women were condemned in the ancient world, said, " Immediately after they are fourteen, women are called ' ladies ' by men. And so, when they see that they have nothing else than to be bedfellows of men, they begin to beautify themselves, and put all their hopes on that. It is, therefore, worthwhile for us to take pains, to make them understand that they are honoured for nothing else but only for appearing modest and self-respecting." Epictetus and Peter agree.

There is at least one passage in the Old Testament which lists the various items of female adornment, and threatens the day of judgment in which they will be destroyed. The passage is in *Isaiah* 3: 18-24. It speaks of the tinkling ornaments of the feet, and the tires like the moon, the chains and the bracelets and the spangled ornaments, the bonnets and the headbands and the earrings, the rings and the nose jewels, the dresses, the mantles, the wimples, and the crisping pins, the glasses, the fine linens, the hoods and the veils.

In the world of the Greeks and the Romans it is interesting to collect the references to personal adornments. There were as many ways of dressing the hair as there were bees in Hybla. Hair was waved, and dyed, sometimes black, more often auburn. Wigs were worn, especially blonde wigs, which are found even in the Christian catacombs; and hair to manufacture them was imported from Germany, and even from as far away as India. Hairbands, pins and combs were made of ivory, and boxwood, and tortoiseshell; and sometimes of gold, studded with gems.

Purple was the favourite colour for clothes. One pound weight of the best Tyrian purple wool, strained twice through, cost 1,000 *denarii*, £43 10s. A Tyrian cloak of the best purple cost well over £100. In one year silks, pearls, scents and jewellery were imported from India to the value of £1,000,000. Similar imports of luxury came from Arabia. Diamonds, emeralds, topazes, opals and the sardonyx were favourite stones. Struma Nonius had a ring valued at £21,250. Pearls were loved most of all. Julius Caesar bought for Servilia a pearl which cost him £65,250. Earrings were made of pearls, and Seneca spoke of women with two or three fortunes in their ears. Slippers were encrusted with them; Nero even had a room whose walls were covered with them. Pliny saw Lollia Paulina, wife of Caligula, wearing a dress so covered with pearls and emeralds that it had cost £450,000. Christianity came into a world of luxury and decadence combined.

In face of all this Peter pleads for the graces which adorn the heart, the gentle and the quiet spirit, which are precious in the sight of God. These were the jewels which adorned the holy women of old. Did not Sara, with wifely submission, call Abraham " Lord "? (*Genesis* 18: 12). Isaiah had called Sara the mother of God's faithful people (*Isaiah* 51: 2); and, if Christian wives are adorned with the same graces of modesty, humility, and chastity, they too will be her daughters, and will be within the family of the faithful people of God.

A Christian wife lived in a heathen society where she would be tempted to luxurious and senseless extravagance; she lived a life where she might well go in fluttering fear of the caprices of her heathen husband. But she must live in selfless service, in goodness, and in serene trust; that would be the best sermon which she could preach to win her husband for Christ. Without a word she must win those who were disobedient to the word. There are few passages where the value of the beauty of a lovely Christian life are so vividly stressed.

THE HUSBAND'S OBLIGATION

I Peter 3: 7

> Likewise, you husbands, live understandingly with your wives, remembering that women are the weaker sex, and assigning honour to them as fellow-heirs of the grace of life, so that there may be no barrier to your prayers.

SHORT as this passage is, it has in it much of the very essence of the Christian ethic. The great characteristic of the Christian ethic is that it is what may be called a *reciprocal* ethic. It is an ethic which never places all the responsibility or all the duty on one side. If it speaks of the duties of slaves, it also speaks of the obligations of masters. If it speaks of the duty of children, it also speaks of the obligations of parents (cp. *Ephesians* 6: 1-9; *Colossians* 3: 20—4: 1). Peter has just laid down the duty of wives; and now he goes on to lay down the duty of husbands. Any marriage must be based on reciprocal duty and reciprocal obligation. Any marriage in which all the privileges are on one side and all the obligations are on the other is bound to be an imperfect marriage with every chance of failure. It must be noted that this itself was a new conception in the ancient world. We have already seen the woman's total lack of rights in the ancient world. We already quoted Cato's statement of the rights of the husband; but we did not finish that quotation; we finish it now: " If you were to catch your wife in an act of infidelity, you can kill her with impunity without a trial; but, if she were to catch you, she would not venture to touch you with her finger, and, indeed, she has no right." That is to say, in the Roman moral code all the obligation is on the wife, and all the privilege is with the husband. It is the mark of the Christian ethic that it never grants a privilege without a corresponding obligation.

What then are the obligations of the husband?

(i) He must be *understanding*; he must be considerate. He must be sensitive to the feelings of his wife. Somerset Maugham's mother was a very beautiful woman with the world at her feet; his father was by no means handsome. Someone once asked his mother: " Why do you remain faithful to that ugly little man you married? " Her answer was: " Because he never hurts me." It was understanding and considerateness which forged the constant and unbreakable bond. The cruelty which is hardest to bear is often not deliberate, but the product of sheer thoughtlessness.

(ii) He must be *chivalrous*; he must remember that women are the weaker sex, and he must treat them with perfect courtesy. In the ancient world chivalry to women was well-nigh unknown. It was, and still is, no uncommon sight in the East to see the man riding on a heavily-laden donkey while the woman trudges by his side. It was Christianity which introduced chivalry into the relationships between men and women.

(iii) He must remember that the woman has *equal spiritual rights*. She also is a fellow-heir of the grace of life. Women did not share in the worship of the Greeks and the Romans. Even in the Jewish synagogue women had no share in the service, and in the orthodox synagogue still have no share. When women were admitted to the synagogue at all, they were segregated from the men, who formed the congregation, and hidden behind a lattice or a screen, because there was no part for women in Jewish worship. Here in Christianity there emerged a revolutionary principle. Women have equal spiritual rights; granted that, the whole relationship between the sexes was changed.

(iv) Finally, unless a man realizes and fulfils these obligations there is a barrier between his prayers and God. As Bigg puts it: " The sighs of the injured wife come between the husband's prayers and God's hearing." Here is a great truth. Our relationships with God can never be right, when our relationships with our fellow-men are wrong. It is when we are one with each other that we are also one with God.

THE MARKS OF THE CHRISTIAN LIFE (I)

1 *Peter* 3: 8-12

> Finally, you must all be of one mind; you must have sympathy with each other, and you must live in brotherly love; you must be compassionate and humble; you must not return evil for evil, nor insult for insult; on the contrary, you must return blessing; for it was to give and to inherit blessing that you were called.

He who wishes to love life,
    And to see good things,
Let him keep his tongue from evil,
    And his lips from speaking guile:
Let him avoid evil, and let him do good;
    Let him seek peace, and pursue it,
Because the eyes of the Lord are upon the righteous,
    And His ears are open to their request;
But the face of the Lord is against those who do evil.

HERE Peter, as it were, gathers together the great qualities of the Christian life.

(i) Right in the forefront Peter sets *Christian unity*. It is worth while to collect the great New Testament passages about this Christian unity, in order to see how great a place unity occupies in New Testament thought. The basis of the whole matter is in the words of Jesus, when He prayed for His people that they might all be one; that they might be perfected into one; that they might be one, even as He and His Father are one (*John* 17: 21-23). In the great and thrilling early days of the Church this prayer was fulfilled, for they were all of one heart and of one soul (*Acts* 4: 32). Over and over again Paul exhorts men to this unity and prays for it. He reminds the Christians of Rome that, though they are many, they are one body, and he pleads with them to be of one mind (*Romans* 12: 4, 16). In writing to the Christians of Corinth he uses the same picture of the Christians as members of one body, in spite of all their differing qualities and gifts (I *Corinthians* 12: 12-31). He pleads with the quarrelling Corinthians that there should be no divisions among them, that they should be perfectly joined together in the same mind (I *Corinthians* 1: 10). He tells them that strifes and divisions are carnal things, marks that they are living on purely human standards, without the mind of Christ (I *Corinthians* 3: 3). Because they have partaken of the one bread, they too must be one bread and one body (I *Corinthians* 10: 17). Finally, he tells them that they must be of one mind, and that they must live in peace (2 *Corinthians* 13: 11). In Christ Jesus the dividing walls are down, and Jew and Greek are united into one (*Ephesians* 2: 13, 14). Christians must maintain the unity of the Spirit in the bond of peace, remembering that there is one Lord, one faith, one baptism, one God and Father of all (*Ephesians* 4: 3-6). The Philippians must stand fast in one spirit, striving together with one mind for the faith of the gospel; they will make Paul's happiness complete, if they have the same love, and have one accord, and one mind; the quarrelling Euodias and Syntyche are urged to be of one mind in the Lord (*Philippians* 1: 27; 2: 2; 4: 2).

All through the New Testament there rings this plea for Christian unity. It is more than a plea; it is an announcement that the Christian cannot live the Christian life, unless in his personal relationships he is at unity with his fellow-men; and that the Church cannot be the Christian Church, if there are divisions within it. It is tragic to realize how far men are from realizing this unity in their personal lives, and how far the Church is from realizing it within herself. C. E. B. Cranfield writes so finely of this that we cannot do other than quote his whole comment in full, lengthy though it is: " The New Testament never treats this agreeing in Christ as an unnecessary though highly desirable spiritual luxury, but as something essential to the true being of the Church. Divisions, whether disagreements between individual members or the existence of factions and parties and—how much more!—our present-day denominations, constitute a calling in question of the Gospel itself and a sign that those who are involved are carnal. The more seriously we take the New Testament, the more urgent and painful becomes our sense of the sinfulness of the divisions, and the more earnest our prayers and strivings after the peace and unity of the Church on earth. That does not mean that the like-mindedness we are to strive for is to be a drab uniformity of the sort beloved of bureaucrats. Rather is it to be a unity in which powerful tensions are held together by an over-mastering loyalty, and strong antipathies of race and colour, temperament and taste, social position and economic interest, are overcome in common worship and common obedience. Such unity will only come when Christians are humble and bold enough to lay hold on the unity already given in Christ and to take it more seriously than their own self-importance and sin, and to make of these deep differences of doctrine, which originate in our imperfect understanding of the Gospel and which we dare not belittle, not an excuse for letting go of one another or staying apart, but rather an incentive for a more earnest seeking in fellowship together to hear and obey the voice of Christ." There speaks the prophetic voice to our modern condition.

THE MARKS OF THE CHRISTIAN LIFE (2)

I *Peter* 3: 8-12 (*continued*)

(ii) Second, Peter sets *sympathy*. Here again the New Testament urges this duty upon us. We are to rejoice with them who do rejoice, and to weep with them who weep (*Romans* 12: 15). When one member of the body suffers all the other members suffer with it; and when one member of the body is honoured, all the members rejoice with it (I *Corinthians* 12: 26), and it must be so with Christians, who are the body of Christ. One thing is clear, sympathy and selfishness cannot co-exist. So long as the self is the most important thing in the world, there can be no such thing as sympathy. Sympathy depends on the willingness to forget self, to step outside self, and to identify oneself with the pains and sorrows of others. It is only when we die to self that we can live to others. Sympathy comes to the heart when Christ reigns within the heart.

(iii) Third, Peter sets *brotherly love*. Here again the matter goes back to the words of Jesus. " A new commandment give I unto you, that ye love one another. . . .

By this shall all men know that ye are my disciples, if ye have love one to another " (*John* 13: 34, 35). Here the New Testament speaks with unmistakable definiteness and with almost frightening directness. " We know that we have passed from death unto life, because we love the brethren. He that loveth not his brother abideth in death. Whosoever hateth his brother is a murderer " (I *John* 3: 14, 15). " If a man say, I love God, and hateth his brother, he is a liar " (I *John* 4: 20). The simple fact is that love of God and love of man go hand in hand; the one cannot exist without the other. If in the life of a man or of a Church there is no love of men, then quite certainly in that man and in that Church there is no true love of God. The simplest test of the reality of our religion is whether or not it makes us love our fellow-men.

(iv) Fourth, Peter sets *compassion*. There is a sense in which pity is in danger of becoming one of the lost virtues. The conditions of modern life, especially the conditions of our own age, tend to blunt the edge of the mind to sensitiveness in pity. As C. E. B. Cranfield puts it: " We got used to hearing on the radio of a thousand-bomber raid as we ate our breakfast. We have got used to the idea of millions of people becoming refugees." We can, for instance, read of the thousands of casualties on the roads with no reaction at all within our hearts, forgetting that each one of them means a broken body and a broken heart for someone. In the conditions of modern twentieth century life it is easy to lose the cutting edge of pity, and it is still easier to be satisfied with a sentimentalism which feels a moment's comfortable sorrow, and which does nothing about it. Pity is of the very essence of God; compassion is of the very being of Jesus Christ; a pity so great that God sent His only Son to die for men, a compassion so intense that it took Christ to the Cross. There can be no Christianity without compassion.

(v) Fifth, Peter sets *humility*. Christian humility comes from two things. It comes, first, from the sense of creatureliness. It comes from the feeling of the creature in the presence of his Creator. The Christian is humble because he is constantly aware of his utter dependence on God, and because he constantly remembers that of himself he can do nothing. It comes, second, from the fact that the Christian has a new standard of comparison. It may well be true that, when he compares himself with his neighbour, he is as good as any man. It may well be true that, when he compares himself with his fellow-men, he has nothing to fear from the comparison. But the Christian's standard of comparison is Christ, and, when he compares himself with the sinless perfection of incarnate love divine, he is ever in default. When the Christian remembers his dependence on God, and when he keeps before him the standard of Christ, he will be ever kept in humility.

(vi) Lastly, and as a climax, Peter sets *forgiveness*. It is to receive forgiveness from God, and to give forgiveness to men that the Christian is called. And the one cannot exist without the other; it is only when we forgive others their sins against us that we are forgiven our sins against God (*Matthew* 6: 11, 14, 15). The mark of the Christian is that he forgives others as God has forgiven him (*Ephesians* 4: 32).

Finally, as was natural for him, Peter sums the whole matter up by quoting the picture of the good man in *Psalm* 34, with its picture of the man whom God receives, and the man who God rejects.

THE CHRISTIAN'S SECURITY IN A THREATENING WORLD

1 *Peter* 3: 13, 14

> Who will hurt you, if you are ardent lovers of goodness? Even if you do have to suffer for the sake of righteousness, you are blessed. Have no fear of them; do not be troubled; but in your hearts give Christ a unique place.

IN this passage we can see how Peter was soaked in the Old Testament. There are two Old Testament foundations for this passage. It is not so much that Peter actually quotes these Old Testament passages, as that he could not have written the passage at all unless the Old Testament passages had been in his mind. The very first sentence of the passage is a reminiscence of *Isaiah* 50: 9: " Behold, the Lord God will help me; who is he that shall condemn me?" Again, when Peter is talking about the banishing of fear he is thinking of *Isaiah* 8: 13, where the prophet says, "Sanctify the Lord of hosts Himself; and let Him be your fear, and let Him be your dread."

There are three great conceptions in this passage.

(i) Peter begins by insisting on a passionate love of goodness. A man may have more than one attitude to goodness. Goodness may be to him a burden; goodness may be to him a bore; goodness may be to him something which he vaguely and sentimentally and nebulously desires, but the price of which he is not willing to pay in sweat and effort. The word we have translated an *ardent lover* is interesting. It is the word *ȝēlōtēs*; that is the word which is translated *Zealot*. The Zealots were the fanatical patriots, who were pledged and sworn to liberate their native land by every possible means. They were men who were prepared to take their lives in their hands, to sacrifice ease and comfort, home and loved ones, in this passionate love for country. What Peter is saying is: " Love goodness with that passionate intensity with which the most fanatical patriot loves his country." Sir John Seeley said, "No heart is pure that is not passionate; no virtue safe which is not enthusiastic." It is only when a man falls in love with goodness that the wrong things lose their fascination and their power.

(ii) Peter goes on to speak about the Christian attitude to suffering. It has been well pointed out that we are involved in two kinds of suffering. There is the suffering in which we are involved because of our *humanity*. Because we are men, there comes physical suffering, there comes death, there comes sorrow, there comes distress of mind and weariness and pain of body. All these things are part of the human situation for every man. But there is also the suffering in which we may be involved because of our *Christianity*. There may be unpopularity, a certain amount of persecution; there may be sacrifice for principle and the deliberate choosing of the difficult way; there is the necessary discipline and toil of the Christian life. Yet in the Christian life there is a certain blessedness which runs through it all. The question is how does this blessedness come? What is the reason for it?

(iii) Peter's answer is this. The Christian is the man to whom God and Jesus Christ are the supremacies in life. To him his relationship to God in Christ is life's greatest value. Now, if a man's heart is set on earthly things, on earthly possessions, on earthly happiness, on earthly pleasures, on earthly ease and comfort, he is of all men most vulnerable. For, in the nature of things, he may lose these things at any moment. There may come at any time a reversal of fortune, and he may find himself stripped of them all. Such a man is desperately easily hurt and wounded. On the other hand, if a man gives to Jesus Christ the unique place in his life, if the most precious thing for him is his relationship to God, that is something which can never be taken from him; no experience can despoil him of it; nothing can take it from him. Therefore, he is completely secure. His treasure is untouchable by the chances and the changes of this life. So, then, even in suffering the Christian is still blessed. When the suffering is for Christ, he is certainly demonstrating his loyalty to Christ, and he is sharing the sufferings of Christ. When the suffering is part of the human situation, it still cannot despoil him of the most precious things in life. No man escapes suffering, but for the Christian suffering cannot touch the things which matter most of all.

THE CHRISTIAN ARGUMENT FOR CHRIST

I *Peter* 3: 15, 16

> Always be prepared to make your defence to anyone
> who calls you to account concerning the hope that
> is in you; but do so with gentleness and reverence.
> Keep your conscience clear, so that, when you are
> abused, those who revile your good behaviour in Christ
> may be put to shame.

IN a hostile and suspicious world it was, and still is, inevitable that the Christian will be called upon to defend the
faith he holds and the hope by which he lives. Here Peter
has certain things to say about the Christian defence, and
the Christian argument for Christ.

(i) It must be *reasonable*. It is a *logos* that the Christian
must give, and a *logos* is a reasonable and intelligent
statement of his position. A cultivated Greek believed
that it was the mark of an intelligent man that he was able
to give and to receive a *logos* concerning his actions and
belief. As Bigg puts it, he was expected " intelligently
and temperately to discuss matters of conduct." To do so
we must know what we believe; we must have thought it
out; we must be able to state it intelligently and intelli-
gibly. Our faith must be a first-hand discovery, and not
a second-hand story. It is, in fact, one of the tragedies of
the modern situation that there are so many Church
members who, if they were asked what they believe,
could not tell anyone, and who, if they were asked why
they believe it, would be equally helpless. The Christian
must go through the mental and spiritual toil of thinking
out his faith, so that he can tell what he believes and
why he believes it.

(ii) His defence must be given *with gentleness*. There are
many people who state their beliefs with a kind of arrogant
belligerence. Their attitude is that anyone who does
not agree with them is either a fool or a knave. They seek
to ram their beliefs down other people's throats, and to
bludgeon others into accepting their beliefs. The case for

Christianity must be presented with winsomeness and with love, and with that wise tolerance which realizes that it is not given to any man to possess the whole truth. " There are as many ways to the stars as there are men to climb them." Men can be wooed into the Christian faith when they cannot be bullied into it.

(iii) His defence must be given *with reverence*. That is to say, any argument in which the Christian is involved must be carried on in a tone and in an atmosphere which God can hear with joy. No debates have been so acrimonious as theological debates. The tragic thing is that no differences have caused such bitterness as religious differences. In any presentation of the Christian case, and in any argument for the Christian faith, the accent to the end of the day must be the accent of love.

(iv) Finally, Peter lays it down that the only compelling argument is the argument of the Christian life. Let a man so act that his conscience is clear. Let him meet criticism with a life which is beyond reproach. Such conduct will silence slander and will disarm criticism. The only unanswerable argument for Christianity is a Christian life. " A saint," as someone has said, " is someone whose life makes it easier to believe in God."

THE SAVING WORK OF CHRIST

1 Peter 3: 17—4: 6

> For, it is better to suffer for doing right, if that should be the will of God, than to suffer for doing wrong. For Christ also died once and for all for sins, the just for the unjust, that He might bring us to God. He was put to death in the flesh, but He was raised to life in the Spirit, in which also He went and preached to the spirits who are in prison, the spirits who were once upon a time disobedient, in the time when the patience of God waited in the days of Noah, while the ark was being built, in which some few—that is, eight souls—were brought in safety through the water.

And water now saves you, who were symbolically represented in Noah and his company, I mean the water of baptism; and baptism is not merely the removal of dirt from the body, but the pledge to God of a good conscience, through the resurrection of Jesus Christ, who is at the right hand of God, because He went to heaven, after angels and authorities and power had been made subject to Him.

Since, then, Christ suffered in the flesh, you too must arm yourselves with the same conviction, that he who has suffered in the flesh has ceased from sin, and as a result of this the aim of such a man now is to spend the time that remains to him of life in the flesh no longer in obedience to human passions, but in obedience to the will of God. For the time that is past is sufficient to have done what the Gentiles will to do, to have lived a life of licentiousness, lust, drunkenness, revellings, carousings, and abominable idolatry. They think it strange when you do not rush to join them in the same flood of profligacy, and they abuse you for not doing so. They will give account to Him who is ready to judge the living and the dead. For this is why the gospel was preached even to the dead, so that, although they have already been judged in the flesh like men, they might live in the Spirit like God.

THIS is not only one of the most difficult passages in Peter's letter; it is one of the most difficult passages in the whole New Testament; and it is also the basis of one of the most difficult articles in the creed, the article which says: " He descended into Hell." It is, therefore, better first of all to read it as a whole, and then to study it in its various sections.

THE EXAMPLE OF THE WORK OF CHRIST

I *Peter* 3: 17, 18a

For, it is better to suffer for doing right, if that should be the will of God, than to suffer for doing wrong. For Christ also died once and for all for sins, the just for the unjust, that He might bring us to God.

WE have said that this passage is one of the most difficult in the whole New Testament, but it begins with something which anyone can understand. The point that Peter is making is that, even if the Christian is compelled to suffer cruelly and unjustly for his faith, he is only walking the way that his Lord and Saviour has already walked. The suffering Christian must always remember that he has a suffering Lord. In the narrow compass of these two verses Peter has the greatest and the deepest things to say about the work of Christ, and about the death of Christ.

(i) He lays it down that the work of Christ is *unique*, and that it never need be repeated. Christ died *once and for all* for sins. When Christ died, He died once and for all (*Romans* 6: 10). The priestly sacrifices in the Temple have to be repeated day and daily, but Christ made the perfect sacrifice once and for all when He offered Himself up (*Hebrews* 7: 27). Christ was once and for all offered to bear the sin of many (*Hebrews* 9: 28). We are sanctified through the offering of the body of Christ once and for all (*Hebrews* 10: 10). The New Testament is completely sure that on the Cross something happened which never needs to happen again, and that in that happening sin is finally defeated. On the Cross God dealt with man's sin in a way which is adequate for all sin, for all men, for all time. The sacrifice of the Cross, unlike all other sacrifices, is so efficacious that it never needs to be repeated.

(ii) He lays it down that that sacrifice was *for sin*. Christ died once and for all *for sins*. This again is completely New Testament belief. Christ died for our sins, says Paul, according to the scriptures (I *Corinthians* 15: 3). Christ gave Himself for our sins (*Galatians* 1: 4). The function of the High Priest, and Jesus Christ is the perfect High Priest, is to offer sacrifice for sins (*Hebrews* 5: 1, 3). He is the propitiation for our sins (I *John* 2: 2). The phrase in the Greek for *for sins* is either *huper* or *peri hamartiōn*. Now it so happens that in the Greek version of the Old Testament the regular phrase for a *sin-offering* is *peri hamartias*. (*Hamartias* is the singular form for *hamartiōn*). It is by that phrase that the word *sin-offering* is represented, for instance, in *Leviticus* 5: 7 and 6: 30. That is to say, Peter is laying it down that the death of Christ is the sacrifice which atones for the sin of men. We may put it this way. Sin is that which interrupts the relationship which should exist between God and men. The whole object of sacrifice is to restore that lost relationship. The death of Christ upon the Cross is that which, however we explain it, avails to restore the lost relationship between God and man. As Charles Wesley put it in verse:

> No condemnation now I dread:
> Jesus, and all in Him, is mine!
> Alive in Him, my living Head,
> And clothed in righteousness divine,
> Bold I approach the eternal throne,
> And claim the crown, through Christ my own.

It may be that we will never agree in our theories of what happened on the Cross, for, indeed, as Charles Wesley said in that same hymn: " 'Tis mystery all." But on one thing we can agree—through what happened on the Cross of Christ we enter into a new relationship with God.

(iii) He lays it down that that sacrifice was *vicarious*. Christ died once and for all for sins, *the just for the unjust*. That the just should suffer for the unjust is an extraordinary thing. At first sight it looks like nothing other than injustice. As Edwin H. Robertson put it: " Only forgiveness without reason can match sin without excuse." The suffering of Christ was for us; and the mystery of it all is that He who deserved no suffering bore that suffering for us who deserved to suffer. He sacrificed Himself to restore our lost relationship with God.

(iv) He lays it down that the work of Christ was *to bring us to God*. Christ also died once and for all for sins, the just for the unjust, *that He might bring us to God*. The word for *to bring* is *prosagein*. It is a word with two vivid backgrounds. It has a Jewish background. (*a*) It is used in the Old Testament of bringing to God those who were to be priests. It is God's instruction: " Aaron and his sons thou shalt *bring unto* the door of the tabernacle of the congregation " (*Exodus* 29: 4). The point is this—as the Jews saw it, only the priests had the right of close access to God. In the Temple the layman might come so far; he could pass through the Court of the Gentiles, the Court of the Women, the Court of the Israelites—but there he must stop. Into the Court of the Priests, into the nearer presence of God, he could not go; and of the priests only the High Priest could enter into the Holy of Holies. But Jesus Christ brings *us* to God; He opens the way for all men to the nearer presence of God. (*b*) It has a Greek background. In the New Testament the corresponding noun *prosagōgē* is three times used. *Prosagein*, the verb, means *to bring in*; *prosagōgē*, the noun, means the right of *access*, which is the result of the bringing in. Through Christ we have *access* to grace (*Romans* 5: 2). Through Him we have *access* to God the Father (*Ephesians* 2: 18). Through Him we have boldness and *access* and confidence to come to God (*Ephesians* 3: 12). In Greek this had a specialized meaning. At the court of kings there was an official called the *prosagōgeus*, the *introducer*, the *giver of access*, and it was his function to decide who should be admitted to the king's presence, and who should be kept out. He, as it were, held the keys of access. That is to say, it is Jesus Christ, through what He did, who brings men into the presence of God, who gives them access to God, who opens the way to God.

(v) When we go beyond these two verses, further into the whole passage, we can add still two more great truths to Peter's view of the work of Christ. In 3: 19 Peter says that Jesus went and preached to the spirits in prison; and in 4: 6 he says that the gospel was preached to them that are dead. As we shall go on to see, this most probably means that in the time between His death and His resurrection Jesus actually preached the gospel in the abode

of the dead; that is to say, that He preached the gospel
to those who in their life-time had never had the opportunity to hear it. Here indeed is a tremendous thought.
It means that the work of Christ is infinite in its range,
that it includes time and eternity, this world and any
other world. It means that no man who ever lived is outside
the grace and the gospel of God.

(vi) Finally, Peter sees the work of Christ in terms of
complete triumph and victory. He says that after His resurrection Jesus went into heaven, and is at the right hand of
God, angels and authorities and powers having been made
subject to Him (3: 22). The meaning of that is that there is
nothing in earth and heaven outside the empire of Christ.
To all men He brought the new relationship between man
and God; in His death He even brought the good news
to the dead; in His resurrection He conquered death;
even the angelic and the demonic powers are subject to
Him; and He shares the very power and throne of God.
Here is the great belief that there is no created being in
heaven or earth outside the empire and the power of
Christ. Christ the sufferer has become Christ the victor,
and Christ the crucified has become Christ the crowned.

THE DESCENT INTO HELL

I *Peter* 3: 18b-20; 4: 6

> He was put to death in the flesh, but He was raised
> to life in the Spirit, in which also He went and preached
> to the spirits who are in prison, the spirits who were
> once upon a time disobedient in the time when the
> patience of God waited in the days of Noah, while
> the ark was being built. . . . For this is why the gospel
> was preached even to the dead, so that, although they
> have already been judged in the flesh like men, they
> might live in the spirit like God.

WE have already said that we are here face to face with
one of the most difficult passages, not only in Peter's letter,

but in the whole New Testament; and, if we are to grasp what it means, we must indeed follow Peter's own advice and gird up the loins of our mind to study it.

This passage has lodged in the creed in the phrase: " He descended into hell." We must first note that that phrase is very misleading. The idea of the New Testament is not that Jesus descended into *hell*, but that He descended into *Hades*. *Acts* 2: 27, as all the newer translations correctly show, should not be translated: " Thou wilt not leave my soul in hell," but, " Thou wilt not leave my soul in Hades." The difference is this. Hell is definitely the place of the torture and the punishment of the wicked; Hades, in Jewish thought, was the place where all the dead went. The Jews had a very shadowy conception of the life beyond the grave. They did not think in terms of heaven and of hell; they thought in terms of a shadowy world, where the spirits of men moved like grey ghosts in an everlasting twilight, and where there was neither light nor strength nor joy. Such was Hades. It was the twilight shadowland, into which the spirits of all men alike went after death. Isaiah writes: " The grave cannot praise Thee, death cannot celebrate Thee; they that go down into the pit cannot hope for Thy truth " (*Isaiah* 38: 18). The Psalmist wrote: " In death there is no remembrance of Thee; in the grave who shall give Thee thanks? " (*Psalm* 6: 5). " What profit is there in my blood when I go down into the pit? Shall the dust praise Thee? Shall it declare Thy truth? " (*Psalm* 30: 9). " Wilt Thou show wonders to the dead? Shall the dead arise and praise Thee? Shall Thy loving-kindness be declared in the grave? or Thy faithfulness in destruction? Shall Thy wonders be known in the dark? And Thy righteousness in the land of forgetfulness? " (*Psalm* 88: 10-12). " The dead praise not the Lord, neither any that go down into silence " (*Psalm* 115: 17). " Whatsoever thy hand findeth to do, do it with thy might; for there is no work, nor device, nor knowledge, nor wisdom in the grave whither thou goest " (*Ecclesiastes* 9: 10). Such was the Jewish conception of the world after death. It was a grey world of shadows and strengthlessness and forgetfulness, in which men were separated from life and light and God.

As time went on, there emerged the idea of stages and divisions in this shadowland. For some it was to last for ever; but for others it was a kind of prison-house in which they were held until the final punishment and judgment of the wrath of God should blast them (*Isaiah* 24: 21, 22; 2 *Peter* 2: 4; *Revelation* 20: 1-7). So, then, it must first of all be remembered that this whole matter is to be thought of, not in terms of hell, as we understand the word, but in terms of Christ's going to the dead in their grey and shadowy world.

THE DESCENT INTO HELL

I Peter 3: 18b-20; 4: 6 (continued)

THIS doctrine in the creed of the descent into Hades, as we must now call it, is based on two phrases in our present passage. In this passage it says that Jesus went and preached to the spirits who are in prison (3: 19); and it speaks of the gospel being preached to the dead (4: 6). In regard to this whole doctrine there have always been differing attitudes amongst thinkers.

(i) There are those who wish to eliminate it altogether. There is the attitude of *elimination*. That elimination is attempted along two lines. (a) Peter says that in the Spirit Christ preached to the spirits who are in prison, the spirits who were once upon a time disobedient in the time when the patience of God waited in the days of Noah, when the ark was being built. It is argued that what this means is that it was *in the time of Noah himself* that Christ did this preaching; that in the Spirit long ages before this Christ was preaching and appealing to the wicked men of Noah's day; that it was not after they had died and gone to Hades that Christ preached to them in the time between His own death and resurrection, but that actually in the days of Noah, the pre-existing Christ in the Spirit preached and appealed to these sinners. This would completely eliminate the whole idea of the descent into Hades, and would transfer this preaching by Christ to this world in the ancient days of Noah. Many great scholars have accepted, and do accept, that view; but we do not think that it is the view which comes naturally from Peter's words.

(b) If we look at Moffatt's translation, we find that Moffatt has something quite different. He translates: " In the flesh He (Christ) was put to death, but He came to life in the Spirit. It was in the Spirit that Enoch also went and preached to the imprisoned spirits who had disobeyed at the time when God's patience held out during the construction of the ark in the days of Noah." Moffatt introduces *Enoch* into the picture, and Enoch does not appear in the Authorized Version at all. How, then, does Moffatt arrive at this translation?

The name of Enoch does not appear in any Greek manuscript at all. But in the consideration of the text of any Greek author, scholars sometimes use a process which is called *emendation*. The process of emendation means this. Sometimes scholars think that there is something wrong with the text as it stands, that some scribe has copied it wrongly, that it does not make sense as it stands; and they, therefore, suggest that some word should be changed, or that some word should be added, although the change and the addition do not appear in any Greek manuscript. In this passage Rendel Harris suggested that the word *Enoch* was missed out in the copying of Peter's writing and should be put back in.

(Although it involves the use of Greek some readers may be interested to see how Rendel Harris arrived at this famous emendation; and we indicate his kind of reasoning. In the top line of italic print, we have set down the Greek in English lettering, and beneath each Greek word there is its English translation:

thanatōtheis				*men sarki*		
having been put to death				in the flesh		

zōopoiētheis				*de pneumati*		
having been raised to life				in the Spirit		

en	*hō*	*kai*	*tois*	*en*	*phulakē*	*pneumasi*
in	which	also	to the	in	prison	spirits

poreutheis	*ekēruxen*
having gone	he preached.

This then is the passage in question in Greek and in word for word English. (*Men* and *de* are in Greek what are called particles; they are not translated; they merely mark the contrast between *sarki* and *pneumati* flesh and spirit). It was Rendel Harris's suggestion that between *kai* and *tois* the word *Enōch* had dropped out. His explanation is that, since most manuscript copying was done to dictation, scribes were very liable to miss out words which followed each other, if they sounded very similar. In this passage

> *en hō kai*   and   *Enōch*

sound very much alike, and Rendell Harris thought it very likely that the word *Enōch* had for that reason been mistakenly omitted).

What reason is there for bringing *Enoch* into this passage at all? Enoch has always been a fascinating and mysterious person. " And Enoch walked with God; and he was not; for God took him " (*Genesis* 5: 24). In between the Old and the New Testaments many legends sprang up about Enoch, and there were very famous and important books which were written under his name. One of the legends was that Enoch, though a man, acted as " God's envoy " to the angels who sinned by coming to earth and lustfully seducing mortal women (*Genesis* 6: 2). In the Book of Enoch it is said that Enoch was sent down from heaven to announce to these angels their final doom (*Enoch* 12: 1), and that he proclaimed to them that for them, because of their sin, there was neither peace nor forgiveness for ever (*Enoch*

12 and 13). So, then, according to Jewish legend, Enoch did, in fact, go to Hades and preach doom to the fallen and sinning angels. And so Rendel Harris thought that this passage refers, not to Jesus, but to Enoch, and Moffatt so far agreed with him as to put Enoch into his translation. That is an extremely interesting and ingenious suggestion, but without a doubt it must be rejected, because there is no evidence for it at all; and it is not natural to bring Enoch into the picture, for the whole picture is of the work of Christ.

THE DESCENT INTO HELL

I Peter 3: 18b-20; 4: 6 (continued)

WE have now seen that the attempt at the *elimination* of this passage fails.

(ii) The second attitude to this passage is the attitude of *limitation*. This attitude—and it is the attitude of some very great New Testament interpreters—believes that Peter is indeed saying that Jesus went to Hades and preached, but that He by no means preached to all the inhabitants of Hades. Different interpreters limit that preaching in different ways.

(*a*) It is argued that Jesus preached in Hades *only* to the spirits of the men who were sinful and disobedient in the days of Noah. Those who hold this view often go on to argue that, since these sinners in the days of Noah were desperately wicked, and desperately disobedient, so much so that God sent the flood and destroyed them (*Genesis* 6: 12, 13), we may believe that no man is outside the mercy of God. These men were the worst of all sinners; they were given another chance of repentance; therefore, the worst of men still have a chance in Christ.

(*b*) It is argued that Jesus preached to the fallen angels, and that He preached, not salvation, but final and irrevocable and awful doom. We have already mentioned these angels. Their story is told in *Genesis* 6: 1-8. They were tempted by the beauty of mortal women; they came to earth, seduced earthly women, and begat children; and because of their action, it is inferred, the wickedness of man was great and his thoughts were evil continually. *2 Peter* 2: 4 speaks of these sinning angels as being imprisoned in chains in hell, awaiting judgment. It was to them that Enoch did, in fact, preach; and there are those who think that what this passage means is not that Christ preached mercy and another chance; but that, in token of His complete triumph, He preached terrible doom to those angels who had sinned.

(c) It is argued that Christ preached *only* to those in the past who had been righteous, and that He led them out of Hades into the paradise of God. The idea is this. We have seen how the Jews believed that all the dead went to Hades, the grey, shadowy land of forgetfulness. The argument is that *before* Christ that was indeed so; but that Christ opened the gates of heaven to mankind; and that, when He did so, He went to Hades and told the glad news to all the righteous men of all past generations and led them out to God. That is indeed a magnificent picture. Those who hold this view often go on to say that, because of Christ, there is now no times in the shadows of Hades for the Christian, but the way to the paradise of God is open as soon as this world closes on us.

THE DESCENT INTO HELL

1 *Peter* 3: 18b-20; 4: 6 (*continued*)

(iii) There is the attitude that what Peter is saying is that Jesus Christ, between His death and His resurrection, went to the world of the dead and preached the gospel there. Peter says that Jesus Christ was put to death in the flesh, but raised to life in the Spirit, and that it was in the Spirit that He so preached. The meaning of this is that Jesus lived in a human body and was under all the limitations of time and space in the days of His flesh; that He died with that body battered and broken and bleeding upon the Cross. But when He rose again He rose with a spiritual body, in which He was rid of the necessary weaknesses of humanity, in which He was liberated from the necessary limitations of time and space, and in which the whole universe became His sphere. It was in this spiritual condition of perfect freedom that this preaching to the dead took place.

We must now ask what are the great and timeless truths in this doctrine? As it stands the doctrine is stated in categories which are outworn and overpassed. It speaks of the *descent* into Hades. The very word *descent* thinks in terms of three-storey universe in which heaven is localized above the sky, and Hades beneath the earth. But, laying aside all the physical and geographical categories of this doctrine, we can still find in it truths which are eternally valid and precious. It conserved three great truths.

(a) If Jesus Christ descended into Hades, then Jesus Christ really and truly died. His death was no sham bit of play-acting. His death is not to be explained in terms of a swoon on the Cross, or anything like that. He really and truly experienced death, and rose again. It enables us to believe in a Christ who went through the human experience of birth and life and death. At its simplest, the doctrine of the descent into Hades lays down the complete identity of Christ with our human condition, even to the experience of death.

(b) If Christ descended into Hades, then it means that the triumph of Christ is literally universal. This, in fact, is a truth which is ingrained into the New Testament. It is Paul's dream that at the name of Jesus every knee should bow, of things in heaven and things in earth and things under the earth (*Philippians* 2: 10). In the *Revelation* the song of praise comes from every creature which is in heaven, and on the earth, and under the earth (*Revelation* 5: 13). He who ascended into Heaven is He who first descended into the lower parts of the earth (*Ephesians* 4: 9, 10). The total submission of the universe to Christ is woven into the thought of the New Testament.

(c) If Christ descended into Hades, and preached there, then there is no corner of the universe into which the message of grace has not come. There is in this passage the solution of one of the most haunting questions raised by the Christian faith—What is to happen to those who lived before Jesus Christ, and to those to whom the gospel never came? There can be no salvation without repentance, and how can repentance come to those who have never been confronted with the love and the holiness of God? If there is no other name by which men may be saved, what is to happen to those who never heard that name? This is the point that Justin Martyr fastened on long ago: " The Lord, the Holy God of Israel, remembered His dead, those sleeping in the earth, and came down to them to tell them the good news of salvation." The doctrine of the descent into Hades conserves the precious truth that no man who ever lived is left without a sight of Christ, and without the offer of the salvation of God.

There are many who in repeating the creed have found the phrase, " He descended into hell," either meaningless or bewildering, and who have tacitly agreed to set it on one side and to forget it. It may well be that we ought to think of this as a picture painted in terms of poetry rather than a doctrine stated in terms of theology; it may well be that this is a picture for the heart to feed upon rather than for insertion into the formula of a creed. But in it there are three great truths—the truth that Jesus Christ not only tasted death, but drained the cup of death, the truth that the triumph of Christ is universal, the truth that there is no corner of the universe into which the grace of God has not reached out.

THE BAPTISM OF THE CHRISTIAN

1 Peter 3: 18-22

> For Christ also died once and for all for our sins, the
> just for the unjust, that He might bring us to God.
> He was put to death in the flesh, but He was raised to
> life in the Spirit, in which also He went and preached
> to the spirits who are in prison, the spirits who were
> once upon a time disobedient in the time when the
> patience of God waited in the days of Noah, while the
> ark was being built, in which some few—that is, eight
> souls—were brought in safety through the water.
> And water now saves you, who were symbolically
> represented in Noah and his company, I mean the water
> of baptism; and baptism is not merely the removal
> of dirt from the body, but the pledge to God of a
> good conscience, through the resurrection of Jesus
> Christ, who is at the right hand of God, because He
> went to heaven, after angels and authorities and
> powers had been made subject to Him.

THIS passage is really a digression. Peter has been speaking
about the wicked men who were disobedient and corrupt
in the days of Noah; they were ultimately destroyed. But
in the destruction by the flood eight people were saved in
the ark—Noah and his wife, his sons Shem, Ham and
Japhet, and their wives. They were brought to safety
through the water in the ark. Immediately the idea of
being *brought to safety through the water* turns Peter's
thoughts to Christian baptism, for baptism is also a bringing
to safety through the water. What Peter literally says is
that baptism is an *antitype* of Noah and his people in the
ark. This word introduces us to a special way of looking
at the Old Testament. There are two closely connected
words. There is *tupos*, type, which means a *seal*, and there
is *antitupos*, antitype, which means the *impression of the
seal*. Now clearly between the seal and its impression
there is the closest possible correspondence; the seal and
its impression correspond to each other. So there are
people and events and customs in the Old Testament which
are types, and which find their antitypes in the New

Testament. The Old Testament event or person is like the seal; the New Testament event or person is like the impression; the two correspond, answer to each other. In a more modern way we might put it that the Old Testament event symbolically represents and foreshadows the New Testament event. The science of finding types and antitypes in the Old and the New Testaments is very highly developed. But to take very simple and obvious examples, the Passover Lamb and the scape-goat, who bore the sins of the people are types of Jesus; and the work of the High Priest in making sacrifice for the sins of the people is a type of Jesus' saving work. Here Peter sees the bringing safely through the waters of Noah and his family as a type of baptism; it is a corresponding, a symbolic picture of baptism.

In this passage Peter has three great things to say about baptism. It must be remembered that at this stage of the Church's history we are still dealing with adult baptism, the baptism of people who had come straight from heathenism into Christianity, and who were professing their faith, and taking upon themselves a new way of life and living.

(i) Baptism is not merely a physical cleansing; it is a spiritual cleansing of the whole heart and soul and life. It is not merely a bath of water to wash the body; it is a bathing with grace to cleanse the life. Its effect must be on a man's very soul, and on his whole life.

(ii) Peter calls baptism *the pledge of a good conscience to God* (verse 21). There is a very vivid picture here. The word which Peter uses for *pledge* is *eperōtēma*; in Greek this was a technical business and legal word; in Latin the word for the same process is *stipulatio*. In every business contract there was a definite question and answer which made the contract legal and binding. The question was: " Do you accept the terms of this contract, and bind yourself to observe them?" And the answer, before witnesses was: "Yes." Without that question and answer the contract was not valid. The technical word for that question and answer clause is *eperōtēma* in Greek, *stipulatio* in Latin. Peter is, in effect, saying that in baptism God said to the man coming direct from heathenism: "Do you accept the terms of my service? Do you accept its privileges and promises, and do you undertake its responsibilities and its demands?" And in the act of being baptized the man answered: "Yes." We use the word *sacrament*. The word *sacrament* is derived from the Latin word *sacramentum*, which means *a soldier's oath of loyalty* on entering the army. Here we have basically the same picture. We cannot very well apply this question and answer in infant baptism, unless it be to the parents; but, as we have said, baptism in the very early Church was the baptism of adult men and women coming spontaneously from heathenism into the Church; and the modern parallel is entering upon membership of the Church. When we enter upon Church membership, God asks us: "Do you accept the conditions of my service, with all privileges and all its responsibilities, with all its promises and all its demands?" and we answer; "Yes." It would be well if all Church members were clearly to understand what they are doing when they take upon themselves membership of the Church.

(iii) The whole idea and effectiveness of baptism is dependent on the resurrection of Jesus Christ. It is the grace of the Risen Lord which cleanses us. It is to the Risen, Living Lord that we pledge ourselves; it is to the Risen, Living Lord that we look for strength and grace to keep the pledge that we have given. Once again in the case of infant baptism, we must take these great conceptions and apply them to the time when we enter upon full and deliberate and self-chosen membership of the Church.

THE OBLIGATION OF THE CHRISTIAN

1 *Peter* 4: 1-5

> Since, then, Christ suffered in the flesh, you too must arm yourselves with the same conviction, that he who has suffered in the flesh has ceased from sin, and as a result of this the aim of such a man now is to spend the time that remains to him of life in obedience to the will of God. For the time that is past is sufficient to have done what the Gentiles will to do, to have lived a life of licentiousness, lust, drunkenness, revellings, carousings, and abominable idolatry. They think it strange when you do not rush to join them in the same flood of profligacy, and they abuse you for not doing so. They will give account to Him who is ready to judge the living and the dead.

THE Christian in virtue of the fact that he is a Christian is committed to abandon the ways of heathenism and of godlessness and live as God would have him to do.

Peter says, " He who has suffered in the flesh has ceased from sin." What exactly does he mean? It is very difficult to say what he means. There are three real and distinct possibilities.

(i) There is a strong line in Jewish thought that suffering is in itself a great purifier, that, as the fire purifies the gold, so suffering purifies the soul. In the *Apocalypse of Baruch* the writer, speaking of the experiences of the people of Israel, says, " Then, therefore, were they chastened that they might be sanctified " (13: 10). In regard to the purification of the spirits of men *Enoch* says, " And in proportion as the burning of their body becomes severe, a corresponding change will take place in their spirit for ever and ever; for before the Lord of spirits there will be none to utter a lying word " (67: 9). The terrible sufferings of the time are described in 2 *Maccabees*, and the writer says, " I beseech those that read this book that they be not discouraged, terrified or shaken for these calamities, but that they judge these punishments not to be for destruction but for chastening of our nation. For it is a token of his great goodness, when evil-doers are not suffered to go on in their ways any long time, but forthwith punished. For not as with other nations, whom the Lord patiently forbeareth to punish, till the day of judgment arrive, and they be come to the fulness of their sins, so dealeth He with us, lest that, being come to the height of sin, afterwards He should take vengeance on us. And though He punish sinners with adversity, yet doth He never forsake His people " (6: 12-16). The idea here is that suffering sanctifies, and that not to be punished is the greatest penalty and punishment which God can lay upon a man. " Blessed is the man whom Thou chastenest, O Lord," said the Psalmist (*Psalm* 94: 12). " Happy is the man that God correcteth," said Eliphaz (*Job* 5: 17). " Whom the Lord loveth He chasteneth and scourgeth every son whom He receiveth " (*Hebrews* 12: 6). If this is the idea, it means that he who has been disciplined by suffering has been cured from sin. That is a great thought. It enables us, as Browning said, " to welcome each rebuff that turns earth's smoothness rough." It enables us to see the meaning behind the experiences of life, and to thank God for the experiences which hurt, but which save the soul. But great as this thought is, it is not strictly relevant here.

(ii) When Peter says that he who has suffered in the flesh has ceased from sin, Bigg thinks that he is speaking in terms of the experience which his people had of persecution, and unpopularity, and suffering for the Christian faith. Bigg puts it this way: " He who has suffered in meekness and in fear, he who has endured all that persecution can do to him rather than join in wicked ways can be trusted to do right; temptation has manifestly no power over him." The idea is that if a man has come through persecution, and has not denied the name of Christ, and has stood fast for the faith, then he comes out on the other side of it with a character so tested and tried, and a faith so strengthened, that temptation cannot touch him any more. Again there is a great thought here, the thought that every trial and every temptation which come to us are meant, not to make us fall, but to make us stronger and firmer and better. Every temptation resisted makes the next temptation easier to resist, and every temptation conquered makes us better able to meet and to face and to overcome the next attack. As we have said, that is a splendid thought, but again it is doubtful if it comes in very relevantly here.

(iii) There is one further explanation, and it is most probably the right one. Let us set down our text: " He who has suffered in the flesh has ceased from sin." Peter has just been talking about baptism. Now the great New Testament picture of baptism is in *Romans* 6. In that chapter Paul says that the experience of baptism is like being buried with Christ in death and raised with Christ to newness of life. It is like dying to sin, and rising to live to righteousness. It is like sharing every experience of Christ, His life, His temptations, His sufferings, His death, and, finally, His resurrection. We think that this is what Peter is thinking of here. He has spoken of baptism; and now he says, " He who in baptism has shared the sufferings and the death of Christ, is risen to such newness of life with Him that sin has no more dominion over him " (*Romans* 6: 14). Again, as ever, we must remember that this is adult baptism, the baptism of the man who is voluntarily coming over from paganisn into Christianity. In that act of baptism the man is identified with Christ; he shares the sufferings and even the death of Christ; and he shares Christ's risen life and risen power, and is, therefore, victor over sin.

When that has happened a man has said a long good-bye to his former way of life. The rule of pleasure, pride and passion is gone, and the rule of God has begun. This was by no means easy. A man's former associates would laugh at the new " puritanism " which had entered into his life. But the Christian knows very well that the judgment of God will come, and then the judgments of earth will be reversed, and the pleasures that are eternal will compensate a thousandfold for the transitory and the hurtful pleasures which had to be abandoned in this life.

THE ULTIMATE CHANCE

I *Peter* 4: 6

> For this is reason why the gospel was preached to the dead, that, although they have been judged in the flesh like men, they may live in the Spirit like God.

THIS very difficult passage ends with a very difficult verse. Once again we have the idea of the gospel being preached to the dead. At least three different meanings have been attached to the word *dead*. (i) It has been taken to mean those who are *dead in sin*; not those who are physically dead, but those who are under the killing influence of sin. (ii) It has been taken to mean *those who died before the Second Coming of Christ*. They are dead; but they heard the gospel before they died; and they will not miss the glory. (iii) It has been taken to mean quite simply *all the dead*. There can be little doubt that this third meaning is correct; Peter has just been talking about the descent of Christ to the place of the dead, and here he comes back to the idea of Christ preaching to the dead.

But what does it mean to say that, though they have been judged in the flesh like men, the gospel has been preached to them that they may live in the Spirit like God?

No fully satisfactory meaning has ever been found for this verse; but we think that the best explanation is as follows. For mortal man, death is the penalty of sin. It was sin which brought death into the world. As Paul wrote: " By one man sin entered into the world, and death by sin, and so death passed upon all men, for that all have sinned " (*Romans* 5: 12). Had there been no sin, there would have been no death; death is the penalty of sin; and, therefore, death in itself is a judgment. So Peter says, all men have already been judged when they die. Because they are men, they are under the judgment of death. But in spite of that Peter has this amazing idea that Christ descended to the world of the dead and preached the gospel there, and that very fact means that, even though they had been judged by death, the dead had still another chance to grasp the gospel and to live in the Spirit of God.

In some ways this is one of the most wonderful verses in the Bible, for, if our explanation of it is anywhere near the truth, it gives us a breath-taking glimpse of nothing less than a gospel of a second chance.

THE APPROACHING END

I *Peter* 4: 7a

The end of all things is near.

HERE is a note which is struck consistently all through the New Testament. It is the summons of Paul that it is time to wake out of sleep, for the night is far spent and the day is at hand (*Romans* 13: 12). " The Lord is at hand," he writes to the Philippians (*Philippians* 4: 5). " The coming of the Lord cometh nigh," writes James (*James* 5: 8). John says that the days in which his people are living are the last time (I *John* 2: 18). " The time is at hand," says the John of the *Revelation*, and he hears the Risen Christ testify: " Surely I come quickly " (*Revelation* 1: 3; 22: 20).

There are many for whom these and all such passages are problems, for, if they are taken literally and at their face value, the New Testament writers were mistaken; nineteen hundred years have passed and the end is not yet come. These passages raise a problem which any thinking student of the Bible is compelled to face. There are four ways of looking at such passages.

(i) We may hold quite simply that the New Testament writers were in fact mistaken; they looked for the return of Christ and the end of the world in their own day and generation; and these events did not take place. If we adopt that point of view the curious thing is that the Christian Church allowed these words to stand. It would not have been difficult quietly to excise them from the New Testament documents; and yet they allowed them to stand. It was not until late in the second century that the New Testament began to be fixed in the form in which we have it today; and, when it was fixed, books with statements such as these became unquestioned parts of it. The clear conclusion is that the people of the early Church did not think that they were mistaken, and still believed these words to be true.

(ii) There is a strong line of New Testament thought which, in effect, holds that the end *has* come. The consummation of history was the coming of Jesus Christ. In Him time was invaded by eternity. In Him God entered into the human situation. In Him the prophecies were all fulfilled. In Him the end has come. Paul speaks of himself and his people as those on whom the ends of the world have come (I *Corinthians* 10: 11). Peter in his first sermon speaks of Joel's prophecy of the outpouring of the Spirit and of all that should happen in the last days, and then says that these days have come, that at that very time men were actually living in those last days which the prophet had foretold (*Acts* 2: 16-21). If we accept that, it means that in Jesus Christ the end of history came. The battle has been won; there remain only skirmishes with the last remnants of opposition, a kind of final mopping-up process. It will mean that at this very moment we are living in the "end time," in what someone has called "the epilogue to history." That is a very common and orthodox point of view; but the trouble about it is that it does fly in the face of facts. Evil is as rampant as ever; man is as rebellious as ever; the world is still far from having accepted Christ as King. It may be the "end time," but the dawn seems as far distant as ever it was.

(iii) It may be that we have to interpret the word *near* in the light of history. History is a process of almost unimaginable length. It has been put this way. Suppose all time to be represented by a column the height of Cleopatra's Needle with one single postage stamp upon the top of it, then the length of recorded history is represented by the thickness of the postage stamp, and the unrecorded history which went before it by the height of the whole column. When we think of time in terms like that the word *near* becomes an entirely relative word. The Psalmist was literally and historically right when he said that in God's sight a thousand years were no more than like a watch in the night (*Psalm* 90: 4). In that case the word *near* can cover centuries and generations, and still be correctly used. But it is quite certain that the biblical writers did not take the word *near* in that sense, for they had no conception of history in terms like that.

(iv) The simple fact is that behind this there is one inescapable and most personal truth. *For everyone of us, the time is near.* For every one of us the hour is hastening on. The one thing which can be said of every man—and the only thing which can be said of every man—is that we will die. For every one of us the Lord is at hand. We cannot tell the day and the hour when we shall go to meet our God; and, therefore, all life must be lived in the shadow of eternity.

" The end of all things is near," said Peter. The early thinkers may have been wrong if they thought that the total end of the world was round the corner, but they have left us with the warning that for every one of us personally and inescapably the end is near, and their exhortations and warnings in face of that universal fact are as valid for us today as ever they were.

THE LIFE LIVED IN THE SHADOW OF ETERNITY

I Peter 4: 7b, 8

> Be, therefore, steady and sober in mind, so that you
> will really be able to pray as you ought. Above all
> cherish for each other a love that is constant and
> intense, because love hides a multitude of sins.

WHEN a man realizes the nearness of Jesus Christ, he is
bound to commit himself to a certain kind of life. In view
of that nearness Peter here makes four demands.

(i) He says that we must be steady in mind. We might
translate that: " Preserve your sanity." The verb Peter
uses is *sōphronein*; connected with that verb is the noun
sōphrosunē, which the Greeks derived from the verb
sōzein, which means *to keep safe*, and the noun *phronēsis*,
which means *the mind*. *Sōphrosunē* is the wisdom which
characterizes a man who is pre-eminently sane; and
sōphronein means *to preserve one's sanity*. The great
characteristic of sanity is that it sees things in their proper
proportions; it sees what things are important and what
things are not important; it is not swept away by sudden
and capricious and transitory enthusiasms; it is prone
neither to unbalanced fanaticism nor to unrealizing indifference. It is only when we see the affairs and the activities
of earth in the light of eternity that we see them in their
proper proportions and their proper importances. It is
when God is given His proper place that all things take
their proper places.

(ii) He says that we must be sober in mind. We might
translate: " Preserve your sobriety." The verb Peter
uses is *nēphein*. Originally that verb meant *to be sober*
in contradistinction to *being drunk*. It then came to mean
to act soberly and sensibly. This does not mean that the
Christian is to be lost in a gloomy joylessness; but it does
mean that his approach to life must not be frivolous and
irresponsible. To take things seriously is to be aware of
their real importance, to be ever mindful of their conse-

quences in time and in eternity, to be always aware of their effects on ourselves and on others, to approach life, not as a jest, but as a serious matter, for which we are answerable and responsible.

(iii) He says that we must do this in order to pray as we ought. We might say that Peter meant: " Preserve your prayer life." When a man's mind is unbalanced, when he lets his own prejudices run away with him, when his approach to life is frivolous and selfish and irresponsible, he obviously cannot pray as he ought. He will not know in such a case for what he ought to ask; and he will ask for the wrong things. We only learn to pray when we take life so wisely and so seriously that we begin to say in all things: " Thy will be done." The first necessity of prayer is the earnest desire, not to get what we wish, but to discover the will of God for ourselves.

(iv) He says that we must cherish for each other a love that is constant and intense. That is to say, he urges us: " Preserve your love." The word that Peter uses to describe this Christian love is *ektenēs*. *Ektenēs* has two meanings, and we have included both in the translation. It means *outstretching* in the sense of *constant* and *consistent*, never-failing. Our love must be the love that never fails. But *ektenēs* means more than that. It means stretching out as a runner stretches out. As C. E. B. Cranfield reminds us it describes a horse at full gallop, and it denotes " the taut muscle of strenuous and sustained effort, as of an athlete." Here is a fundamental Christian truth. Christian love is not an easy, sentimental reaction. It demands everything a man has got of mental and spiritual nerve and muscle and sinew. It means loving the unlovely and the unlovable; it means loving in spite of insult and injury; it means loving when love is not returned, but is spurned. Bengel translates *ektenēs* by the Latin word *vehemens, vehement*. The Christian love is the love which never fails, and the love into which every atom of man's strength is directed.

So, then, the Christian, in the light of eternity, must preserve his sanity, preserve his sobriety, preserve his prayers, and preserve his love.

THE POWER OF LOVE

I *Peter* 4: 7b, 8 (*continued*)

" Love," says Peter, " hides a multitude of sins." There are three things which this saying may mean; and it is not necessary that we should choose between them, for they are all there, and they are all valid, and they are all precious.

(i) It may mean that *our* love can overlook many sins. " Love covereth all sins," says the writer of the *Proverbs* (*Proverbs* 10: 12). If we love a person, it is easy to forgive. It is not that love is blind, but it is that love loves a person just as he is, faults and all. Love makes patience easy. It is much easier to be lovingly patient with our own children than with the children of strangers. If we really love our fellow-men, we can accept their faults, and bear with their foolishness, and even endure their unkindness and their cruelty. Love indeed can cover a multitude of sins.

(ii) It may mean, that, if we love others, God will overlook a multitude of sins in us. In life we meet two kinds of people. We meet people who have no faults at which the finger may be pointed; there is nothing in them which can be criticized; they are moral, orthodox, and supremely respectable; but they have little sympathy; they have no understanding; they are hard and austere and unable to understand why others make mistakes and fall into sin. We also meet people who have all kinds of faults; they are guilty of habits and practices and indulgences which are anything but respectable, and which make the respectable raise their eyebrows; but they are kind; they have sympathy; their first instinct is to forgive and to help and to comfort; and they seldom or never condemn. It is the second kind of person to whom the heart warms; and in all reverence we may say that it is so with God. God will forgive much to the man who loves and helps his fellow-men.

(iii) It may mean that *God's* love covers the multitude of our sins. We know that that is blessedly and profoundly true. It is the wonder of grace that sinners as we are God loves us, that that is indeed why He sent His Son.

Here is a blessed saying, for, however we take it, love indeed covers a multitude of sins.

CHRISTIAN RESPONSIBILITY

1 *Peter* 4: 9, 10

> Be hospitable to one another, and never grudge it. As each has received a gift from God, so let all use such gifts in the service of one another, like good stewards of the grace of God.

PETER'S mind is dominated in this section of his letter by the conviction that the end of all things is near. It is of the greatest interest and the greatest significance to note that he does not use that conviction to urge men to withdraw from the world and to enter on a kind of private campaign to save their own souls; he uses it to urge men to go out into the world and to serve their fellow-men. The approaching end was for Peter not a reason for separating oneself from the world in a determined effort to win a selfish salvation; it was a reason for becoming still more deeply involved in the world in the service of others. As Peter sees it, a man will be happy, if the end finds him, not withdrawn into a monastery or living as a hermit, but out in the world serving his fellow-men.

(i) First, Peter urges upon his people the duty of hospitality. Without hospitality the early Church could not have existed. The travelling missionaries who spread the good news of the gospel had to find somewhere to stay, and there was no place for them to stay except in the homes of Christians. Such inns as there were were impossibly dear, impossibly filthy, and notoriously immoral. Without the private hospitality of Christian homes the work of the early missionaries would have come to a standstill. Thus we find Peter lodging with one Simon a tanner (*Acts* 10: 6), and Paul and his company were to lodge with one Mnason of Cyprus, an old disciple (*Acts* 21: 16). Many and many a nameless one in the early Church by opening the doors of his house and home made Christian missionary work possible.

But not only did the missionaries need hospitality; the local Churches also needed it. For two hundred years there was no such thing as a Church building. The Church was compelled to meet in the houses of those who had bigger rooms, and who were prepared to lend these rooms for the services of the congregation. Thus we read of the Church which was in the house of Aquila and Priscilla (*Romans* 16: 5; I *Corinthians* 16: 19), and of the Church which was in the house of Philemon (*Philemon* 2). Without those who were prepared to open their homes, the early Church could not have met for worship at all.

It is little wonder that again and again in the New Testament the duty of hospitality is pressed upon the Christians. The Christian is to be given to hospitality (*Romans* 12: 13). A bishop is to be given to hospitality (I *Timothy* 3: 2); the widows of the Church must have lodged strangers (I *Timothy* 5: 10). The Christian must not forget to entertain strangers, and must remember that some who have done so have entertained angels unawares (*Hebrews* 13: 2). The bishop must be a lover of hospitality (*Titus* 1: 8). And it is ever to be remembered that it was said to those on the right hand: " I was a stranger, and ye took me in," and the condemnation of those on the left hand was: " I was a stranger, and ye took me not in " (*Matthew* 25: 35, 43).

In the early days the Church depended on the hospitality of its members; and to this day no greater gift can be offered than the welcome of a Christian home to the stranger in a strange place.

(ii) Such gifts as a man has he must place ungrudgingly at the service of the community. This again is a favourite New Testament idea which is expanded by Paul in *Romans* 12: 3-8 and I *Corinthians* 12. The Church needs every gift that every man can have. It may be a gift of speaking, of music, of the ability to visit people. It may be a craft or skill which can be used in the practical service of the Church. It may be a house which a man possesses or money which he has inherited. There is no gift which cannot be placed at the service of Christ.

The Christian has to regard himself as a steward of God. In the ancient world the steward was very important. He himself might be a slave, but his master's goods were in his hands. There were two main kinds of stewards, the *dispensator*, the dispenser, who was responsible for all the domestic arrangements of the household, and who laid in and divided out the household supplies; and the *vilicus*, the bailiff, who was in charge of his master's estates, and who acted as landlord to his master's tenant. The steward knew well that nothing of the things over which he had control belonged to him; they all belonged to his master. In his administration of them his one duty was to consult his master's interests, and in everything he did he was answerable to his master.

The Christian must always be under the conviction that nothing he possesses of material goods or personal qualities is his own; that everything he possesses belongs to God; that he must ever use what he has in the interests of God, as God would use it; and that he is always answerable to God. If that be so, the Christian will be certain that all that he has must be used in the service of his fellow-men.

THE SOURCE AND OBJECT OF ALL CHRISTIAN ENDEAVOUR

I Peter 4: 11

> If anyone speaks, let him speak as one uttering sayings sent from God. If anyone renders any service, let him do so as one whose service comes from the strength which God supplies, so that God may be glorified in all things through Jesus Christ to whom belong glory and power for ever and ever. Amen.

HERE Peter is thinking of the two great activities of the Christian Church, the activity of preaching and the activity of practical service. The word which Peter uses for *sayings* is *logia*. That is a word with a kind of divine background. The heathen used it for the oracles which came to them from their gods; the Christians used it for the words of scripture, and the words of Christ. So Peter is saying, " If a man has the duty of preaching, let him preach not as a man offering his own opinions or propagating his own prejudices, but as a man with a message from God." It was said of one great preacher: " First he listened to God, and then he spoke to men." It was said of another that, when he preached ever and again he paused, " as if listening for a voice." Therein lies the secret of preaching power.

Further, Peter goes on to say that if a Christian is engaged in practical Christian service, he must render that service as one who renders it in the strength which God supplies. It is as if Peter said, " When you are engaged in Christian service, you must not do it or give it as if you were conferring a personal favour, or distributing bounty from your own store, but in the consciousness that what you give, you first received from God." Such an attitude preserves the giver from all pride and the gift from all humiliation.

The aim of everything is that God should be glorified. The preaching is not done to display the preacher, but to bring men face to face with God. The service is rendered not to bring thanks and prestige to the giver of it, but to

turn men's thoughts to God. E. G. Selwyn reminds us
that the motto of the great Benedictine Order of monks
is four letters—IOGD—which stand for the Latin words
(*ut*) *in omnibus glorificetur Deus*, which means *in order
that in all things God may be glorified*. A new grace and
glory would enter the Church, if all Church people, ceased
doing things for themselves, and did them for God. We
would do well to carry the letters IOGD before us, to put
them up where we can ever see them, so that we might
never forget that all things must be done for the glory of
God—and the obliteration of self.

THE INEVITABILITY OF PERSECUTION

I *Peter* 4: 12, 13

> Beloved, do not regard the fiery ordeal through which
> you are passing, and which has happened to you to
> test you, as something strange, as if some alien exper-
> ience were happening to you, but rejoice in so far as
> you share the sufferings of Christ, so that you may also
> rejoice with rapture, when His glory shall be revealed.

IN the nature of things persecution must have been a much
more daunting experience for Gentiles than it was for
Jews. The average Gentile had little experience of it;
but the Jews have always been the most persecuted people
upon earth; persecution has been part of their heritage.
Peter was writing to Christians who were Gentiles, and
he had to try to help them by showing them persecution
in its true terms. It is never easy to be a Christian. The
Christian life can still bring its own loneliness, its own
unpopularity, its own problems, its own sacrifices, and its
own persecutions. It is, therefore, well to have certain
great principles in our minds.

(i) It was Peter's view that persecution is inevitable.
It is human nature to dislike, to resent, and to regard
with suspicion anyone who is different; the Christian is
necessarily different from the man of the world. The

particular impact of the Christian difference makes the matter more acute. To the world the Christian brings the standards of Jesus Christ. In his own way, and, as far as he can, he confronts the world with Christ. That is another way of saying that the Christian is inevitably a kind of conscience to any group or society in which he moves; and many a man would gladly eliminate the troublesome twinges of conscience. The very goodness of Christianity can be an offence to a world in which goodness is a handicap.

(ii) It was Peter's view that persecution is a test. It is a test in a double sense. Any man's devotion to any principle can be measured by his willingness to suffer and to sacrifice for it; therefore, any kind of persecution is a test of a man's faith. But it is equally true that it is only the real Christian who will be persecuted. The Christian who compromises with the world, who plays down the difference between the Christian way and the world's way, who accommodates himself to the world, will certainly not be persecuted. In a double sense persecution is the test of the reality of a man's faith.

(iii) But now we come to the uplifting things. Persecution is a sharing in the sufferings of Jesus Christ. When a man has to suffer and sacrifice for his Christianity he is walking the way his Master walked, and sharing the Cross his Master carried. This is a famous and favourite New Testament thought. If we suffer with Him, we will be glorified with Him (*Romans* 8: 17). It is Paul's desire to enter into the fellowship of the sufferings of Christ (*Philippians* 3: 10). If we suffer with Him, we shall reign with Him (2 *Timothy* 3: 11). If we remember that, then anything we must suffer and sacrifice for the sake of Christ becomes a privilege and not a penalty.

(iv) Persecution is the way to glory. The Cross is the way to the crown. Jesus Christ is no man's debtor, and His joy and crown await the man who, through thick and thin, has been true to Him.

THE BLESSEDNESS OF SUFFERING FOR CHRIST

1 *Peter* 4: 14-16

> If you are reproached for the name of Christ, you are
> blessed, because the presence of the glory and the
> Spirit of God rest upon you. But let none of you
> suffer as a murderer, or a thief, or an evil-doer, or as a
> busybody. But if anyone suffers as a Christian, let
> him not be ashamed, but let him by this name bring
> glory to God.

HERE Peter says the greatest thing of all. He says that, if
a man suffers for Christ, the presence of the glory rests
upon him. In the Greek this is a very strange phrase.
Literally, the Greek is *the presence of the glory.* We think
this can only mean one thing. The Jews had the conception
of what they called the *Shekinah.* The *Shekinah* was the
luminous glow of the very presence of God. This is a
conception which constantly recurs in the Old Testament.
" In the morning," said Moses, " then shall ye see the
glory of the Lord " (*Exodus* 16: 7). " The *glory* of the Lord
abode upon Mount Sinai, and the cloud covered it six
days," when the law was being delivered to Moses (*Exodus*
24: 16). In the tabernacle God was to meet with Israel,
and the tabernacle was to be sanctified with His *glory*
(*Exodus* 29: 43). When the tabernacle was completed,
" then a cloud covered the tent of the congregation, and
the *glory* of the Lord filled the tabernacle " (*Exodus* 40: 34).
When the ark of the covenant was brought into Solomon's
temple, we read that " the cloud filled the house of the
Lord, so that the priests could not stand to minister because
of the cloud; for the *glory* of the Lord had filled the house
of the Lord " (1 *Kings* 8: 10, 11). Repeatedly this idea
of the *Shekinah*, the glowing, luminous glory of God in
visible light, occurs in the Old Testament.

It is Peter's conviction that something of that glow of
glory rests on the man who suffers for Christ. When
Stephen was on trial for his life, and when it was certain
that he would be condemned to death, to those who looked

on him his face was as the face of an angel (Acts 6: 15).
The reproach of suffering for Christ becomes a glory;
something of the very glory of God rests on the man who
suffers for Christ.

Peter goes on to point out that it is as a Christian that
a man must suffer, and not as an evil-doer. The evils
which Peter singles out are all clear enough until we come
to the last. A Christian, Peter says, is not to suffer as an
allotriepiskopos. The trouble is that there is no other
instance of this word in Greek, and Peter may well have
invented it. We have to try to work out its meaning. It
can have three possible meanings, all of which would be
relevant. It comes from two words. *Allotrios* means
belonging to another; *episkopos* means *looking upon* or
looking into. The word, therefore, means *looking upon,
or into, that which belongs to another*.

(i) To look on that which is someone else's goods might
well be to cast covetous eyes upon them. That is how both
the Latin Bible and Calvin take this word; they take it
to mean that the Christian must not be *covetous*.

(ii) To look upon that which belongs to another might
well mean to be too interested in other people's affairs,
to be a meddling busybody. That, in fact, is by far the most
probable meaning of the word. There are Christians
who are meddlesome busybodies, and who do an infinite
deal of harm with their unwise and misguided interference
and criticism and interventions. This would mean that the
Christian must never be an *interfering busybody*. That
gives good sense; we believe that it gives the best sense.

(iii) But there is a third possibility. *Allotrios* means
that which belongs to someone else; that is to say, *that
which is alien and foreign to oneself*. If we look for the
meaning of the word along that line *allotriepiskopos* will
mean *looking upon that which is foreign or alien to oneself*.
That would mean of a Christian, being guilty of conduct,
being guilty of entering upon undertakings, which are
alien to a Christian, and which do not befit the Christian

life. This, then, would be a warning that a Christian must never interest himself in things, or engage in a trade, or enter on a course of action, which is alien and foreign to the life that a Christian should lead.

While all three meanings are possible, and while all three warnings are relevant, we think that the third meaning is the right one. It is Peter's injunction that, if a Christian has to suffer for Christ, he must suffer in such a way that his suffering brings glory to God and to the name he bears. His life and conduct must be the best argument that he does not deserve the suffering which has come upon him. By his general conduct in life, and by his attitude to the suffering he has to bear, he must commend the name he bears.

ENTRUSTING ALL LIFE TO GOD

I *Peter* 4: 17-19

> For the time has come for judgment to begin from the household of God. And, if it begins from us, what will be the end of those who disobey the good news which comes from God? And, if the righteous man is scarcely saved, where will the impious man and the sinner appear? So, then, let those who suffer in accordance with the will of God, entrust their souls to Him who is a Creator on whom you can rely, and continue to do right.

As Peter saw it, it was all the more necessary for the Christian to do right, because judgment was about to begin.

Judgment was to begin with the household of God. Ezekiel hears the voice of God proclaiming judgment upon His people, and the voice says, " Begin at my sanctuary " (*Ezekiel* 9: 6). Where the privilege has been greatest, there the judgment will be sternest.

And, if judgment is to fall upon the Church of God, what will be the fate of those who have been utterly regardless of, and disobedient to, the invitation and command of God? Peter confirms his appeal with a quotation from *Proverbs* 11: 31: " If the righteous man is scarcely saved, where will the impious man and the sinner appear? "

Finally, Peter exhorts his people to continue to do good, and, whatever happens to them to entrust their lives to God, who is the Creator on whom they can rely. The word which Peter uses for to entrust is a vivid word; it is the word *paratithesthai*, which is the technical word for *depositing money with a trusted friend*. In the ancient days there were no banks and few really safe places in which to deposit money. So, before a man went on a journey, he often left his money in the safe-keeping of a friend. Such a trust was regarded as one of the most sacred things in life. The friend was absolutely bound by all honour and all religion to return the money intact.

Herodotus (6: 86) has a story about such a trust. A certain Milesian came to Sparta, for he had heard of the strict honour of the Spartans, and entrusted his money to a certain Glaucus. He said that in due time his sons would reclaim the money and would bring tokens which would establish their identity beyond doubt. The time passed; the sons came. Glaucus treacherously said that he had no recollection of any money being entrusted to him, and said that he wished four months to think about it. The Milesians departed sad and sorry. Glaucus consulted the gods as to what he ought to do, and they warned him that he must return the money. He did so, but before long he died, and all his family died with him, and in the time of Herodotus there was not a single member of his family left alive, because the gods were angry that he had even contemplated breaking the trust reposed in him. Even to think of evading such a trust was a mortal sin. If a man entrusts himself to God, God cannot fail him. If such a trust is sacred to men, how much more is it sacred to God? This is the very word which is used of Jesus, when He said " Father, into Thy hands I commend my spirit" (*Luke* 23: 46). Jesus unhesitatingly committed and entrusted His life to God, certain that in the end God would not fail Him—and so may we. The old advice is still the good advice—Trust in God and do the right.

THE ELDERS OF THE CHURCH

1 *Peter* 5: 1-4

So, then, as your fellow-elder, and a witness of the sufferings of Christ, as a sharer in the glory which is going to be revealed, I urge the elders who are among you, shepherd the flock of God which is in your charge, not because you are coerced into doing so, but of your own free-will as God would have you to do, not to make a shameful profit out of it, but with enthusiasm, not as if you aimed to be petty tyrants over those allotted to your care, but as being under the obligation to be examples to the flock; and, when the Chief Shepherd appears, you will receive the unfading crown of glory.

THERE are few passages which show more clearly the importance of the eldership in the early Church. It is to the elders that Peter specially writes, and he, who was the chief of the apostles, does not hesitate to call himself a fellow-elder. It will be worth our while to look at something of the background and history of the eldership, the most ancient and the most important office in the Church.

(i) The eldership has a Jewish background. The Jews traced the beginning of the eldership to the days when the children of Israel were journeying through the wilderness to the Promised Land. There came a time when Moses felt the burdens of leadership too heavy for him to bear by himself alone, and to help him seventy elders were set apart and granted a share of the spirit of God (*Numbers* 11: 16-30). Thereafter the elders became a permanent feature of Jewish life. We find the elders as the friends of the prophets (2 *Kings* 6: 32); as the advisers of kings

(I *Kings* 20: 8; 21: 11); as the colleagues of the princes in the administration of the affairs of the nation (*Ezra* 10: 8). Every village and city had its elders; they met at the gate of the village or city and dispensed justice to the people (*Deuteronomy* 25: 7). The elders were the administrators of the synagogue; they did not preach, but they saw to the good government and the order of the synagogue, and they exercised discipline over its members. The elders formed a large section of the Sanhedrin, the supreme court of the Jews, and they are regularly mentioned along with the Chief Priests and the rulers and the Scribes and the Pharisees (*Matthew* 16: 21; 21: 33; 26: 3, 57; 27: 1, 3; *Luke* 7: 3; *Acts* 4: 5; 6: 11; 24: 1). In the vision of the *Revelation* in the heavenly places there are twenty-four elders around the throne. It is clear that the elders are woven into the very structure of Judaism, both in its civil and its religious affairs.

(ii) The eldership has a Greek background. Especially in Egyptian communities we find that elders are the leaders of the community and that they are responsible for the conduct of public affairs, much as town councillors are today responsible for the affairs of the community. We find a woman who had suffered an assault appealing to the elders for justice. When corn is being collected as tribute on the visit of a governor, we find that " the elders of the cultivators " are the officials concerned. We find them connected with the issuing of public edicts, the leasing of land for pasture, the ingathering of taxation. In Asia Minor, also, the members of councils and corporations were called elders. Even in the religious communities of the pagan world we find " elder priests " mentioned who were responsible for discipline. In the Socnopaeus temple we find the elder priests dealing with the case of a priest who is charged with allowing his hair to grow too long and with wearing woollen garments—an effeminacy and a luxury of which no priest should have been guilty.

We can see that long before Christianity took over the title the title of *elder* was a title of honour both in the Jewish and in the Graeco-Roman world.

THE CHRISTIAN ELDERSHIP

I Peter 5: 1-4 (*continued*)

WHEN we turn to the Christian Church we find that the eldership is its basic office.

It was Paul's custom to ordain elders in every community to which he preached, and in every Church which he founded. On the first missionary journey elders were ordained in every Church (*Acts* 14: 23). Titus is left in Crete to ordain elders in every city (*Titus* 1: 5). The elders had charge of the financial administration of the Church; it is to them that Paul and Barnabas delivered the money sent to relieve the poor of Jerusalem in the time of the famine (*Acts* 11: 30). The elders were the councillors and the administrators of the Church. We find them taking a leading part in the decisions of the Council of Jerusalem at which it was decided to fling open the doors of the Church to the Gentiles. So much so is this the case that at that Council the elders and the apostles are spoken of together as the chief authorities of the Church (*Acts* 15: 2; 16: 4). When Paul came on his last visit to Jerusalem, it was to the elders that he reported, and it was the elders who suggested the course of actions that he should follow (*Acts* 21: 18-25). One of the most moving passages in the New Testament is Paul's farewell to the elders of Ephesus. We find there that the elders, as Paul saw them, are the overseers of the flock of God, and the defenders of the faith (*Acts* 20: 28, 29). We learn from James that the elders had a healing function in the Church through prayers and anointing with oil (*James* 5: 14). From the Pastoral Epistles we learn that the elders were rulers and teachers, and that they were by that time paid officials of the Church

(I *Timothy* 5: 17; the phrase *double honour* is better translated *double pay*).

When a man enters the eldership, no small honour is conferred upon him, for he is entering on the oldest religious office in the world, an office whose history can be traced through Christianity and Judaism for four thousand years. When a man enters the eldership, no small responsibility falls upon him, for he has been ordained as a shepherd of the flock of God, and a defender of the faith.

THE PERILS AND PRIVILEGES OF THE ELDERSHIP

I *Peter* 5: 1-4 (*continued*)

IN this passage Peter sets down in a series of contrasts the perils and the privileges of the eldership. And, it is to be noted, that everything which Paul here says is applicable, not only to the eldership, but also to all Christian service inside and outside the Church.

The elder is to accept office, not under coercion, but willingly. This does not mean that a man is to grasp and grab at office; it does not mean that he is gaily to enter upon office without a self-examining thought. Any Christian man will have a certain reluctance to accept high office, because he knows only too well his own unworthiness and his own inadequacy. There is a sense in which it is by compulsion that a man accepts office and enters upon Christian service. " Necessity," said Paul, " is laid upon me; yea, woe is unto me, if I preach not the gospel " (I *Corinthians* 9: 16). " The love of Christ constraineth me," he said (2 *Corinthians* 5: 14). But there is a way of accepting office and of rendering service as if it was a grim and unpleasant duty, as if it was a weariness, as if it was a burden to be resented. It is quite possible for a man to be asked to do something, and for him to do it, but to do it in such an ungracious way that the whole action is spoiled.

Peter does not say that a man should be conceitedly or irresponsibly eager for office; but he does say that every Christian should be tremblingly eager to render such service as he can, although he is fully aware how unworthy he is to render it.

The elder is to accept office, not to make a shameful profit out of it, but eagerly. The word for *making a shameful profit* is the adverb *aischrokerdēs*. The noun from this is *aischrokerdeia*, and it was a characteristic which the Greek loathed. Theophrastus, the great Greek delineator of character, has a character sketch of this *aischrokerdeia*. *Meanness*—as it might be translated—is the desire for base gain. The mean man is the man who never sets enough food before his guests, and who gives himself a double portion when he is carving the joint. He waters the wine; he only goes to the theatre when he can get a free ticket. He never has enough money to pay the fare, and always borrows from his fellow-passengers. When he is selling corn, he uses a measure in which the bottom is pushed up, and even then he carefully levels the top. He counts the half radishes left over from dinner in case the servants eat any. Rather than give a wedding present, he will go away from home when a wedding is in the offing. Meanness is an ugly fault. It is quite clear that there were people in the early Church who accused the preachers and missionaries of being in the job for what they could get out of it. Paul repeatedly declares that he coveted no man's goods, that he worked with his hands to meet his own needs, that he was burdensome to no man (*Acts* 20: 33; I *Thessalonians* 2: 9; I *Corinthians* 9: 12; 2 *Corinthians* 12: 14). It is certain that the payment any early office-bearer received was pitifully small, and the repeated warnings that the office-bearers must not be lovers of " filthy lucre " shows that there were those who coveted more (I *Timothy* 3: 3, 8; *Titus* I: 7, 11). The point that Peter is making—and it is a point that is for ever valid—is that no man dare accept office or render service for what he can get out of it. His desire must ever be to give and not to get.

The elder is to accept office, not to be a petty tyrant, but to be the shepherd and the example of the flock. Human nature is such that it is true that for many people prestige and power are even more attractive than money. There are those who love authority, even if that authority be exercised in a narrow sphere. Milton's Satan thought it better to reign in hell than to serve in heaven. Shakespeare spoke about man, proud man, dressed in a little brief authority, playing such fantastic tricks before high heaven as would make the angels weep. The great characteristic of the shepherd is his selfless care and his sacrificial love for the sheep. Any man who enters on office with the desire for the pre-eminence, with the idea of exercising authority, with the idea of becoming a ruler, has got his whole point of view upside down. Jesus said to His ambitious disciples, " Ye know that they which are accounted to rule over the Gentiles exercise lordship over them; and their great ones exercise authority upon them. But it shall not be so among you; but whosoever shall be great among you shall be your servant, and whosoever of you will be the chiefest shall be the servant of all " (*Mark* 10: 42-44).

THE IDEAL OF THE ELDERSHIP

I *Peter* 5: 1-4 (*continued*)

THERE is one thing in this passage which defies translation, and which is yet one of the most precious and significant things in it. In verse 3 the Authorized Version has it that elders are forbidden to be lords over God's heritage. It will be noted that the word *God's* is printed in the Authorized Version in italic letters, which means that it is not present in the Greek, and has been added by the translators to clarify the sense. We have translated it that the elders are not to aim to be petty tyrants over those who are *allotted* to their care. The phrase which the Authorized Version translates *God's heritage,* and which we have translated *those who are allotted* is curious in Greek; it is *tōn klēron,* which is a genitive plural. The significance is in this word *klēros.* (*Klēros* is the nominative). *Klēros* is a word of extraordinary interest.

(i) It begins by meaning a *dice* or a *lot.* It is so used in *Matthew* 27: 35 which tells how the soldiers beneath the Cross were throwing dice (*klēroi*) to see who should possess the seamless robe of Jesus.

(ii) Second, it means an office gained or assigned by *lot.* It is the word used in *Acts* 1: 26 which tells how the disciples cast lots to see who should inherit the office of Judas the traitor.

(iii) It then comes to mean an inheritance allotted to someone, as it is used in *Colossians* 1: 12 where it is used for the *inheritance* of the saints.

(iv) In classical Greek it very often means a public allotment or estate of land. These allotments were distributed by the civic authorities to the citizens; and very often the distribution was made by drawing lots for the various pieces of land available for distribution.

Now, even if we were to go no further than this, it would mean that the office of the eldership, that any piece of service offered to us, is never *earned* by any merit of our own; it is always *allotted* to us by God. It is not something that we have deserved; it is something which is given to us by the grace of God.

But we can go further than this. *Klēros* means something which is allotted to man; it is something which has been specially assigned to him. Now in *Deuteronomy* 9: 29 we read that Israel is the *inheritance* of God, and the word is *klēros.* That is to say, Israel is the people specially allotted to God, specially assigned to God, by God's own will and choice. Israel is the *klēros* of God; the congregation is the *klēros* of the elder. Just as Israel is allotted to God, an elder's duties in the congregation are allotted

to him. That must mean this—that the whole attitude
of the elder, or of anyone who takes up any service, to his
people must be the same as the attitude of God to His
people. Here we have another great thought. In verse 2
there is a phrase in the best Greek manuscripts which is
not in the Authorized Version. We have translated it:
" Shepherd the flock of God, which is in your charge, not
because you are coerced into doing so, but of your own free-
will *as God would have you to do*." The phrase we have
translated *as God would have you to do* is in Greek *kata
theon*, and that could well mean quite simply *like God*.
Peter says to the elders, " Shepherd your people *like God*."
Just as Israel is God's special allotment, the people we have
to serve in the Church or anywhere else are our special
allotment; and our whole attitude to them must be the
attitude of God; we must shepherd them like God.

What a vision opens out! What an ideal! And what
a condemnation! It is our task to show to people the
forbearance of God, the forgiveness of God, the seeking
love of God, the illimitable service of God. God has allotted
to us a task to do, and we must do it as God Himself would
do it. That is the supreme ideal of service in the Christian
Church.

MEMORIES OF JESUS

1 *Peter* 5: 1-4 (continued)

ONE of the lovely things about this passage is Peter's whole
attitude throughout it. He begins by, as it were, taking
his place beside those to whom he speaks. " Your fellow-
elder " he calls himself. He does not speak down to them;
he speaks alongside them. He does not separate himself
from them, and raise himself above them; he comes to
share the Christian problems and the Christian experience
with them. But in one thing Peter is different; he has
memories of Jesus, and these memories colour this whole

passage. Even as he speaks, the memories are crowding into Peter's mind.

(i) He describes himself as a witness of the sufferings of Christ. At first sight we might well be inclined to question that statement, for we are told that, after the arrest in the garden, " All the disciples forsook Him and fled " (*Matthew* 26: 56). But, when we think a little further, we shall come to see that it was given to Peter to see the suffering of Jesus in a more poignant way than it was given to any other human being. Peter followed Jesus into the courtyard of the High Priest's house; there in a time of weakness he three times denied his Master; then the trial came to an end, and Jesus was taken away; and there comes what may well be the most tragic sentence in the New Testament: " And the Lord turned and looked upon Peter . . . and Peter went out and wept bitterly " (*Luke* 22: 61, 62). In that look of Christ, Peter saw the suffering of the heart of a leader whose follower had failed him in the hour of his bitterest need. Of a truth Peter was a witness of the suffering that comes to Christ when men deny their Lord; and that is precisely why he was so eager that his people might be staunch in loyalty and faithful in service.

(ii) He describes himself as a sharer in the glory which is going to be revealed. That statement has a backward and a forward look. Peter had already had a foretaste and glimpse of that glory on the Mount of Transfiguration. There the sleeping three had been awakened, and, as Luke puts it, " when they were awake they saw His glory " (*Luke* 9: 32). Peter had seen the glory. But he also knew that there was glory to come, for Jesus had promised to His disciples a share in the glory when the Son of Man should come to sit on the throne of His glory (*Matthew* 19: 28). Peter remembered both the experience and the promise of glory.

(iii) There can surely be no doubt that, when Peter spoke of shepherding the flock of God, he was remembeing the task that Jesus had given to himself, when he had bidden him to feed His sheep (*John* 21: 15-17). The reward of love was the appointment as a shepherd; and Peter was remembering the task which Christ had given him to do.

(iv) When Peter spoke of Jesus as the Chief Shepherd, many a thought and memory must have been in his mind. Jesus had likened Himself to the shepherd who sought at the peril of his life for the sheep which had gone lost (*Matthew* 18: 12-14; *Luke* 15: 4-7). He had sent out His disciples to gather in the lost sheep of the house of Israel (*Matthew* 10: 6). He was moved with pity for the crowds, for they were as sheep without a shepherd (*Matthew* 9: 36; *Mark* 6: 34). And, above all, Jesus had likened Himself to the Good Shepherd who was ready to lay down His life for the sheep (*John* 10: 1-18). The picture of Jesus as the Shepherd was a precious one, and the privilege of being the shepherds of the flock of Christ was for Peter the greatest privilege that the servants of Christ could enjoy.

THE GARMENT OF HUMILITY

I *Peter* 5: 5

> In the same way, you younger people must be submissive to those who are older. In your relationships with one another you must clothe yourselves with the garment of humility, because God opposes the proud, but gives grace to the humble.

HERE Peter returns to the thought that the banishment and the denial of self must be the mark of the Christian. He clinches his argument with a quotation from the Old Testament: " God opposes the proud, but gives grace to the humble " (*Proverbs* 3: 34).

But here again it may well be that the memories of Jesus are in Peter's heart, and that they are colouring all his thought and language. Peter tells his people that they must *clothe themselves* with the garment of humility. The word he uses for *to clothe oneself* is a very unusual word;

it is the word *egkombousthai*; this word is derived from the word *kombos* which describes anything tied on with a knot; and connected with it there is the word *egkombōma*. An *egkombōma* was a garment tied on with a knot. It was commonly used for protective clothing; it was used for a pair of sleeves drawn over the sleeves of a robe and tied behind the neck. And it was used for a slave's apron. There was a time when Jesus had put upon Himself just such an apron. At the Last Supper John says of Jesus that He took a towel and girded Himself, and that He took water and began to wash His disciples' feet (*John* 13: 4, 5). Jesus girded Himself with the apron of humility; and so must His followers.

It so happens that this word *egkombousthai* is used of another kind of garment. It is also used of putting on a long, flowing stole-like garment which was the sign of honour and pre-eminence.

So, to complete the picture, we must put both pictures together. Jesus once put on the slave's apron and undertook the humblest of all duties, the duty of washing His disciples' feet; so we too must in all things put on the apron of humility in the service of Christ and of our fellow-men; but that very apron of humility will become the garment of honour for us, for it is he who is the servant of all who is greatest in the Kingdom of Heaven.

THE LAWS OF THE CHRISTIAN LIFE (1)

I *Peter* 5: 6-11

So, then, humble yourselves under the mighty hand of God, so that in His good time He may exalt you.

Cast all your anxiety upon Him, because He cares for you.

Be sober; be watchful. Your adversary the devil prowls around like a roaring lion, seeking someone to devour. Stand up to him, staunch in the faith, knowing how to pay the same tax of suffering as your brethren in the world.

And after you have experienced suffering for a little while, the God of every grace, who called you to His eternal glory in Christ, will Himself restore, establish, strengthen, settle you.

To Him be dominion for ever and ever. Amen.

HERE Peter speaks in imperatives, laying down certain laws for the Christian life.

(i) There is the law of Christian humility before God. The Christian must humble himself under the mighty hand of God. The phrase *the mighty hand of God* is common in the Old Testament; and it is oftenest used in connection with the deliverance which God wrought for His people when He brought them out of Egypt. " With a strong hand," said Moses, " the Lord brought thee out of Egypt " (*Exodus* 13: 9). " Thou hast begun to show Thy servant Thy greatness, and Thy mighty hand " (*Deuteronomy* 3: 24). God brought His people forth out of Egypt with a mighty hand (*Deuteronomy* 9: 26). The idea is that God's mighty hand is on the destiny of His people, if they will humbly and faithfully accept His guidance. After all the varied experiences of life Joseph could say to the brothers who had once sought to eliminate him: " As for you, ye thought evil against me; but God meant it unto good " (*Genesis* 50: 20). The Christian never resents the experiences of life, and never rebels against them, because he knows that the mighty hand of God is on the tiller of his life, and that God has a destiny for him.

(ii) There is the law of Christian serenity in God. The Christian must cast all his anxiety upon God. " Cast your burden on the Lord," said the Psalmist (*Psalm* 55: 22). " Take no anxious thought for the morrow," said Jesus (*Matthew* 6: 25-34). The reason why we can do this with confidence is that we can be certain that God cares for us. As Paul had it, we can be certain that He who gave us His only Son will with Him freely give us all things (*Romans* 8: 32). We can be certain that, because God cares for us, life is out, not to break us but to make us; and, with that assurance, we can accept any experience which comes to us, knowing that God works everything together for good to them who love Him (*Romans* 8: 28).

(iii) There is the law of Christian effort and of Christian vigilance. We must be sober and watchful. The fact that we cast everything upon God does not give us the right to sit back and to do nothing. Cromwell's advice to his troops was: " Trust in God, and keep your powder dry." Trust and effort go hand in hand. And Peter knew how hard this vigilance was, for he must have remembered how in Gethsemane he and his fellow-disciples had slept when they should have been watching with Christ (*Matthew* 26: 38-46). The Christian is the man who trusts, but who, at the same time, puts all his effort and all his vigilance into the business of living for Christ.

(iv) There is the law of Christian resistance. The devil is ever out to see whom he can ruin. Again Peter must have been remembering how the devil had overcome him and how he had denied his Lord. The devil is man's sworn opponent, and a man's faith must be like a solid wall against which the attacks of the devil exhaust themselves in vain. The devil is like any bully; he retreats when he is gallantly and bravely resisted in the strength and in the company of Jesus Christ.

THE LAWS OF THE CHRISTIAN LIFE (2)

I *Peter* 5: 6-11 (*continued*)

(v) Finally, Peter speaks of the law of Christian suffering. He says that, after the Christian has experienced and gone through suffering, God will restore, establish, strengthen and settle him. Every one of the words which Peter uses has behind it a vivid picture. Each one of them tells us something about that which suffering is designed by God to do for a man.

(*a*) Through suffering God will *restore* a man. The word for *to restore* is difficult in this case to translate.

It is the word *kartarizein*. It is the word which is commonly used for setting a fracture; it is the word which is used in *Mark* 1: 19 for mending nets. It means to supply that which is missing, to mend that which is broken, to restore that part which is lacking or wanting. So suffering, if it is accepted in humility and trust and love, can add to a man's character that which is lacking; it can repair the weaknesses, and add the greatness which so far is not there. It is said that Sir Edward Elgar once listened to a young girl singing one of the solos from one of his own works. She had a voice of exceptional purity and clarity and range, a voice like that of a boy soprano. She had an almost perfect technique which made light of the technical difficulties of the solo. When she had finished singing, Sir Edward said softly, ' She will be really great when something happens to break her heart." Barrie tells of how his mother lost her favourite son, and then he says, " That is where my mother got her soft eyes, and that is why other mothers ran to her when they had lost a child." Suffering had done something for her that an easy way could never have done. Suffering is meant by God to add the grace notes to life.

(b) Through suffering God will *establish* a man. The word is *stērixein*, which means to make as firm and solid as granite. Suffering of body and sorrow of heart do one of two things to a man. They either make him collapse; or, out of them, he comes with a solidity of character which he could never have gained anywhere else. He comes out of them like the athlete who, from the rigour of his training, and the total effort of his performance, has emerged with a new toughness of fibre, a new staying-power, a new power which no demand on him can overcome. He emerges like the toughened steel that has been tempered in the fire.

(c) Through suffering God will *strengthen* a man. The verb is *sthenoun*, which means *to fill with strength*. Here is the same meaning again. A life with no effort and no discipline almost necessarily becomes a flabby life. No one really knows what his faith means to him until that faith has been tried in the furnace of affliction. There is something doubly precious about a faith which has come through pain and sorrow and disappointment and loss, and which has emerged burning more brightly than ever it did. The wind will extinguish a weak flame; but the wind will also fan a strong flame to a still greater blaze. And it is so with faith.

(d) Through suffering God will *settle* a man. The verb is *themelioun,* which means *to lay the foundations.* It is only when we have to meet sorrow and suffering that we are driven down to the very bedrock of faith. It is then that we discover what are the things which cannot be shaken. It is in the moment when life falls in that we discover the things which are merely decorations, and the things which are basic essentials. It is in life's trials that we discover the great truths on which life is founded, and which we cannot do without.

We must remember that suffering is very far from doing these precious things for every man. Suffering may well drive a man to bitterness, to resentment, to despair; it may well take away such faith as he ever had. But if it is accepted in love, in trust, in the certainty that a father's hand will never cause his child a needless tear, then out of suffering there come things which the easy way can never bring.

A FAITHFUL HENCHMAN OF THE APOSTLES

I *Peter* 5: 12

> I have written this brief letter to you through Silvanus, the faithful brother, as I reckon him to be, to encourage you and to testify that this is the true grace of God. Stand fast in it.

HERE Peter bears his witness that what he has written is indeed the grace of God, and he bids his people, amidst their difficulties, to stand fast in it.

He says that he has written *through Silvanus*. The Greek phrase (*dia Silouanou*) means that Silvanus was his agent and instrument in writing. Silvanus is the full form of the name Silas, and he is almost certainly to be identified with the Salvanus of Paul's letters and the Silas of the story of *Acts*. When we gather up the references to Silas or Silvanus we find that he was indeed one of the leaders and the pillars of the early Church.

Along with Judas Barsabas, Silvanus was sent to Antioch with the epoch-making decision of the Council of Jerusalem that the doors of the Church were to be opened to the Gentiles; and in the account of that mission Silvanus and Judas are called chief men among the brethren (*Acts* 15: 22, 27). Not only did he bring the message simply as the bearer of it, but he commended it in powerful words for Silvanus was also a prophet (*Acts* 15: 32). During the first missionary journey Mark had left Paul and Barnabas and had returned home from Pamphylia (*Acts* 13: 13); in preparing for the second missionary journey Paul had refused to have Mark with him again; the result was that Barnabas had taken Mark as his companion, and Paul had taken Silvanus (*Acts* 15: 37-40). From that time forward Silvanus was for long Paul's right-hand man. He was with Paul in Philippi, and there he was arrested and imprisoned with Paul (*Acts* 16: 19, 25, 29). He rejoined Paul in Corinth, and with him preached the gospel there (*Acts* 18: 5; 2 *Corinthians* 1: 19). So closely was he associated with Paul that in both the letters to the Thessalonians he is joined with Paul and Timothy as the senders of the letters (I *Thessalonians* 1: 1; 2 *Thessalonians* 1: 1). It is clear that Silvanus was a most notable man in the early Church.

As we have seen in the introduction, it is most probable that Silvanus was far more than merely the scribe who wrote this letter for Peter, and the bearer who delivered it. One of the difficulties of I *Peter* is the excellence of the Greek. It is Greek with such a classical tinge that it seems impossible that Peter the Galilaean fisherman should have written it for himself. Now Silvanus was not only a man of weight in the Church; he was also a Roman citizen (*Acts* 16: 37), and he would be much better educated than Peter was. Most probably Silvanus had a large share in the writing of this letter. We are told that in China, when a missionary wishes to send a message to his people, he often writes it in the best Chinese that he can achieve, and that then he gives it to a Christian Chinese to correct and to put into proper form; or, he may even tell the Christian Chinese what he wishes to say, leaving him to put it into literary form, and then approve of it afterwards. That is most likely what Peter did. He either gave his letter to Silvanus to polish into excellent Greek, or else he told Silvanus what he wished said and left Silvanus to say it, and then added these last three verses as his personal greeting.

Silvanus was one of these men whom the Church can never do without. He was content to be only a name, content to take the second place, content to serve almost in the background so long as God's work was done. For Silvanus it was enough that he was the assistant of Paul, even if Paul for ever overshadowed him. For Silvanus it was enough to be the penman of Peter, even if it meant only a bare mention of his name at the end of the letter. But for all that it is something to go down to history as the faithful henchman on whom both Peter and Paul depended. In ancient and in modern times we need Silvanus in the Church, and many who cannot be a Peter or a Paul can still be a faithful Silvanus without whom Peter and Paul could not have done their work.

GREETINGS

I Peter 5: 13

> She who is at Babylon, and who has been chosen as
> you have been chosen, greets you, and so does Mark
> my son.

ALTHOUGH it sounds so simple, this is indeed a troublesome
verse. It presents us with certain questions which are
difficult of solution.

(i) From whom are these greetings being sent? The
Authorized Version has " the Church that is at Babylon
elected together with you, saluteth you." But in the
Authorized Version the phrase *the Church that is* is in
italics, which means that there is no equivalent of it in the
Greek. In the Greek there is no word for *Church*. It is
simply *the one elected together with you at Babylon*, and
the phrase is feminine. There are two possibilities.

(a) It is quite possible—perhaps even probable—that
the Authorized Version is correct. That is the way in which
Moffatt takes it when he translates the phrase " your
sister Church in Babylon." The phrase could well be
explained as being based on the fact that the Church is
the Bride of Christ, and can be spoken of in this way. On
the whole the commonest view of this passage is that it is a
Church which is meant.

(b) But it does have to be remembered that there is
actually no word for *Church* in the Greek, and this might
equally well refer to some well-known Christian lady. If it
does, by far the best suggestion is that the reference is to
Peter's wife. We know that Peter's wife did actually
accompany him in his preaching journeys (I *Corinthians*
9: 5). Clement of Alexandria (*Stromateis* 7.11.63) tells
us that she died a martyr, executed in Peter's own sight,
while he encouraged her by saying to her, " Remember
the Lord." Peter's wife was clearly a well-known figure
in the early Church.

We would not wish to speak dogmatically on this question. It is perhaps more likely that the reference is to a Church; but it is not impossible that Peter is here associating his wife and fellow-evangelist in the greetings which he sends.

(ii) From where was this letter written? The greetings are sent from *Babylon*. There are in regard to this three quite definite possibilities.

(*a*) There was a Babylon in Egypt. It was near Cairo, and it had been founded by Babylonian refugees from Assyria, and was called by the name of their ancestral city. But by this time it was almost exclusively a great military camp; and in any event the name of Peter is never connected with Egypt; and this Babylon may be disregarded.

(*b*) There was the city of Babylon in the east. To this Babylon the Jews had been taken in captivity. Many had never come back. It was indeed a centre of Jewish scholarship. The great commentary on the Jewish Law is called the *Babylonian Talmud*. So important were the Jews of Babylon that Josephus had issued a special edition of his histories for them. There is no doubt that there was a large and important colony of Jews there; and it would have been quite natural for Peter, the apostle of the Jews, to preach and to work there. But we do not find the name of Peter ever connected with Babylon; there is neither trace nor tradition of him having ever been there. Scholars so great as Calvin and Erasmus have taken this Babylon to be the great eastern city, but, on the whole, we think that the probabilities are against it.

(*c*) Regularly the city of Rome was called Babylon, both by the Jews and by the Christians. That is undoubtedly the case in the *Revelation* where Babylon is the great harlot, drunk with the blood of the saints and the martyrs (*Revelation* 17 and 18). The distinctiveness, the Godlessness, the lust and luxury of ancient Babylon were, so to speak, reincarnated in Rome. Now Peter is definitely connected in tradition with Rome; and the likelihood is that it was from there that the letter was written.

(iii) Lastly, who is the Mark, whom Peter calls his son, and from whom he sends greetings? If we take the elect lady to be Peter's wife, then Mark might quite well be literally Peter's son. But in this case it is much more likely that Mark is the Mark who wrote the gospel. Tradition has always closely connected Peter and Mark, and has always handed down the story that Peter was intimately connected with Mark's gospel. Papias, who lived towards the end of the second century, and who was a great collector of early traditions, describes Mark's gospel in this way: " Mark, who was Peter's interpreter, wrote down accurately though not in order, all that he recollected of what Christ had said or done. For he was not a hearer of the Lord or a follower of His; he followed Peter, as I have said, at a later date, and Peter adapted his instructions to practical needs, without any attempt to give the Lord's words systematically. So that Mark was not wrong in writing down some things in this way from memory, for his one concern was neither to omit nor to falsify anything he had heard." According to Papias, Mark's gospel is nothing other than the preaching material of Peter. In the same way Irenaeus says that after the death of Peter and Paul at Rome, " Mark, the disciple and interpreter of Peter, also handed down to us in writing what had been preached by Peter." It is the consistent story of tradition that Mark was indeed a son to Peter, and all the likelihood is that these greetings are from him.

So, then, we may gather up the possibilities in this verse. " She who is at Babylon, and who has been chosen, as you have been chosen," may either be the Church, or she may be the wife of Peter, herself a martyr. Babylon may be Babylon in the east, but is more likely the great and wicked city of Rome. Mark might just possibly be the son of Peter, about whom we know nothing else, but is more likely to be Mark, the writer of the gospel, who was to Peter as a son.

AT PEACE WITH ONE ANOTHER

I Peter 5: 14

Greet each other with a kiss of love. Peace be to you all that are in Christ.

THE most interesting thing here is the injunction to give each other the kiss of love. The kiss was for centuries an integral and precious part of Christian fellowship and worship; and the history of it, and of its gradual elimination, is of the greatest interest.

With the Jews it was the custom for a disciple to kiss his Rabbi on the cheek, and to lay his hands upon his master's shoulder. That is what Judas did to Jesus (Mark 14: 44). To the Jews the kiss was the greeting of welcome and respect, and we can see how much Jesus valued it, when we see how He was grieved when it was not given to Him (Luke 7: 45). Paul's letters frequently end with the injunction to salute each other with a holy kiss (Romans 16: 16; I Corinthians 16: 20; 2 Corinthians 13: 12; I Thessalonians 5: 26).

In the early Church the kiss became an essential part of Christian worship. " What prayer is complete," asks Tertullian, " from which the holy kiss is divorced? What kind of sacrifice is that from which men depart without the peace? " (Dex Oratione 18). The kiss, as we see from Tertullian, was called the peace. The kiss was specially a part of the communion service. Augustine says that, when Christians were about to communicate, " they demonstrated their inward peace by the outward kiss " (De Amicitia 6). The kiss was usually given after the catechumens had been dismissed, when only members of the Church were present, and after the prayer before the elements were brought in. Justin Martyr says, " When we have ceased from prayer, we salute one another with a kiss. There is then brought to the president bread and a cup of wine " (1.65). The kiss was preceded by the prayer " for the gift of peace and of unfeigned love, undefiled by hypocrisy or deceit," and the kiss was the sign that " our souls are mingled together, and have banished all remembrance of wrongs " (Cyril of Jerusalem, Catechetical Lectures 25.5.3). The kiss was the sign that all injuries were forgotten, all wrongs forgiven, and that those who sat at the Lord's Table were indeed one in the Lord.

This was a lovely custom, and yet it is clear that it was sadly open to abuse. And it is equally clear from the warnings so often given that abuses did creep in. Athenagoras insists that the kiss must be given with the greatest care, for, "if there be mixed with it the least defilement of thought, it excludes us from eternal life " (Leg. 32). Origen insists that the kiss of peace must be " holy, chaste and sincere," not like the kiss of Judas (In Rom. 10: 33). Clement of Alexandria condemns the shameless use of the kiss, which ought to be mystic, for with the kiss " certain persons make the Churches resound, and thereby occasion foul suspicions and evil reports " (Paedag. 3: 11). Tertullian speaks of the natural reluctance of the heathen husband to think that his wife should be so greeted in the Christian Church (Ad. Ux. 2: 4).

In the Church of the west these inevitable problems gradually brought the end of this lovely custom. By the time of the Apostolic Constitutions in the fourth century, the kiss is confined to those of the same sex—the clergy are to salute the bishop, the men the men and the women the women. In this form the kiss of peace lasted in the Church of the west until the thirteenth century. Sometimes substitutes for the kiss were introduced. In some places a little wooden or metal tablet, with a picture of the crucifixion on it, was used. It was kissed first by the priest, and then passed to the congregation, who each kissed it and handed it on, each man to his neighbour, in token of their mutual love for Christ and in Christ. In the oriental Churches the custom still obtains; it is not extinct in the Greek Church; the Armenian Church substituted a cour-teous bow.

We may note certain other uses of the kiss in the early Church. At baptism the person baptized was kissed, first by the baptizer, and then by the whole congregation, as a sign of his welcome into the household and family of Christ. A newly ordained bishop was given " the kiss in the Lord." The marriage ceremony was ratified by a kiss, a natural action taken over from paganism. Those who were dying first kissed the Cross and were then kissed by all present. The dead were kissed before burial.

To us the kiss of peace may seem something that is very far away. It came from the day when the Church was a real family and a real fellowship, when Christians really did know and really did love one another. It is one of the tragedies of the Church that the modern Church, often with its vast congregations who do not know each other, and who do not even wish to know each other, could not use the kiss of peace except as a formality. It is a lovely custom which was bound to cease to exist when the reality of fellowship went lost within the Church.

" Peace be to you all that are in Christ," says Peter; and so he leaves his people to the peace of God which is greater than all the troubles and the distresses the world can bring.

THE LETTERS OF PETER

INTRODUCTION TO SECOND PETER

The Neglected Book and its Contents

It may well be said that *Second Peter* is one of the neglected books of the New Testament. It is a book which very few people will claim to have read, still less to have studied in detail. E. F. Scott says of it that " it is far inferior in every respect to *First Peter* "; and he goes on to say that " it is the least valuable of the New Testament writings." As we shall see, it was only with the greatest difficulty that *Second Peter* gained entry into the New Testament at all, and that for many years the Christian Church seemed to be unaware of its existence. But, before we approach the history of the letter, let us look at the contents of it.

The Lawless Men

Second Peter was written to combat the beliefs and the activities of certain men who were a threat to the Church. It begins by insisting that the Christian is a man who has escaped from the corruption of the world (1: 4), and must always remember that he has been purged of his old sins (1: 9). There is laid upon him the duty of ethical holiness and moral goodness, which culminates in the great Christian virtue of love (1: 5-8).

Let us set out the characteristics of the men whom *Second Peter* rebukes. They are men who twist Scripture to make it suit their own purpose (1: 20; 3: 16). They bring the Christian faith into disrepute (2: 2). They themselves are covetous of gain and exploiters of their fellowmen (2: 3; 2: 14, 15). They are doomed, and they will share the fate of the sinning angels (2: 4), the men before the Flood (2: 5), the citizens of Sodom and Gomorrah (2: 6), and the false prophet Balaam (2: 15). They are bestial creatures, ruled by their brute instincts (2: 12), and dominated by their lusts (2: 10; 2: 18). Their eyes are full of adultery (2: 14). They are presumptuous, self-willed, and arrogant (2: 10, 18). They spend even the daylight hours in unrestrained and luxurious revelry (2: 13). They speak of liberty, but what they call liberty is unbridled licence, and they themselves are the slaves of their own lusts (2: 19). Not only are they deluded themselves, they also delude and beguile others, and lead them astray (2: 14; 2: 18). They are worse than those who never knew the right, because they knew what goodness is and have relapsed into evil, like a dog returning to its vomit, and a sow returning to the mud, after it has been washed (2: 20-22).

It is clear that Peter is describing men who were anti-nomians, men who used God's grace as an excuse and a justification for sinning. In all probability they were Gnostics, who said that only spirit is good, and that matter is essentially evil, and that, therefore, it does not matter what we do with the body, and that we can glut and sate its appetites, and it makes no difference. They lived the most immoral lives; and they encouraged others to do so; and they justified their actions by perverting grace and interpreting Scripture to suit themselves.

The Denial of the Second Coming

Further, these evil men denied the Second Coming (2: 3, 4). They argued that this was a stable world, in which things remain unalterably the same, and that God was so dilatory that it was possible to assume that the Second Coming was never going to happen at all. The answer of *Second Peter* is that this is not a stable world; that it has, in fact, been destroyed by water in the Flood, and that it will be destroyed by fire in the final conflagration (3: 5-7). What they regard as dilatoriness on the part of God is in fact God withholding His hand in patience to give men still another chance to repent (3: 8, 9). But the day of destruction is coming (3: 10). A new heaven and a new earth are on the way; therefore, goodness is an absolute necessity if a man is to be saved in the day of judgment (3: 11-14). With this Paul agrees, however difficult his letters may be to understand, and however false teachers deliberately misinterpret them (3: 16). The duty of the Christian is to stand fast, firmly founded in the faith, and to grow in grace and in the knowledge of Jesus Christ (3: 17, 18).

The Doubts of the Early Church

Such, then, are the contents of this letter. For long this letter was regarded with doubt, and with something very like misgiving. There is no trace of it at all until after A.D. 200. It is not included in the Muratorian Canon, which dates to A.D. 170 and which was the first official list of New Testament books. It did not exist in the Old Latin Version of the Scriptures; and it did not exist in the New Testament of the early Syrian Church.

The great scholars of Alexandria either did not know it or were doubtful about it. Clement of Alexandria, who wrote outlines of the books of Scripture, does not appear to have included *Second Peter*. Origen says that Peter left behind one epistle which is generally acknowledged; " perhaps also a second, for it is a disputed question." Didymus commented on it, but concluded his work by saying: " It must not be forgotten that this letter is spurious; it may be read in public; but it is not part of the canon of Scripture."

Eusebius, the great scholar of Caesarea, who made a careful investigation of the Christian literature of his day, comes to the conclusion: " Of Peter, one Epistle, which is called his former Epistle, is acknowledged by all; of this the ancient presbyters have made frequent use in their writings as indisputably genuine; but that which is circulated as his second Epistle we have received to be not canonical, although, since it appeared to be useful to many, it has been diligently read with the other Scriptures."

It was not until well down in the fourth century that *Second Peter* came to rest in the canon of the New Testament.

The Objections

It is the well-nigh universal judgment of scholars, both ancient and modern, that Peter is not the author of *Second Peter*. Even John Calvin regarded it as impossible that Peter could have spoken of Paul as *Second Peter* speaks of him (3: 15, 16), although he was willing to believe that someone else wrote *Second Peter* at Peter's request. But he was not willing to believe that the letter, as it stands, came from Peter's hand. What then are the arguments against Peter's authorship of this letter.

(i) There is, first, the extreme slowness, and even reluctance, of the early Church to accept it. If it had been truly Peter's, there can be no doubt that the Church would have welcomed it and honoured it from the first. But, as we have seen, the case was very different. For the first two centuries the letter is never quoted at all in any certain instance; it is regarded with doubt and suspicion for more than an other century; and only late in the fourth century was it accepted.

(ii) The contents make it difficult to believe that it is Peter's. There is no mention of the Passion, the Resurrection and the Ascension of Jesus Christ; no mention of the Church as the true Israel; no mention of that faith which is undefeatable hope and trust combined; no mention of the Holy Spirit, of prayer, of baptism; and none of that passionate desire to call men to the supreme example of Jesus Christ. If one took away these great verities from *First Peter* there would be little or nothing left, and yet none of them occurs in *Second Peter*.

(iii) It is wholly different in character and style from *First Peter*. This was realized as early as Jerome. Jerome wrote: " Simon Peter wrote two Epistles which are called Catholic, of which the authenticity of the second is denied by many because of the difference of the style from the first." The Greek style of this letter is very difficult. Clogg calls it ambitious, artificial and often obscure, and remarks that it is the only book in the New Testament which is improved by translation. Bishop Chase wrote: " The Epistle does produce the impression of being a somewhat artificial piece of rhetoric. It shows throughout signs of self-conscious effort. The author appears to be ambitious of writing in a style which is beyond his literary power." He concludes that it is hard to reconcile the literary character of this letter with the supposition that Peter wrote it. Moffatt says: " Second Peter is more periodic and ambitious than *First Peter*, but its linguistic and its stylistic efforts only reveal by their cumbrous obscurity a decided inferiority of conception, which marks it off from *First Peter*." It might be claimed, as Jerome did claim, that, while Silvanus was Peter's amanuensis for *First Peter*, he used a different amaneunsis for *Second Peter*, and that therein there lies the explanation of the change in style. But J. B. Mayor compares the two letters. He quotes some of the great passages of *First Peter*, and then he says: " I think that none who read these words can help feeling that, not even in Paul, not even in John, is there to be found a more beautiful or a more living description of the secret of primitive Christianity, of the force that overcame the world, than in the perfect quaternion of faith and hope and love and joy, which pervades this short epistle (i.e. *First Peter*). No one could make the same assertion with regard to *Second Peter*: thoughtful and interesting as it is, it lacks that intense sympathy, that flame of love, which marks *First Peter*. . . . No change of circumstances can account for the change of tone of which we are conscious in passing from one epistle to the other." It is the conclusion of that great and conservative scholar that no explanation, other than difference of authorship, can explain, not so much the difference in style, as the whole difference in atmosphere between *First* and *Second Peter*. It is true that from the purely linguistic point of view there are 369 words which occur in *First Peter* which do not occur in *Second Peter*; and there are 230 words which occur in *Second Peter* and not in *First Peter*. But this is more than a difference in style. A writer can change his style and his vocabulary to suit his audience and his occasion. But the change between the two letters is a change in atmosphere and attitude so wide that it is hardly possible that the same person should have written both.

(iv) There are certain things within *Second Peter* which point well-nigh irresistibly to a late date. Clearly so much time has passed that men have begun to abandon hope of the Second Coming altogether (3: 4). The apostles are spoken of as figures of the past (3: 2). The fathers, that is the founders of the Christian faith, are now figures of the almost dim and distant past; there have been generations between this letter and the first coming of the Christian faith (3: 4).

There are references which require the passing of the years to explain them. The reference to Peter's approaching death looks very like a reference to Jesus' prophecy in *John* 21: 18, 19, and the Fourth Gospel was not written until about A.D. 100. The statement that Peter is going to leave something which will continue his teaching after he has gone looks very like a reference to Mark's Gospe (1: 12-14).

But, above all, there is the reference to the letters of Paul (3: 15, 16). From that passage it is quite certain that Paul's letters are known and used throughout all the Church; they are public property, and furthermore they are regarded as Scripture, and on a level with " the other Scriptures " (3: 16). It was not until at least A.D. 90 that Paul's letters were collected and published, and quite certainly it would take many years for them to acquire the position of sacred Scripture. It is well-nigh impossible that anyone should write like this until midway through the second century A.D.

All the evidence converges to prove that *Second Peter* is a late book. It is not until the third century that it is quoted at all. The great scholars of the early Church did not themselves regard it as Peter's although they did not question its usefulness. The letter itself has references which require the passing of the years to explain them. The great interest of *Second Peter* lies in the very fact that it was the last book in the New Testament to be written, and the last book to gain an entry into the New Testament.

In Peter's Name

How, then, did it become attached to the name of Peter? The answer to that is that it was deliberately attached to his name. This may seem to us a strange proceeding, but we must remember that in the ancient world this was a practice which was very common and quite normal. In the classical world Plato's letters were not written by Plato, but by a disciple in the master's name. The Jews repeatedly used this method of writing. Between the Old and the New Testament books were written under the names of Solomon, Isaiah, Moses, Baruch, Ezra, Enoch and many another. And in New Testament times there is, in fact a whole literature, around the name of Peter. They are The Gospel of Peter, The Preaching of Peter, The Apocalypse of Peter.

There was one salient fact which makes this method of writing even more intelligible. The heretics themselves used it. The heretics issued misleading and pernicious books under the names of the great apostles; they claimed that these books were the secret teaching of the great founders of the Church handed down by word of mouth to them. Faced with this the Church retaliated in kind, and issued books in which men set down for their own generation the things they were quite sure that the apostles would have said had they been facing this new situation. There is nothing either unusual or discreditable in a book being issued under the name of Peter, although Peter did not write it. When some great and unknown teacher did this he was only doing what was commonly done in his day and

341

generation. He was a humble man, and he was putting the message which the Holy Spirit had given him into the mouth of Peter, because he felt that his own name was quite unworthy to appear upon the book.

We will not find *Second Peter* easy to read; but here is a book of first-rate importance because it was written to men who were undermining the Christian ethic and the Christian doctrine, and who had to be stopped before the Christian faith itself was wrecked by the perversion of the truth.

SECOND PETER

THE MAN WHO OPENED DOORS

2 Peter 1: 1

> Symeon Peter, a servant and apostle of Jesus Christ,
> writes this letter to those to whom there has been
> allotted a faith equal in honour and privilege with our
> own, through the impartial justice of our God and
> Saviour Jesus Christ.

THIS letter opens with a very subtle and beautiful allusion
for those who have eyes to see it, and knowledge enough
of the New Testament to grasp it. Peter writes to " those
to whom there has been allotted a faith equal in honour
and privilege with our own "—and he calls himself
Symeon Peter. Who were these people? There can really
be only one answer to that. These people must
once have been Gentiles in contradistinction to the
Jews who were uniquely the chosen people of God. Those
who had once been no people are now the chosen people
of God (I *Peter* 2: 10); those who were once aliens and
strangers to the commonwealth of Israel, and who were
once far off, have been brought nigh (*Ephesians* 2: 11-13).
Peter puts this very vividly, using a word which would
at once strike an answering chord in the minds of those
who heard it. Their faith is *equal in honour and privilege*.
The word in Greek is *isotimos*; *isos* means *equal* and *time*
means *honour*. Now this word was particularly used in
connection with strangers and foreigners who were given
equal citizenship in a city where they were strangers and
aliens. Josephus, for instance, writing of Antioch, says
that in Antioch the Jews were given all the rights of citizenship, and were made *isotimoi, equal in honour and privilege*,
with the Macedonians and the Greeks who lived there.
So Peter addresses his letter to those who had once been
despised Gentiles, but who had been given equal rights of

citizenship with the Jews, and even with the apostles themselves, in the city and the kingdom of God.

Two things have to be noted about this great and wonderful privilege which had been extended to the Gentiles. (*a*) It had been *allotted* to them. That is to say, they had not earned it, and they had not deserved it; it had fallen to them through no merits of their own, as some prize falls to a man by the fall of the lot, and by no effort of his own. In other words, their new citizenship and their new honour was all of grace. (*b*) It came to them through the impartial justice of their God and Saviour Jesus Christ. It came to them because with God there is no respect of persons, there is no " most favoured nation clause," there is no *herrenvolk*, or master-race; God's grace and God's favour and God's privileges goes out impartially to every nation upon earth.

Now what has this to do with the name *Symeon*, by which Peter is here called? In the New Testament, Peter is oftenest of all called Peter; he is fairly often called Simon, which was, indeed, his original name, before Jesus gave him the name of Cephas or Peter (*John* I: 41, 42); but only once in the whole of the rest of the New Testament is Peter called *Symeon*. Where is that one occasion? It is in the story of the Council of Jerusalem in *Acts* 15, that Council of the Church which decided that the door of the Church should be opened wide to the Gentiles. There James says, " Symeon hath declared how God at the first did visit the Gentiles, to take out of them a people for His name " (*Acts* 15: 14). The fact is that the only other time when Peter is called *Symeon* is on the great occasion when he was the leading spirit in throwing open the doors of the Church to the Gentiles. Here in this letter Peter begins with greetings to the Gentiles who have been granted, by the grace of God, privileges of equal citizenship in the kingdom with the Jews and with the apostles, and he is called by the name of *Symeon*; and the one other time when he is called by that name is on the occasion when he was the principal instrument whereby that privilege was granted.

When Peter is called Symeon, the name has in it the memory that Peter is the man who opened doors. He opened the doors to Cornelius, the Gentile centurion (*Acts* 10); his great authority was thrown on the side of the open door at the Council of Jerusalem (*Acts* 15). To call Peter by the name of Symeon is to remember him as the opener of doors.

THE GLORIOUS SERVITUDE

2 *Peter* 1: 1 (*continued*)

PETER calls himself the *servant* of Jesus Christ. The word for servant is *doulos*; and it means more than *servant*, it means *slave*. Strange as it may seem, here is a title, which is apparently a title of humiliation, and which the greatest of men took as the title of the greatest of honour. Moses the great leader and law-giver was the *doulos* of God (*Deuteronomy* 34: 35; *Psalm* 105: 26; *Malachi* 4: 4). Joshua the great commander was the *doulos* of God (*Joshua* 24: 19). David the greatest of the kings was the *doulos* of God (2 *Samuel* 3: 18; *Psalm* 78: 70). In the New Testament Paul is the *doulos* of Jesus Christ (*Romans* 1: 1; *Philippians* 1: 1; *Titus* 1: 1), a title which James (*James* 1: 1), and Jude (*Jude* 1) both proudly claim. In the Old Testament the prophets are the *douloi* of God (*Amos* 3: 7; *Isaiah* 20: 3). And in the New Testament the *servant* of Christ becomes the title of the Christian man; he is Christ's *doulos* (*Acts* 2: 18; 1 *Corinthians* 7: 22; *Ephesians* 6: 6; *Colossians* 4: 12; 2 *Timothy* 2: 24). There is deep meaning here.

(i) To call the Christian the *doulos* of God means that he is inalienably possessed by God. In the ancient world a master possessed his slaves in the same sense as he possessed his tools. A servant can change his master; but a slave cannot. The Christian inalienably belongs to God.

(ii) To call the Christian the *doulos* of God means that he is unqualifiedly at the disposal of God. In the ancient world the master could do what he liked with his slave. He had the same power over his slave as he had over his inanimate possessions. He had the power of life and death over his slave. The Christian belongs to God, for God to send him where He will, and to do with him what He will. The Christian is the man who has no rights of his own, for all his rights are surrendered to God.

(iii) To call the Christian the *doulos* of God means that the Christian owes an unquestioning obedience to God. Ancient law was such that a master's command was a slave's only law. Even if a slave was told to do something which actually broke the law, he could not protest, for, as far as he was concerned, his master's command was the law. In any situation the Christian has but one question to ask: " Lord, what wilt *Thou* have me to do? " The command of God is his only law.

(iv) To call the Christian the *doulos* of God means that he must be constantly in the service of God. In the ancient world the slave had literally no time of his own, no holidays, no time off, no working-hours settled by agreement, no leisure. All his time belonged to the master. The Christian cannot, either deliberately or unconsciously, compartment life into the time and the activities which belong to God, and the time and the activities in which he does what he likes. The Christian is necessarily the man every moment of whose life and time is spent in the service of God.

We may note one further point. Here Peter speaks of the impartial justice of *our God and Saviour Jesus Christ*. The Authorized Version translates, " the righteousness of God and our Saviour Jesus Christ," as if this referred to two persons, God and Jesus; but as Moffatt and the American Revised Standard Version both show, in the Greek there is only one person involved, and the phrase should read, *our God and Saviour Jesus Christ*. The great interest of this is that it does what the New Testament very, very seldom does. It actually calls Jesus God. The only real parallel to this is the adoring cry of Thomas, when he recognized his Lord for what He was: " My Lord and my God " (*John* 20: 28). This is not a matter to argue about at all; it is not even a matter of theology; for to Peter and to Thomas to call Jesus by the name of God was not a matter of theology, but an outrush of the adoration of the heart. It was simply that in the depths of the emotion of their heart and in the glory of their wonder they felt that human terms could not contain this person whom they knew as Lord.

THE ALL-IMPORTANT KNOWLEDGE

2 Peter 1: 2

May grace and peace be multiplied to you by the knowledge of God, and of Jesus, our Lord.

PETER puts this in an unusual way. Grace and peace are to come from *knowledge*, the knowledge of God and of Jesus Christ, our Lord. What does he mean by this? Is he turning Christian experience into something which is dependent on knowledge? Or, is there some other meaning here? First, let us look at the word which he uses for knowledge. The word is *epignōsis*. This word can be interpreted in two directions.

(*a*) It can mean *increasing knowledge*. *Gnōsis* is the normal Greek word for *knowledge*, and here it is preceded by the preposition *epi* which means *towards, in the direction of*. *Epignōsis* then could be interpreted as knowledge which is always moving further in the direction of that which it seeks to know. Grace and peace are multiplied to the Christian, they increase more and more, as he comes to know Jesus Christ better and better. As it has been put: " The more Christians realize the meaning of Jesus Christ, the more they realize the meaning of grace and the experience of peace." The better we know Jesus, the greater the wonder of grace, and the more real our experience of the peace which passeth understanding.

(b) *Epignōsis* has a second meaning. Often in Greek it means *full knowledge*. Plutarch for instance, uses it of the scientific knowledge of music as opposed to the knowledge of the mere amateur. So it may be that the implication here is that knowledge of Jesus Christ is what we might call " the master-science of life." The other sciences may bring new skill, new knowledge, new abilities, but the master-science, the knowledge of Jesus Christ, alone brings the grace men need, and the peace for which their hearts crave.

But there is still more here. Peter has a way of using words which were commonly on the lips of the pagans of his day, and of charging them with a new fulness of meaning. Now knowledge was a much used word in pagan religious thought in the days when this letter was written. To take but one example, the Greeks defined *sophia*, which means *wisdom*, as knowledge of things both human and divine. The Greek seekers after God sought after that knowledge in two main ways.

(a) They sought it by philosophic speculation. They sought to reach God by the sheer power of human thought. There are clear and obvious troubles there. For one thing, God is infinite; the mind of man is finite; and the finite can never reach or grasp the infinite. Long ago Zophar had asked: " Canst thou by searching find out God? " (*Job* 11: 7). If God is ever to be known, He must be known, not because man's mind discovers Him, but because He chooses to reveal Himself. For another thing, if religion is based on philosophic speculation, then obviously at its highest it can be the preserve of only the few, for it is not given to every man to be a philosopher; and the simple souls will be left for ever on the lower reaches, distant from God. Whatever Peter meant by *knowledge*, he did not mean that.

(b) They sought it by mystical experience. They sought it by mystical experience with the divine, until they could say, " I am Thou, and Thou art I." This was the way of the Mystery Religions. The Mystery Religions were all passions plays; they were all the dramatically acted story of some God who suffered and died and rose again. The initiate was carefully prepared by instruction in the inner meaning of the story, by long fasting and continence, by the deliberate building up of psychological tension. The play was then played out with a magnificent liturgy, with sensuous music, with carefully calculated lighting, with the burning of incense. The aim was that, as the initiate watched, he should so enter into this experience that he became actually one with the suffering, dying, rising, and eternally triumphant God. Again there are troubles here. For one thing, not every one is mystical; not every one is capable of mystical experience. For another thing, any such experience is necessarily transient; it must fade into the light of common day. It may leave an effect, but it cannot be a continual experience. Mystical experience is the privilege of the few, and it is always the exceptional experience.

(c) If, then, this knowledge of Jesus Christ does not come by philosophic speculation, and if it does not come by mystical experience, what is it, and how does it come? In the New Testament knowledge is characteristically *personal* knowledge. Paul does not say, " I know *what* I have believed "; he says, " I know *whom* I have believed " (I *Timothy* I: I2). The Christian knowledge of Christ is personal acquaintance with Christ; it is knowing Christ as a person, and entering day by day into a closer and more intimate relationship with Him.

When Peter speaks of grace and peace coming through the knowledge of God and of Jesus Christ, he is not intellectualizing religion; he is saying that Christianity means an ever-deepening personal relationship with Jesus Christ.

THE GREATNESS OF JESUS CHRIST FOR MEN

2 Peter 1: 3-7

> Since His divine power has bestowed upon us all
> things that are necessary for true life and true religion,
> through the knowledge of Him who called us to His
> own glory and excellence, and since through these
> gifts there have been bestowed upon us precious and
> very great promises, that through them we might
> escape the world's corruption caused by lust, and
> become sharers in the divine nature—since all this is
> so, bend all your energy to the task of equipping your
> faith with courage, your courage with knowledge,
> your knowledge with self-control, your self-control
> with stedfastness, your stedfastness with piety, your
> piety with brotherly affection, your brotherly affection
> with Christian love.

IN the earlier part of this section, in verses 3 and 4, there is a
tremendous and comprehensive picture of Jesus Christ.

(i) He is the *Christ of power*. In Him there is the divine
power, which cannot be ultimately defeated or frustrated.
In this human world one of the tragedies of life is that love
is so often frustrated, because love cannot give what it
wants to give, cannot do what it wants to do, must so often
stand helpless, while the loved one meets disaster. But it
is to be remembered always that the love of Christ is
backed by the power of Christ, and is, therefore, a victorious
love.

(ii) He is the *Christ of generosity*. He bestows on us all
things necessary for true life and true religion. It is to be
noted that the word Peter uses for religion is *eusebeia*,
and the characteristic meaning of this word is *practical
religion*. What Peter is saying is that Jesus Christ tells
us what life is, and then enables us to live life, as life ought
to be lived. He gives us the religion which is not withdrawal
from life but which is triumphant involvement in life.

(iii) He is the *Christ of the precious and very great promises*.
That does not so much mean that He brings us the great
and precious promises as it means that in Him the great

and precious promises come true. Paul put the same thing in a different way when he said that all the promises of God are yea and Amen in Christ (2 *Corinthians* I: 20). That is to say Christ says, " Yes. So let it be," to all the promises of God. He confirms and guarantees them. It has been put this way—once we know Jesus Christ, every time we meet a promise in Scripture which begins with the word " Whosoever," we can immediately say to ourselves, " That means me."

(iv) He is the *Christ by whom we escape the world's corruption*. Peter had to meet the antinomians; the antinomians were the people who used the grace of God as an excuse and a reason to sin. They declared that grace was the greatest thing in the world, and that grace was wide enough to cover every sin. Therefore, why worry about sin? Sin does not matter any more. The grace of Christ will win forgiveness for it. Sin but gives to this amazing grace fresh opportunities to operate and to abound. But for any man to speak like that is simply to show that he is thirled to sin. He *wants* to sin. But Jesus Christ is the person who can rid us of the fascination of the world's lust, and who can cleanse and purify us by His presence and His power. To walk with Christ is to walk in safety from the world's taint. It is quite true that so long as we live in this world sin will never completely lose its fascination over us; but in the presence of Christ we have our defence against that fascination.

(v) He is the *Christ who makes us sharers in the divine nature*. Here again Peter is using an expression which the pagan thinkers well knew. They spoke much about sharing in the divine nature. But there was this difference—they believed that man as man had a share in the divine nature. They regarded man as essentially divine, as it were, all by himself. All men had to do was to live in accordance with the divine nature which was already in them. The whole trouble about that is that life flatly contradicts it. On every side we see bitterness, hatred, lust, crime; on every side we see moral failure, moral helplessness, moral frustration; in every age we see men utterly failing to reach their ideals and utterly helpless to make their dreams come true. What Christianity says is that men are *capable of becoming* sharers in the divine nature. Christianity realistically faces man's actuality, but at the same time sets no limit to man's potentiality. " I am come," said Jesus, " that they might have life, and that they might have it more abundantly " (*John* 10: 10). As one of the great early fathers said, " He became what we are to make us what He is." Man has it in him to share nothing less than the nature of God—but only in Jesus Christ does that destiny come true, and only in Him can that potentiality be realized.

EQUIPMENT FOR THE WAY

2 Peter 1: 3-7 (*continued*)

IN this passage Peter says that we must bind all our energies *to equip* ourselves with a series of great qualities and virtues. The word he uses for *to equip* is the word *epichorēgein*, and a very interesting word it is. He uses the same word again in verse 11 when he speaks of us being *richly gifted* with the right of entry into the eternal kingdom.

This is one of these many Greek words which have a vivid and pictorial background. The verb *epichorēgein* comes from the noun *chorēgos*, which literally means *the leader of a chorus*. Perhaps the greatest gift that Greece, and especially Athens, gave to men, was the great plays and dramas of men like Aeschylus, Sophocles and Euripides, works of literature and art which are still among the most cherished possessions of the world. All these plays needed large choruses, for the choruses were integral parts of them. It was, therefore, very expensive to produce such plays. In the great days of Athens there were public-spirited citizens who voluntarily and willingly took on the duty, at their own expense, of collecting, maintaining, training and equipping such choruses. It was at the great religious festivals that these plays were produced. For instance, at the city Dionysia there were produced three tragedies, five comedies and five dithyrambs. Men had to be found to find and equip and train the choruses for them all. It could cost such a man as much as 3,000 drachmae; and it was the pride of such men to train and to equip their choruses as nobly and as splendidly as they could. The men who undertook these duties, voluntarily, out of their own pocket, and out of love for their city were called *choregoi*, and the verb *choregein* is the verb for undertaking such a duty. The word, therefore, has a certain lavishness in it. It never means to equip in any cheese-paring and miserly way; it means lavishly and willingly to pour out everything that is necessary for a noble performance. The word *epichoregein* went out into a larger world, and it grew to mean, not only to equip a chorus, but to be responsible for any kind of equipment; it can mean to equip an army with all necessary provisions and supplies; it can mean to equip the soul with all the necessary and lovely virtues for life. But always at the back of it there is this idea of a willing and lavish generosity in the equipment.

So Peter urges his people to equip their lives with every virtue; and that equipment must not be the provision of a kind of necessary minimum, but a lavish and a generous equipment. The very word is an incitement to be content with nothing less than the loveliest and the most splendid life.

But there is something else at the back of this. In verses 5 and 6 Peter goes on saying that we must, as the Authorized Version has it, *add* virtue to virtue, until the whole culminates in Christian love. Behind this there is a Stoic idea; the Stoics insisted that in life there must continuously be what they called *prokope* which is *moral progress*. The word *prokope* is a word that can be used for *the advance of an army towards its objective*. In the Christian life there must be this steady moral advance. Moffatt quotes a saying that, " the Christian life must not be an initial spasm followed by a chronic inertia." It is very apt to be just that; it is apt to be a moment of enthusiasm, when the wonder of Christianity is realized, and then a failure to work out the Christian life in this continuous progress.

That brings us to still another basic idea here. Peter bids his people *to bend every energy* to do this. That is to say, in the Christian life the supreme effort of man must co-operate with the grace of God. As Paul has it: " Work out your own salvation with fear and trembling, for it is God that worketh in you both to will and to do of His good pleasure " (*Philippians* 2: 12, 13). It is quite true that everything is of faith; but a faith which does not issue in life is not faith at all, as Paul would heartily have agreed. Faith is not only commitment to the promises of Christ; faith is also commitment to the demands of Christ. Bigg well points out that Aristotle, in the *Nicomachean Ethics*, has a discussion on the source of happiness. He says that there are three theories of the source of happiness. (i) Happiness is something which can come by training, by learning, and by the formation of right habits. (ii) Happiness is a matter of divine allotment; it is the gift of God. (iii) Happiness is all a matter of chance, and is at the mercy of fickle fortune. The truth is that, as the Christian sees it, happiness depends *both* on God's gift and on our effort. We do not earn salvation, but at the same time we have to bend every energy towards our progress towards the Christian objective of a lovely life. Bengel, in commenting on this passage, asks us to compare the Parable of the Ten Virgins, five of whom were wise, and five of whom were foolish. He writes: " The flame is that which is imparted to us by God and from God without our own labour; but the oil is that which a man must pour into life by his own study and his own faithful effort, so that the flame may be fed and increased."

Faith does not exempt a man from works; the generosity of God does not absolve a man from effort. Life is at its noblest and its best when our effort co-operates with God's grace, to produce the necessary loveliness.

THE LADDER OF VIRTUES

2 Peter I: 3-7 (continued)

LET us then look at the list of the virtues which have to be added one to another. It is worth while noting that in the ancient world such lists were common. It was a world in which books were not nearly so common, so cheap, and so readily available as they are today. Instruction, therefore, had for the most part to be carried in the pupil's head; and easily memorized lists were one of the commonest ways of inculcating instruction. One ingenious way of teaching the child the names of the virtues was by means of a game played with counters which could be won or lost, and each of the counters had on it the name of one of the virtues. Lists of virtues are common in the New Testament. Paul gives us the fruit of the Spirit—love, joy, peace, long-suffering, gentleness, goodness, fidelity, meekness, self-control (*Galatians* 5: 22, 23). In the Pastoral Epistles the man of God is bidden to follow after righteousness, godliness, faith, love, patience, meekness (I *Timothy* 16: 11). In *The Shepherd of Hermas* (*Visions* 3.8.1-7), faith, self-control, simplicity, innocence and reverence, understanding and love are daughters one of another. In the *Epistle of Barnabas* (2) fear and endurance are the helpers of faith; patience and self-control are our allies; and when these are present a man can develop and possess wisdom, prudence, understanding and knowledge. Let us then look one by one at the stages in this list which this letter gives to us.

(i) It begins with *faith* (*pistis*); everything goes back to that. And for Peter faith is the conviction that what Jesus Christ says is true, the utter certainty that we can commit ourselves to His promises and launch ourselves on His demands. It is the unquestioning certainty that the way to happiness and peace and strength on earth and in heaven is to accept Him at His word.

(ii) To faith there must be added what the Authorized Version calls *virtue*, and what we have called *courage*. The word is *aretē*; this word is very rare in the New Testament, but it is the supreme Greek word for virtue in every sense of the term. It means *excellence*. It has two special directions in which its meaning moves. (*a*) In Greek *aretē* is what we might call *operative*, or *efficient*, *excellence*. To take two examples of its usage from widely differing spheres—it can be used of land which is fertile, and productive, and rich to bear crops; and it can be used of the mighty and effective deeds of the gods. *Aretē* is that virtue which makes a man a good and an effective citizen and friend; it is that virtue which makes him an expert in the actual art and technique of living well. (*b*) In Greek *aretē* often means *courage*. Plutarch says that God is a hope of *aretē* courage, not an excuse for cowardice. In 2 *Maccabees* we read the story of how Eleazar died rather than be false to the laws of God and his fathers; and the story ends by saying that he left his death for an example of noble courage (*aretē*) and a memorial of virtue, not only to young men, but also to all the nation (2 *Maccabees* 6: 31). In this passage it is not necessary to choose between these two meanings; they are both there. Faith must issue, not in the retirement of the cloister and the cell, but in a life that is effective in the service of God and man; faith must issue in the courage always to show whose it is, and whom it serves.

(iii) To courage there must be added *knowledge*. The word is *gnōsis*. In ethical Greek language there are two words which have a very similar meaning with a very significant difference. *Sophia* is wisdom, in the sense of " knowledge of things both human and divine, and of their causes." *Sophia* is knowledge of first causes, and of deep and ultimate things. On the other hand *gnōsis* is *practical knowledge*; it is the knowledge what to do in any given situation; it is the knowledge to apply to particular situations the ultimate knowledge which *sophia* gives. *Gnōsis* is that knowledge which enables a man to decide rightly and to act honourably and efficiently in the day to day circumstances and situations of life. So, then, to faith there must be added courage and effectiveness; to courage and effectiveness there must be added the practical wisdom to deal with life.

THE LADDER OF VIRTUES

2 Peter 1: 3-7 (*continued*)

(iv) To this practical knowledge there must be added *self-control*, or *self-mastery*. The word is *egkrateia*, and it means literally *the ability to take a grip of oneself*. This is a virtue of which the great Greeks spoke, and wrote, and thought much. In regard to a man and his passions Aristotle distinguishes four states in life. There is *sōphrosunē*, in which passion has been entirely subjugated to reason; the fight is won, and reason reigns supreme; we might call it *perfect temperance*. There is *akolasia*, which is the precise opposite; it is the state in which reason is entirely subjugated to passion; the fight is lost, and passion reigns supreme; we might call it *unbridled lust*. In between these two states there is *akrasia*, in which reason fights but passion prevails; the battle is still on, but at the moment it is a losing battle; we might call it *incontinence*. There is *egkrateia*, in which reason fights against passion and prevails; the battle is still on, but it is a winning battle; we call it *self-control*, or *self-mastery*.

This *egkrateia* is one of the great Christian virtues; and the place it holds in the Christian ethic is an example of the realism of the Christian ethic. The Christian ethic does not contemplate a situation in which a man is emasculated of all passion, in which he is drained of virility, in

357

which he is de-sexed and emptied of every passion; it envisages a situation in which a man's instincts and passions remain, but remain under perfect control and mastery, and so become his servants and not his tyrants.

(v) To this self-control there must be added *steadfastness*. The word *hupomonē*. Chrysostom called *hupomonē* " The Queen of the Virtues." In the Authorized Version it is usually translated *patience*; but *patience* is in English too passive a word. In Greek *hupomonē* has always a background of courage. Cicero defines *patientia*, its Latin equivalent, as: " The voluntary and daily suffering of hard and difficult things, for the sake of honour and usefulness." Didymus of Alexandria writes on the temper of Job: " It is not that the righteous man must be without feeling, although he must patiently bear the things which afflict him; but it is true virtue when a man deeply feels the things he toils against, but nevertheless despises sorrows for the sake of God." This Christian steadfastness, *hupomonē*, does not simply sit down and accept and endure. There is always a forward look in it. It is said of Jesus, by the writer to the Hebrews, that for the joy that was set before Him, He *endured* the Cross, despising the shame (*Hebrews* 12: 2). That is *hupomonē*. *Hupomonē*, Christian steadfastness, is the brave and courageous acceptance of everything that life can do to us, and the transmuting of even the worst event into another step on the upward way.

(vi) To this steadfastness there must be added *piety*. The word is *eusebeia*, and it is quite untranslatable; even the word *piety* is a word which carries with it a suggestion at least sometimes of something which is not altogether attractive and winsome. The great characteristic of the word *eusebeia* is that it looks in two directions. The man who has *eusebeia* always correctly worships God, and gives God His due; but the man who has *eusebeia* always correctly serves his fellow-men, and also gives men their due. The man who is *eusebēs* (the corresponding adjective) is the man who is in a right relationship both with God and his fellow-men. *Eusebeia* is piety and religion, but it is piety and religion in their most practical aspects.

We may best of all see the meaning of this word by looking at the man whom the Greeks held to be the finest example of it; that man was Socrates, and Xenophon describes him as follows: " He was so pious and devoutly religious that he would take no step apart from the will of heaven; so just and upright that he never did even a trifling injury to any living soul; so self-controlled, so temperate, that he never at any time chose the sweeter instead of the better; so sensible, so wise, and so prudent that in distinguishing the better from the worse he never erred " (Xenophon, *Memorabilia* I.5.8-11). In Latin the word is *pietas*; and Warde Fowler describes the Roman idea of the man who possesses that quality: " He is superior to the enticements of individual passion and of selfish ease; (*pietas* is) a sense of duty which never left a man, of duty first to the gods, then to father and to family, to son and to daughter, to his people and to his nation."

Eusebeia is the nearest Greek word for *religion*; and, whenever we begin to define it and to see what it meant, we see at once the intensely practical character of the Christian religion. Whenever a man becomes a Christian, he acknowledges a double duty, a duty to God, and a duty to his fellow-men.

(vii) To this piety there must be added *brotherly affection*. The word is *philadelphia*, which literally means *love of the brethren*. The point is this—there is a kind of religious devotion which separates a man from his fellow-men. The claims of his fellow-men become an intrusion on his prayers, his study of God's word, and his meditation. The ordinary demands of human relationships become nothing other than a nuisance. Epictetus, the great Stoic philosopher, never married. Half-jestingly he said that he was doing far more for the world by being an unfettered philosopher than if he had produced " two or three dirty-nosed children." " How can he who has to teach mankind run to get something in which to heat the water to give the baby his bath? " What Peter is saying is that there is something wrong with the religion which at any time finds the claims and the demands of personal relationships a nuisance and an interruption.

(viii) The whole ladder of Christian virtue must end in Christian love. Not even affection for the brethren is enough; the Christian must end with a love which is as wide and inclusive as that love of God which makes God cause his sun to rise on the just and on the unjust, and which makes Him send His rain on the evil and the good. The Christian must end by showing to all men the love which God has shown to himself.

ON THE WAY

2 Peter I: 8-11

> For, if these things exist and increase within you, they will make you not ineffective and not unfruitful in your progress towards the knowledge of our Lord Jesus Christ. For whoever does not possess these things is blind, short-sighted, and has lapsed into forgetfulness that the sins of his old way of life have been cleansed away. So, brothers, be the more eager to confirm your calling and your choice. For, if you do practise these virtues, you will never slip; for you will be richly gifted with the right of entry into the eternal kingdom of our Lord Jesus Christ.

HERE Peter strongly urges his people to keep climbing up this ladder of virtues which he has set before them, and to be continually on the way. The more we know of any subject the more we are fit to know. It is always true that " to him that hath it shall be given." Progress is the way to more progress. Moffatt says of ourselves and Jesus Christ:

" We learn Him as we live with Him and for Him." As
the hymn has it:

> May every heart confess Thy name,
>   And ever Thee adore,
> And, seeking Thee, itself inflame
>   To see Thee more and more.

To keep climbing up the ladder of the virtues is to come
ever nearer and nearer to knowing Jesus Christ; and the
further we climb, the further we are yet able to climb.

On the other hand, if we refuse to make the effort of the
upward climb, certain things happen. (*a*) We grow blind;
we are left without the guiding light that the knowledge
of Jesus Christ brings. As Peter sees it, to walk without
Christ is necessarily to walk in the dark, and not to be
able to see the way. (*b*) We grow what Peter calls *muōpazōn*.
This word can have either of two meanings. It can mean
short-sighted. It is easy to become short-sighted in life, to
see things only as they appear at the moment and to be
unable to take the long view of things, to have our eyes
so fixed upon earth that we never think of the things
which are beyond. But this word can also mean *blinking,
shutting the eyes*. Again, it is easy in life to shut our eyes
to that which we do not wish to see, to walk, as it were in
blinkers, which limit our view to the things that we wish
to see about ourselves and about the world. To walk
without Christ is to be in danger of taking the short-
sighted or the blinkered view of life.

Further, Peter says, to fail to climb the ladder of virtue
is to forget that the sins of the old way of life have been
cleansed away. Here Peter is thinking of baptism. At
that time baptism was adult baptism; it was a deliberate
act of decision to leave the old way and to enter upon the
new way. The man who, after baptism, does not begin
upon the upward climb and the upward way has forgotten,
or never realized, the meaning of the experience through
which he has passed. For many of us the parallel to baptism
in this sense is entry into the membership of the Christian

Church. To enter into membership of the Church, and then to remain exactly the same, is to fail to understand what membership of Christ's Church means, for our entry into it must be the first step of the climb upon the upward and the onward way.

In view of all this Peter urges his people to make every effort to confirm their calling by God. Here is a most significant demand. In one way all is of God; it is God's call which gives us entry into the fellowship of His people; without His grace and His mercy we could do nothing and we could expect nothing. His call is the call to the privilege of fellowship with Himself. But that does not absolve us from every possible effort. Let us take an analogy, which, although it is not perfect and complete, will yet help us to understand. Suppose a man who is wealthy and kind picks out a poor lad, who would never otherwise have had the chance, and offers him the privilege of a university education. The benefactor is giving the lad something which he could never have achieved for himself; he is setting before him an immense and unexpected privilege. But the lad cannot make use of that privilege and cannot enter into it unless he is prepared to work and to study and to toil, and the harder he works the more he will enter into the privilege which has been offered to him. The gracious free offer and the personal hard work have to combine before the privilege becomes fully effective. It is so with us and God. God has called us in His free mercy and His unmerited grace; but at the same time we have to bend every effort to toil upwards and onwards on the way.

If we follow this upward way, Peter says, we shall in the end be richly gifted with the right of entry into His eternal kingdom; and we shall not slip upon the way. By this Peter does not mean that we will never sin and that we will never make a mistake. The picture in his mind is the picture of a march, and what he means is that we will never fall out upon the march, and so be left behind. If we set out upon this upward and this onward way, the effort will be great, but God's help will also be great, and in spite of all the toil, He will enable us not to fall out, but to keep going, until we reach our journey's end.

THE PASTOR'S CARE

2 Peter 1: 13-15

> It is for this reason that I intend constantly to remind you of these things, although you already know them, and although you are already firmly established in the truth which you possess. I think it is right, so long as I am in this tent, to rouse you by reminding you, for I know that the time to put off my tent is coming soon, as indeed our Lord Jesus Christ has told me. Yes, and I will make it my endeavour to see to it that after my departure you will constantly remember these things.

HERE there speaks the pastor's care. In this passage Peter shows us two things about the preaching of the preacher, and the instruction and admonition of the teacher. First, preaching is very often reminding a man of what he already knows. It is the bringing back to his memory that truth which he has forgotten, or at which he refuses to look, or whose meaning he has not fully appreciated and realized. It often happens that the task of the preacher and the teacher is to say to men: " Remember what you know, and be what you are." Second, Peter is going to go on to uncompromising rebuke and to very definite, and even threatening, warning, but he begins with something that is very like a compliment. He begins by saying that his people already possess the truth, and that they are firmly established in it. It will always remain true that a preacher, a teacher, a parent will achieve more by encouragement than by scolding. We will do more to reform people and to keep them safe by, as it were, putting them on their honour than by flaying them with invective and rebuke. Peter was wise because he knew well that the first essential to make men listen is to show that we believe in them.

In this passage Peter looks forward to his early death. He talks of his body as his tent, as Paul does (2 *Corinthians* 5: 4). The picture of the body as a tent became a favourite one with the early Christian writers. The writer of *The Epistle to Diognetus* says, " The immortal soul dwells in a mortal tent." The picture comes from the journeyings of the patriarchs in the Old Testament. They had no abiding residence; they lived in tents, because they were on the way and on the pilgrimage to the Promised Land. The Christian knows well and always remembers that his life in this world is not a permanent residence, but a journey towards the world beyond. We get the same idea in verse 15. There Peter speaks of his approaching death as his *exodos*, his departure. This word *exodos* is, of course, the word which is used for the departure of the children of Israel from Egypt, and their setting out to the Promised Land. So Peter sees death, not as the end, not as the going out into nothingness and into the dark, but as the going out into the Promised Land of God.

Peter says that Jesus Christ has told him that for him the end will soon be coming. This may be a reference to the prophecy of Jesus about Peter which is related in *John* 21: 18, 19, when Jesus foretells that there will come a day when Peter also will be stretched out upon a cross. That time is now about to come.

Peter says that he will take steps to see that what he has got to say to them will be held before their memory even when he is gone from this earth. That may well be a reference to the Gospel according to St. Mark. The consistent tradition is that Mark's gospel is the preaching material of Peter. Irenaeus says that, after the death of Peter and Paul, Mark, who had been the disciple and interpreter of Peter, handed on in writing the things which it had been Peter's custom to preach. Papias, who lived towards the end of the second century, and who collected so many traditions about the early days of the Church, hands down the same tradition about Mark's gospel:

" Mark, who was Peter's interpreter, wrote down accurately, though not in order, all that he recollected of what Christ had said or done. For he was not a hearer of the Lord, or a follower of His; he followed Peter, as I have said, at a later date, and Peter adapted his instruction to practical needs, without any attempt to give the Lord's words systematically. So that Mark was not wrong in writing down some things in this way from memory, for his one concern was neither to omit or to falsify anything that he had heard." Tradition consistently connects the preaching of Peter and the Gospel of Mark; and it may well be that the reference here means that Peter's teaching was made still available to Peter's people in Mark's Gospel after Peter's death.

In any event, the pastor's aim was to bring to his people God's truth while he was still alive, and to take steps to keep it in their memories even after he was dead. He wrote, not to preserve his own name, but to preserve the name of Jesus Christ.

THE MESSAGE AND THE RIGHT TO GIVE IT

2 Peter 1: 16-18

> For it was not cleverly invented fables that we followed when we made known to you the power and the coming of our Lord Jesus Christ; it was because we were made eye-witnesses of His majesty. This happened to us on that occasion when He received honour and glory from God the Father, when this voice was borne to Him by the majestic glory—" This is my Son, the Beloved, in whom I am well pleased." It was this voice that we heard, borne from heaven, when we were with Him in the sacred mountain.

HERE Peter comes to the message which it was his great aim to bring to his people. His message was concerning " the power and the coming of our Lord Jesus Christ." As we shall see quite clearly as we go on, the great aim of this letter is to recall men to certainty in regard to the

Second Coming of Jesus Christ. The heretics whom Peter is attacking no longer believed in the Second Coming; it was so long delayed that people had begun to think that it would never happen at all; and *Second Peter* is above all the letter which seeks to recall men to a belief in the Second Coming of Jesus Christ.

Such, then, was Peter's message. Having stated it, he goes on to speak of his right to state it. And in this he does something which is, at least at first sight, surprising. His right to speak is that he was with Jesus on the Mount of Transfiguration, and that there he saw the glory and the honour which were given to Him, and heard the voice of God speak to Him. That is to say, Peter uses the transfiguration story, not as a foretaste of the Resurrection of Jesus, as it is commonly regarded, but as a foretaste of the triumphant glory of the Second Coming. The transfiguration story itself is told in *Matthew* 17: 1-8; *Mark* 9: 2-8; *Luke* 9: 28-36. Was Peter right in seeing in it a foretaste of the Second Coming rather than a prefiguring of the Resurrection.

There is one particularly significant thing about the transfiguration story. In all three gospels, in *Matthew*, *Mark*, and *Luke*, it immediately follows the prophecy of Jesus which says that there were some standing there who would not pass from the world until they had seen the Son of Man coming in His kingdom (*Matthew* 16: 29; *Mark* 9: 1; *Luke* 9: 27). That would certainly seem to indicate that the transfiguration and the Second Coming are in some way linked together.

Whatever we may say, this much is certain, that Peter's great aim in this letter is to recall his people to a living belief in the Second Coming of Christ, and that he bases his right to do so on what he saw on the Mount of Transfiguration.

In verse 16 of this passage there is one very interesting word. There Peter says, " We were made *eye-witnesses* of His majesty." The word he uses for an *eye-witness* is *epoptēs.* In the Greek usage of Peter's day this was a technical word. We have already spoken about the Mystery Religions. These Mystery Religions were all of the nature of passion plays, in which the story of a god who lived, suffered, died, and rose again, never to die again, was played out. It was only after a long course of instruction and preparation that the worshipper was finally allowed to be present at the passion play, and to be offered the experience of becoming one with the dying and rising God. When he reached the stage of being allowed to attend the actual passion play, he was an initiate, and the technical word to describe him was in fact *epoptēs*; he was a prepared and privileged eye-witness of the experiences of God. So Peter says that the Christian is an eye-witness of the sufferings of Christ. With the eye of faith the Christian sees the Cross; in the experience of faith he dies with Christ to sin, and rises to righteousness. His faith has made him one with Jesus Christ in His death and in His risen life and power.

THE WORDS OF THE PROPHETS

2 Peter I: 19-21

> So this makes the word of the prophets still more certain for us; and you will do well to pay attention to it, as it shines like a lamp in a dingy place, until the day dawns and the Morning Star rises within your hearts. For you must first and foremost realize that no prophecy in Scripture permits of private interpretation; for no prophecy was ever borne to us by the will of man, but men spoke from God, when they were carried away by the Holy Spirit.

THIS is a particularly difficult passage, because in both halves of it the Greek can mean two quite different things. We shall look at these different possibilities, and in each case we shall take the less probable first.

(i) The first sentence of this passage in Greek can well mean: " In prophecy we have an even surer guarantee, that is, of the Second Coming." If Peter did say this, he means that the words of the prophets are an even surer guarantee of the reality of the second coming than his own experience on the Mount of Transfiguration. However unlikely it may seem, it is by no means impossible that he did say just that. When Peter was writing there was a tremendous interest in the words of prophecy; to the people of his age the supreme proof of the truth of Christianity was in fact drawn from the fulfilment of prophecy. We get case after case of people who were converted in the days of the early Church, not by reading the New Testament books, but by reading the Old Testament books, and seeing in the life of Jesus the fulfilment of prophecy. It would be quite in line with that to declare that the strongest argument for the Second Coming is that the prophets foretold it.

(ii) But we think that the second possible translation must be preferred. This passage can equally well mean: " What we saw on the Mount of Transfiguration makes it even more certain that what is foretold in the prophets about the Second Coming must be true." If we take it this way, it means that the glory of Jesus on the Mount of Transfiguration is the strongest guarantee that the prophets were right when they foretold the Second Coming of the Lord.

However we take this, the meaning of it is that the glory of Jesus on the mountain top and the visions of the prophets combine to make it certain the the Second Coming is a living reality which all men must expect, and for which all men must prepare.

But, as we have said, there is also a double possibility about the second part of this passage. " No prophecy of the Scripture," as the Authorized Version has it, " is of any private interpretation."

(i) Many of the early scholars took this to mean: " When any of the prophets interpreted any situation in history, or when they told how history was going to unfold itself, they were not expressing a private opinion of their own; they were passing on to men a revelation which God had given to them." This is, indeed, a perfectly possible meaning. In the Old Testament the mark of a false prophet was that he was speaking *of himself*, as it were, *privately*, and that he was not saying what God had told him to say. Jeremiah condemns the false prophets: "They speak a vision of their own heart; and not out of the mouth of the Lord" (*Jeremiah* 23: 16). Ezekiel says, "Woe unto the false prophets who follow their own spirit, and have seen nothing" (*Ezekiel* 13: 3). Hippolytus describes the way in which the words of the true prophets came: "They did not speak of their own power, nor did they proclaim what they themselves wished, but first they were given right wisdom by the word, and were then instructed by visions."

If we take this meaning, the passage means that, when the prophets spoke, it was no private opinion, no intelligent guess, no human forecast they were giving; it was a revelation from God, and, therefore, their words must be most carefully heeded.

(ii) The second way to take this passage is to take it of *our* interpretation of the prophets. A situation was confronting Peter in which the heretics and the evil men were interpreting the prophets to suit themselves; they were twisting the prophetic messages to fit their own views and their own desires. If that is the case, and we think it certainly is, what Peter is saying is: "No man can go to Scripture and interpret it according to his own private views and opinions; he cannot interpret Scripture and prophecy privately and as it suits himself."

Now this is of first-rate practical importance. What Peter is saying is that no man has the right to interpret Scripture for himself and by himself, to use his own words, *privately*. How then must Scripture be interpreted? To answer that question we must ask another question. How did the prophets receive their message? The prophets received their message from the Spirit. It was sometimes even said that the Spirit of God used the prophets as a writer uses a pen, or as a musician uses a musical instrument. It could even be said that the prophets were entirely passive instruments in the hand of the Spirit of God. In any event the Spirit gave the prophet his message. The obvious conclusion is that it is only through the help of that same Spirit that the prophetic message can be interpreted and understood. As Paul had already said, spiritual things are spiritually discerned (I *Corinthians* 2: 14, 15). As the Jews viewed the Holy Spirit, the Spirit has two functions—the Spirit brings God's truth to men, *and* enables men to understand and to recognize that truth when it is brought. So, then, Scripture is not to be interpreted by private cleverness and private ingenuity and even private prejudice; Scripture is to be interpreted by the help of the Holy Spirit, since it was first given by the Holy Spirit.

What does that mean practically? It means two things.

(*a*) Throughout all the ages and the generations the Spirit has been working and moving in devoted scholars who under the guidance of God studied and opened the Scriptures to men. If then, we wish to interpret Scripture, we must never arrogantly insist that our own interpretation of it must be correct; we must humbly go to the works of the great devoted scholars to learn what they have to teach us, because of what the Spirit taught them.

(*b*) But there is more than that. The one place in which the Spirit specially resides, and the one place in which the Spirit is specially operative is the Church; and, therefore, Scripture must be interpreted in the light of the teaching, the belief, and the tradition of the Church. God is our Father in the faith, but the Church is our mother in the faith. If a man finds that his interpretation of Scripture is quite at variance with the teaching of the Church, then he must humbly examine himself, and he must ask whether his guide has not been his own private wishes rather than the guidance of the Holy Spirit.

It is Peter's insistence that Scripture does not consist of any man's private opinions, but is the revelation of God to men through God's Spirit; and that, therefore, the interpretation of Scripture must not depend on any man's private opinions, but must ever be guided by the same Spirit who guided scholarly men whose hearts were given to Christ, and who is still specially operative within the Church.

FALSE PROPHETS

2 *Peter* 2: 1

> There were times when false prophets arose among the people, even as amongst you too there will be false teachers, men who will insidiously introduce destructive heresies, and deny the Lord who bought them; and by so doing they will bring swift destruction on themselves.

THAT there should arise false prophets and false teachers within the Church was something only to be expected, for in every generation false prophets had been responsible for leading God's people astray, and for bringing tragedy and disaster on the nation. It is worthwhile looking at the false prophets in the Old Testament story, and seeing their characteristics, for the characteristics were recurring in the time of Peter, and are still recurring today.

(i) The false prophets were more interested in gaining popularity than in telling the truth. Their policy was to tell people what people wanted to hear. The false prophets said, " Peace, peace, when there is no peace " (*Jeremiah* 6: 14). They saw visions of peace, when the Lord God was saying that there was no peace (*Ezekiel* 13: 16). In the days of Jehosaphat, Zedekiah, the false prophet, donned his horns of iron and said that Israel would push the Syrians out of the way as he pushed with these horns; Micaiah the true prophet foretold disaster if Jehosaphat went to war. Of course, Zedekiah was popular, and naturally his message was accepted, but Jehosaphat went forth to war with the Syrians, and perished tragically (I *Kings* 22). In the days of Jeremiah, Hananiah prophesied the swift end of the power of Babylon, while Jeremiah prophesied the servitude of the nation to Babylon; and of course the prophet who told people what they wished to hear was popular (*Jeremiah* 28). Diogenes, the great cynic philosopher, spoke of the false teachers of his day whose method it was to follow wherever the applause of the crowd lead. One of the first characteristics of the false prophet is that he tells men what they want to hear, and will not tell him the truth they need to hear. His aim is popularity and his touchstone is applause.

(ii) The false prophets were interested in personal gain. As Micah said, " The priests teach for hire, and the prophets divine for money " (*Micah* 3: 11). They teach for filthy lucre's sake (*Titus* 1: 11), and they identify godliness and gain, making their religion a money-making thing (I *Timothy* 6: 5). We can see these exploiters of the Christian people at work in the early Church. In *The Didachē, The Teaching of the Twelve Apostles*, which is what might be called the first service-order book, it is laid down that a prophet who asks for money, or who asks for a table to be spread in front of him, is a false prophet. " Traffickers in Christ," *The Didachē* calls such men (*The Didachē* 11). The false prophet is a covetous creature who regards men as dupes to be exploited for his own ends.

(iii) The false prophets are dissolute in their own personal life. Isaiah writes: " The priest and the prophet have erred through strong drink; they are swallowed up in wine " (*Isaiah* 28: 7). Jeremiah says, " I have seen also in the prophets of Jerusalem a horrible thing; they commit adultery and walk in lies; they strengthen also the hands of evil-doers. . . . They cause my people to err by their lies and by their lightness " (*Jeremiah* 23: 14, 32). The false prophet's personal life is a seduction to evil rather than an attraction to good.

(iv) The false prophet is above all a man who leads other men further away from God instead of closer to God. The prophet and the dreamer who invites the people: " Let us go after other gods," must be mercilessly destroyed (*Deuteronomy* 13: 1-5; 18: 20).

These were the characteristics of the false prophet in the ancient days; these were the characteristics of the false teachers who were troubling Peter's people; and to this day these characteristics still recur.

THE SINS OF THE FALSE PROPHETS AND THEIR END

2 Peter 2: 1 (*continued*)

IN this verse Peter has certain things to say about these false prophets and their actions.

(i) They insidiously introduce destructive heresies. The Greek word for *heresy* is *hairesis*, and it is a word with a very curious and a very interesting history. It comes from the Greek verb *haireisthai*, which means *to choose*; and originally it was a perfectly good and honourable word. It simply meant a line of belief and action which a man had chosen for himself. In the New Testament itself we read of the *hairesis* of the Sadducees, the Pharisees, and the Nazarenes (*Acts* 5: 17; 15: 5; 24: 5). It was perfectly possible to speak of the *hairesis* of Plato, and to mean nothing more than those who were Platonist in their thought and their philosophy. It was perfectly possible to speak of a group of doctors who believed in, and practised, a certain method of treatment as a *hairesis*. All that a *hairesis* meant was a belief which one had personally chosen for oneself, and to which one by choice adhered. But very soon in the Christian Church the word *hairesis* quite changed its complexion. In Paul's thought heresies and schisms go together as things to be condemned (1 *Corinthians* 11: 18, 19); *haireseis* (the plural form of the word) are part of the works of the flesh; a man that is a heretic is to be warned, and even given a second chance, and then rejected (*Titus* 3: 10).

Why the change? The whole point is that before the coming of Christianity, and before the coming of Jesus, who is the way, the truth, and the life, there was no such thing as definite, God-given truth. A man was presented with a number of alternatives any of which he might choose honestly to believe. But with the coming of Jesus, God's truth came to men, and men had either to accept or to reject that truth. In other words, with the revelation of God in Christ, it is no longer a question of choosing the particular line of belief which happens to appeal to us; it is a question of accepting, or rejecting, the revealed truth of God. A heretic then becomes a man who believes what *he* wishes to believe instead of accepting the truth of God which he must believe.

What was happening in the case of Peter's people was that certain men, who claimed to be prophets, were insidiously persuading men to believe the things they wished to be true rather than the things which God has revealed as true. They did not set themselves up as opponents of Christianity. Far from it. Rather they set themselves up as the finest fruits of Christian thinking. Insidiously, unconsciously, imperceptible, so gradually and so subtly that they did not even notice it, people were being lured away from God's truth to men's private opinions, for that is what heresy is.

(ii) These men denied the Lord who had bought them. This idea of Christ buying men for Himself is an idea which runs through the whole New Testament. It comes from His own word, when He said that He had come to give His life a ransom for many (*Mark* 10: 45). The idea was that men were slaves to sin and evil, and that Jesus Christ had purchased them at the cost of His life for Himself, and, therefore, for freedom and liberty. " Ye are bought with a price," says Paul (I *Corinthians* 7: 23). " Christ has

redeemed us (bought us out) from the curse of the law "
(*Galatians* 3: 13). In the new song in the *Revelation* the
hosts of heaven tell how Jesus Christ bought them with
His blood out of every kindred and tongue and people and
nation (*Revelation* 5: 9). This clearly means two things. It
means that the Christian, by right of purchase, belongs
absolutely to Christ. And it means that a life which cost
so much cannot be squandered on sin or on cheap and
worthless things.

The heretics in Peter's letter are *denying* the Lord who
bought them. What does that mean? It could mean that
they are saying that they do not know Christ; and it
could mean that they are denying His authority. But it
is not as simple as that; one might say that it is not as
honest as that. We have seen that these men claimed to be
Christians; more, they claimed to be the wisest and the
most advanced of Christians. Let us take a human analogy.
Suppose a man says that he loves his wife, and then suppose
that he is consistently and deliberately unfaithful to her,
then by his acts of infidelity he denies, and gives the lie
to, his words of love. Suppose a man protests sincere and
eternal friendship to someone, and then suppose he is
consistently disloyal and consistently unhelpful to the
person he calls his friend, then his actions deny, and give
the lie to, his protestations of friendship. What these evil
men, who were troubling Peter's people, were doing, was
that they were saying that they loved and served Christ,
and at the same time the things they preached and taught,
and the things they did, were a complete denial of Him.
One of the most terrible ways to deny Christ is to seek
to undo all that he has done by influencing for evil the men
for whom He died.

(iii) The end of these evil men was destruction. They
were insidiously introducing destructive heresies, but these
destructive heresies would in the end destroy themselves.
There is no more certain way to ultimate condemnation
than to teach another to sin.

THE WORK OF FALSEHOOD

2 Peter 2: 2, 3

> And many will follow the way of their blatant immoralities, and through them the true way will be brought into disrepute. In their evil ambition they will exploit you with cunningly forged arguments. Their sentence was settled long ago, and now it is not inactive, and their destruction is not asleep.

In this short passage we see four things about the false teachers and their teaching.

(i) We see the *cause* of false teaching. The cause is *evil ambition*. The word is *pleonexia*; *pleon* means *more* and *exia* comes from the verb *echein*, which means *to have*. *Pleonexia* is *the desire to possess more*. But this word *pleonexia* acquired a certain flavour. It is by no means always a sin to desire to possess more; there are many cases in which that is a perfectly honourable desire, as in the case of virtue, or knowledge, or skill. But *pleonexia* comes to mean the desire to possess that which a man has no right to desire, still less to take. So it can mean covetous desire for money and for other people's goods; lustful desire for the person of someone; unholy ambition for honour and prestige and power. False teaching comes from this evil ambition to possess something which a man has no right to possess. It comes from the desire for nothing less than the place of Christ, for its desire is to put its own ideas in the place of the truth of Jesus Christ. The false teacher is guilty of nothing less than of usurping the place of Christ.

(ii) We see the *method* of false teaching. Its method is the use of cunningly forged arguments. Falsehood is easily resisted when it is presented as falsehood; it is when it is cunningly dressed and disguised as truth that it becomes threatening and menacing. There is only one touchstone. Any teacher's teaching must be tested by the words and the presence of Jesus Christ Himself. If that is done, its falsity will be fully exposed.

(iii) We see the *effect* of the false teaching. Its effect was twofold. It encouraged men to take the way of blatant immorality. The word is *aselgeia*, and, as we have already seen, that word describes the attitude of the man who is lost to shame; he is past the stage of wishing to conceal his sin and of being ashamed of it; he takes what he wants and he takes it when and where he wants it; and he cares for the judgment of neither man nor God, and he sets no value on his own good name. We must remember that which was at the back of the teaching of these false teachers. They were perverting the grace of God into a justification for sin. They were telling men that grace was inexhaustible and that, therefore, they were free to sin as they liked, for grace would forgive. They were presenting God's grace in a way which made grace a reason for sin.

But this false teaching had obviously a second effect. It brought Christianity into disrepute. If Christianity produced people who acted like that, then obviously people were going to have no use for Christians and for the Christian Church. In the early days, and just as much now, every Christian is a good or bad advertisement for Christianity, and for the Christian Church. It was Paul's accusation to the Jews that through them the name of God had been brought into disrepute (*Romans* 2: 24). In the Pastoral Epistles the younger women are urged to behave with such modesty and chastity that the Church will never be brought into disrepute (*Titus* 2: 5). Any type of teaching which produces a kind of person who repels men from Christianity instead of attracting them to it is false teaching, and the work of those who are enemies of Christ.

(iv) We see the *ultimate end* of false teaching; and that ultimate end is destruction. Sentence was passed on the false prophets long ago; the Old Testament pronounced their doom (*Deuteronomy* 13: 1-5). It may look as if that sentence had become inoperative or was slumbering, but it was still valid, and the day would come when the false

377

teachers would pay the terrible price of their falsehood.
No man who leads another man astray will ever escape his
own judgment.

THE FATE OF THE WICKED AND THE RESCUE OF
THE RIGHTEOUS

2 Peter 2: 4-11

> If God did not spare even angels who had sinned, but
> condemned them to the lowest hell, and committed
> them to the pits of darkness, where they remain kept
> for judgment; if He did not spare the ancient world,
> but preserved in safety Noah, the preacher of right-
> eousness, with seven others, when He despatched the
> flood on a world of impious men; if He reduced the
> cities of Sodom and Gomorrah to ashes, when He
> sentenced them to destruction, and so gave an example
> of what would happen to those who would one day
> act with impiety, but rescued righteous Lot, who was
> distressed by the blatantly immoral conduct of lawless
> men, for, to such a man, righteous in his looking
> and in his hearing, it was torture for his righteous
> soul to live his daily life amidst such people, and
> amidst such lawless deeds—if all this is so, you can be
> sure that the Lord knows how to rescue truly religious
> men from trial, and how to preserve the unrighteous
> under punishment, until the day of judgment comes,
> especially those whose lives are dominated by the
> polluting lusts of the flesh, and who despise the
> celestial powers. Audacious, self-willed men they are;
> they do not shrink from speaking evil of the angelic
> glories, whereas angels who are greater in strength
> and power do not bring an accusation of evil against
> them in the presence of the Lord.

HERE is a passage which for us combines undoubted power
and equally undoubted obscurity. The white heat of its
rhetorical intensity glows through it to this day; but it
moves in allusions which would be familiar and terrifyingly
effective to those who heard it for the first time, but which
have become unfamiliar and obscure to us today. It cites
three notorious examples of sin, and its destruction; and

in two of the cases it shows how, when sin was obliterated, righteousness was rescued and preserved by the mercy and the grace of God. Let us look at these examples of sin one by one.

I.—THE SIN OF THE ANGELS

Before we retell the story which lies behind this in Jewish thought and legend, there are two separate words at which we must look. Peter says that God condemned the sinning angels to the lowest depths of hell. Literally the Greek says that God condemned the angels to *Tartarus*; the verb is *tartaroun*. Tartarus was not a Hebrew conception at all; it was Greek. In Greek mythology Tartarus is the lowest hell; it is as far beneath Hades as the heaven is high above the earth. In particular it was the place into which there had been cast the Titans and the Giants who had rebelled against Zeus, the Father of gods and men. Tartarus, then, was the lowest and the most terrible hell, in which those who had rebelled against divine power were kept in eternal punishment.

The second word at which we must look is the word which speaks of the *pits* of darkness. Here there is a doubt. There are two Greek words, which are both rather uncommon, and which are confused in this passage. The one word is the unusual word *siros* or *seiros*. *Siros* originally meant a great earthenware jar for the storing of grain; then it came to mean the great underground pits and chambers in which grain was stored, and which served as granaries. The word is *siros*, and that very word has come into English *via* Provençal in the form *silo*, which still describes the towers in which grain is stored. Still later the word went on to mean a pit in which a wolf or other wild animal is trapped. If, then, we think that this is the word which Peter uses, and according to the best manuscripts it is, it will mean that the wicked angels were cast into great subterranean pits, and kept there in darkness and in punishment. This well suits the idea of a

Tartarus beneath the lowest depths of Hades. But there is a very similar word *seira*, which means a *chain*. This is the word which the Authorized Version translates when it speaks of *chains of darkness* (verse 4); and it is the word which Jude was thinking of when he speaks of *everlasting chains* for the wicked angels (verse 6), for the word which Jude uses is *desmoi*, which means *chains* or *fetters*. The Greek manuscripts in *Second Peter* vary between *seiroi*, pits, and *seirai*, chains. But the better manuscripts have *seiroi*, pits, and *pits of darkness* makes better sense than *chains of darkness*; so we may take *seiros* as right, and we may assume that here the Authorized Version is in error.

The story of the fall of the angels is a story which rooted itself deeply in Hebrew thought, and which underwent much development as the years went on. The original story is in *Genesis* 6: 1-5. There the angels are called *the sons of God*, as they commonly are in the Old Testament. In *Job*, *the sons of God* come to present themselves before the Lord, and Satan comes amongst them (*Job* 1: 6; cp. 2: 1; 38: 7). The Psalmist speaks of the sons of the Mighty (*Psalm* 89: 6). These angels came to earth and seduced mortal women. The result of this lustful union was the race of giants. And through them wickedness came upon the earth. Clearly this is an old, old story belonging to the childhood of the race. This story was much developed in the Book of Enoch, and it is from Enoch that Peter is drawing his allusions, for in his day that was a book which everyone would know. In *Enoch* the angels are called *The Watchers*. Their leader in rebellion was Semjaza or Azazel. At his instigation they descended to Mount Hermon in the days of Jared, the father of Enoch. They took mortal wives, and instructed them in magic and in arts which gave them power. They begat the race of the giants, and the giants begat the *nephillim*, the giants who inhabited the land of Canaan, and of whom the people were afraid (*Numbers* 13: 33). These giants became cannibals and were guilty of every kind of lust and crime, and especially of insolent arrogance to God and man. The apocryphal literature has many references to these giants and their pride. *Wisdom* (14: 6) tells how the proud giants perished. *Ecclesiasticus* (16: 7) tells how the ancient giants fell away in the strength of their foolishness. They had no wisdom, and they perished in their folly (*Baruch* 3: 26-28). Josephus says that they were arrogant and contemptuous of all that was good, and that they trusted in their own strength (*Antiquities* I.3.1). Job says that God charged His angels with folly (*Job* 4: 18). This old story makes a strange and fleeting appearance in the letters of Paul. In I *Corinthians* II: 10 Paul says that women must have their hair covered in the Church, *because of the angels*. Behind that strange saying lies the old belief that it was the loveliness of the long hair of the women of the olden times which moved the angels to desire; and Paul wishes to see that the angels are not tempted again. In the end even men complained of the sorrow and the misery and the cruelty brought into the world by these giants, through the sin of the angels. The result was that God sent out His archangels. Raphael bound Azazel hand and foot and shut him up in darkness; Gabriel slew the giants; and the Watchers, the sinning angels, were shut up in the abysses of darkness under the mountains for seventy generations, and then confined for ever in everlasting fire. Here is the story which is in Peter's mind; and which Peter's readers well knew. The angels had sinned, and God had sent His destruction, and they were shut up for ever in the pits and abysses of darkness and the depths of hell. That is what happens to rebellious sin.

But the story does not stop there; and it reappears in another of its forms in this passage of *Second Peter*. In verse 10 Peter speaks of those who live lives dominated by the polluting lusts of the flesh, and who despise the celestial powers. The word is *kuriotēs*, which is the name of the one of the ranks of angels. They speak evil of the angelic glories. The word is *doxai*, which again is a word for one of the ranks of angels. They slander the angels, and they bring the angels into disrepute.

Now here is where the second turn of the story comes in. Obviously this story of the angels is a very ancient story and very primitive. It is the kind of story that belongs to the childhood of the race. And, further, as soon as men begin to think, and to see the implications of the old stories, it is an awkward and an embarrassing story, for it ascribes lust to the holy angels. So, in the later Jewish and Christian thought, two lines of thought develop. First, it is denied that the story involves angels at all. The sons of God are said to be good men, who were the descendants of Seth, and the daughters of men are said to be evil women who were the daughters of Cain, and who corrupted the good men. There is no scriptural evidence for this distinction and this way of escape. Second, the whole story was allegorised. It was claimed, for instance by Philo, that it was never meant to be taken literally, and that it describes the fall of the human soul under the attack of the seductions of lustful pleasures. Augustine declared that no man can take this story literally, and no man can talk of the angels like that. Cyril of Alexandria said that the story could not be taken literally, for did not Jesus say that in the after-life men will be like angels and there will be no marrying or giving in marriage (*Matthew* 22: 30)? Chrysestom said that, if the story was taken literally, it was nothing short of blasphemy. And Cyril went on to say that the story was nothing other than an incentive to sin, if it was taken as a true and literal story of the angels.

It is clear that men began to see that this was indeed a dangerous story. Now here we get our clue as to what Peter means when he speaks of men who despise the celestial powers, and bring the angelic glories into disrepute, by speaking slanderously of them. The men whom Peter was opposing were men who were turning their religion never be selfish. A man can never keep to himself the grace which he has received. It is always his duty to bring light to those who sit in darkness, guidance to the wanderer, and warning to those who are going astray. The good man must himself be on the way to God; and to others he must be a signpost pointing to God, and a voice inviting to God.

3.—THE DESTRUCTION OF SODOM AND GOMORRAH AND THE RESCUE OF LOT

THE third example of sin and its destruction, and of goodness and its rescue, which Peter takes, is the destruction of Sodom and Gomorrah and the rescue of Lot.

The terrible and dramatic story is told in *Genesis* 18 and 19. The story begins with Abraham's plea that God should not destroy the righteous with the guilty, and his request to God that, if even ten just men are found in these cities, they may be spared (*Genesis* 18: 16-33). Then there follows one of the grimmest and most horrible stories in the Old Testament. The angelic visitors came to Lot, and he persuaded them to stay with him; but his house was surrounded by the men of Sodom demanding that these strangers might be brought out to them that they might use them for the wicked purposes of their terrible and unnatural lust (*Genesis* 19: 1-11). By that terrible deed, at once, the abuse of hospitality, the insulting of angels, and the raging of unnatural and uncontrollable lust, the doom of the cities is sealed. As the destruction of heaven came upon them Lot and his family were saved, except his wife, who turned and lingered and looked back, and who turned into a pillar of salt (*Genesis* 19: 12-25). " And it came to pass, when God destroyed the cities of the plain, that God remembered Abraham, and sent Lot out of the midst of the overthrow, when He overthrew the cities in which Lot dwelt " (*Genesis* 19: 29). Here again is the story of the into an excuse for, and a justification for, blatant immorality. Cyril of Alexandria makes it clear that in his day the story could be used as an incentive to sin. Most probably what was happening was this—the wicked men of Peter's time were citing the example of the angels as a justification for their own sin. They were saying, " If angels came from heaven, and took mortal women, why should not we? What the angels did cannot be wrong for man to do." They were despising the angels; they were bringing the angels into disrepute; they were slandering the angels; they were making the conduct of the angels an excuse for their own sin.

But we have to go still further with this passage. In verse II this passage finishes very obscurely. It says that angels who are greater in strength and in power do not bring a slanderous charge against them in the presence of God. What does Peter mean by this? Once again he is speaking allusively, in a way that would be clear enough to the people of his day, but which is obscure to us, because we do not know the legends and traditions to which he is referring. His reference may be to either of two stories. (a) He may be referring to the story to which Jude refers in *Jude* 9. That story is that the archangel Michael was entrusted with the duty of burying the body of Moses. Satan claimed the body on the ground that all matter belonged to him, and on the ground that once Moses had murdered an Egyptian. Michael did not bring a railing charge against Satan; all that he said was: " The Lord rebuke you." The point is that even an angel so great as Michael would not bring an evil charge against an angel so dark as Satan. He left the matter to God. If Michael did not despise and slander an evil angel, how can men bring slanderous charges against the angels of God? (b) But Peter may here well be referring to a further development of the *Enoch* story. *Enoch* tells that when the conduct of the giants on earth became unbearable and intolerable, men made their complaint to the archangels Michael,

Uriel, Gabriel and Raphael. The archangels took this complaint to God; but they did not rail against the evil angels who were responsible for it all; they made no charge against them; they did not slander them; they simply took the story to God, for God to deal with (*Enoch* 9). Even the archangels did not slander the evil angels; they left everything to God.

As far as we can see today, the situation behind Peter's allusions is that the wicked men who were the slaves of lust claimed that the angels were their examples and their justification; they slandered the angels; Peter reminds them that not even archangels dared to slander other angels, and demands how men can dare to do so.

This is a strange and a difficult passage; but the meaning of it is clear. Even angels, when they sinned in lust, were punished. How much more shall men be punished? Angels could not rebel against God, and escape the consequences of their rebellion. How shall men escape? And men need not seek to put the blame on others, not even on angels; nothing but their own rebellious lust is responsible for their own sin.

2.—THE MEN OF THE FLOOD AND THE RESCUE OF NOAH

The second illustration of the destruction of wickedness which Peter chooses may be said to lead on from the first. It was the sin introduced into the world by the sinning angels which lead on to that intolerable sin which ended in the destruction by the deluge (*Genesis* 6: 5). In the midst of this destruction God did not forget those who had clung to Him, who had resisted evil, and who had lived in goodness. Noah, together with seven others, was saved. The seven others were his own wife, his sons, Shem, Ham, and Japhet, and their wives. In Jewish legend and tradition Noah had acquired a very special place. Not only was he regarded as the one man who had been saved; he was also regarded as the preacher who had done his best to turn men from the evil of their ways. Josephus says, " Many angels of

God lay with women and begat sons, who were violent and who despised all good, on account of their reliance on their own strength. . . . But Noah displeased and distressed at their behaviour, tried to induce them to alter their dispositions and conduct for the better " (*Antiquities* I.3.I). Noah had acquired the reputation of being a preacher for God in an evil world.

The attention in this passage is concentrated, not so much on the people who were destroyed, as on the man Noah who was saved. Noah is offered as the type of man who, amidst the destruction of the wicked, receives the salvation of God. The outstanding qualities of Noah were two.

(i) In the midst of a rebellious, disobedient and sinning generation he remained faithful and obedient to God. In the later days Paul was to urge his people to be, not conformed to the world, but transformed from the world (*Romans* 12: 2). It may well be said that often the most dangerous sin of all is conformity. To be the same as others is always easy; to be different from others is always difficult. But from the days of Noah until now he who would be the servant of God must be prepared to be different from the world.

(ii) The later legends pick out another characteristic of Noah. Noah is the preacher of righteousness. The word for preacher used here is *kērux*, which literally means *a herald*. Epictetus called the philosopher the *kērux* of the gods, the herald of the gods to men. The preacher is the man who brings to men an announcement and a proclamation from God. There is here something of very considerable significance. The good man is not concerned only with the saving of his own soul; he is just as much concerned with the saving of the souls of other people. He does not, in order to preserve his own purity and innocence divorce himself from men and live apart. He is concerned to bring God's message to them. His concern is not only to save himself, but also to rescue others. Salvation destruction of sin, and the rescue of righteousness. Once again, as in Noah, we can see in Lot the characteristics of the righteous man.

(i) Lot lived in the midst of evil, and the very sight of it was a constant distress to him, and a continual torture to his soul. Moffatt reminds us of the saying of Newman: " Our great security against sin lies in being shocked at it." Herein is something very significant. It often happens that, when evils first emerge, people are shocked and disturbed at them; but, as time goes on, they begin to cease to be shocked at them and to accept them as a matter of course. There are many things at which we ought to be shocked and horror-stricken. In our own generation there is the problem of prostitution and of promiscuity, the problem of drunkenness, the extraordinary gambling fever which has the country in its grip, the breakdown of the marriage bond, the problem of violence and crime, death upon the roads, the still-existing slum conditions. And in many cases the tragedy is that these things have ceased to shock in any real sense of the term. They are accepted as part of the normal order of things. They may be regarded as unfortunate and regrettable, but not as shocking in the literal sense of the term. For the good of the world, and for the good of our own souls, we must keep alive the sensitiveness which is shocked by sin.

(ii) Lot lived in the midst of evil, and yet he escaped the taint of it. Amidst the sin of Sodom he remained true to God and obedient to God. If a man will accept it and remember it, he has in the grace of God, and in the memory of the presence of God, an antiseptic and a prophylactic which will preserve him from the infection of sin. No man need be the victim and the slave of the environment in which he happens to find himself.

(iii) When the worst came to the worst, Lot was willing to make the clean break with the environment in which he lived. He was willing, however much he did not want to do so, to rise up and leave it for ever. It was because his wife was not prepared to make the clean break that she perished. There is a strange verse in the Old Testament story. It says that, when Lot lingered, the angelic messengers took hold upon his hand (*Genesis* 19: 16). There are times when the influence of heaven tries even to force us to step out of some evil and tainting position or situation or environment. It may come to any man to have to make the choice between settlement and security, and the new start and the clean break; and there are times when a man can only save his soul by breaking clean away from his job and his environment and his present situation, and beginning all over again. It was in that that Lot found his salvation; and it was in failure in that that Lot's wife lost her salvation.

THE PICTURE OF THE EVIL MAN

2 Peter 2: 4-11 (continued)

VERSES 9-11 of this passage give us a picture of the evil man. Peter with a few swift, vivid strokes of the pen paints the outstanding characteristics of the man who may properly be called the bad man.

(i) He is *the desire-dominated man*. His life is dominated by the polluting lusts of the flesh. Such a man is guilty of two sins. (*a*) Every man has two sides in his nature. He has a physical nature; he has instincts, passions and impulses which he shares with the animal creation. These instincts are good—*if they are kept in their proper place*. They are even necessary for the preservation of the individual life and for the continuation of the race. But they must be kept within their proper place. The word *temperament* literally means a *mixture*. The picture behind the word is that human nature is a mixture in which a large variety of ingredients are all mixed together. It is clear that the virtue and the efficacy of any mixture depends on each ingredient being there in its proper proportion. Wherever there is either excess or defect in the case of any ingredient or ingredients the mixture is not what it ought to be. Man has a physical nature; and man has also a spiritual nature; and manhood depends on a correct mixture of the two. The desire-dominated man is the man who has allowed his animal nature to usurp a place it should not have; he has allowed the ingredients to get out of proportion; the recipe for manhood has gone wrong. First, then, the desire-dominated man is the man who has lost the proper proportions in God's recipe for human nature. (b) But there is a reason for this loss of proportion—and the reason is nothing other than *selfishness*. The root evil of the lust-dominated life is that it proceeds on the assumption that nothing matters but the gratification of its own desires, and the expression of its own feeling. It has ceased to have any respect or care for others. It has erected itself in the centre of the picture. Selfishness and desire go hand in hand. The bad man is the man who has allowed one side of his nature a far greater place than it ought to have, and who has done so because he is essentially selfish and completely inconsiderate of others.

(ii) He is the *audacious man*. The word in Greek is *tolmētēs*, which comes from the verb *tolman*, which means *to dare*. There are two kinds of daring. There is the daring which is a noble thing, the mark of true courage and bravery. There is the daring which is an evil thing, the daring which dares to do things it has no right to dare to do. As the character in Shakespeare had it: " I dare do all becomes a man. Who dares do more is none." There are certain things which a man has no right to dare to do. To do them means the defying of conscience and the defying of the law of God. The bad man is the man who dares to defy the will of God as it is known to him.

(iii) He is the *self-willed man*. *Self-willed* is not really an adequate translation. The word in Greek is *authadēs*, which the Greeks derived from the two words *autos*, *self*, and *hadōn*, *pleasing*, and they used it of a man who had no idea of anything other than pleasing himself. In it there is always the element of obstinacy. If a man is *authadēs*, neither logic, nor common-sense, nor appeal, nor a sense of decency will keep him from doing what he wants to do and what he has decided to do. As R. C. Trench says, " Thus obstinately maintaining his own opinion, or asserting his own rights, he is reckless of the rights, opinions and interests of others." The man who is *authadēs* is stubbornly and arrogantly and even brutally determined on his own way. The bad man is the man who has no regard for either human appeal or divine guidance.

(iv) He is *the man who is contemptuous of the angels.* We have already seen how this goes back to allusions in Hebrew legend and tradition which are obscure to us. But it has a wider meaning. The bad man is a man who insists on living in one world. To him the unseen world is totally unimportant; the spiritual world does not exist; the heavenly influences have no power upon him, and he never hears the voices from beyond. He is of the earth earthy. He is the man who has forgotten that there is a heaven, and who is blind and deaf when the sights and sounds of heaven break through to him in life.

DELUDING SELF AND DELUDING OTHERS

2 *Peter* 2: 12-14

But these, like brute beasts, knowing no law but their instincts, born only for capture and corruption, speak evil of the things about which they know nothing; they will be destroyed with their own corruption, and, like a man who is cheated, they will even lose the reward at which their iniquity aimed. They regard daylight debauchery as pleasure. They are spots and blots, revelling in their dissipations, carousing in their cliques amongst you. They have eyes full of adultery, eyes which can never gaze their fill on sin. They entrap souls which are not firmly founded in the faith. They have a heart which is trained in unbridled ambition for the things they have no right to have. They are accursed.

HERE Peter launches out into a long passage of magnificent invective. It is a passage through which there glows the fiery heat of flaming moral indignation.

The evil men are like brute beasts; they are the slaves of the instincts which they share with the beasts. But a beast is born for capture and death, says Peter; it has no other end, and no other destiny. Even so, there is something self-destroying in fleshly pleasure. To make such pleasure the be-all and the end-all of life is in the end a suicidal policy. Such pleasure is corrupt and has in it the seeds of corruption and destruction. The aim of the man who gives himself to such fleshly things is pleasure; and his tragedy is that in the end he loses even the pleasure. The point which Peter is making is this, and it is an eternally valid one—if a man dedicates himself to these fleshly pleasures, if he makes them his only joy, in the end he so ruins himself in bodily health and in spiritual and mental character, that he cannot even enjoy them. To put it quite simply and bluntly, the glutton destroys his appetite in the end; the drunkard ruins his health; the sensualist destroys his own body; the self-indulgent ruins his own character and his own peace of mind. The man who dedicates himself to these things is seeking for pleasure; for a while he may enjoy what he calls pleasure, but in the end he ruins his health, wrecks his constitution, destroys his mind and character, and begins his experience of hell when he is still upon earth.

These men regard daylight debauchery, dissipated revelling, abandoned carousing as pleasure. They are blots on the Christian fellowship; they are like the blemishes on an animal, which make it unfit to be offered to God. Once again we must note that what Peter is saying is not only religious truth; it is also sound common sense. The pleasures of the body, the pleasures of luxurious feasting and drunken revelry, the pleasures of the libertine are demonstrably subject to the law of diminishing returns. In themselves they lose their thrill, so that as time goes on it takes more and more of them to satisfy. The luxury must become ever more luxurious; the wine must flow ever more freely; everything must be done to make the thrill sharper and more intense. Further, a man becomes less and less able to enjoy them. His physical capacity and his physical ability to enjoy such things in the nature of things declines. He has given himself literally to a life that has no future, and to pleasure which ends in pain.

So Peter goes on. In verse 14 he uses an extraordinary phrase which will not translate into English at all. We have translated it: " They have eyes which are full of adultery." The phrase in Greek literally is: " They have eyes which are full of an adulteress." Most probably, as has been suggested, the meaning is they see a possible adulteress in every woman. They regard every woman with the eye of lustful calculation, wondering if and how she can be persuaded to agree to gratify their lusts. " The hand and the eye," said the Jewish teachers, " are the brokers of sin." As Jesus said, such people look in order to lust (*Matthew* 5: 28). They have to come to such a stage that they cannot look on anyone without lust's calculation.

As Peter speaks of this, there is a terrible deliberateness about it. They have hearts trained in unbridled ambition for the things they have no right to have. We have taken a whole phrase to translate the one word *pleonexia*; *pleonexia* means the desire to have more of the things which a man has no right even to desire, let alone to have. The picture is a terrible one. The word which is used for *trained* is the word which is used for an athlete, exercising and training himself for the games. These people have actually trained and equipped and taught their minds and hearts to concentrate on nothing but the forbidden desire. They have deliberately fought with conscience until they have destroyed it; they have deliberately wrestled with God until they have thrown God out of life; they have deliberately struggled with their finer feelings until they have strangled them; they have deliberately trained themselves to concentrate on the forbidden things. Their lives have been a dreadful battle to destroy virtue and to train themselves in the techniques of sin.

There remains in this passage still one further charge. It would be bad if these people deluded only themselves; it is worse that they delude others. They entrap souls which are not firmly founded in the faith. The word used for *to entrap* is *deleazein*, which means *to catch with a bait*. A man becomes really a bad man when he sets out to make others as bad as himself. The hymn has it:

> All the mischief we have wrought,
> All forbidden things we've sought,
> All the sin to others taught:
> Forgive, O Lord, for Jesus' sake.

Every man must bear the responsibility for his own sins, but to add to that the responsibility for the sins of others, is an intolerable burden.

ON THE WRONG ROAD

2 *Peter* 2: 15, 16

> They have left the straight road and have gone awandering, and have followed the road of Balaam, the son of Beor, who loved the profit which unrighteousness brings, and who was convicted of his lawlessness. A dumb ass spoke with a man's voice and checked the prophet's folly.

PETER likens the evil men of his time to the prophet Balaam. In the popular Jewish mind and legends Balaam had come to stand as the type of all false and pernicious prophets. His story is told in *Numbers* 22 to 26. Balak, the King of Moab, was alarmed at the steady and apparently irresistible advance of the Israelites. In attempt to check this advance he sent for Balaam to come and curse the Israelites for him, offering Balaam very great rewards if he would come. To the end of the day Balaam refused to curse the Israelites, but the story makes one thing quite clear, that Balaam's covetous heart longed after the rich rewards which Balak was offering, even if he was afraid to take them. Balaam at Balak's second request played with fire enough to agree to meet Balak. It was on that journey that the ass stopped in the way, because it saw the angel of the Lord standing in its path and rebuked Balaam.

As we have said, it is true that on this occasion Balaam did not succumb to Balak's bribes, but if ever a man desperately wanted to accept a bribe, that man was Balaam. After that story, in *Numbers* 25 there follows another story. It tells how the Israelites were seduced into the worship of Baal, and into lustful alliances with Moabite women. Although it does not actually say so in this chapter of *Numbers*, Jewish belief was that Balaam was behind this seduction and was responsible for leading the children of Israel astray. And when the Israelites entered into possession of the land, "Balaam the son of Beor they slew with the sword" (*Numbers* 31: 8). In view of all this Balaam became increasingly the type and example of the false and misleading prophet. Balaam had two characteristics which were repeated in the evil men of Peter's day.

(i) Balaam was *covetous*. As the *Numbers* story unfolds we can see Balaam's fingers itching to get at the gold of Balak, and his eyes glinting with covetousness. True, he did not take it; but the evil desire to take it was there. The evil men of Peter's day were covetous; they were out for what they could get; they were ready to exploit their membership of the Church to make unholy gain.

(ii) Balaam *taught Israel to sin*. Above all Balaam went down to history as the man who taught Israel to sin. He led the people out of the straight and into the crooked way. He persuaded them to forget their promises to God, and their loyalty to God. The evil men of Peter's day were seducing Christians from the Christian way, and were causing them to break the pledges of loyalty which they had given to Jesus Christ.

The man who loves gain and who lures others to evil for ever stands condemned.

THE PERILS OF RELAPSE

2 Peter 2: 17-22

These people are waterless springs; mists driven by a squall of wind and the gloom of darkness is reserved for them. With talk at once arrogant and futile, they ensnare by appeals to shameless, sensual passions those who are only just escaping from the company of those who live in error, promising them freedom, while they themselves are the slaves of moral corruption; for a man is in a state of slavery to that which has reduced him to helplessness.

If they have escaped the pollution of the world by the knowledge of the Lord and Saviour Jesus Christ, and if they allow themselves again to become involved in these things, and to be reduced to moral helplessness by them, the last state is for them worse than the first. It would be better for them not to have known the way of righteousness, than to have known it, and then to turn back from the holy commandment which was handed down to them. In them the truth of the proverb is plain to see: "A dog returns to his own vomit," and, "The sow which has been washed returns to rolling in the mud."

PETER is still rolling out his tremendous denunciation of the evil men.

They flatter only to deceive. They are like wells with no water, and like mists blown past by a squall of wind. Think of a traveller in the desert being told that ahead of him there lies a spring where he can quench his thirst, and think of him arriving at that spring to find it dried up and useless. Think of the husbandman praying for rain for his parched crops, and then seeing the cloud that promised rain blown uselessly by. As Bigg has it: "A teacher

395

without knowledge is like a well without water." These men are like Milton's shepherds whose " hungry sheep look up and are not fed." These men promise a gospel, and in the end have nothing to offer the thirsty soul.

Their teaching is a combination of arrogance and futility. Christian liberty and Christian freedom always have a danger in them. Paul tells his people that they have indeed been called to liberty, but that they must not use that liberty for an occasion to the flesh (*Galatians* 5: 13). Peter tells his people that indeed they are free, but they must not use their freedom as a cloak of maliciousness (I *Peter* 2: 16). These false teachers offered freedom, but the kind of freedom they offered was freedom to sin as much as a man liked. Their appeal was not to the challenge of nobility, but to the satisfaction of lust. They appealed, not to the best, but to the worst in a man. Peter is quite clear why they did this. They did this because they themselves were slaves to their own lusts. Seneca said, " To be enslaved to oneself is the heaviest of all servitudes." Persius spoke to the lustful debauchees of his day of " the masters that grow up within that sickly breast of yours." These teachers were offering liberty, when they themselves were slaves, and the liberty they were offering was the liberty to become a slave of lust. Their message was *arrogant*, because it was the contradiction of the message of Christ and the Church; their message was *futile*, because he who followed it would find himself a slave. Here again in the background there is the fundamental heresy which makes grace into an excuse and a justification for sin instead of a power and a summons to nobility.

If they had once known the real way of Christ, and if they had relapsed into this, their case is even worse. They are like the man in the parable whose last case was worse than his first (*Matthew* 12: 45; *Luke* 11: 26). Why should that be? If a man has never known the right way, he cannot be condemned for not following it. If he has never seen the truth, and if he has never heard the message of Christ, he cannot be condemned for not accepting and obeying it. But, if he has known it, and has then deliberately taken the other way, then he sins against the light; he has known the best and he has chosen the worst; he has sinned in the full knowledge of what he is doing. And if that be so, it were better for him that he had never known the truth, for his knowledge of the truth has become his condemnation. A man should never forget the responsibility which knowledge brings.

So Peter ends with contempt. These evil men are like dogs who return to their vomit (*Proverbs* 26: 11), or like a sow which has been scrubbed and then goes back to rolling in the mud. These men have seen Christ, but they are so morally degraded by their own choice, that they prefer to wallow in the depths of sin rather than to climb the heights of virtue. It is a dreadful warning that a man can make himself such that in the end the tentacles of sin are inextricably around him, and virtue for him has lost its beauty.

THE PRINCIPLES OF PREACHING

2 Peter 3: 1, 2

Beloved, this is now the second letter that I have written to you, and my object in both of them is to rouse by reminder your pure mind to remember the words spoken by the prophets in former times, and the commandment of the Lord and Saviour, which was brought to you by your apostles.

IN this passage we see very clearly displayed the principles of preaching which Peter observed.

(i) He believed in the value of *repetition*. He knows that it is necessary that a thing must be said over and over again, if it is to penetrate the mind. When Paul was writing to the Philippians he said that to repeat the same thing over and over again was not a weariness to him, and for them it was the only safe way (*Philippians* 3: 1). It is by continued repetition that the rudiments of knowledge are in the end settled in the mind of the child. There is something of significance here. It may well be that often we are too desirous of novelty, too eager to say new things, while what is needed is a repetition of the eternal truths which men so quickly forget, and the significance of which they so often refuse to see. There are certain foods of which a man does not get tired; they are necessary for his daily sustenance; and they are set before him every day. We speak about a man's *daily bread*. And there are certain great Christian truths which have to be repeated again and again, and which must never be pushed into the background in the desire for novelty.

(ii) He believed in *the need for reminder*. Again and again the New Testament makes it clear that preaching and teaching are so often, not the introducing of new truth, but the reminding of a man of that which he already knows, and the summoning him to be that which he already is. Moffatt quotes a saying of Dr. Johnson: " It is not sufficiently considered that men more frequently require to be reminded than informed." The Greeks spoke of " time which wipes all things out," as if the human mind were a slate and time a sponge which passes across it with a certain obliterating and erasing quality. We are so often in the position of men whose need is not so much to be taught as it is to be reminded of that which we already know.

(iii) He believed in *the value of a compliment*. It is his intention—so he says—to rouse *their pure mind*. The word he uses for pure is the word *eilikrinēs*, which may have either of two meanings. It may mean that which is sifted until there is no admixture of chaff left; or it may mean that which is so flawless that it may be held up to the light of the sun. Plato uses this very same phrase—*eilikrinēs dianoia*—in the sense of *pure reason*, reason which is keen and clear and pure and unaffected by the seductive influence of the senses; we might call it uncontaminated reason. By using this phrase Peter appeals to his people as having minds uncontaminated by heresy and unbelief and lustful desire. It is as if he said to them: " You really are fine and splendid people—if you would only remember it." The approach of the preacher should so often be that his hearers are not wretched creatures who deserve to be damned, but splendid creatures who must be saved. They are not so much like rubbish fit to be thrown out and burned as they are like jewels which have to be rescued from the mud and mire into which they have fallen. The appeal is not so much to innate sin as it is to innate nobility. Donald Hankey tells of " the beloved captain " whose men would follow him anywhere. He tells how he and his squad looked at each other, and how he looked at them and they looked at him, and they were filled with the determination to be what he believed them to be. We always get further with people when we make them feel that we believe in them, than when we make them feel that we despise them.

(iv) He clearly believed in *the unity of Scripture*. As he saw it there was a pattern in Scripture. There were, first, the prophets who foretold Christ; there was, second, Christ Himself who came; and there were, third, the apostles who brought the good news of Christ. To Peter the Bible was a book which centred in Christ. The Old Testament foretold Christ; the gospels tell of the Christ who came; and the apostles seek to bring the message of that Christ to men. The only way to read the Bible is to put Christ in the centre of it. It is the book which begins by telling of the preparation for the coming of Christ; which goes on to tell of the actual coming of Christ; and which ends by bringing to all men the gospel of Christ. From beginning to end the message of the Bible is Christ.

THE DENIAL OF THE SECOND COMING

2 *Peter* 3: 3, 4

> To begin with, you are well aware that in the last
> days there will come mockers with their mocking,
> guiding their steps by the law of their own lusts, and
> saying, " What has happened to the promise of His
> Coming? For, since the day when our fathers fell
> asleep, everything remains the same as it was from the
> foundation of the world."

THE characteristic of the heretics which worried Peter
most of all was their denial of the Second Coming of Jesus.
Literally, their question was: " Where is the promise of
His Coming? " That was a form of Hebrew expression
which implied that the thing about which the questioner
asked did not exist at all. " Where is the God of judgment?"
asked the evil men of Malachi's day (*Malachi* 2: 17).
" Where is thy God? " the heathen demanded of the
Psalmist (*Psalm* 42: 3; 79: 10). " Where is the word
of the Lord? " his enemies asked Jeremiah (*Jeremiah*
17: 15). And in every case the implication of the question,
and the belief of the questioner is that the thing or the
person asked about is a delusion and does not exist. The
heretics of Peter's day were denying altogether that Jesus
Christ would ever come again. It will be best here at the
beginning to summarize their arguments and Peter's
answer to them.

The argument of Peter's opponents was twofold (verse 4).
" What has happened," they demanded, " to the promise
of the Second Coming? " Their first argument was that the
promise had been so long delayed that it was safe to take
it that now it would never be fulfilled. They regarded the
Second Coming as something which would have happened
long ago, if it was going to happen, and they regarded
belief in it as something which could now be safely dis-
carded. Their second assertion was that their fathers
have died, and the world is going on precisely as it always
went on. Their argument is that this is characteristically

a stable universe, and convulsive upheavals like the Second Coming do not happen in a universe like this.

Peter's response is two fold. He deals with the second argument first (verses 5-7). His argument is that, in fact, this is not a stable universe, that once the universe was destroyed by water in the time of the Flood, and that a second destruction, this time by fire, is on the way. So far from this being a stable universe in which everything remains for ever the same, it is a universe which has been destroyed once, and which is on the way to being destroyed again.

His second answering argument is in verses 8 and 9. His opponents speak of the delay and the dilatoriness of God, a delay so long that we can safely assume that the Second Coming is not going to happen at all. Peter's answer to that is a double answer. (a) We must see time as God sees it. With God a day is as a thousand years, and a thousand years is as a day. " God does not pay every Friday night." God has all the eternities to work it. When we think of God, we must abandon all our notions of time, for time does not exist for God. (b) In any event God's apparent slowness to act is not dilatoriness. It is, in fact, mercy. He holds His hand in order to give sinning men another chance to repent and to find salvation. God withholds His hand, not from indifference, and not from dilatoriness, but to give men still another chance to repent and so to escape destruction.

Peter then goes on to his conclusion (verse 10). The conclusion is that the Second Coming is on the way; and that it will come with a sudden terror and destruction which will dissolve the universe in melting heat.

Then, finally, there comes his practical demand in face of all this. If we are living in a universe on which Jesus Christ is going to descend, and if we are living in a universe which is hastening towards the destruction of the wicked, then surely it behoves us to live in piety and in holiness so that we may be spared and saved when the terrible day does come. The Second Coming is used as a tremendous motive for moral amendment, so that a man may prepare himself literally to meet his God. Such, then, is the general scheme of this chapter, and now we must proceed to look at it section by section.

DESTRUCTION BY FLOOD

2 Peter 3: 5, 6

> What they wilfully fail to see is that long ago the heavens were created and that the earth was composed out of water and through water; and that through these waters the ancient world perished, when it was overwhelmed in a deluge of water.

THIS is Peter's first argument that the world is not eternally stable, and that things are not eternally and for ever the same. The point that he is making is that the ancient world was destroyed by water, just as the present world is going to be destroyed by fire. The detail of this passage is, however, difficult.

He says that the earth was composed out of water and through water. In the *Genesis* story in the beginning there was a kind of watery chaos. " The Spirit of God moved upon the face of the waters. . . . God said, Let there be a firmament in the midst of the waters, and let us divide the waters from the waters " (*Genesis* 1: 2, 6). Out of this watery chaos the world was formed. Further, it is through water that the world is sustained, because life is sustained by the rain which comes down from the skies. What Peter means is that the world was created out of water, and that it is sustained by water; and it was through these waters that the ancient world was destroyed.

Further to clarify this passage we have to note that the flood legend developed. It became more than the wiping out of sinners; it became the destruction of the whole world. As so often in *Second Peter* and *Jude* the picture behind this comes not directly from the Old Testament but from the Book of Enoch. In *Enoch* 83: 3-5 Enoch has a vision: " I saw in a vision how the heaven collapsed and fell to the earth, and, where it fell to the earth, I saw how the earth was swallowed up in a great abyss." In the later stories the flood involved not only the obliteration of sinners but the total destruction of heaven and earth. So the warning which Peter is giving may be put like this: " You say that as things are, so they have ever been, and so they ever will be. You build your hopes on the idea that this is a stable and unchanging universe. You are deluded and wrong, for the ancient world was formed out of water and was sustained by water, and it perished in the deluge and the flood. Your hopes are built on a wrong idea of what actually did happen in history."

We may say that this is only an old legend, more than half-buried in the dim antiquities of the past. But we cannot go on to say that a passage like this has no significance and no meaning for us. When we strip away from this passage the old Jewish legend, and the later Jewish development of it, we are still left with this permanent truth—that the man who will read history with honest and with open eyes can see within it the moral law at work, and God's dealings with men. Froude, the great historian, said that history is a voice sounding across the centuries that in the end it is always ill with the wicked and well with the good. When Oliver Cromwell was arranging his son Richard's education, he said, " I would have him know a little history." In fact, the lesson of history is that there is a moral order in the universe, and that he who defies that moral order does so at his peril.

DESTRUCTION BY FIRE

2 Peter 3: 7

> But by the same word the present heavens and earth are treasured up for fire, reserved for the day of judgment, and the destruction of impious men.

It is Peter's conviction that, as the ancient world was destroyed by water, the present world will be destroyed by fire. He says that that is stated " by the same word." What he means is that the Old Testament tells of the story of the flood in the past, and warns of the destruction by fire in the future. There are many passages in the prophets which he would take quite literally and which must have been in his mind. Joel foresaw a time when God would show blood, and fire, and pillars of smoke (*Joel* 2: 30). The Psalmist has a picture in which, when God comes, a fire shall devour before Him (*Psalm* 50: 3). Isaiah speaks of a flame of devouring fire (*Isaiah* 29: 6; 30: 30). The Lord will come with fire; by fire and by His sword will the Lord plead with all flesh (*Isaiah* 66: 15, 16). Nahum has it that the hills melt, and the earth is burned at his presence; His fury is poured out like fire (*Nahum* I: 5, 6). In the picture of Malachi the day of the Lord shall burn as an oven (*Malachi* 4: I). If the old pictures be taken literally, Peter has plenty of material for his prophecy.

The Stoics also had a doctrine of the destruction of the world by fire. But the Stoic doctrine was a grim thing. The Stoics held that the universe completed a cycle; that it was consumed in flames; and then that everything started all over again, precisely and exactly as it was. They had the strange idea that at the end of the cycle the planets are in exactly the same position as they were in when the world began. In some way, " This produces the conflagration and destruction of everything which exists," says Chrysippus. He goes on: " Then again the universe is restored anew in a precisely similar arrangement as before . . . Socrates and Plato and each individual man will live again, with the same friends and fellow-citizens. They will go through the same experiences and the same activities. Every city and village and field will be restored, just as it was. And this restoration of the universe takes place, not once, but over and over again—indeed to all eternity without end. . . . For there will never be any new thing other than that which has been before, but everything is repeated down to the minutest detail." History as an eternal tread-mill, the eternal and unceasing recurrence of the sins, the sorrows and the mistakes of men—that is one of the grimmest views of history that the mind of man has ever conceived.

It must always be remembered that, as the Jewish prophets saw it, and as Peter saw it, this world will be destroyed with the conflagration of God, but the result will not be obliteration, and the result will not be the grim repetition of what has been before; the result will be a new heaven and a new earth. One thing is true—that for the Biblical view of the world there is something beyond destruction; there is the new creation of God. The worst that the prophet can conceive is not the death agony of the old world so much as the birth pangs of the new world.

THE MERCY OF GOD'S DELAY

2 *Peter* 3: 8, 9

> Beloved, you must not shut your eyes to this one fact, that with the Lord one day is as a thousand years, and a thousand years as one day. It is not that God is dilatory in fulfilling His promise, as some people reckon dilatoriness; but it is that for your sakes He patiently withholds His hand, because He does not wish any to perish, but wishes all to take the way to repentance.

THERE are in this passage three great truths on which to nourish the mind and rest the heart.

(i) Time is not the same to God as it is to man. As the Psalmist had it: " A thousand years in Thy sight are but as yesterday when it is past, and as a watch in the night " (*Psalm* 90: 4). When we think of the world's hundreds of thousands of years of existence, it is easy to feel paralysed and dwarfed into insignificance; when we think of the slowness of human progress, it is easy to become discouraged into pessimism. There is comfort in the thought of a God who has all eternity to work in, and in the memory that to God a thousand years are but a day. It is only against the background of eternity that things appear in their true proportions and assume their real value.

(ii) But we can also see from this passage that time is always to be regarded as an opportunity. Every day which comes to us is a gift of mercy. As Peter saw it, the years God gave the world were a further opportunity for men to repent and to turn to God. Every day which comes to us is God's gift to us. Every day is an opportunity to develop and to purify ourselves; to render some service to our fellow-men; to take one step nearer and closer to God. We do well not to forget God's gift of time.

(iii) Finally, in this passage there is another echo of a truth which so often lies in the background of New Testament thought. God, says Peter, does not wish any to perish. God, says Paul, has shut them all up together in unbelief, that He might have mercy on all (*Romans* 11: 32). The Pastoral Epistles in a tremendous phrase speaks of God who will have all men to be saved (I *Timothy* 2: 4). Ezekiel hears God ask: " Have I any pleasure at all that the wicked should die, and not that he should return from his ways and live? " (*Ezekiel* 18: 23).

Ever and again there shines in Scripture the glint of light of the larger hope. We are not forbidden to believe that somehow and some time the God who loved the world will bring the whole world to Himself.

THE DREADFUL DAY

2 *Peter* 3: 10

> But when it does come, the Day of the Lord will **come** as a thief, and in it the heavens will pass away with **a** crackling roar; the stars will blaze and melt; **and** the earth and all its works will disappear.

IT inevitably happens that a man has to speak and think in the terms which he knows. That is what Peter is doing here. He is speaking of the New Testament doctrine of the Second Coming of Jesus Christ, but he is describing it in terms to the Old Testament doctrine of the Day of the Lord.

The Day of the Lord is a conception which runs all through the prophetic books of the Old Testament. The Jews saw time in terms of two ages. There is *this present age*, which is wholly bad, wholly given over to sin, and wholly past remedy. It is beyond mending and is ripe for destruction. On the other hand, there is *the age to come*, which is the golden age of God. How was the one to turn into the other? The change could not be made by human effort or human achievement. The change could not happen by a process of evolution and development, for the world is on the way to destruction, and is incurably evil. As the Jew saw it, there is only one way in which the change can happen; it must happen by the direct action and intervention of God. The time of that action they called the Day of the Lord. It was to come suddenly and without warning. It was to be a time when the universe was shaken and shattered to its foundations. It was to be a time when the judgment and the obliteration of sinners would come to pass, and, therefore, it would be a time of terror. " Behold the Day of the Lord cometh, cruel both with wrath and fierce anger, to lay the land desolate; and He shall destroy the sinners thereof out of it " (*Isaiah* 13: 9). " The Day of the Lord cometh, for it is nigh at hand; a day of darkness and of gloominess, a day of clouds and of thick darkness " (*Joel* 2: 1, 2). " That Day is a day of wrath, a day of trouble and distress, a day of waste and desolation, a day of darkness and gloominess, a day of clouds and thick darkness " (*Zephaniah* 1: 14-18). " The sun will be turned into darkness and the moon into blood, before the great and terrible Day of the Lord " (*Joel* 2: 30, 31). " The stars of the heaven and the constellations thereof shall not give their light; the sun shall be darkened in his going forth, and the moon shall not cause her light to shine. . . . Therefore will I shake the heavens, and the earth shall remove out of her place, in the wrath of the Lord of hosts, and in the day of His fierce anger " (*Isaiah* 13: 10-13).

What Peter did, and what many of the New Testament writers did, was to identify the Old Testament pictures of the Day of the Lord with the New Testament conception of the Second Coming of Jesus Christ. His picture of the Second Coming of Jesus is drawn in terms of the Old Testament picture of the Day of the Lord.

He uses one very vivid phrase. He says that the heavens will pass away with a crackling roar (*roizēdon*). That word is used for the whirring of a bird's wings in the air, for the sound a spear makes as it hurtles through the air, for the crackling of the devouring flames of a forest fire.

We need not take these pictures with a crude literalism. It is enough to see that Peter sees the Second Coming of Christ as a time of terror for those who are the enemies of Christ.

One thing has to be held in the memory. The whole conception of the Second Coming is full of difficulty. But one fact remains—there comes a day when God breaks into every life, for there comes a day when we must die; and for that day we must be prepared. We may say what we will about the Coming of Christ as a future event. We may feel that this is a doctrine which we have to lay on one side; but we cannot escape from the certainty of the entry of God into our own life as an ever-present reality and as an utter certainty.

THE MORAL DYNAMIC

Peter 3: 11-14

Since these things are going to be dissolved like that, what kind of people ought you to be, living a life of constant holiness and true piety, you who are eagerly awaiting and doing your best to hasten on the Day of the Lord, by whose action the heavens will burn and be dissolved, and the stars blaze and melt! For it is new heavens and a new earth, as He promised, for which we wait, in which righteousness has its home. So, then, beloved, since these are the things for which you eagerly wait, be eager to be found by Him at peace, without spot and blemish.

THE one thing in which Peter is supremely interested is the moral dynamic of the Second Coming. If these things are going to happen, if the world is hastening to judgment, then obviously a man must live a life of piety and of holiness. If there are to be a new heaven and a new earth, and if that heaven and earth are to be the home of righteousness, then obviously a man must seek with all his mind and heart and soul and strength to be fit to be a dweller in that new world, in which there will be no room for the unrighteous. To Peter, as Moffatt puts it, " it was impossible to give up the hope of the advent without ethical deterioration." In actual practice Peter was right. If there is nothing in the nature of a Second Coming, if there is nothing in the nature of an end and a goal to which the whole creation moves, then life is going nowhere. That, in fact, was the heathen position. If there is no end or goal, either for the world or for the individual life, other than extinction, certain attitudes to life become well-nigh inevitable. These attitudes emerge in the heathen epitaphs on tombs.

(i) If there is nothing to come, a man may well decide to make what he can of the pleasures of this world. So we come on an epitaph like this: " I was nothing: I am nothing. So thou who art still alive, eat, drink, and be merry." A man might as well make the most of the one world which he possesses, if there is no other to possess.

(ii) If there is nothing to live for, then a man may well be utterly indifferent. Nothing matters much if the end of everything is extinction, in which a man will not even be aware that he is extinguished. So we come on such an epitaph as this: " Once I had no existence; now I have

none. I am not aware of it. It does not concern me."
When life and the world are on the way to nothingness,
the value is gone out of life.

(iii) If there is nothing to live for but extinction, and
if the world is going nowhere, there can enter into life a
kind of lostness. Man ceases to be in any sense a pilgrim
for there is nowhere to which he can be a pilgrim. He
must simply drift in a kind of lostness, coming from nowhere
and on the way to nowhere. So we come on an epigram
like that of Callimachus. " Charidas, what is below? "
" Deep darkness." " But what of the paths upward? "
" All a lie." " And Pluto? " (The god of the underworld).
" Mere talk." " Then we're lost." Even the heathen found
a certain almost intolerable quality in a world and in a life
without a goal.

When we have stripped the doctrine of the Second
Coming of all its temporary and its local imagery and
apparatus, the one tremendous truth which it conserves
is that life is going somewhere—and without that conviction
there is literally nothing left to live for.

HASTENING THE DAY

2 Peter 3: 11-14 (continued)

THERE is in this passage still another great conception.
Peter speaks of the Christian as not only eagerly awaiting
the Coming of Christ, but as actually hastening it on.
How is it possible to hasten on the Coming of Christ?
The New Testament itself tells us certain ways in which
this may be done.

(i) It may be done by prayer. Jesus taught us to pray:
" Thy Kingdom come " (Matthew 6: 10). The earnest
prayer of the Christian heart hastens the coming of the
King. If in no other way it does so in this—that he who
prays opens his own heart for the coming of the King into it.

(ii) It may be done by *preaching*. Matthew tells us that Jesus said, " And this gospel of the Kingdom shall be preached in all the world for a witness to all nations; and then shall the end come " (*Matthew* 24: 14). All men must be given the chance to know and to love Jesus Christ, before the goal and end of creation is reached. The missionary activity of the Church is the hastening of the coming of the King.

(iii) It may be done by *penitence* and *obedience*. Of all things this would be nearest to Peter's mind and to Peter's heart. The Rabbis had two sayings: " It is the sins of the people which prevent the coming of the Messiah. If the Jews would genuinely repent for one day, the Messiah would come." The other form of the saying means the same: " If Israel would perfectly keep the law for one day, the Messiah would come." In true penitence and in real obedience a man opens his own heart to the Coming of the King, and brings nearer that coming throughout the world. We do well to remember that it is our own coldness of heart and our own disobedience which delays the Coming of the King.

PERVERTERS OF SCRIPTURE

2 *Peter* 3: 15, 16

Regard the Lord's willingness to wait as an opportunity of salvation, as indeed our beloved brother Paul has written to us, in the wisdom which has been given to him, and as he says in all his letters, when he touches on these subjects, letters which contain some things which are difficult to understand, things which those who lack knowledge and a firm foundation in the faith twist, as they do the rest of the Scriptures, to their own destruction.

PETER here cites Paul as teaching the same things as he himself teaches. It may be that he is citing Paul as agreeing that a pious and a holy life is necessary in view of the approaching Second Coming of our Lord. More likely, he is citing Paul as agreeing that the fact that God withholds His hand is to be regarded, not as delay and indifference on God's part, but as an opportunity to repent and to believe the gospel and to accept Jesus Christ. Paul speaks of those who despise the riches of God's goodness and forbearance and long-suffering, forgetting that that kindness of God is designed to lead a man to repentance (*Romans* 2: 4). More than once Paul stresses this forbearance and this long-suffering of God (*Romans* 3: 25; 9: 22). Both Peter and Paul were agreed that the forbearance and the long-suffering of God, the fact that God withholds His hand, are never to be used as an excuse for sinning, but always as a means of repentance and an opportunity of amendment.

With its reference to Paul and with its tinge of criticism of him, this is one of the most intriguing passages in the New Testament. It was this passage which made John Calvin certain that Peter did not himself write *Second Peter*, because, he says, Peter would never have spoken about Paul like this. What do we, in fact, learn from this passage?

(i) We learn that Paul's letters by this time were known and used throughout the Church. They are spoken of in such a way as to make it clear that they have been collected and published, and that they are generally available and widely read. Now we are fairly certain that this did not happen until about the year A.D. 90. About that year Paul's letters were collected and published in Ephesus. This means that this letter which is called *Second Peter* cannot have been written before that, and that, therefore, it cannot really be the work of Peter, who was martyred in the middle sixties of the century.

(ii) It tells us that Paul's letters have come to be regarded as Scripture. The misguided men twist them as they do the other Scriptures. This again goes to prove that *Second Peter* must come from a time well on in the history of the early

Church, for it would take many generations before the letters of Paul ranked alongside the Scriptures of the Old Testament.

(iii) It is a little difficult to see just what the attitude to Paul is in this passage. Paul is writing, so this letter says, " in the wisdom which has been given to him." Bigg says neatly that that phrase can be equally a commendation or a caution! The truth is that Paul suffered the fate of all outstanding men. He had his critics. He suffered the fate of all those who fearlessly face, and fearlessly state, the truth. He had those who regarded him as great but dangerous.

(iv) There are things, says this letter, in Paul's letters which are hard to understand, and which ignorant people twist to their own ruin. The word which is used for *hard to understand* is *dusnoētos*, which is used of the utterance of an oracle. As we know, the utterances of Greek oracles were always ambiguous. There is the classic example of the king who was about to go to war. He consulted the oracle at Delphi; he was given the answer: " If you go to war, you will destroy a great nation." He took this as a prophecy that he would destroy his enemies; but it happened that he was so utterly defeated that by going to war he destroyed his own country. This was typical of the dangerous ambiguity of the ancient oracles. Now it is that very word which Peter uses of the writings of Paul. They have things in them which are as difficult to interpret as the ambiguous utterance of an oracle.

Not only, Peter says, are there things in Paul's writings that are hard to understand; there are things which a man may twist to his own destruction. What are the things in Paul's thought and teaching which could be twisted into something which is destructive of true religion. Three things come immediately to mind. Paul's doctrine of *grace* was, in fact, twisted into an excuse and a justification, and even a reason, for sin (*Romans* 6). Paul's doctrine of Christian *freedom* was, in fact, twisted into an excuse for unchristian licence (*Galatians* 5: 13). Paul's doctrine of *faith* was twisted into an argument that Christian action was unimportant, as we see in *James* (*James* 2: 14-26).

G. K. Chesterton drew his famous picture of orthodoxy. Orthodoxy, he said, was like walking along a narrow ridge, almost like a knife-edge. One step to either side was a step to disaster. Jesus is God and man; God is love and holiness; Christianity is grace and morality; the Christian lives in this world and also lives in the world of eternity. Overstress either side of these great truths, and at once destructive heresy emerges. One of the most tragic things in life is when a man twists Christian truth and holy Scripture into an excuse and a defence, and even a reason, for doing what He wants to do, and does not accept it as a guide for doing what God wants him to do.

A FIRM FOUNDATION AND A CONTINUAL GROWTH

2 *Peter* 3: 17, 18

> As far as you are concerned, beloved, you have been forewarned. You must, therefore, be on your guard not to be carried away by the error of lawless men, and so to fall from your own foundation; rather, you must see to it that you grow in grace and in understanding of our Lord and Saviour Jesus Christ.
>
> To Him be glory both now and to the day of eternity.

HERE, in conclusion, Peter tells us certain things about the Christian life.

(i) The Christian is a man who is forewarned. That is to say, the Christian cannot plead ignorance. He knows the right way and its rewards; he knows the wrong way and its disasters. He has no right to expect an easy way, for he has been told that Christianity means a cross, and he has been warned that there will always be those who are ready and eager to attack and to pervert the faith. To be forewarned is to be forearmed; but to be forewarned is also a grave responsibility, for he who knows the right and does the wrong is under a double condemnation.

(ii) The Christian is a man with a basis for life. He ought to be rooted and founded in the faith. There are certain things of which he is absolutely certain. James Agate once declared that his mind was not a bed to be made and remade, but that on certain things it was finally made up. There is a certain inflexibility in the Christian life; there is a certain basis of belief which never changes. The Christian will never cease to believe that, " Jesus Christ is Lord " (*Philippians* 2: 11); and he will never cease to be aware that there is laid on him the duty of making his life fit his belief.

(iii) The Christian is a man with a developing life. The inflexibility of the Christian life is not the rigidity of death. The Christian must daily experience the wonder of grace, and daily grow in the gifts which grace can bring; and the Christian must daily enter more and more deeply into the wonder which is in Jesus Christ. It is only on a firm foundation that a great building can tower into the air; and it is only because it has a deep root that a great tree can reach out to the sky with its branches. The Christian life is at once a life with a firm foundation and with an ever outward and upward growth.

And so the letter finishes by giving glory to Christ, both now and to the end of time.

NOTES